Live On Stage!

Performing Arts for
Middle School

Teacher Resource
Book

Carla Blank Jody Roberts

DALE SEYMOUR PUBLICATIONS®

Managing Editor: Catherine Anderson

Product Manager: Bev Dana

Senior Editor: Jeri Hayes

Project Editor: Geri Stewart

Production/Manufacturing Director:
Janet Yearian

Senior Production/Manufacturing
Coordinator: Claire Flaherty

Design Manager: Jeff Kelly

Cover and Text Design:
Lynda Banks Design

Composition: Andrea Reider

Reviewers/Consultants

Wayne Cook
Program Administrator for Artists
in Residency Program
California Arts Council
Sacramento, California

Ann Crofton
Teacher
Dewitt Perry Middle School
Carrolton, Texas

Karen Gossett
Teacher
Strickland Middle School
Denton Texas Independent
School District
Denton, Texas

Julia Russell
Arts Specialist, Division of
Special Programs
Memphis City Schools
Memphis, Tennessee

Lorraine Shackelford
Director of Theater Education
University of North Carolina,
Greensboro
Greensboro, North Carolina

Julie Strauss
Teacher
Menlo Park School District
Menlo Park, California

Order number DS31500
ISBN 1-57232-209-8

1 2 3 4 5 6 7 8 9 10-ML-00-99 98 97 96

DALE
SEYMOUR
PUBLICATIONS®
P.O. BOX 10888
PALO ALTO, CA 94303

This book is printed
on recycled paper.

To our families

Ishmael and Tennessee

John, David, and Taya

To our teachers

And our students

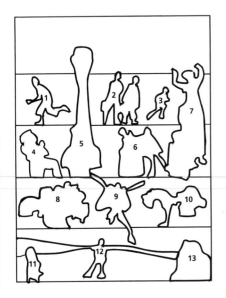

Photo Credits

Cover

© Mark Citret: photos 1, 4–7, 8–10, 11, 12

© Bonnie Kamin: photos 2, 3

Jan Inouye, photographer: photo 13

Inside

Lynda Banks: pages 4, 8, 14, 21, 28, 35–36, 59 (both), 63, 79, 84–85, 87, 172, 216 (right), 217–218, 223

Robert Bryant: pages xxiii, 1, 6, 29, 77, 98, 166, 209, 222, 239

© Mark Citret: pages v, 11, 25, 41, 43–44, 51, 53, 66, 81, 89, 103, 109–110, 115, 139, 141, 145, 149 (bottom), 151, 153, 155, 161, 178, 180, 185, 186, 191, 211, 213, 215, 216 (left), 225–226, 230, 232, 234, 238, 240

Jan Inouye, photographer: page 177

© Bonnie Kamin: pages 37, 61, 93, 133

Susan Lindh Photography: page 19

Nan Phelps: pages 169, 197, 199

Jody Roberts: page 13, 149, 160,

John Roberts: pages 31, 183

Barbara Sansone: pages 194–195

Allen Willis: page 233

Text Credits

Grateful acknowledgment is due the following publisher for permission to use the selections from their publications.

Excerpts from "Creativity vs. Academics: How to Teach the Arts?" by Susan Chira, New York Times, 2/4/93 and from "This Computer Loves to Dance" by Max Wyman, New York Times 6/27/93. Copyright © 1993 by the New York Times Company. Reprinted by permission.

Contents

About the Authors

We are performing artists, teachers, and directors who have worked with diverse groups of people, from toddlers to ninety-year-olds, in classrooms—preschool through postgraduate levels—in community arts programs and social institutions, business programs, and health facilities. We have taught in special education classrooms and in regular classrooms that included disabled students. The participants have included working artists as well as people who had never considered making art or its use in their daily lives.

We came to teaching and directing from different performing backgrounds. Carla's training was based in creative theater and modern dance, and Jody's began with Russian ballet and character dance. Performance was a major ingredient of our training. We both started teaching as teenagers. We had been performing on the East and West coasts when we met in 1971 as graduate students in the Mills College dance program.

In 1977 we founded a performing arts organization, called Roberts & Blank Dance Theater, Inc. By 1981 it became a nonprofit organization, for the purposes of teaching techniques of dance, theater, music, and stage design, and directing a performing company called The Children's Troupe. The Children's Troupe was composed of young people between the ages of six and nineteen who were willing to commit to creating and performing each season's original work. From 1981 to 1992, the Troupe performed in San Francisco Bay Area theaters, festivals, schools, libraries, and community arts facilities. The Children's Troupe presented works with a multicultural world view. In part, this was a natural result of our company drawing from a diverse mix of people. We collaborated on original productions, which were based on investigations of myths, biographical and autobiographical histories, generational and cultural issues, and traditions based on ancient and contemporary theater forms.

Collaboration is integral to our work. It's exciting for us to work with people of varying ages and experiences. Twelve people in collaboration means twelve points of view. Our students collaborated with us and guest artists, among whom were composer, Ed Bogas (of *Peanuts* movie score fame); writer, choreographer, and designer, Remy Charlip; composer and musician, Randy Craig; lighting designer, José Maria Francos: director and playwright, Ken Grantham; composer and choreographer, Meredith Monk; composer and musician, Carman Moore; writer, Ishmael Reed; and landscape architect, John Roberts. With the help of the students and guest artists, we created each season's new work.

Ours is a multidisciplinary approach. As we see it, in the world's history of performing arts, the interweaving of text, sound, music, movement, and design is nothing new. The tradition from which our work evolves makes for great theater. In our productions we often combine sign language, poetry, storytelling, masks, mime, puppets, projections, film, music, and spoken texts.

For seven years, from 1984 to 1991, we were awarded Artists-in-Schools residency grants by the California Arts Council to teach performance art classes supplementing the language arts curriculum in public and private elementary and secondary schools. The students were able and disabled, hearing and nonhearing. Our challenge was to create productions that would accommodate all grade levels.

Through our roles as codirectors, we serve as models for our students, who see us solving problems in their presence. They join in the give and take of exploring ways we can all work together. We agree to disagree. One of the rewards of this way of problem solving is the likelihood of finding unpredictable solutions that take us in new directions. We respect our students as we would any professionals. We treat them as artists working with other artists. Sometimes problems need to be anticipated or solved. Our role is that of facilitators, providing resources, references, and materials.

The school residencies, The Children's Troupe, and other community arts residencies we have conducted have served as ongoing laboratories toward developing theater and movement activities that we have anthologized in *Live On Stage!* These performance guides reflect the basic premise of our teaching and directing: offering structures that provide creative problem-solving opportunities. We use the structures as guides and encourage each performer to find a personal way to work within the structures. The participants, by finding their own solutions, produce performances that reflect their time, place, and themselves.

Acknowledgments

This book could only have happened with the help of our fellow artists, our students, our teachers, and our families.

Carla wishes to thank her first teachers, Rose Mukerji-Bergeson, Miriam Kirkell, and Rose Ann Lohmeyer, for showing her methods of creative and respectful collaboration; and also thanks Mihail Stolarevsky, who helped her understand musical expression. Jody wishes to thank her teachers, Tatiana Dokoudovska and Rebecca Fuller. They provided the inspiration and foundation for our work and this book.

We thank the members of the 1979–1992 Children's Troupes, who helped us develop and refine the methods and structures that are found in these pages. Their wonderful work is presented in photographs throughout this book. Grateful thanks also to Nancy Quinn and Allen Willis, for their expert support and advice that helped us promote and document our work.

Thanks to the California Arts Council for awarding us the Artist-in-Schools residency projects that gave us opportunities to test out our ideas in classroom settings, and the schools who co-sponsored our residencies, including Far West High School in Oakland, and Columbus Middle School, The School of the Madeline, and John Muir Elementary School in Berkeley. In addition, we gratefully thank the San Francisco Foundation, Morris Stulsaft Foundation, Zellerbach Family Fund, Fleishhaker Family Fund, Foremost McKesson Foundation, Benefit Guild of the East Bay, Wells Fargo Bank, Mervyn's, The Upjohn Fund of San Francisco, East Bay Volunteers for the Arts, Berkeley Civic Arts Commission, and Alameda County Art Commission for helping to support our work with The Children's Troupe. We also thank the students and faculty of Arrowsmith Academy in Berkeley, who worked on many of the scriptwriting and full-scale production methods that are offered here. We particularly thank the Fall 1995 drama students, whose photographs appear on these pages, along with The Children's Troupe.

Thanks to Don Fehr, for passing on our manuscript to Bev Dana at Dale Seymour Publications. We especially thank Bev Dana who believed in the book and championed it into publication. Great thanks to Jeri Hayes and Geri Stewart for their thoughtful, sensitive guidance and careful editing, to Theo Crawford for her inputting, and to Lynda Banks for her wonderful text and cover designs. Finally, we thank the staff of Addison-Wesley for their support of this project.

Introduction

Conceptual Framework

Active Learning and the Play Process

In *Live On Stage!*, experience is the teacher. Recent research supports the theory that learning by doing is the most effective way to learn, reaching a greater number of students.

> Educators believe children learn best when they are active rather than passive, when they are asked to find their own answers to questions. . . .The arts demand students' involvement. . . . ("Creativity vs. Academics: How to Teach the Arts?" by Susan Chira, *New York Times,* Feb. 3, 1993)

We experience active learning first in childhood play, and play process is at the heart of the teaching methods in *Live On Stage!*. By tapping into childhood play experiences we gain access to a treasury of intuitive information about creative problem solving, about how to make something from nothing, and about how to work together while having a good time.

Moreover, as participants become aware of the skills that are needed to play performance games, they improve their ability to live in the present, to be spontaneous, and allow themselves and others freedom to try out new ideas. Through practice they can become conscious of these skills and, over time, begin to apply them to their lives.

> . . . when it comes to the forging of new understandings and the creation of new worlds, childhood can be a very powerful ally. Indeed, I contend that the creator is an individual who manages a most formidable challenge: to wed the most advanced understandings achieved in a domain with the kinds of problems, questions, issues, and sensibilities that most characterized his or her life

as a wonder-filled child. It is in this sense that the adult creator draws repeatedly on the capital of childhood. In different eras, different periods of childhood will be drawn upon; it seems that the special burden of the modern era is to mine the early years of childhood. (*Creating Minds* by Howard Gardner, p.32)

Life Skills Taught by the Performing Arts

In the long run, one of the principle goals of this method is to help participants become aware of how they can continue to use creative play experiences to build life skills. Effective performing arts skills and good life skills involve being focused on the present at all times. The rewards of "being present" are built into the experience. The mental processes used in performing arts correspond directly to those needed in the workplace. Collaborations, or teamwork projects, give students opportunities to be part of something bigger than themselves.

- **Focus** Learning how to attend to or concentrate on a task

- **Observation** As audience or observer; as performer or creator of a project
  - Paying attention and noticing details
  - Becoming sensitive to multiple points of view
  - Learning to use observations to think analytically

- **Creative Problem Solving**
  - Being willing to experiment without locking into a single course of events
  - Being able to suspend the inner "critic" during experimentation

- **Follow-through** Learning to participate in a decision-making process that starts with a concept and ends with a product/performance

- **Organization**
  - Learning to be responsible for scheduled commitments
  - Researching and gathering materials
  - Formulating concepts into structures
  - Finding details of content to place within structures
  - Understanding and analyzing the correlations between the details of content or events
  - Reformulating concepts and structures to order information into a final product

- **Presentation** Learning to present oneself clearly and forcefully while maintaining a personal, individual style

- **Communication**
  - Learning to articulate ideas to others
  - Learning to listen to others
  - Learning about other cultures and ideas

- **Teamwork (Ensemble Collaboration)**
  - Learning to work together with respect and cooperation to develop an idea or project
  - Learning to negotiate and compromise

- **Self-discipline**
  - Learning to take responsibility for oneself
  - Following through on a project from beginning to end
  - Being on time and ready to work
  - Taking initiative and completing assignments
  - Participating in repetitive rehearsal drills

Benefits of the Performing Arts in Education

There is much material available to support the premise that performing arts can address many educational goals and help give approaches to problems that teachers face in today's classrooms.

Name a current educational buzzword, and arts educators point to a way that arts teaches (sic) it: multiculturalism, alternative forms of testing, different learning styles, interdisciplinary curriculum, self-esteem, problem solving. (*New York Times*, Ibid.)

Because the performing arts often integrate language arts skills into other activities, students' overall academic skills often improve. Young people who are alienated, discouraged, or consider themselves failures (or have been dismissed as failures) often become inspired to learn through the arts. An arts program at Florida's Cutler Ridge Middle School is notable for showing how the arts can reach students whom others may have given up on.

The Ridge Arts program, which offers two-hour afternoon classes in art, music or drama, includes students whom teachers had labeled troublemakers or indifferent. But to stay in the program they must maintain at least a C average, and teachers have found that attendance and grades shoot up when students join Ridge Arts. (*New York Times*, Ibid.)

We want to help our students develop an interest in and a positive attitude toward using the creative process to analyze and make decisions, so that it spills over into their lives and brings a sense of purpose, excitement, and enthusiasm to all of their work.

Through performance games, students should be able to find ways to participate that are interesting and important to them, and begin applying that information to creatively think through ideas in other school subjects, at home, and in the workplace.

In countless reports executives say they need employees who can analyze problems and work well together despite their disparate ethnic backgrounds. Creating art in and of itself requires such skills. . . "A child must know how to do it, then critique it and be able to verbalize it," said Lilia Garcia, who supervises arts for the Dade County School District in Florida. "Art is based on problem solving: What color do I choose? What feeling do I want to portray? They will use these skills their whole lives." (*New York Times*, Ibid.)

Addressing Different Learning Styles

In performance, there is a need for many different kinds of skills or ways to interact and work together. We want to engage students in ways that they learn best—visually, kinesthetically, verbally, and socially—in order to communicate and work together at an optimum level. The games and activities in *Live On Stage!* offer multiple learning choices through watching, listening, writing, speaking, or doing. Participants can choose to be writers, composers, performers, designers, or technicians.

Cross-Disciplinary Approach

Mixing and sampling information and applying ideas from many disciplines is useful as a tool for creative problem solving, and is referred to as a cross-disciplinary or multidisciplinary approach. *Live On Stage!* is full of practical applications that apply cross-disciplinary methods that connect arts disciplines to other academic disciplines.

When participating in the performance games in *Live On Stage!,* students are given opportunities to research, process, and utilize information from the point of view of many different disciplines. Working across disciplines provides teachers and students with a variety of choices in how to approach learning. It addresses the needs of diverse learning styles; provides a framework to represent and present the cultures and interests of both students and teachers; and incorporates methodology from academic and artistic disciplines. By connecting information across disciplines, students will arrive at deeper insights into their own thinking and appreciation of other times, cultures, and people.

Particularly in the performing arts, it is necessary to learn how interdependent disciplines can be. Most drama productions require collaborations between researchers, writers, visual designers, actors, and technicians. Many other disciplines are often called into play.

In this cross-disciplinary approach, collaborations can involve any number of teachers, students, guest artists, parents, and any other available community resources. The blend of interests and disciplines guides the choices and provides a natural tool for embracing the many ways of learning. With each new group there are new ways to work.

Celebrating Diversity

In the performing arts, diversity is a positive asset. By using cross-disciplinary or multidisciplinary approaches to the performing arts, a variety of artistic perspectives are brought forward, offering students an effective model by demonstrating that there are many different ways to address a single idea.

The arts also provide opportunities to introduce students to other cultures, bridging differences between cultures. With diverse groups of people working together using a cross-disciplinary approach, the work evolves from their lives and interests, and therefore reflects their cultures, races, backgrounds, ages, and beliefs. This way of interacting naturally introduces respect and interest in other cultures and other forms of presentation.

Collaboration and Consensus

There are many precedents in the world history of theater for the development of work through collaboration. Many professional theater companies work collaboratively to build a performance structure that includes all participants, starting from a beginning concept and finishing with a performance. *Les Miserables, A Chorus Line, Mahabarata,* and *Nicolas Nicolby* are well-known recent examples of elaborate collaborations that included actors, writers, designers, directors, and musicians.

The skills of teamwork, critical thinking, problem solving, and organization are all essential to collaboration. The goal is to bring the ideas, background, and skills of two or more people to bear on the work. At the beginning, the work may only be a structure, and from there it becomes a total concept, integrating as many ideas from the participants as possible. This process integrates all the details of the production—the action, text, sound, and design—into what is known as *total theater.*

Collaboration is a three-part process. The first part involves exploration and experimentation of the initial ideas through discussion, improvisation, and other tools for getting the creative juices flowing. The second part establishes the structure of the work through rehearsal. Even if the resulting performance is intended to remain an improvisation, some structure has to exist for the work's core idea to be maintained and communicated. The third part is the time for refining and polishing the work into its best possible performance readiness.

Collaborations require open and steady communication. This is the only absolute in the many ways we have to bring a diverse group of people together, using the richness of each person's life in building the group's collaboration. To define the structure of the work, ideas have to be tried out, and opinions aired. Everybody needs to participate in the exploration of the general topic or germ of an idea that is at hand. Listening and sharing ideas is essential. Participants may contribute personal experiences and discoveries; conduct research through interviews, reading, and observation; or gather interesting materials, images, or text from art or life.

Leadership can take many forms in collaborations. Each group develops ways that work for them. There can be one Leader who guides the group, collating the materials and making the final decisions about structure and content. Or the work may be divided among all participants, with everyone taking responsibility for sections of the work or for particular jobs. The work could also be completely shared by all participants, perhaps using some kind of voting process or discussion forum to facilitate decision making.

The activities in *Live On Stage!* are set up so that everyone is a part of the decision-making process. The goal is to remove the "top-down" hierarchy in the decision-making process and replace it with a horizontal, across-the-board model in which everyone's opinion is valued. In business, this way of problem solving is called *consensus management.* When we relate as facilitators, reference guides, or members of the team—artists among artists—our students learn to value finding their own solutions, remaining flexible to change.

Central to the concepts of *Live On Stage!* is the premise that everyone is creative—creativity is not a "gift" bestowed on a few—and that there is no one particular way in which to create or assist others in their creating. In a world defined this way, everything is negotiable, and consensus is always possible.

 Contents

Live On Stage! is an anthology of teaching methods for incorporating performing arts into any classroom or community setting. The authors, Carla Blank and Jody Roberts, have compiled this resource out of their years of experience as performing artists, educators, and educational consultants. It is filled with a variety of theater and movement techniques, most of which require no special space, training, or materials, enabling teachers to bring quality arts education to their students in the context of the academic curriculum.

Live On Stage! guides the reader, who may have little or no experience in the performing arts, with simple step-by-step directions to games and exercises that are fun to play. They can be easily adapted to fit particular needs, including the needs of special populations, such as physically disabled or learning disabled children. In addition, the book provides variations within activities; suggestions for developing performances; teaching notes that include classroom management tips, ideas for incorporating the activities into various curriculum disciplines, and assessment strategies; a glossary of performing arts and technical theater terms; and a bibliography of books and other sources.

Live On Stage! also contains background notes that provide a historical perspective of movements, styles, and genres in the performing arts. Within these notes and interspersed throughout the book, the authors discuss the history behind techniques that are used by performing artists in the real world, and offer ways to apply these techniques to classroom teaching and group leadership. *Live On Stage!* includes performance techniques used by artists since the 1920s; improvisational theater games that have evolved since the 1950s to modern day performance art; scriptwriting methods that originated with the classic theater of Greece and Rome and the commedia dell'arte; and popular entertainments from the ancient and modern world.

The activities in *Live On Stage!* offer many basic performance structures, including scores, script-writing devices, storytelling formulas, movement exercises, and improvisational forms. Throughout the book, you will find these activities referred to as *performance games,* this book's term for structures used in performing arts disciplines, including theater, dance, and design. They are experiential, process-based building blocks for creative learning.

The performance games can be played in the classroom, in any indoor or outdoor open space, or onstage. The activities are intended to be used flexibly; a single activity can be used as a one-time-only, ten-minute warm-up or improvisation, or be expanded into an ambitious, full-length event with elaborate production values. *Live On Stage!* invites Leaders and Players to make their own variations on the performance games, and find new combinations of structures besides those suggested in these pages. It celebrates different learning styles and provides many ways to approach learning and creating. It may be used to help meet standard objectives set for the language arts, social studies, and mathematics curricula, thereby providing students with a performing arts education without adding to an already crowded academic schedule. All students—not only the gifted and talented—can participate in these performance games with understanding and enjoyment.

Chapter Overview

The book is divided into eleven chapters:

Chapter 1, Orientation Games, presents introductory activities that acquaint students and teachers with one another, the working space, and to performance games as an approach to exploring theater.

Chapter 2, Movement Activities, offers a mixture of contemporary and historical dance and pantomime exercises that require no formal dance training. The activities use simple structures that rely on daily life movements and tasks, simple locomotor skills, social dance forms, improvisation, and personal style.

Chapter 3, Acting Skills, gives students practice in self-presentation so that they will be able to communicate what they intend. The exercises offer structures in which to develop critical thinking and problem-solving skills.

Chapter 4, Improvisational Techniques, looks more closely at how to use improvisation. Communication, collaboration, and cooperation are practiced through exercises that require quick responses to changing situations.

Chapter 5, Scriptwriting, offers various methods to organize, record, and perform oral and written texts. They are easily connected to language arts, social studies, and other curriculum objectives.

Chapter 6, Scores, presents performance structures— alternatives to scripted forms—to help Players discover fresh ways to create theater works.

Chapter 7, Musical Forms, looks at how musical structures can be used as models to inspire new ways to think about performance structures.

Chapter 8, Site-Specific Projects, expands Players' perception of art and provides structures to view, create, respond to, and relate to an environment.

Chapter 9, World Theater, is a resource to familiarize students with diverse theatrical genres. It suggests ways to explore them through research, view them on video and in live theater, critically analyze them, and experiment with them.

Chapter 10, Short Takes, offers quick warm-up exercises to use in workshop classes, rehearsals, and to prepare for performance.

Chapter 11, Showtime! gives advice to guide Players through final rehearsals and performance. It includes directing aids, design and technical considerations, final rehearsal and performance procedures, and suggestions for closure after the event.

Lesson Components

Introduction Each lesson begins with a brief summary of the directions and suggestions for its uses in performance training or applications to academic curriculum.

Skills Highlights particular learning tools that will be practiced in playing the game or activity.

Time Offers a guideline for estimating how long to schedule for each activity, according to the level of production that you are choosing.

Space States space requirements and suggests where the activity can be done.

Materials Lists materials that are necessary and those that can be used to expand production values. Suggests what preparations to make, if any are required.

Directions In Chapters 1 through 8, each lesson provides some suggestions for general rules or methods of approach. They are listed in chronological order, to help you present each activity to your class. Chapter 9, World Theater, uses a slightly different format that gives students opportunities to become familiar with various genres from a variety of perspectives, including research, audience participation, and performance exploration. Chapter 10, Short Takes, gives brief activity descriptions, without going into the components provided in other chapters.

Variations In addition to the general approach suggested in the Directions, many lessons include other ways to perform or structure the materials.

Performance Suggestions Ideas for developing informal projects into more ambitious productions.

Teaching Notes Concrete suggestions to help activities flow smoothly, guide student focus, and emphasize particular skills.

Management Tips Ways to adjust the activities, set up the space, and prepare the students so that they work safely, respectfully, and with understanding.

Connections Cross-disciplinary suggestions for linking lessons to other academic or arts disciplines.

Special Needs Suggestions for adapting activities to meet special education needs, including those of ESL, learning disabled, and physically disabled students.

Background Notes Historical or cultural information that provides a context for the lessons and genres.

Assessment Ways to translate student experiences into critical-thinking explorations, and to evaluate understanding and achievement.

Teacher Observations Suggested guidelines to help assess students' exploratory research, creative process, and performance. Questions relate to the skills emphasized in the activities.

Group Discussion Suggested discussion topics and questions to help facilitate students' processing of their feelings, judgments, and learning during performance or audience experiences.

Student Activities Lists related material and assignments in the Student Book and provides ideas for students to explore in their Journals.

Performance Models Examples of how the authors have used the structures in lesson activities to create performances. These models are meant to be used as jumping-off points for your own creative process.

Student Activities

A Student Activities component is provided at the end of most lessons. There you'll find page references for the Student Book, and where relevant, Journal writing assignments. You will need to review the pages in the Student Book when planning your classroom lessons, as you sometimes may want to assign reading in the Student Book before conducting the classroom activities. For example, chapter Overviews for the Student Book are referenced *after* the first lesson in each chapter of the Teacher Resource Book (e.g., see page 4). It is suggested that students read the chapter Overview before beginning the class work for that chapter.

Since keeping a journal is an optional student activity, Journal assignments are not included in the Student Book.

Student Book Chapters 1–11 of the Student Book correspond the the chapters in the Teacher Resource Book. Chapter 12 in the Student Book is devoted to scripts. Each script is cross-referenced at relevant points in the Teacher Resource Book. The Student Book provides a brief overview of each chapter, telling students what they can look forward to learning and performing. In addition, the Student Book includes background information, historical notes theater vocabulary, scripts, poem-plays, performance and writing models, design projects, research activities, and extensive production information.

Journal It is recommended that students keep a specifically designated journal to complete research and writing assignments and to record personal feelings about their individual and group performances. Journal entries may be turned in to the teacher for evaluation.

 Teaching Notes

How to Use *Live On Stage!*

Live On Stage! is a nonlinear, flexible, and interactive approach to learning. Almost all of the performance games can be adapted to meet the needs of any group, from beginners to more experienced theater students. Select lessons as they are of interest to you and your group, or to complement your curriculum needs.

Skills and methods may overlap from lesson to lesson. Sometimes, cross-references are indicated within Directions, Variations, and Performance Suggestions to indicate where to find design ideas, movement activities, or other creative structures that might apply to your project. Besides the arts references, there are also interdisciplinary connections suggested within Teaching Notes.

You may find it useful to skip around in the book. Chapter 1, Orientation Games, offers ways to begin working with all groups. The activities introduce the Players to each other and the workspace, and establish a basis for a shared vocabulary. You could look at Chapter 10, Short Takes, to find physical and vocal warm-ups to begin any work session. If you want to start a project through improvisation, refer to Chapter 4, Improvisational Techniques, for directing hints. Then, if you decide the group could develop their improvisations into scripts, refer to Chapter 5, Scriptwriting, to get ideas on how to present assignments and choose appropriate structures. Or, you could start a session informally with a half-hour of exercises from Chapter 2, Movement Activities, Chapter 3, Acting Skills, or Chapter 8, Site-Specific Projects. If everyone gets excited about any one of these exercises, and you decide to develop it into a public performance, turn to Chapter 11, Showtime! to think about how to go into production. Once you are into the expansion phase of a project, you could refer to Chapter 10, Short Takes, again, to find rehearsal energizers and performance warm-ups.

There are a few performance games that we advise using only with participants who have worked together for awhile, because they require a more complicated creative process and involve extra steps of analysis. These include Live Movie (page 128), because Players need to understand and use film vocabulary and apply it to a live performance; Part Forms (page 142), because Players need to understand and use music and literary vocabulary and apply it to their work; and ambitious production goals for any game, especially the genres discussed in Chapter 9, World Theater.

Curriculum Connections

Any activity in *Live On Stage!* can be related to curriculum. Following are some general suggestions of ways to incorporate creative projects into other subjects.

Language Arts Read and perform existing plays, poetry, and short fiction works; transform creative writing assignments into performance scripts; practice effective presentation and communication skills

Social Living Create skits on relevant subjects; practice teamwork skills through small-group improvisations

Government/Civics Perform a mock trial; go through an election process beginning with primaries and following through to the final election

History/Social Studies Research, write, and perform autobiographies and biographies as monologues and dialogues; create living history skits or environments based on a time, place, or event; learn dances and theater forms from different times and cultures

Mathematics Use improvisational games to learn progressions, recognize patterns, become familiar with geometric shapes, practice multiples and fractions, or analyze statistical data

Science Practice observing an environment; design and build sound effects equipment and lighting systems; invent optical illusions to use as sets or props

Computers Design or use existing software programs to choreograph dances, compose music, and draft set, lighting, or costume designs; program technical cues; use word processing for writing and editing scripts

Foreign Languages Improvise conversational scenes; combine language and pantomime to kinesthetically express vocabulary

Art Design and make masks, puppets, costumes, special effects, stage sets, backdrops, publicity; explore artworks to inspire ideas; analyze artistic elements to inform movements, design, and character

Music Compose original scores; perform existing choral or instrumental music; analyze musical forms and adapt their structures for performance works

Structure in Performance Games

At the core of each project is structure. For performance work, a *structure* is the way in which the parts are put together to form a whole. Structures serve as safety nets, relating to the work as a skeleton does to the body, supporting ideas to be communicated.

Structures provide problem-solving opportunities or offer guides by which individuals are encouraged to find a personal way to work. It is the structure that gives performers a base from which to explore and experiment with new ideas. A structure can function for a one-time-only experiment, or it can be the basis for a more elaborate production.

Perhaps the oldest and most universal structures can be found in games. Games made for performing function similarly to the rules of games made for sport. Once the Players understand the rules as given, they play the game according to their own interpretations.

The start of a structure may be as simple as a word, a formula, or visual image that generates ideas, associations, and research. Then the question is: Where does the word, formula, or image lead?

After an agreement has been reached about which kind of structure to develop, the process of creating a performance becomes the focus. Through improvisation, the Players keep trying different solutions to the structure, layering details to build the performance.

Presenting the Activities

In playing performance games, anything is permissible within the rules or structure, since there is no right or wrong solution. Often Players will ask for answers that will tell them what to do, or ask you to give them permission to do something. Players may ask questions, such as "How long should it be?" or "Can we talk while playing the game?" or "Can we do this with a partner?" Questions should not be resolved by you. If they come up, ask Players to think about the rules or to state the rules of the game again. Once you are sure the Players understand the structure, advise them to let it be their guide. Following are some guidelines for presenting a new performance game to the Players.

- If you are working in a large open area, define the limits of the space and remove any dangerous objects or safety hazards from the playing area.

- Stand where everyone in the group can see and hear you. If the group is in a circle, stand on the circle, so that your back is to no one.

- Give the name of the game first.

- Explain the directions in a simple and clear manner.

- Check for comprehension of the directions. State them again, if you observe any misunderstanding.

- If appropriate, relate the rules to a well-known reference: a familiar game such as Follow the Leader or a team sport; an experience with improvisation or storytelling; or imagery from cartoons, movies, or television.

- Ask for questions. Clarify any confusion in the rules. Encourage Players to solve the rules in their own way.

- Be open to including any variations or suggestions that might be offered by Players. Give the group the choice of including them in the game.

- Remind Players to take responsibility for their safety. Give Players permission to modify physical tasks that cause pain and suggest how Players can modify actions.

- After playing a game, it is sometimes useful to have a discussion. Listen to how participants felt while playing the game; discuss alternative solutions; ask what skills the group feels the game can strengthen; ask if they would like to develop the game further, or play it again.

General Lesson Plan

Use performance techniques to do the organizing for you. The following list suggests ways to run focused work sessions and build a performance. It could function as an outline to order lesson plans.

1. Preset the performance area by clearing the room of distractions and unnecessary furniture.

2. Begin with warm-up exercises to help students prepare for the work ahead.

3. Give focusing exercises to practice concentration and increase sensory awareness.

4. Present ensemble-building exercises to build trust and teamwork skills.

5. Use improvisational activities to explore ideas and practice adapting to change.

6. Conduct discussions to present directions to performance game activities, analyze classwork, vote on performance choices, give directing notes, assign performance responsibilities, and to ascertain that everyone understands the rules of conduct in performance.

7. Have Players share projects with one another in order to gain presentation experience and to learn appropriate audience behavior.

8. Give closure to a project with a wind-down discussion or cooling-off activity .

9. Restore the performance area to the same condition in which you found it, ready for the next group of occupants.

General Management Tips

Session Duration Schedule the length of work time according to each group's level of interest. Try to keep the duration of sessions within realistic expectations. Some groups need to move quickly from activity to activity. Others benefit from longer work periods. If you intend to take a project into performance, it will be useful to schedule larger blocks of rehearsal time close to the performance date.

Offer Variety and Variations Offer a variety of performance games so that everyone's taste is recognized. Or add challenging variations, to keep energy high and focus engaged.

Shortening or Simplifying a Project Provide some ready-made parts for a project rather than having students start from scratch. You can select the topic and research the materials, divide up the tasks by assigning roles or jobs, revise the script, and stage the production.

Ask for Student Input

- Allow Players to request favorite games or activities to use as warm-ups.

- Ask students to bring in music selections, projects, ideas, costumes or props, and so on.

- Increase Players' participation in the decision-making process so that everyone feels included and that their tastes and values are recognized. For example, after initial exploration of an idea, ask for student input in making editing decisions and choosing a performance order.

- Once students are familiar with the project choices available to them, take a vote to decide which idea will be done. Go with a simple majority or a two-thirds majority decision.

- Include creators in the editing process of their original work.

Make Your Expectations Clear Present assignments orally and in written form. Let people know your expectations and then hold them accountable for fulfilling their responsibilities.

Solve Discipline Problems Try solving problems, including discipline problems, with immediate solutions that serve performance objectives. For example:

- If the class gets too noisy, call for a freeze. Ask them to go through a series of Move/Freeze actions. Or, take time out and do some focus or relaxation exercises.

- If the class gets giddy, acknowledge the giddiness by asking Players to increase the size of the giggles (a useful tool for clowning activities); perform quiet giggles; alternate giggles with a performance of sadness, or jumps, or whatever fits the activity that was going on. Or suggest that Players concentrate on what their characters want or what their performance objective is at that moment.

- Use live or recorded music to calm and organize a group or shift the mood.

- Be positive. Point out examples of good work and good habits: "I really like the way you maintained focus in the large group frieze." Try not to compare one student's work with another's.

Give Personal Feedback When possible, write personal notes or call people aside to share suggestions for ways to solve artistic problems and to let them know they are working well.

Divide Players into Teams Divide large groups into small groups or teams to keep everyone working as much of the time as possible. Encourage team members to work together in planning their performance. Occasionally check the progress of each team to see if Players need some guidance.

Contracts When a large production is about to be undertaken by a group, you might want to consider drawing up a contract to serve as an agreement that the performer will participate in the class or group throughout the performance project, attend all rehearsals on time, be prepared to work at each session, and have a positive attitude. Have all parties, including yourself, the Player, and the Player's parents or guardians, sign the contract. Attach a tentative rehearsal schedule to the contract, so that everyone is agreeing to the actual date and time commitments, as far as is known at the time of signing the contract.

Involving All Students

Look for each individual's strength, experimenting with alternative approaches to find the ways he or she learns best. Then help Players take advantage of these strengths while performing. This principle holds true for everybody, and has particular applications for those with physical or learning disabilities.

The following methods involve visual, spatial, kinesthetic, verbal, and social cues that could be adapted to fit many performance situations. They have proved useful when working with diverse groups to create strong, clear presentations.

Highlight Individuality You can present an organized stage image—and even create a unison effect—and still give Players permission to perform in their own unique styles. For example, ask everyone to walk her favorite walk on a specific path, such as crossing from downstage right to upstage left. The unison effect will be achieved by performers walking on the same path rather than trying to be exactly in step with everyone else. The acceptance of individual styles will eliminate the anxiety of trying to be "perfect," or to look the same as everyone else.

Use Nonlinguistic Aids Use visual aids, rhythmic patterns, sound cues, or other kinds of nonlinguistic approaches to help Players learn and memorize text or kinesthetic tasks, or to help them find a personal performance style. Use repetition to reinforce learning.

Create a Buddy System Build a support system by pairing Players to compensate for differences in experience and to compensate for special needs that might present difficulties, such as memorization problems, spatial disorientation, and physical limitations.

Use Peer Grouping Have Players work in small groups when doing research, studying lines, directing, and rehearsing scenes. Have Players appear in their groups for at least part of the performance; this will provide some security for the performers during the stress of performing.

Give Players Appropriate Responsibilities Give people the amount of responsibility that they are capable of and ready to assume. Too much responsibility can create unnecessary tension that works against the performer and the performance; too little may keep individuals from investing in themselves and the performance. For example, when using an audition process, encourage people to audition for the parts they want. Then have them write down their choices, in order of preference. Balance what they have to say with what you feel would be an appropriate level of challenge.

Provide Alternative Jobs Appeal to students' interests by assigning or allowing them to choose a job responsibility to fit the needs of the project. There are many other important jobs besides acting in the performing arts that can be useful even in an informal production.

- Writers who research, write, and edit the script or score

- Composers, musicians, and singers

- Choreographers and dancers

- Directing assistants, including script recorder and prompter

- Designers who design costumes, lighting, sound, visuals, and the set

- Technical crew: stage manager, sound and lighting operators, property manager, stage crew, and costume manager (Chapter 11, Showtime! includes descriptions of the more intensive production, design, and stage crew jobs.)

- Publicist, who writes press release copy, designs announcements and tickets, and compiles and creates the program

- House manager, who prepares the performing space for the audience and supervises ticket sales and ushers

Sometimes, Players take the attitude that a backstage job is less important than a performing job. Students are usually impressed to hear that, in the theater world, the first people to be paid and the ones who generally get paid at a higher fee are those with behind-the-scenes jobs.

Discuss job descriptions, so that participants understand the responsibilities of each job and why these jobs are necessary to the work. Since many of these jobs—especially the technical designers and crew—require independent work, assign Players who are capable of taking on that responsibility. You will need to check in with the designers and crew to see that they follow-through on doing their work, as they should be held to the same expectations as the performers. If you have a very efficient stage manager, that person can help you by being a liaison and organizer among all the designers and crews.

Working with Special Needs

The performance games in *Live On Stage!* are excellent and tailor-made to facilitate learning for physically disabled, learning disabled, and ESL students. They encourage peer interaction where students can learn through sharing and get reinforcement of concepts through interaction. Much of the learning can be supported with visual aids that can help with comprehension, such as gestures, pictures, and audiovisual aids.

There are many resources that give advice on ways to assist students with special needs. In this section, broad guidelines are suggested that may or may not apply to your specific needs. Special education teachers, specialists, aides, parents or guardians, and tutors are invaluable resources. Ask them for suggestions for effective compensating skills to help individual students process information or manage tasks. Also, enlist their help in getting participants to learn cues, lines, and actions, and to follow through on gathering materials. Make sure a caretaker, special educa-

tion teacher, or translator is participating in the activities as needed.

As with all students, be sure to check that the workspace provides a safe environment and try to anticipate any difficulties students could have in adapting lessons and using their compensating skills. When you present rules verbally, include a choice of variations that speak to the limitations of your students' disabilities.

Special Education Students Following are suggestions that address different types of special needs.

- Give the work sessions some feeling of a routine, if possible. For example, always begin with a warm-up in a circle formation, followed by a short exercise or two to develop trust and ensemble, and then break into teams to do projects.

- Be supportive, calm, and positive. Be clear and consistent about expectations for behavior and classwork. If necessary, discuss pre-established consequences for out-of-bounds behaviors.

- Place students near the Leader, so that it is possible to quietly redirect a student's attention to the work at hand if he begins to lose focus. Try to keep a student's workspace away from distracting stimuli like an air conditioner, heater, door, or window.

- Work in small increments, giving specific one- or two-step directions. When each unit is understood, add on the next idea, and so on.

- Give assignments in ways that require students to use two or more senses, for example, a handout to read and verbal instructions to listen to; a text to read aloud and discuss and related pictures to write about. Check that students record the assignment correctly.

- Use visuals—drawings, photographs, and videos— to help students understand any directions and research information.

- Check comprehension of the directions on a regular basis. For example, check scripts to be sure cues and lines are highlighted accurately and pages are organized.

- Provide alternative methods to do assignments and classwork.
  - If a student has difficulty with writing, allow her to use visual images, such as stick-figure drawings, felt board cutouts, and sand-tray figures, to communicate her ideas.
  - If a student has difficulty with both written language and visual imagery, record his ideas by audio or video, and have someone transcribe it; or give the student notes that he can refer to when writing the assignments.

- If a student reads well, use flash cards to help her with memorization of lines and cues. If it can be integrated into a scene, let her use a prop that holds a cue sheet, such as a clipboard or a book. Or avoid the issue by doing improvisations or reader's theater.

- Set a text to music, say it in a rhythm, or connect it to gestures or actions.

- Provide a peer tutor or ask parents or guardians to find a private tutor.

- Give extra time, if helpful, whenever possible.

Physically Disabled Students Generally, many of the guidelines for special education students apply to the needs of physically disabled students. There are specific notes listed in some activities for adapting them to specific needs.

For students in wheelchairs, or those who walk with physical aids such as braces, crutches, or walkers, make sure that the performing area is accessible. If the stage in your facility is not accessible to them, plan your performing area to include the floor in front of the stage. Or, if that is not possible, choose a project and find an alternative space that will allow everyone to participate. Assign one person to watch out for and remove any stray props, costumes, or unused set pieces that get in the way of entrances and exits and make access to the performing space unsafe. (In performance, this could be a stage crew job.)

Team physically able with physically disabled. If possible, choose projects that will help students learn from one another and how to care for each other. For example, find ways to team a wheelchair-bound student with a student who can walk and ask them to explore movements that can be done together, using the wheelchair. There are many theater groups experimenting with new mobility ideas that take advantage of a wheelchair's capacity to give support, mobility, and speed. Another solution is to assign a physically able tech crew student to assist a disabled tech designer by doing the legwork of hanging and focusing lights, constructing the set or props, or maintaining the equipment.

Most directions can be adapted or modified to help meet the needs of physically handicapped students. For those in wheelchairs, using walkers, or other mechanical supports, try breaking down jobs into component steps, so that they do not sound like overwhelming physical challenges. If they cannot be adapted, provide an alternative activity so that all students feel included and important to the project. James LeBrecht, one of the most respected and innovative theater sound designers in the country, was born with spina bifida and is wheelchair-bound. He says that his disability has provided him with a unique perspective on his profession.

Ask interpreters to translate for deaf students, to facilitate conversations between the deaf and hearing students and yourself. Place interpreters in a prominent position, where they can be seen by both the deaf and hearing students. Also, ask them to help deaf students share the art of sign language, including jokes, picture signs, and grammatical construction.

Team hearing with hearing-impaired students. Hearing students will not only begin to learn sign language, but will also learn how to cue a deaf person by tapping her on the shoulder, making eye contact, and using visual cues. When working with verbal imagery and cueing systems, as in the activities in Chapter 3, Acting Skills, substitute visual imagery for sound cues. Flashing the lights, agreed upon hand signs, and flash cards are three ways to do this.

To help blind students, team them with seeing students. This management technique will help them to familiarize themselves with new performing spaces, learn cues, practice memorizing lines, or participate in crowd scenes. Always provide Braille scripts or cue sheets. Substitute sound cues for visual cues. When working on a project that is presented with an emphasis on visual imagery, such as Cut and Paste (page 123) or Living Pictures (page 125), substitute verbal imagery. Have someone quietly describe images that the rest of the group is seeing when watching live theater, video, or film productions.

ESL Students Honor students' native languages. Encourage them to participate using their native speech. It can enrich performances to interweave various languages, either by repeating lines in more than one language or by having scenes that go from English to some other tongue.

An adult or student translator may be needed so that all students understand directions and discussions. Pair up an ESL student with another student who speaks the first language. If that is not possible, ask an English-speaking student to help the ESL student. Encourage the use of bilingual and/or English dictionaries at all times.

Keep directions concise and easy to understand. If a student chooses not to speak aloud, offer him the option of using gesture or mime. To encourage participation, try not to correct or edit too much, unless you are going into a performance situation, and then do corrections on a one-to-one basis. Or, ask an ESL teacher to help by editing grammar in verbal or written performance scripts, and to help the students practice memorization tasks.

Encourage ESL students to indicate when they do not understand you. Check their comprehension on a regular basis, privately. Adjust or shorten assignments if needed to allow for success. Providing alternative assignments or independent projects, including watching pertinent television shows or doing picture presentations by making charts, graphs, or maps, could be beneficial to the student and the project.

Conclusion

"If everybody is ridiculous, no one is!"
    Augusto Boal, Director

In our teaching, we frequently encounter much fear, embarrassment, and resistance to trying ways to imagine, to experiment, to learn new material, and to communicate. Not only is it difficult for young people to explore different methods of learning and presenting—it can be difficult for anyone, teachers included. A critical self can get in the way of finding innovative methods, and certainly can impede the creation of exciting theater.

We all seem to have an idea of how we maintain our own dignity. And often, playing performance games does not fit a preconceived picture of what "should be" presented. The intent of the games is to create an arena where "right" and "wrong" do not exist. So this is the only value judgment we impose: everyone must try something. If you don't try something, nothing will happen.

The validity of this rule was confirmed by a group of classroom teachers when they joined in workshop sessions to learn how to adapt performance games into their academic curriculum. They found that, just like the students in their classes, when they participated in the work, they learned better.

Change is the nature of the game when you are crossing many disciplines, working collaboratively, and trying to address many learning styles. How else can you acknowledge and integrate all the information presented?

As Leaders and participants, we need to try to remain open to see and perceive what has been shared, to acknowledge what is present at any moment. Working in this manner inspires flexibility, adaptability, awareness, and learning without end. What better tools can anyone offer as preparation to live and work in the changing world?

Orientation Games

The games in this chapter are especially useful for introducing a new group to one another, the group Leader, the working space, and the activities found in *Live On Stage!* The games can also be used to refresh the work of an existing group. Their rules are quickly understood, they offer comfortable challenges to people regardless of their performing experiences, and their structures organize a group to create an immediate performance in which everyone participates.

As they play these games, participants learn through experience the basic skills they can apply to any performance game. Players will discover that each person's ideas will be honored and that everyone will get a chance to try. They will begin to find personal understanding of how to work within the rules of each game to find individual interpretations. They will realize that they have permission to creatively solve problems without judgment by themselves or others.

These orientation games are great ensemble-builders. Many are performed as group activities where participants need to focus on and be aware of one another in order to receive information or make decisions. Players will need to make instantaneous choices based on any changes to the space and their reactions to the actions of other Players. By encouraging participants to support one another in a spirit of give and take, you will help them begin to find a basis for presenting and negotiating ideas—a necessity when creating group performance work.

These orientation games also serve as guides to the Leader, who can gather a great deal of information about a group by observing how each game is played. You can gain insights about participants' interests, strengths, and weaknesses, as well as how they work together as a group. By watching what the students choose to perform, you will also discover what they believe is a performance.

If time allows, play these orientation games for a few sessions, letting impressions wash over you and the group as you try out a variety of ideas. It may be necessary to repeat a game or activity, especially if it wasn't understood the first time around or if it generated a lot of good energy and fun. Then build on this information to plan future sessions and to choose projects.

Direction Calls

n this game, a Leader calls out a series of directions, which Players simultaneously follow, finding their own interpretations. Direction Calls is a useful introductory game for the first session with a new group. During play, participants get acquainted with the space they will work in and the people with whom they will work.

Directions

1. Tell the Players that you will be calling out directions. After listening to each direction call, each Player decides how to interpret the call. All Players will perform their solutions at the same time.

2. Define the boundaries of the playing area. Have Players take one of the following positions to begin the game:

Skills
★ Developing body awareness and spatial perception
★ Following oral directions

Time
5 to 15 minutes

Space
Adaptable to any space, such as a classroom, a gym, a stage, or a playground. If you will be playing the game in a room with furniture, you may wish to clear a central space.

Materials
If you're uncomfortable about making up direction calls spontaneously, write a list prior to meeting with the group.

- Stand on or immediately outside the boundaries of the playing area.
- Stand together in the middle of the playing area.
- Choose a spot anywhere in the playing area.

3. Call out a series of directions, leaving ample time between calls for Players to complete the actions called for. Following are some ideas for direction calls:

- Choose a spot in the room and walk to it/walk away from it.
- Walk to the center/edges of the space.
- Cross the space in diagonal lines.
- Walk around the space and observe how another person walks.
- Imitate another person's walk.
- Give a hand greeting as you pass another person.
- Greet everyone you pass with a bow.
- Walk through the space, avoiding/looking into people's eyes.
- Walk through the space and shake hands/exchange names with everyone you meet.
- Touch elbows with each person you meet, remaining connected until everyone forms a clump.
- Move as a clump to somewhere else in the space.
- Slowly melt down and roll away from the clump.

4. Turn over the responsibility of making direction calls to the Players. Assign callers, ask for volunteers, or give an open invitation to all Players.

Variation

Direct each Player to choose and go to a spot in the working space that will be "Home." Alternate direction calls between moving away from Home and returning Home while performing a specific action or sound.

Examples:
- Go Home, laughing.
- Travel the edges of the space.
- Go Home, giving a lecture.
- Fill up the center of the space.
- Go Home, traveling in slow motion.

Teaching Notes

Management Tips

Observing Players Position yourself where you can observe the Players' movements. Try standing along the boundaries or at a distance outside the boundaries of the playing area.

Adjusting Direction Calls Adjust direction calls to comply with the size and attributes of the space and the capabilities of the Players. For example, if you are playing in a classroom, you may need to keep the physical actions slow and simple (walking, shaking hands) and noise to a minimum. If space allows, Players might enjoy directions calling for more physically active tasks (rolling, hopping, running).

Volume Repeat the directions more than once to help Players hear and process them. If you are going to be in a large space, you may need a megaphone or a microphone. Be aware that voice amplifiers will create a different dynamic. If none is available, define a smaller space within the area, or keep the noise level down by avoiding directions that ask for loud speaking or sound effects. If the noise level interferes with the Players' ability to hear direction calls, ask Players to make only the sounds called for by the directions.

Safety Remind Players to respect one another's space by being careful not to bump or push one another.

Connections

Physical Education Use direction calls that take Players through the skills of a particular sport, such as dribbling, kicking, or throwing a ball; running; jumping; turning cartwheels.

 Assessment

Teacher Observations

During Direction Calls, observe how well Players follow oral directions and how readily they interact to determine when they are ready to take over as their own directors.

Group Discussion

Generate a discussion about variations in individual interpretations of the same direction call.

 Student Activities

Book

pages 1–2 (Overview)

Journal

Ask Players to write about how playing this game was a "performance."

Stop/Listen/Go

n this game, the Leader or a Player calls out the commands, "Stop," "Listen" (+ Action Command), "Go," for other Players to follow. Stop/Listen/Go is a good orientation or warm-up game. Its structure is familiar, easily understood, and fun to play. By listening to the kinds of activities the Players call out and observing how enthusiastically the group solves each call, you will gain a lot of information about the group, their dynamics, and their interests.

 Directions

1. Set up the boundaries of the playing area and explain the following rules to the Players:

- The person who is "It" calls out "Stop!" All Players freeze, wherever and however they are.

- "It" calls out "Listen." Players remain in their friezes. "It" then gives an action command, such as "Jump," "Sing while walking," "Skip," "Give a lecture," "Walk a zigzag," "Laugh," or "Walk through molasses."

Skills
★ Developing leadership and teamwork skills
★ Giving, interpreting, and performing action commands

Time
5 to 15 minutes

Space
Adaptable to any open space

Materials
None

- "It" calls out "Go" and Players come out of their frieze and perform the action called for, moving anywhere in the playing space, until "It" calls out "Stop" again.

2. Begin the game by becoming "It" yourself. Remind Players to freeze whenever they hear the word "Stop," to remain in their friezes through the command "Listen" and the action command, and to begin moving as directed when they hear the word "Go."

3. Once it is clear that Players understand how to play the game, leadership can be offered to the group. Designate one Player to be "It," or ask for a volunteer. Rotate so that everyone has a turn to be "It."

 Teaching Notes

Management Tips

Timing Commands Ask that the Player who is "It" knows what command she wants to give before she calls "Stop." Remind "It" to give the Players enough time to try the action command before calling out "Stop."

Sharing Leadership As the pace of the game increases, there may be several Players who want to be "It." The "It" role is usually up for grabs, and it becomes a challenge for Players to learn how to share leadership. You can help to avoid confusion by setting a minimum time limit (about ten to twenty seconds) that must pass before a new command can be called.

Simplifying Commands The "Listen" command can be omitted, depending on the age and listening skills of the Players. Sometimes a three-step command is overwhelming.

Connections

Commands could be related to various curriculum subjects by asking for calls that relate to a specific time, place, or historic event or figure; ask for pantomimes of jobs or characters; or require the use of specific math skills. For example, if the group is studying the American Revolution, the calls could be "Boston Tea Party!" or "Washington crossing the Delaware."

 Assessment

Teacher Observations

Use the following questions to guide your observations and to help you assess your group's abilities.

- Do Players like to make the calls or do they wait for you to give examples? This will give you information about how comfortable Players are about trying out new ideas and solutions in front of one another.

- Do the calls ask for kinesthetic or linguistic tasks? Do they involve spatial changes? Your observations will help you determine whether the group is linguistically, visually, or kinesthetically inclined; the Players' strengths; and the areas that might need some practice.

- Are Players able to share the space without collisions? If not, you may need to work on activities such as Move/Freeze (page 27) to encourage large motor control through kinesthetic and spatial awareness, and teamwork activities such as Tug of War (page 53), Sculptures (page 12), or Follow the Leader (page 219) to encourage group work.

- How well does the group work together? Do they respect one another's ideas or do they tend to be more interested in being a Leader/caller? If you would like to encourage their leadership skills and give them permission to try new ideas, Follow the Leader (page 219), Musical Chairs (page 220), and Enter/Exit (page 47) are useful games.

Group Discussion

Ask Players to discuss the kinds of action commands that were given.

- What kinds of commands were the easiest/most difficult to understand?

- What kinds of commands were the easiest/most difficult to perform?

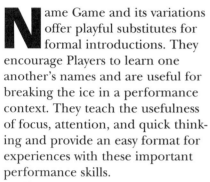

Name Game

Name Game and its variations offer playful substitutes for formal introductions. They encourage Players to learn one another's names and are useful for breaking the ice in a performance context. They teach the usefulness of focus, attention, and quick thinking and provide an easy format for experiences with these important performance skills.

These name games illustrate how *Live On Stage!* activities validate individual ways of working and encourage Players to free themselves from their inner critic. By performing everything they see and hear, Players understand that whatever they do is available for performance. Generally, the effect is to reduce anxieties caused by expectations for some imagined level of performance, while producing a lot of playful fun.

Skills
★ Performing self-introductions
★ Observing and imitating details of physical and vocal expression

Time
5 to 15 minutes

Space
Adaptable to any space

Materials
Musical or percussion accompaniment may be added to the Name + Rhythm variation.

★ Directions

1. Ask Players to stand or sit in a circle. Explain that one by one, Players will introduce themselves. Everyone else observes and listens to each person's introduction.

2. After each Player performs his or her introduction, everyone repeats the introduction simultaneously, trying to imitate all details of vocal and physical style as closely as possible. This means that Players imitate any information given by each person in his performance, including tone of voice, laughter, eyeball rolls, sighs, weight shifts, hand gestures, and so on.

3. The performance of introductions and imitations progresses around the circle until everyone has had a turn.

Variations

Name That Name Players draw each letter of their names in space, making the letters as large as possible.

Name + Run-Around Players run or walk the shapes of the letters in their names as a floor pattern.

Name + Rhythm By clapping, stamping, drumming, using vocalization, or by making sounds in some other manner, break down each name into syllables, giving each syllable a beat and/or a sound. Either the Leader or the person whose name is being performed repeats the name and rhythm over and over, then the rest of the group joins in. The Players or the Leader can decide whether

the group should remain in the circle or move around the space. The rhythm of each person's name is made by all Players, either by using percussion instruments or making body music with hand jive, clapping, stamping, or using the body as a drum.

Name + Action Each Player says his name and performs an action. The action can be anything, such as an everyday attitude, a dance movement, or a cliché gesture.

Name + Rhyme Each Player says her name then adds another sound or word that rhymes with it. Other Players then repeat the name and rhyme, imitating the Player's actions in their performance.

Name + Specific Category The group chooses a category. Each Player says her name and adds both a sound and an action that are related to the category.
Examples:
Name + Animal: "My name is Shadow, Meow." Action: stretch and clean face.
Name + Machine: "This is AT&T. Please leave a message at the tone." Action + sound: push pretend buttons while making beeping tones.
Name + Food: "I'm green and slimy spinach." Action: floppy and loose arms and legs, like a tangled leaf.

Add-a-Pearl Play the basic game, adding any of the variations. For example: Name + Category, Action, or Rhymer. After each Player's performance, the group repeats all Players' performances, in order.

Example:

First Player says his name + _____.

Group repeats First Player's name + _____.

Second Player says her name + _____.

Group repeats the First Player's name + _____ and the Second Player's name + _____.

Continue around the circle until all Players have introduced themselves and all names + _____ are performed in a string, from the first to the last Player.

Teaching Notes

Management Tips

Keep the Solutions Positive and Nonjudgmental

- Participate by playing the game and sharing your perceptions of sounds and actions. Students will model your examples.

- Approach the imitations in a positive manner. For example, if you observe someone scratching his chin, heaving a big sigh, folding her arms, or gazing into the distance, say, "Hey, that's a good action. Let's all do that one."

- Encourage fun and playfulness by encouraging Players to do everything as big and boldly as possible.

- Ask Players to imitate what they have observed, not their judgment on the observation. For example, Players should try to imitate a hand gesture for the sake of learning how to perform the gesture, rather than making fun of the person who originally made it.

Connections

Language Arts The Name + Rhyme variation can be used to practice rhyming techniques.

Assessment

Teacher Observations

- Observe how the Players imitate or mirror one another's actions to discover the observation strengths and weaknesses of your group.

- Look for changes of dynamics, levels, shapes, and timing. All of these are qualities that create the texture of a performance.

- Observe whether your students are enjoying working together.

If so, they are ready to progress to other challenges. If not, look first for games that use team-building skills in order to build participants' confidence in themselves and the group.

Group Discussion

Ask Players to discuss whether or not this game improved their observation and listening skills, and how.

Student Activities

Journal

Ask Players to record their responses to the following questions:

- What did you learn about yourself and the way you present yourself during Name Game?

- Were you surprised by some of the mannerisms or expressions the other Players noticed and imitated during your introduction?

Home Base

ome Base works well as an orientation game, and generally can serve as a warm-up activity. Players become aware of how they help create the stage picture through their relationship to the space and the other Players. The spatial structure of Home Base is derived from the configuration of bases on a baseball diamond. The participants choose their own individual locations for home, first, second, and third bases within the playing area. This game introduces Players to practicing self-direction within a cueing system.

Directions

1. Before playing the game, set the boundaries of the playing area. Ask the Players to look around the space and find a place to call home base. Tell Players to go to home base. Next, ask Players to find and go to another location, which will be called first base. Repeat this process until Players have each chosen the locations for all four bases.

Skills
- ★ Recalling spatial patterns in sequence
- ★ Responding instantaneously to oral commands
- ★ Following safety guidelines in group movement

Time
10 to 15 minutes

Space
Adaptable to any open space

Materials
None

2. Have Players walk to each of their four bases in order: home, first, second, then third. Each Player will have a unique pattern. Have Players walk through their base patterns a few times, until they all know exactly where their bases are located.

3. Explain that you are going to call any one of the four bases, and that you will also tell the participants a specific way to travel to that base. For example: "Go to second base on one leg," "Go to home base laughing," "Travel to third base as fast as possible," or "Go to first base backwards." Direct Players to travel as directed until they reach the designated base.

4. Continue calling bases and travel methods until Players become confident of their floor patterns. Then invite Players to call out directions.

Variations

Group Travel Everyone goes to one Player's home base. As a group, Players travel to that person's four bases, following the Leader's calls. Alternate Players whose bases will be used.

Small Group Travel Divide the group into four smaller groups. Each group adopts one group member's bases. All groups simultaneously follow the caller's commands.

Teaching Notes

Management Tips

Safety Issues This is a good game to establish the rule that Players need to respect one another's personal space by being careful not to bump

or push each other as they travel. To avoid crashes, have Players practice their traveling patterns in slow motion so everyone can see one another's path and adjust to any potential crashes. If Players do not understand, have them model with each other different ways to avoid colliding by slowing down, speeding up, or looping around another Player.

Assessment

Teacher Observations

- After some practice, do Players improve in their ability to perceive and control their spatial awareness in relation to others?
- Are Players able to memorize or keep track of a complicated spatial pattern as they experiment with different commands?

Group Discussion

Ask Players to discuss their experiences and feelings about sharing a performing space with other performers who were following different spatial patterns.

Student Activities

Journal

Have Players write about what they like and/or dislike about choosing, memorizing, and following their own spatial patterns.

Add-a-Pearl

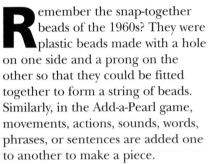

Remember the snap-together beads of the 1960s? They were plastic beads made with a hole on one side and a prong on the other so that they could be fitted together to form a string of beads. Similarly, in the Add-a-Pearl game, movements, actions, sounds, words, phrases, or sentences are added one to another to make a piece.

The success of this game relies on everyone maintaining focus, with each Player finding simple solutions for an action and/or a sound. By the last person's contribution, there is a lot to remember. The resulting piece could have a story line, read as a dance, or appear as a string of random bits.

Add-a-Pearl works well as an introductory activity. By the end of the game the class has made a quick and simple performance piece.

Skills
★ Creating movement and sound phrases
★ Memorizing and reproducing movement and sound sequences

Time
5 to 15 minutes. If Add-a-Pearl is developed into a performance project, you will need to add rehearsal time.

Space
Adaptable to any open space. If only sounds, phrases, or sentences are used, even a small enclosed space will work.

Materials
None

Directions

1. Have Players sit or stand in a line or circle formation. Large groups should be divided into teams of four to twelve Players per team.

2. Have one Player begin by making a single sound and/or movement idea.

Examples:
• Wave hand and say "Hello."
• Jump four times and say "Yes" on the fourth jump.
• Bow and say "We're out of here."

3. The whole group repeats the first Player's sound and/or movement idea.

4. The second Player then performs her own sound and/or movement idea. The whole group repeats the first Player's idea, then the second Player's idea.

5. This continues until all Players have contributed to the string of ideas. With each addition, the whole group repeats the string of ideas. At the end, all ideas are performed by everyone in the order they were contributed.

Variations

Changing Places Divide Players into small groups of three to six Players. Have Players in each group stand in a line.

1. Player 1 performs a sound/movement, which travels down the line. Player 1 then goes to the end of the line.

2. Player 2 is now the head of the line. He adds a new sound and/or movement phrase to the first Player's phrase. Both phrases pass down the line. Then Player 2 goes to the end of the line.

3. Players continue adding phrases and stringing them together as they pass down the line until all Players have had a turn being head of the line.

Categories Limit the sound and/or movement to one category, such as names, animals, ages of people, or jobs. For example, if the category is parts of the body:

1. Ask the group to improvise a particular action. "Show me ways to move the head only." Choose one action you observed and perform it. Then ask the group to imitate it, specifying the number of times it is to be repeated. "Let's do this head action four times." (If possible, use the name of the person who offered the action.)

2. Ask everyone to improvise any foot action. Choose one and decide how many times to repeat this action. Then have everyone perform the desired repetitions of first the head action, then the foot action.

3. Continue the string of choices as long as seems appropriate, up to ten choices. When the movement selection has been completed, it will look something like this:
4 head shakes
2 foot stomps
3 hand waves
1 shoulder shrug
(and so on)

Reversing Order, Changing Rhythm

All of the Add-a-Pearl movement series can be performed in reverse once they are learned. Experiment with speeding up and slowing down the rhythms.

Performance Suggestions

Solos Add-a-Pearl can be performed as simultaneous solos. The timing of each Player's performance may be slightly different.

Group Unison If Add-a-Pearl is performed as a group, Players will have to memorize the series and rehearse it so that everyone is doing the same thing at the same time.

Audience Participation Try playing this game with audience members participating and Players taking the Leader's role.

 Teaching Notes

Management Tips

Reinforce Individuality If your group has trouble working in unison, emphasize Players' individuality. Encourage their differences in accomplishing the same task, eliminating perceived judgments about what is "correct." This simple adaptation will give Players positive reinforcement of their individuality and will remove the stigma of being considered uncoordinated if a Player has difficulty achieving a particular shape.

Connections

Foreign Language This game is an excellent teaching tool for learning names of body parts in other languages and for practicing short phrases.

 Assessment

Teacher Observations

Use the following questions to determine your group's readiness to create and remember longer performance works.

- Were Players willing and able to think of and demonstrate movement and/or sound ideas?
- How successful were Players at observing and imitating other Players' ideas?

- Were Players able to memorize and reproduce a long sequence of movement and/or sound ideas?

Group Discussion

Encourage Players to discuss how they would like to develop Add-a-Pearl into a performance piece.

 Student Activities

Journal

Ask Players to explain how they feel about and deal with memorization. Pose the following questions:

- Is it easy or difficult for you to memorize a series of actions and sounds? Tell why.
- Do you use any "tricks" to help you memorize things? If so, describe them.

Sculptures

In this game, Players work in pairs. One partner plays the sculptor, and the other partner plays the sculpture that is to be molded. Then partners reverse roles. Sculptures helps to build trust, open communication, and teamwork. By working together with partners, participants learn to trust one another and are then able to transfer this to working together in a larger group. Sculptures can be a very relaxing and calming activity and therefore useful in bringing participants' focus to an awareness of themselves and their interactions with others.

Skills

★ Developing body awareness: isolating body parts, experimenting with balance

★ Practicing teamwork: partner trust, communication

Time

15 to 30 minutes

Space

Any indoor or outdoor open space

Materials

Small hand props and bits of costume and cloth could be made available to add to the sculpture. Music can be used to create a sound environment. Mussorgsky's *Pictures at an Exhibition* is fun to use when Players view one another's completed sculptures.

 Directions

1. Ask Players to choose a partner. Explain that one partner will be a sculptor, who will mold the other partner into a sculpture. Everyone will get a chance to be both the sculptor and the sculpture.

2. Tell Players who are going to be sculptures to start by lying down on the floor, or to stand in a neutral position. They will pretend to be a lump of unformed clay for the sculptor to shape.

3. Then direct sculptors to experiment moving their sculptures into various shapes until they find the shape that they want the sculpture to be. To help Players become comfortable with working together, suggest that sculptors start by gently manipulating the arms and legs of their sculpture partners while they are lying down. Once the sculpture is relaxed enough to allow the work to happen, a sculptor can move slowly and gently to carry the arms, legs, and head to try out different body positions. If they wish to create a sculpture that is sitting, kneeling, or standing, sculptors should take care to assist their sculptures in rising to an upright position and help them maintain balance.

4. When the sculptors find the shape they wish to keep, they tell the sculptures that they are finished. Sculptures should memorize their positions.

5. Designate a museum display area. When all sculptors have completed their sculptures, have the sculptures display their final poses in the museum. All the sculptors can then view one another's work.

6. Have partners reverse roles.

Variations

Large Group Sculptures

1. Divide Players into two to four teams. One team works as sculptors to compose one art piece, using the other half of the Players as their material. Decide whether sculptors may speak to one another or should remain silent while they work together making their sculpture. When the sculptors decide that the piece is completed, have them step back to view their artwork.

2. Have each sculptor exchange places with a Player who is a part of the sculpture, assuming the exact position of the Player they have replaced in the sculpture. As Players are replaced, they become viewers of the sculpture.

3. Repeat the process so that both teams perform both roles.

4. Discuss how it felt to be part of a sculpture and how it felt to be a sculptor.

Tableaux Vivants Leader or group chooses images from famous sculptures, paintings, photographs, or drawings. In solos or in teams, Players recreate the images. The images can be performed as one stationary image or as a series of images. (See Tableaux Vivants, page 197.)

 Teaching Notes

Management Tips

Working Safely Remind students of the basic rule of treating one another with respect. You might want to model how partners could work together by demonstrating safe ways to move a partner into various positions. Or, ask partners who are working together particularly well to demonstrate for the others. Advise Players to notice any resistance or hesitation from their partners as a cue to be especially careful.

Working Together If some partners are having difficulty working together, either have them alternate roles more quickly so that they understand both the roles of sculptor and sculpture, or have them actually change to new partners. On the rare occasion when partnering is too much of a challenge, allow the Players to work alone to mold themselves into sculptures.

Sculpting Methods You may wish to suggest one of the following three ways that sculptors can use to communicate to their partners how to move. The first is by using touch, the second is by using gesture signals that do not require touch, and the third is by mirroring each other.

• **Using Touch** First establish partner trust by modeling for Players how to lift various appendages of their partners' bodies. Demonstrate each task, such as lifting the right leg and putting it down, lifting the left arm and putting it down,

lifting the head and putting it down. When lifting the head, show how to support it using two hands so that the sculpture feels protected at all times. Advise sculptors to work slowly and smoothly without making any sudden or unexpected adjustments to their sculpture's body.

• **Using Gesture** Model for Players ways to communicate changes of position.

– Use as an example the image of a marionette and puppet master. Suggest that the Players have imaginary strings attached to appendages that can be lifted and lowered. The sculptor is the puppet master who raises and lowers arms and legs by lifting and lowering strings attached to the puppet. Have partners practice lifting and lowering arms, legs, and head using this method.

– Encourage players to invent or use existing sign language or cliché language to communicate changes in position.

• **Mirroring** The sculptor shows the position he wants and the sculpture mirrors, or imitates, the sculptor.

Maintaining Positions If Players who are the sculptures begin by lying down on the floor, one dilemma is to maintain the same position when changing from the horizontal to the vertical. This can be a lot of fun, offering a challenge of balance and physical and spatial awareness. It also becomes a partnering problem to make the changes, encouraging teamwork as the Players learn to work together. If Players find this shift of position too difficult, suggest the sculptors help move their sculptures to the standing or sitting position before setting the final shape. Players may decide to make adjustments to the final position to accommodate balance problems or other unanticipated difficulties that may arise because sculptures have to maintain their positions for a long time until all sculptors are finished and have viewed one another's finished work.

Connections

Art Art appreciation and history can come alive by having Players recreate existing images from photographs, drawings, paintings, or sculptures. Encourage Players to notice all details in the image and to try to find ways to include setting, costume, lighting, spatial design, or any other important information in the existing work.

Language Arts/History From classroom readings, have Players create their own ideas of how events or characters might look. Research and discussion about period costume, mannerisms, social customs, and physical environments of a place or time might help Players in forming their images.

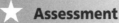

Assessment

Teacher Observations

- Were Players able to work creatively and cooperatively with a partner?
- Did partners appear to communicate effectively and trust one another?
- Were sculptors careful with their partners when moving them into position?

Group Discussion

Use the following questions to lead the group in a discussion of both roles.

- What did you like/dislike about being a sculptor/sculpture?
- When you were the sculptor, were you able to mold your sculpture into the shape you wanted? If not, what went wrong?
- When you were the sculpture, did you trust your partner to move you without hurting you? Were you able to relax and let the sculptor move you?

Use the following discussion questions if you utilized any of the Connections activities.

- What was learned by becoming a part of history, a character, or an image?
- Did the experience give new insights into what was read or seen? If so, in what way?

Student Activities

Journal

Have Players record what they learned about balance during this activity. Pose these questions:

- Did you and your partner try any positions that didn't work? Describe them.
- Why didn't they work? How did you change them?

Points of View

When building an ensemble or establishing teamwork skills, it should be understood that differences of opinions will occur and are part of working respectfully in a group. The activities in Points of View demonstrate experientially that there can be as many different points of view as there are people playing the game. Through discussing these experiences, Players will discover how points of view can vary.

The term *point of view* is a metaphor, used in common speech to describe many kinds of physical, social, and psychological relationships to events. It may mean either the particular physical vantage point from which we look at something, or the opinions, judgments, and attitudes that influence our perceptions when we look at something.

Changes in our point of view can be effected by our perspective as influenced by any of the following conditions.

Skills
★ Observing a specific focal point
★ Recalling and sharing descriptions of what was seen during observations
★ Discussing individual differences in points of view and why these differences exist

Time
10 to 30 minutes

Space
Adaptable to any space

Materials
None

- **Age** When we are young we may understand the reasons that caused an event differently than when we are old.

- **Experience** If we have direct experience of an event, we may understand it differently than if we learn of it through a photograph.

- **Relationship** Perspective is influenced by the nature of our relationship to the object or event. It may look different to an observer according to whether it had a direct effect on his life, and if that effect was positive, negative, or of no consequence.

- **Observation Skills** Our use of focus and our ability to notice detail will affect our perspective and point of view.

- **Beliefs** Our judgment of what is fact and what is opinion will affect our point of view. Two sensitive examples of how many "truths" can be passionately believed are illustrated in discussions about the "discovery" of America and the reasons for the use of the atomic bomb in the World War II.

The following exercises are dramatic examples of the fact that there can be as many points of view as there are observers, that a person's or group's point of view can change from moment to moment, and that many points of view of the same experience can be very different, while still being "correct" or truthful.

 Directions

There are two different ways to approach Points of View. You can choose to do an activity first, and then base a discussion on the Players' experience of the activity. Or, you can begin with a discussion in which you define the term, *point of view,* and elicit Players' opinions about how points of view can differ from person to person.

Activity 1

1. Ask the group to choose a specific point in the room, where everyone will look. The choice can be perceived as uninteresting and very limited, such as a stain on the floor or a clock; or it can offer more complex information, such as a painting, a shelf of items, or a corner of a room.

2. Direct Players to observe the chosen point of focus for one minute while sitting at their desks; standing clustered around the point of focus; or standing in scattered positions anywhere in the playing area.

3. After one minute, ask Players to describe what they saw during their one-minute observation. Hold a group discussion about the variety of descriptions.

Activity 2

1. Direct Players to sit or stand in a line.

2. Ask Players to focus on a defined area chosen by group agreement or designated by you, such as a corner of a room or a window that is at a distance from the line.

3. Tell Players to observe the chosen focal point for at least one minute. When one minute has passed, tell them to turn away from that point.

4. Ask each Player to describe everything she saw in the area, from her point of view. It is interesting to hear the differences in observations that can occur from one end of the line to the other, especially when using a window or an open doorway as the focal point or frame.

5. Discuss the variety of descriptions given, as well as possible reasons for the differences.

6. After all Players have shared their observations, ask them to look at the focal point once again to see if they observe anything new or different. Discuss the changes in their observations.

7. Ask Players to change places with each other. Change right, center, and left positions to give participants a different physical point. Then repeat the activity.

Variations

Observation Recall Ask a Player to turn away from his view and describe what he saw. Have everyone else group around that Player's location to observe what he saw while listening to him recall the view.

Written Observations After Players have observed a specific point, have them write down everything they thought during their one-minute observation. Ask all Players to read their notes to the group.

 Teaching Notes

Management Tips

Discussion Discussion is an important aspect of this activity and leads to the development of critical thinking skills, such as learning

to distinguish between opinion and fact, and analyzing how visual perception functions and influences thought.

Observation Skills Points of View can be a tool to help increase perceptual awareness and Players' ability to notice and recall detail.

Using the Activities These activities can be used to center and calm participants at the start of a session; as part of a warm-up; to bring a group together when making transitions between activities; or to end a session.

Focusing If you feel the group is having difficulty focusing, try offering a more specific focus, such as color, for Players to observe.

Connections

Language Arts Connect this activity to the use of points of view in writing. How does a writer decide who is going to tell the story, poem, or play? Is it written in first, second, or third person? Is the narrator omniscient, directly involved, or an onlooker?

Science Students could study the anatomy of the eye and learn how the eye functions, its pathways to the brain, and the ways that the brain translates this information. Recent research suggests that perception is also influenced by associative memory and decision-making areas of the brain; perhaps influences, other than images on the retina, affect our perceptions and recall.

Visual Arts Discuss the relationship of design to visual and emotional perception. Advertising media offer readily available materials that can be used in discussing design elements such as size, color, spatial relationships, and texture, and how they can be used to create and influence taste and cultural trends.

 Assessment

Teacher Observations

- Did students understand the different meanings of the term *points of view?*

- Were students able to maintain focus for one minute and share their observations?

- Were students able to distinguish differences in each other's observations? Were they able to analyze the possible source of these differences? Were they able to accept that differences in points of view are possible?

Group Discussion

Discuss with Players the different aspects of how we perceive.

- What influences our perceptions besides the sensory perception of images on the retina?

- How can people see the same thing and describe it in completely different ways?

- What distinguishes fact from opinion?

 Student Activities

Book

pages 3–4 (Overview)

Journal

Have Players try the following journal suggestion:

Pick a color and for one day record everything you see that is that color. Describe what you saw, including any variations in the color and what you think might have made the color appear to be a different hue, such as lighting, relationship to other things, or texture. For example, look for trees and bushes, observing all the different kinds of green.

Signature Piece

Signature Piece helps Players see the alphabet in new ways and offers alternative activities for learning how to read and write. Using their bodies as building materials, Players create letters, names, and words. Through visual, kinesthetic, and teamwork experiences, Players can use Signature Piece as a springboard for autobiographical statements. The combination of shaping the letters and calling out one's name provides a structure for an inventive presentation of self.

 Directions

1. To begin the game, have Players stand in a circle. Ask Players to form their bodies into the shape of the first letter of their first names. They can make the shape by standing, sitting, or lying down.

Skills

★ Experimenting with creative movement
★ Transforming a graphic pattern into a kinesthetic pattern
★ Practicing audience etiquette
★ Responding constructively to peer performances

Time

15 to 30 minutes

Space

Adaptable to any large open space. The floor should be swept clean so that people can lie down.

Materials

Mats or rugs could be used. In performance, music or sound environment may be added.

2. Have Players share their shapes, one by one. Observing Players should see whether or not they can recognize each letter shape. If they cannot, ask them to suggest adjustments that might make the letter shape clearer. When everyone agrees that the letter shape is readable, have all Players copy that shape.

3. Direct Players to work independently to find a way to create and perform each letter of their first names. Tell them also to create transitions to connect the letters. They also decide how to combine the letters so that transitions connect smoothly from one letter into the next. Encourage Players to explore different ideas by changing tempo, size, and dynamics and by experimenting with beginnings and endings of letters. For example, to change tempo, try forming each letter quickly and sharply, then dissolving each letter smoothly and slowly; or make combinations of different qualities. To change size, experiment with forming the letters using the hands only, involving the total body, or *en masse* in a group.

4. Ask Players to perform their signature piece solos for the group. If time is limited, divide Players into groups to share their signature pieces.

Variations

Group Name Shapes Have Players work together in small groups to form the letters of one person's name. It's fun to have each person direct the performance of his own name. This can be solved a number of ways.

• **Letter Progressions** Perform as a progression from the first through the last letter of a Player's name. Choices include unison performance of each letter, call and response of each letter, echoing each letter, rounds, or canons.

– In echoing, one Player performs a letter that is repeated both orally and physically in a manner similar to the sound of an echo.

– In call and response, one Player performs a letter or a full name, and another Player or Players respond with the same letter or full name, so that they make an alternating pattern with each other. This pattern can be repeated exactly the same, as in a mirroring exercise, or there can be some addition or change of detail added in the response.

– Rounds can be performed by teams or by two or more soloists. One soloist or team begins shaping each letter of a name. The other soloists or teams repeat the letters in order, with each new "voice" starting at the same predetermined cue within the performance immediately preceding theirs. The repetitions overlap, with all voices continuing until a set number of repetitions are completed.

– Canons are similar to rounds, except each new "voice" can be started at any point during or after the first presentation. Set the number of repetitions, if desired.

- **Whole Name at Once** Several players make the letters of one name. Each letter is shaped by one or more Players. Order the letters so that an audience can read the names from left to right. The audience sees the whole name spelled out at once.

- **Any Word Shape** Choose any word(s) to perform. If desired, specify a subject area or part of speech from which Players are to limit their choices.

- **Writing in the Air** Write the letters in the air. Flashlights in darkness, long ribbons, or sparklers can make this seem very magical.

- **Floor Patterns** Walk or run the shapes of the letters as floor patterns.

- **Giant Letters** Several Players make one gigantic letter shape. This can be done lying down on the floor or in any other way the Players choose to solve the problem. Props, such as sturdy chairs or bleachers, may increase the possibilities.

Performance Suggestions

The Children's Troupe choreographed a twenty-minute opening dance called "Signature Piece" for a performance work entitled *Handtalk*, done in collaboration with children's book author and performance artist Remy Charlip. "Signature Piece" was performed by sixteen deaf and hearing performers. To begin, each performer entered and introduced herself by speaking and signing her name. Then all the names were performed as solo and group pieces, with overlapping entrances and exits.

Teaching Notes

Management Tips

Visibility If there is to be an audience, be aware of any sightline problems. Check to see if Players' letter shapes will be visible if made while lying or sitting on the floor of the performing space. If they will not be seen, ask that all solutions be standing shapes.

Acknowledging Audience Point of View Remind Players that each letter shape is to be formed so that it reads from the audience's point of view. This means that the Players will form their shapes and words backwards, so that an audience can read them from left to right. The same rule applies when using languages that read up to down or right to left. Players may feel awkward reversing everything from their own point of view.

Special Needs

- Deaf and hearing Players can combine finger spelling with whole body shapes.

- Players with large muscle limitations can form letters using fingers and arms. More than one person can form each letter.

Connections

Language Arts

- Use different languages or intersperse several translations of a name or any word, for example: Michael, Misha, Miguel, Michel.

- Reinforce learning new vocabulary words by making letter shapes. *Antidisestablishmentarianism* might inspire quite a performance piece!

Mathematics Players use their bodies to create number shapes and to show progressions or sequences of numbers, for example: counting 1 to 10; showing only odd or even numbers; performing multiples of twos, fives, and so on.

- Number shapes can be formed by the same number of Players as the number, for example: two Players make the number 2; thirty Players make the number 30.

- Players could perform computations—adding, subtracting, multiplying, or dividing—showing the equation and the answer to the computation. Players can act out the computation, for example: 2 people divide 10 Players into 2 groups of 5 each; 4 Players gather 6 more Players to equal 10 Players; 4 Players + 4 Players + 4 Players + 4 Players = 16 Players.

Assessment

Teacher Observations

- Did Players present their signature pieces so that they could be read from the audience's point of view? If not, did observing Players point out problems? Were Players then able to make necessary adjustments?

- Did the use of familiar material, such as a personal name, help participants relax in meeting the challenge of public presentation?

- Did the presentations reflect the personal style of each participant?

Group Discussion

It helps to have Players take turns being the audience, because they will see any audience reading problems immediately—those caused by reversals or by unclear shaping of characters. Use the following questions to help Players evaluate performance issues.

• Are the letters readable from a distance?

• Are the letters too small, reversed, or done too quickly to register on the eye of the observer?

If Players directed one another in Group Name Shapes, use the following questions to discuss the collaborative process.

• Did you get the results that you envisioned?

• Was there collaboration between Players in the process of creating the group name? In the collaboration, were changes made because other Players offered new ideas, could not perform what the Director wanted, or because new ideas came from working together?

• How did you feel about collaborating?

 Student Activities

Journal

Ask Players to describe how their signature pieces represent who they are.

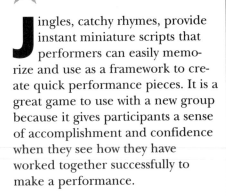

Jingles

Jingles, catchy rhymes, provide instant miniature scripts that performers can easily memorize and use as a framework to create quick performance pieces. It is a great game to use with a new group because it gives participants a sense of accomplishment and confidence when they see how they have worked together successfully to make a performance.

 Directions

1. To play Jingles, provide or have Players create a four- to eight-line chant or call. Old slogans, limericks, conundrums, jump rope ditties, cheerleading calls, and advertisement jingles are examples of interesting source materials.

Skills
★ Working cooperatively to create a performance
★ Inventing actions to accompany text

Time
15 to 30 minutes

Space
Adaptable to any space

Materials
Percussion instruments can be used to heighten rhythm patterns in the jingles. Libraries generally stock many books containing limericks, conundrums, chants, jump rope chants, and so on.

Examples of Jingles:

Chant

One for the money
Two for the show
Three to get ready
And four to GO!

American Counting Game

(Often used to choose teams or to determine who is "It.")
Acka Boca
Soda crocka
Acka Boca Boo
In goes Uncle Sam
And out goes Y-O-U

Cheerleading Call

Which way did they go?
To the left, to the right?
To the right, to the left?
Which way did they go?
To the north, to the south
To the east, to the west?
Which way did they go?

Old English Chant

The noble Duke of York
He had ten thousand men
He marched them right straight up the hill
And right back down again.
And when they're up they're up
And when they're down they're down
And when they're only halfway up
They're neither up nor down.

Conundrum

Pete and Repete were sitting on a fence.
Pete fell off. Who was left?
Repete.

Jump Rope Ditty

Miss Mary Mack, Mack, Mack
All dressed in black, black, black
With silver buttons, buttons, buttons
All down her back, back, back
She asked her mother, mother, mother
For fifteen cents, cents, cents
To see the elephants, elephants, elephants
Jump the fence, fence, fence
They jumped so high, high, high
They reached the sky, sky, sky
And they never came back, back, back
'Til the fourth of July, 'ly, 'ly

Limerick

There once was a yak from Kazoon
Who slipped into a lagoon
He called for his mother
Who said, "There's no other
Way home in our town of Kazoon."

2. Divide Players into small teams. Tell team members to work together to decide how they want to make a performance out of the chosen jingle. The only guidelines are that Players must in some way speak the words in the jingle and invent a series of actions to accompany the jingle.

3. Allow teams to work for five to ten minutes, then ask teams to perform their jingles for one another.

Performance Suggestions

A series of jingles can be strung together to make an amusing performance. Jingles make delightful entr'actes within a larger performance piece. (See Entr'Actes, page 211.)

 Teaching Notes

Management Tips

Rehearsing Encourage Players to practice acting out their jingle performance solutions. Sometimes a group thinks all they have to do is talk it over. Advise them to add actions to their words and rehearse their solutions before they share with an audience.

Connections

Language Arts Jingles could be connected to the study of various uses of language, including rhyming couplets, figures of speech such as simile and metaphor, rhythmic patterns, meter, and phrasing. Jingles could also be used to analyze compositional form and style. For example, students could study advertising jingles to determine how the writers used images, rhythm, and timing to get the attention of their audience.

Science Jingles can aid in the memorization of important facts. Students could make up their own jingles in which they connect the content to their study of weather, energy, rocks and minerals, or other topics.

 Assessment

Teacher Observations

- Were team members able to work cooperatively and come to consensus in devising solutions to Jingles?
- Did teams rehearse their jingles before they presented them?
- Did teams create performances that included the jingle words and accompanying actions?

Group Discussion

After each group performs its jingle solution for the class, use the following questions to guide a peer evaluation.

- Could you understand the words in the jingle?
- Did all Players perform the same solution?
- How did the actions relate to the words?

 Student Activities

Book

pages 5–6 (Performance Model)

Journal

Have Players write about their favorite commercial jingles. Ask them to respond to the following questions:

- What is your favorite? Why?
- How does it get and hold your attention?
- Do you enjoy it each time you hear it or see it?

Run-on Stories

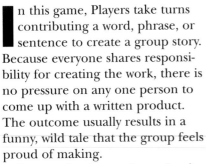

In this game, Players take turns contributing a word, phrase, or sentence to create a group story. Because everyone shares responsibility for creating the work, there is no pressure on any one person to come up with a written product. The outcome usually results in a funny, wild tale that the group feels proud of making.

Run-on Stories can be as simple or as elaborate as desired. The potential for an extravaganza performance hides in this simple kernel of an idea. A run-on story can be poetic or narrative; imaginary or realistic; relate to historical themes or current events and issues; or have a scientific basis. Simply make an additional command that cues the Players about the focus for their contributions to the story.

After recording the story, the group may perform it in a variety of ways, including those in Performance Suggestions.

Skills
★ Creating and dramatizing a group story

Time
10 to 30 minutes

Space
Adaptable to any space

Materials
Recording materials such as tape recorders or pen and paper. Rhythm instruments or recorded music are optional.

★ Directions

1. Before the group begins telling a story, select a storytelling method from the following options.

Storytelling Methods

- **Basic Run-On** Each Player adds a contribution to the story until everyone has had a least one turn and the story is ended.

- **Chorus** After each Player adds a contribution to the story, all Players, as a chorus, retell the story, starting at the beginning and continuing through the latest addition.

- **Gestures and Sound Effects** Each Player includes gestures and sound effects with his or her portion of the story. The gestures and sound effects should be included in any retelling of the story.

- **Rhythmic Story** Put the story on a rhythm pattern that becomes an underlying beat to the story. Hand claps, clapping on the floor, rhythm sticks, or recorded music can set the beat. Everyone speaks on the rhythm. A rhythmic story could take the form of a rap.

2. Select a storytelling format. If you decide to build a story around a particular topic and/or genre, allow class time to discuss the topic before proceeding.

Story Formats

- **Opening Sentences/Phrases** The group builds a story from an introductory phrase or sentence. Either provide the opening sentence/phrase yourself or ask for suggestions from the group.

  Examples:
  - Once upon a time
  - Long ago and far away
  - Welcome to the greatest show on earth!
  - They came from all over
  - It was a dark and stormy night

- **Topics/Forms** The group builds a story around a particular topic or story form. Ensure that everyone understands the topic or form. This may involve group discussions, research, and/or sharing examples of a specific story form.

  Examples:

  ### Story Forms
  - Tall tales
  - Trickster myths (See "Tricky Tales" script, pages 230–260, in the Student Book.)
  - Fairy tales (fractured or not)
  - Soap operas or melodramas

  ### Story Topics
  - Historical or political events
  - Social issues
  - Action taking place in one day
  - Scientific themes
  - Special occasions

3. Have Players take turns contributing one word, phrase, or sentence until the story sounds complete. This might involve more than one go around, depending on the size of the group, the ages of the participants, and the nature of the story.

4. Determine whether or not you want to record the run-on story in writing or on audiotape or videotape for future reference. Run-on stories may be spontaneous with each telling or set and rehearsed. The group may create a new story every time they tell or perform it, never writing down or recording the story in any manner.

5. If you have recorded the story and want the Players to act it out, first read the story as told, while the Players listen. Then read the story again while the group acts it out. See Performance Suggestions for ways to perform the story.

Performance Suggestions

Once a story is recorded, there are various ways to go about making the performance, based on the text.

Narrator The Leader or a Player takes the role of Narrator, reading the group's writing. The rest of the Players perform the story. Each player performs everything in the story, portraying all characters—human and animal—and all inanimate objects—tables, doors, streetlights, or walls—that are present in the story.

Call and Response The Narrator reads the story (Call), with Players repeating each line in unison (Response). Each Player portrays every character and object in the story. The Narrator and Players can improvise from the written script, adding dialogue, actions, or other embellishments. If the story performance is repeated more than one time, the group can discuss other ways to expand or amend the story, and ways to perform these changes in the next run-through.

Dialogue and Cues The story is told by the Players. Everyone can perform everything or each Player can choose to be one or more characters, depending on the size of the group and the number of characters in the story. It is also possible for several Players to play the same character or for a Narrator to speak the parts of characters that no one else has chosen. Characters speak the lines as written, or improvise new dialogue. The Narrator can also act as a commentator on the action.

Director Assigns Roles The Director (who may be the Leader or one of the participants) assigns each Player a role to play. Roles could include objects, such as a table, door, sun, moon, tree, or rock. The story is performed as written, or expanded through improvisation.

Teams Working in small groups, each team solves the story its own way, then shares its solutions with other teams.

Special Word Cues Any word or words can be chosen as cues that will cause all Players to perform some agreed-upon movement. The movement may be arbitrarily silly or strange and have no connection or meaning to the word or story. For example, Players could select some part of speech, such as articles (*the, and, a, an*), and assign a movement to each word that everyone performs each time the word occurs in the story (clap on *the*, jump on *and*, turn around on *a*, and sit on *an*). Or the movement could have some emotional or symbolic connection to the story and particular word. For example, all Players decide to turn their backs to the audience upon hearing one specific word in their story about people who are not communicating with each other.

Teaching Notes

Management Tips

Positioning Players Have the Players sit so that they can hear one another clearly. A semicircle formation works well. If they are going to do physical actions to accompany the story, Players must also be able to see one another.

Limiting Contributions Keep individual contributions short. Remind Players, if they continue on too long, of the basic rule to give only a word, phrase, or sentence.

Encouraging Creativity Encourage all Players to contribute and to not edit themselves. Everyone can come up with one word, at least. To encourage Players' creativity, you may want to tell Players that the story does not need to "make sense" or have a beginning, middle, and end structure that ties up all the loose ends.

Storytelling Suggestions If you ask Players to act out the story while you read it aloud, try the following suggestions.

- Repeat sections or phrases of the story to make sure all the Players have heard what they have to respond to.

- The storytelling device of repeating a phrase so that it becomes louder and louder or softer and softer can add texture and emphasis to the story. For example, Narrator says, "What did you say? I didn't hear that." The Players respond with a louder repetition of the last phrase told in the story.

- Other ways to energize the Players include adding asides to the story or comments on the action in ways that encourage Players to expand their characterization or find new solutions to the actions suggested by the story line. During the improvisation, ask questions that help Players find fresh information or refine what they have. Frame the questions in ways that help to elicit new actions, details of character and image, and solutions to the plot. For example, if Players have composed a run-on story that includes a journey, and you are working to expand the run-on story into a longer scene, you might want to ask questions such as those in the following sample.

Example:

Narrator: "How far did he have to go?"

Character: "All the way to the North Pole."

Narrator: "How did he get to the North Pole?"

Character: "The wind blew him there."

Narrator: "How else did he get to the North Pole?"

Character: "He followed Admiral Byrd."

Connections

Language Arts

- Use this activity to enhance your study of storytelling/fictional narrative. After Players have created their run-on story, ask them to analyze its story elements. If necessary, guide the discussion with questions such as the following.

  - What kind of a story is it?
  - What is the plot? Is there a beginning, middle, and end? Describe them.
  - Does the story have a complication, a climax, and a solution? What are they?
  - Who are the characters? Is there a protagonist, an antagonist, or an antihero?

- Use Run-on Stories to help teach parts of speech by using the Special Word Cues performance suggestion or by requiring that contributions always include an adverb, an active verb, a proper noun, or other part of speech.

Foreign Languages The story can be told in any language, or combination of languages, providing a playful way to practice a new language or expand vocabulary.

Social Studies Choose a particular storytelling format or topic that relates to a specific culture or historical period.

Special Needs

Sign language interpreters may be needed and should be situated within the circle so that everyone can see them easily.

 Assessment

Teacher Observations

- Were all Players able to contribute to the run-on story? Did their contributions show that they had been closely following other Players' contributions and the expanding story line?

- How did Players act out the story? Did they pantomime actions? Did they show details of characterization? Were they creative in their enactments of characters and objects?

Group Discussion

Engage Players in a discussion about the experience of creating a run-on story.

- What did you like/dislike about creating a run-on story?

- Did the resulting story make sense? Was there a clear plot?

- Was the story similar to any story you have heard or read before? How?

- How do you think acting out the story changed it? Did it become more interesting, funnier, or more confusing?

 Student Activities

Journal

If possible, record the story on audiotape; if the story is performed, use a video camera. Have Players listen or watch themselves, then respond to the following questions in their journals.

- Was your perception of how you sounded and/or looked the way you felt as you performed?

- How would you change the story or the way it was acted out to make it more interesting?

CHAPTER 2

Movement Activities

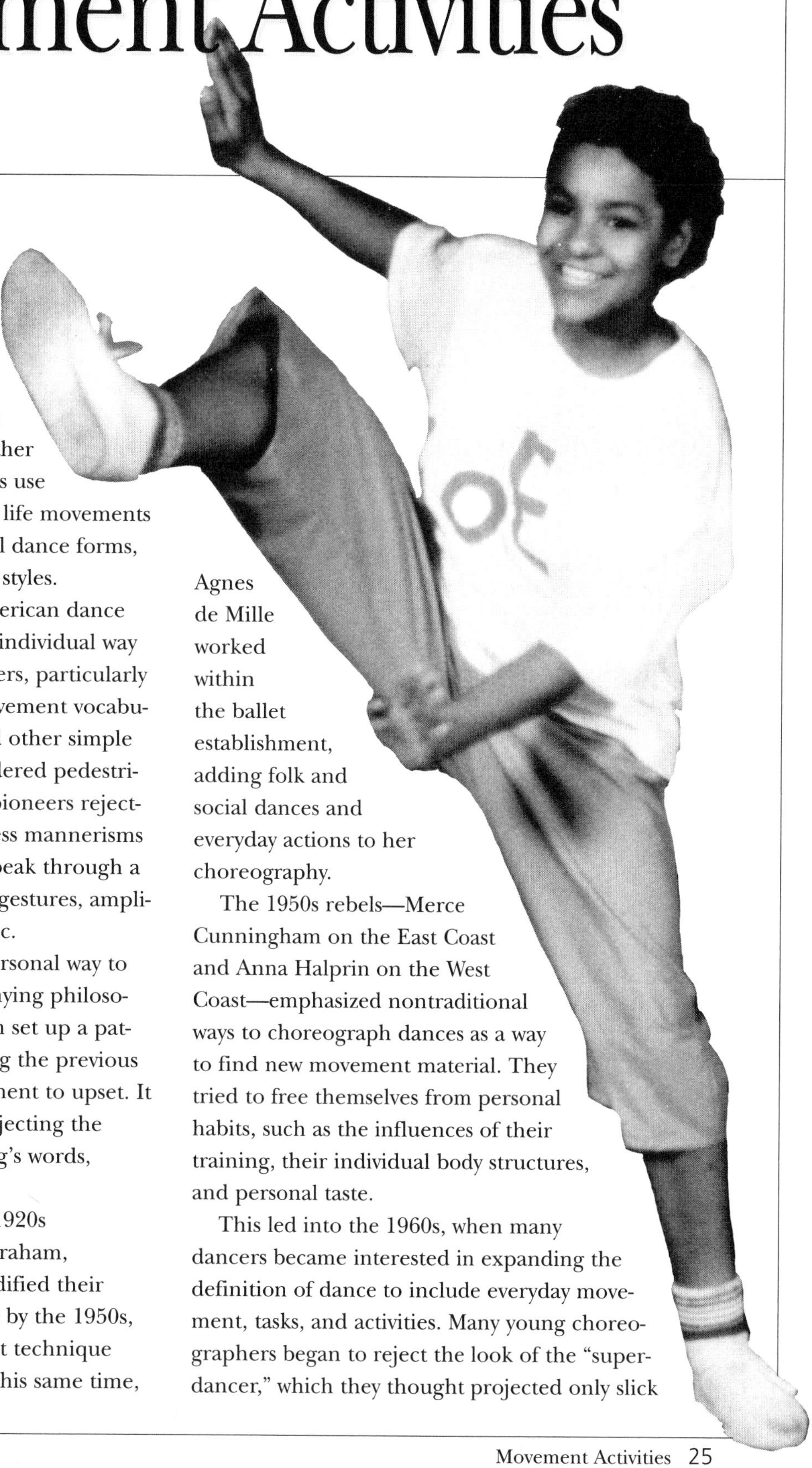

A nyone who can move
can find a way to play
the games in this chapter.
Players do not need to be dancers
to participate in these activities. They
require no formal dance training, since
they ask for everyday human actions rather
than specialized dance steps. The games use
simple structures that are built on daily life movements
and tasks, simple locomotor skills, social dance forms,
improvisation, and personal movement styles.

The history of twentieth-century American dance
has provided many precedents for this individual way
of working. Early modern dance pioneers, particularly
Isadora Duncan, based their whole movement vocabulary on walking, running, skipping, and other simple
locomotor movements that were considered pedestrian by the academy of the time. These pioneers reject-
ed what they considered the meaningless mannerisms
of ballet, which found it necessary to speak through a
codified vocabulary of steps and mime gestures, amplified by elaborate stage design and music.

Instead, each dancer developed a personal way to
move, frequently creating an accompanying philosophy. This belief in individual expression set up a pattern of one dance generation perceiving the previous
generation's revolution as an establishment to upset. It
created a modern dance tradition of rejecting the
past, or, in art critic Clement Greenberg's words,
establishing "the tradition of the new."

The modern dance pioneers of the 1920s
through the 1940s, including Martha Graham,
Doris Humphrey, and Hanya Holm, codified their
techniques and movement vocabularies by the 1950s,
making them as established as the ballet technique
that they had rebelled against. During this same time,

Agnes
de Mille
worked
within
the ballet
establishment,
adding folk and
social dances and
everyday actions to her
choreography.

The 1950s rebels—Merce
Cunningham on the East Coast
and Anna Halprin on the West
Coast—emphasized nontraditional
ways to choreograph dances as a way
to find new movement material. They
tried to free themselves from personal
habits, such as the influences of their
training, their individual body structures,
and personal taste.

This led into the 1960s, when many
dancers became interested in expanding the
definition of dance to include everyday movement, tasks, and activities. Many young choreographers began to reject the look of the "super-
dancer," which they thought projected only slick

technical proficiency. They experimented with ways to free themselves from older methods of using space, time, and gravity. Dances were developed from natural movement, ordinary actions, sports, or games; referred to meditation and chance techniques of non-Western traditions; and set up physical challenges, such as using riggings for wall climbing and other feats, that forced them into new ways of moving. During this time, many dancers seldom appeared on traditional proscenium stages, but performed instead in public spaces, lofts, museums, or galleries. Walls, roofs, hills, beaches, alleys, parking lots, and street scenes all became the sets or structures for their work.

Around 1962, in New York City, dancers formed a cooperative that included artists from various disciplines. Their work became known as the Judson Memorial Church Workshops, because their meetings and experimental concerts took place at that Washington Square site. The choreographic methods developed during the 1960s continue to influence dance. Today's choreographers, in both ballet and modern dance, draw inspiration from the structures and philosophies of the Judson Church establishment to help push them into new territory.

Currently, there is a shift of focus in dance performance work that comes perhaps as a result of the proliferation of the generations of dancers and dance teachers working in many different schools of training. Dance philosophies and styles are not so rigid. For example, moments of superdance and daily life actions appear on the same stage. Most dancers have studied many different dance styles in the course of their training, and in their own work they are likely to incorporate ideas and movements from many styles and times. The American "tradition of the new" continues to draw inspiration from the dance of other cultures in both their traditional and contemporary forms. Many people are trying hard to reconstruct past work so that it is not lost and may continue to be included in our movement memory.

The following activities come from two primary sources: simplified variations of existing pieces by various choreographers; and new structures created by students during theater workshops.

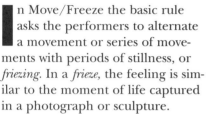

Move/Freeze

In Move/Freeze the basic rule asks the performers to alternate a movement or series of movements with periods of stillness, or *friezing*. In a *frieze*, the feeling is similar to the moment of life captured in a photograph or sculpture.

This particular game works with any age group because its structure is simple and easily attainable, it is open to personal creativity, and the final product looks good in any group. It has rich potential to develop skills of focus and concentration for both individuals and the group as a whole. It allows the performer to shine as a soloist, while teaching teamwork skills.

Skills

★ Responding to sound or visual cues by alternately moving and freezing

★ Striking and maintaining frieze positions that appear to capture a moment in time

★ Developing body awareness and control

Time

5 to 10 minutes. If a performance project is being developed, more time will be necessary for rehearsal.

Space

Adaptable to any large, open space

Materials

Costumes, small hand props, and set pieces can be used to enhance the performance. Music or sound effects can be added.

Move/Freeze is a positive tool to quiet or calm a group into working together. It can be used in introductory classes as a warm-up. It can also serve as the basis of a performance piece. When sound and/or text are added to the action, Move/Freeze can look quite elaborate and take on many levels of meaning or interpretation.

★ Directions

1. Tell Players that in Move/Freeze they are going to follow cues to alternate moving and holding a frieze. Explain that a frieze is like the moment in time captured in a photograph, a painting, or a sculpture.

2. Decide what the cue will be and share it with Players. It can be a visual cue or a sound cue. (see Management Tips.) Explain that when they hear or see the cue, they are to stop moving and maintain a frieze until the cue is given again.

3. Ask the Players to move around the space. You can give them a specific directive, such as "keep walking" or "move in place," or allow Players free choice in their movements.

4. Give the cue to direct Players to freeze. Experiment with the length of time Players maintain their friezes. Continue cueing as Players alternate moving and freezing. Once Players understand the basic activity, try some of the following variations for greater challenge.

Variations

Rhythmic Patterns Set Move/Freeze on a rhythmic pattern of equal counts.

Examples:
- walk for 5 counts/hold frieze 5 counts
- 5 counts of hand gestures/hold frieze 5 counts
- 5 counts foot pattern/hold frieze 5 counts

Choose a series of activities to perform with friezes on a rhythmic pattern of equal counts.

Examples:
- 4 counts peek around an imaginary wall/hold frieze 4 counts
- 4 counts funny faces/hold frieze 4 counts
- 4 counts open choice/hold frieze 4 counts
- 4 counts run in place/hold frieze 4 counts

Vary the rhythmic pattern.

Examples:
- 8 counts move/hold frieze 2 counts
- 3 counts move/hold frieze 6 counts

Changing Emotion, Level, or Character Ask Players to perform a 10-count change of emotion, level, or character, adding freezes either after each count or at the end of the 10-count phrase.

Examples:
- 10-count change from happy to sad
- 10-count change from high to low
- 10-count change from villain to hero

Changing Places Give a series of action commands that ask Players to change direction in space. Have Players alternate the movements with freezes.

Examples:
- Run a diagonal/freeze
- Run to the center/freeze
- Follow another person's walk/freeze
- Run to the edges/freeze
- Run a circle or square/freeze
- All clump together and walk/freeze
- Add character to any of the above

Movement Series Mix together a series of movement commands, ending the series with a freeze command.

Examples:
- Jump/turn around/land on a spot/freeze
- Face front/face back/fall down/roll over/stand up/freeze

Changing Friezes in Place Tell Players to choose a spot or place in the performing area. Have them go to that place and freeze. Players may maintain a frieze in any position for any length of time, then change their friezes at random intervals.

Parade In group formations, such as a single line, parallel lines, circles, or spirals, move through space performing a series of move/freeze actions.

Social Dance Move/Freeze Choose a social dance from the past or present that all Players can easily perform. Set up a counting rhythm that alternates the dance pattern with friezes.

Examples:
- Conga line
- Bunny hop
- Stroll
- Electric slide

Challenges Divide Players into two teams. Have teams face each other in group formations such as two parallel lines. One team offers a move/freeze pattern. The opposing team repeats the pattern by mirroring what they have observed. Alternate which team leads and which team follows.

Circle Formations Have Players stand in a circle. One Player offers a move/freeze pattern. All other Players repeat the pattern. Continue around the circle until every Player has had a turn as Leader.

Performance Suggestions

Accompaniment Add sound accompaniment to any of the variations.

Monologues The performer sings or speaks a monologue while performing any of the variations.

Dialogues/Chorus The group speaks in dialogue or as a chorus while performing any of the variations.

 Teaching Notes

Management Tips

Group Dynamics Move/Freeze is a useful tool to calm large groups of students. Players learn when it is appropriate to move and when it is appropriate to be still, and this can translate into any classroom situation. With practice, it allows each person to find his internal controls, so that eventually the external cueing system translates into an internal cueing system.

Repetition The performance skills of control and awareness that this activity addresses are so important and useful that you may want to repeat it over a series of meetings until the group has developed mastery.

Cues A sound cue can be recorded or live music, an alarm, a bell, a whistle, or a chime. Try alternating sound with silence to provide a way to cue Players when to move and when to freeze. Visual cues can be made by turning the lights off and on, holding up colored cards, or with sign language. You may wish to use a cue that is a carryover from your classroom management system.

Connections

Visual Arts Encourage Players to physically recreate friezes that they have seen in artworks. Discussions could focus on shape, line, balance, energy, and mood.

Music Play Move/Freeze to different types of music. First, analyze the rhythm and then choose a pattern. Use counts as cues for when Players move and freeze. Players could interpret the music in their movement or work counter to it.

Social Studies Use the Social Dance variation, selecting a dance or dances that are representative of the culture you are studying or the cultural backgrounds of the Players. The friezes could also reflect the style of a culture.

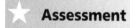 **Assessment**

Teacher Observations

Use the following questions to assess Players' mastery of awareness and control in this activity.

- Can Players stop moving when a freeze cue has been given?

- When do Players begin to move? Do they anticipate the cue or move slightly after a cue is given?

- Can Players maintain their energy in a freeze in a way that is similar to the moment of life captured in a photograph or sculpture?

- If they are playing Move/Freeze on a rhythm pattern, are Players moving in rhythm?

- Can Players remember a series of move/freeze commands?

Group Discussion

Encourage Players to discuss how they would develop Move/Freeze into a performance work.

 Student Activities

Book

pages 7–8 (Overview)

pages 9–10 (Vocabulary)

Journal

- Ask Players to describe how they felt and what they thought about while maintaining their friezes.

- Have Players describe why control and awareness are so important to a performance.

Triangle

Triangle is a walking game in which Players move together in a triangle formation. Three Leaders, one at each apex, call out directional cues that the Players must follow. While playing the game, participants practice teamwork and leadership skills, focus and concentration, and develop an awareness of directional concepts and spatial orientation.

Directions

1. Direct Players to stand close together, facing the same direction, to create the shape of a triangle. Explain that in this game, Players are to maintain this triangle shape while they walk in straight lines, moving anywhere in the performing space.

2. Explain that the three Players at the three apexes of the triangle are the Leaders. It is up to the three Leaders to decide the direction changes the triangle will make.

Skills
★ Practicing teamwork and leadership skills
★ Maintaining focus and concentration to move in group formation
★ Developing spatial awareness

Time
5 to 20 minutes

Space
Adaptable to any large, open space

Materials
None

Any one of the three Leaders can call out a direction cue by calling out a Leader's name. For example, if the three Leaders' names are John, Portia, and Jim, the cue to change direction will be either "Change, John," "Change, Portia," or "Change, Jim."

3. When the group hears a new cue, such as "Change, John," John chooses a new direction and faces that direction. The rest of the Players, upon hearing the cue and seeing where John faces, quickly turn as a unit, facing John's direction choice. All continue to walk, facing the new direction, until the next cue is called.

4. Have Players alternate positions so that others get a chance to lead the group.

Variations

Simplified Directional Changes After Players have established their triangle shape, assume the role of Leader and call out the name of one of the Players standing at the three apexes. The whole group turns and moves in the direction of that apex. In this variation, there are only three directional choices.

Stage Direction Cues To give Players practice following stage movement cues, instruct Leaders to call out direction cues by using the names of parts of the stage to identify the directional choice.

Examples:
Move toward Stage Right.
Go Downstage.
Go to Upstage Left corner.

Other Formations Choose another geometric shape for the Players to form.

Performance Suggestions

Costumes In a public performance, it helps the audience if the Players wear a uniform costume. Without incurring expense, a group could choose something that they all have in their wardrobes, such as blue jeans and white tee shirts. Alternatively, Players could wear color-coordinated clothes, such as only red and black, or all white.

Teaching Notes

Management Tips

Making a Triangle Formation If Players have difficulty making a triangle formation, tell them to think of the way bowling pins are arranged: one in the first row, two in the second row, three in the third row, and so on. If the number in your group doesn't fit this formation exactly, have the middle rows spread out or squeeze in closer together.

Defining the Shape with a Prop You may wish to define the outside edges of the triangle with an object such as rope, plastic tubing, or elastic material. This prop should be held waist-high, parallel to the ground, by those Players standing on the outside of the triangle.

Connections

Mathematics Use this game to give Players a concrete understanding of two-dimensional geometric shapes.

Special Needs

If any of your Players are unable to move with the group in formation, allow them to participate by calling out the direction change cues.

 Assessment

Teacher Observations

- Did the group follow cues well? How quickly was it able to change direction?
- Was the group able to maintain the triangle shape when it changed direction?
- Did the group get better at moving in formation with practice?

Group Discussion

Use the following questions to lead the Players in a discussion about moving in group formation.

- Did you use any special tricks to maintain your spacing with the Players around you? Describe them.
- Did any accidents occur, such as crashes, a breakup of the formation, running out of room before a Leader called the next cue? What do you think caused these accidents?

 Student Activities

Book

pages 11–12 (Background Reading)

Journal

- Ask Players to write about real-life activities that require moving in group formations (e.g., parades, military marches).
- Have Players write about why cooperation and collaboration are so important to the success of movement activities.

Channels

Channels develops Players' awareness of space and their relationships to others in space. Players must visualize an imaginary grid on the floor of the performance space, then travel back and forth within imagined parallel channels. While traveling in their channels, Players concentrate on performing one sound and/or movement idea, changing to a new performance idea each time they change directions. The concept for Channels was adapted from Anna Halprin's 1965 performance score, *Parades and Changes.*

 Directions

1. Before playing the game, ask the Players to visualize an imaginary grid of channels on the floor of the performing space. The top and bottom edges of the grid will be the front and back of the performing area. The channels are perpendicular to the front (downstage) and back (upstage) lines. There will be as many channels as there are Players.

2. Assign each Player a channel. Have the Players line up side by side, at least an arm's length apart, on the back, or upstage line of the grid, facing the front, or downstage line of the grid.

3. Explain that Players will travel back and forth within their channels. In proscenium theater terms, this would be described as traveling downstage and upstage. Tell Players to use one idea or phrase of sound and/or movement as they move in their channels from upstage to downstage. They should repeat this idea or phrase as many times as necessary to travel the entire length of the channel. (See Variations for sound and movement ideas.)

4. When Players arrive at the downstage line, tell them to move in the opposite direction, toward the upstage line, while performing a different sound and/or movement idea. Players continue traveling downstage and upstage in their parallel channels, performing a new sound and/or movement idea each time they change their traveling direction, until you feel that they have made sufficient progress toward mastering the concepts of this activity. (See Assessment, Teacher Observations)

Variations

Frieze When Players reach the downstage and upstage lines, they remain in a frieze until all Players have joined them.

Changing Body Facings When Players move toward the downstage line they face forward. When they move toward the upstage line they face backward (backs to the audience). Or try it vice versa, so that Players are traveling backward. Or tell Players to always face forward, whether moving downstage or upstage.

Changing Channels Have Players change channels at either the upstage or downstage line. This could be done each time they arrive at an end (one or both), or on a verbal cue from you.

Hello/Good-Bye Players begin on the upstage line facing downstage. They move downstage performing sounds and movements that communicate "Hello." Players return to the upstage line performing sounds and movements that communicate "Good-bye."

Body Isolations As Players travel up and down their channels using locomotors, call out cues that tell them to focus their actions through a particular part or parts of the body.

Skills

★ Visualizing an imaginary grid on the floor of the performance space
★ Maintaining a consistent spatial relationship with other moving Players
★ Creating and performing sound and/or movement ideas

Time

10 to 20 minutes

Space

Adaptable to any open space

Materials

A sound environment may be provided for additional texture.

Examples:
Heads only, shoulders only, knees and elbows, fingers plus head

Clichés Players focus on cliché gestures and expressions while traveling up and down their channels.

Examples of cliché gestures:
thumbs up, thumbs down, foot tapping, waving, rolling the eyeballs, hands on the hips, hands across the chest

Examples of cliché expressions:
"cool," "Hey, dude!" "fed up," "All right!" "you know," "hmmmm," "um," and "yo"

 Teaching Notes

Management Tips

Marking Channel Lines If Players are experiencing difficulty moving on an imaginary grid, you may wish to mark the parallel channel lines with chalk or tape. If you are playing in a gymnasium or playground, take advantage of any existing floor markings when setting up the imaginary grid.

Maintaining Parallel Channels Suggest that Players use spotting to maintain their parallel channels. Tell them to search for a mark or object on the floor, the wall, or in the distance to focus on as they travel downstage. They may need to find another spot to focus on while traveling upstage.

Connections

Dance Ask Players to practice a single dance step or movement they are studying in class each time they traverse their channels.

Foreign Languages Channels would be a fun activity for practicing new vocabulary, pronunciation, or conversation. For example, each time Players change directions, they pronounce a new word and make up a sentence using that word. If possible, their movements could relate to what they are saying.

Special Needs

- Players who are sight-impaired may need a physical demarcation of their channels. If possible, allow them to play next to a wall, or set up a path with ropes, chairs, or books. Another option would be to allow a sight-impaired Player to travel close behind a seeing Player in the same channel, tracking the Player by using sound or by placing a hand on her shoulder.

- This score makes a good wheel-chair dance.

 Assessment

Teacher Observations

Use the following questions to assess your students' progress in this movement activity.

- Are Players able to travel in their parallel channels, maintaining consistent spacing with others?

- Do Players seem able to concentrate on a single sound and/or movement idea while traversing their channels?

- Are Players able to instantaneously change their sound or movement ideas when they change directions, or do they seem to have difficulty creating new ideas?

- Did you notice any ideas that would work especially well in a performance of Channels?

Group Discussion

Ask Players to discuss the aspects of playing Channels that they found difficult or challenging. For example, visualizing and staying in a parallel channel, creating new ideas with each direction change, or moving while performing a sound or movement idea. Ask them to explain how they solved these problems.

 Student Activities

Journal

Ask Players to describe how a performance of Channels would look if they were directing it.

Line-Up

Line-up provides a simple and easy-to-understand structure for Players to work in ensemble. To begin the game, Players scatter in the playing area and improvise their own sounds and actions. A line-up is created when two or more Players join another Player and imitate his sounds and movements. To perceive the total stage picture, Players need to be aware of their relationship to everyone else. This encourages them to use peripheral vision, to think and react quickly, and to see the importance of the group, rather than the solo, vision.

Line-up is a variation of follow-the-leader games and is loosely based on a line dance performance structure choreographed by Trisha Brown in 1976 and 1977, in which lines of dancers kept forming and reforming.

Skills
★ Improvising sound and movement ideas
★ Imitating other Players' sounds and movements
★ Creating transitions between distinct sound and/or movement ideas
★ Learning to consider the whole stage picture when performing ensemble

Time
10 to 30 minutes

Space
Adaptable to any open space

Materials
Live or recorded music may be added.

 Directions

1. Have Players scatter randomly throughout the playing area. Tell them to begin Line-up by improvising their own movement and/or sound activities.

2. Explain that anyone may choose at any time to join any other Player's sound and/or movement activity. To do so, they imitate that Player after joining her in a line formation. The line-up can be in a front to back, side to side, back to back, or front to front relationship. Or a Player can wait to see if other Players will join his activity. Instruct Players that if no one has joined their activity within ten seconds, they should join another line-up.

3. Encourage Players to change lines every ten to twenty seconds. The excitement increases when lines constantly change size, shape, levels, and place. The more alert the Players remain to what everyone in the group is performing, the better the game.

4. Once the Players understand the rules of Line-up, you can increase performance demands by adding the dimension of transitions. Ask Players to be aware of what they do as they change lines and activities. You may wish to have the group explore the following ways to use transitions.

• Traveling from line to line can become a separate activity, unlike the activity in any existing line.

• Players use transition times to gradually transform from the sound/movement of the line they are leaving into the sound/ movement of the line they are joining. By the time they arrive in the new line, they are performing the new activity.

• It is possible that some transition activities may become a line-up if someone joins another's transition.

Teaching Notes

Management Tips

Time-Lapse Cues You can indicate ten- or twenty-second time lapses by a cueing signal, such as finger snaps, whistling, turning musical sounds on and off, or a verbal cue.

Line-up Formations There are many interpretations of what constitutes line-up formations. Besides performing side by side, front to front, back to back, and front to back, Players can also relate to each other while creating diagonals, curves, and perpendicular floor patterns in which Players are close to or distant from one another.

Music Use music to contribute different qualities to the performance of the game. Changing music during the game can shift the mood and rhythm of the performance, or give a cohesiveness to the group. It's fun to have the performers continue through changes of silence and sound.

Teacher Observations

Use the following questions to help assess the Players' learning experience during this activity.

- Did Players seem comfortable improvising sounds and movements? What kinds of movements did they perform (dance steps, everyday actions, pantomimes, cliché gestures, locomotors)? What kinds of sounds did they choose (words, sentences, noises, singing)?

- How adept were the Players at imitating the sounds and movements of others?

- Were Players quick to join other line-ups if no one joined them? Did lines constantly change and grow? What kinds of formations did Players create?

- Did Players seem to be aware of creating an overall stage picture through their movements, transitions, and formations, or were they focused more on their own individual activities?

Group Discussion

Ask Players to describe what they thought the overall stage picture looked like during Line-up.

- What kinds of line-up formations were created during the course of the game?

- How many lines were there at one time?

- How many people were in each line-up?

- How often did line-ups change?

- What kinds of activities were occurring in the lines?

- How did the various activities, stage movements, and formation changes work together as a single performance piece?

Journal

Have Players try to recreate their thought processes as they played Line-up. To start Players thinking, ask the following questions.

- How did you decide which line to join and when to change lines?

- Were you comfortable improvising sounds and movements?

- Were you more focused on creating an overall picture or on your own individual activity? Why are both important?

Balancing Act

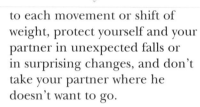

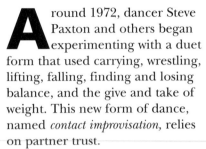

Around 1972, dancer Steve Paxton and others began experimenting with a duet form that used carrying, wrestling, lifting, falling, finding and losing balance, and the give and take of weight. This new form of dance, named *contact improvisation*, relies on partner trust.

Contact improvisation has developed into a form of "dance sport" with a worldwide network of participants. It has profoundly influenced the way dancers partner one another, especially in that it has released men from always performing the traditional male partnering role of supporting, lifting, and catching women. Much choreography since the 1970s contains a wide variety of partnering combinations—anyone can be seen balancing the weight of someone else.

Skills

★ Developing partner trust
★ Experimenting with balance, support, and basic movement partnering techniques
★ Improvising a series of actions in which partners are always in contact and supporting each other's weight

Time

30 minutes to an hour

Space

Any large, open space, either indoors or outdoors

Materials

Gymnastic mats. Sound environments may be added to change the dynamics and enhance the performance.

Balancing Act uses principles of contact improvisation to help Players find new movement information. Working with partners, they find actions that can only be accomplished with a partner's help.

★ Directions

1. Before beginning Balancing Act, make sure that Players are warmed up and stretched out. (See Movement Warm-ups in Chapter 10, Short Takes, page 216.)

2. Explain that Players are going to experiment with a partner to find actions that require them to support each other's weight. Allow Players to choose partners. Direct partners to space themselves out as much as possible in the working space.

3. Before allowing partners to begin their balancing explorations, discuss the following safety rules with them.

- Be responsible for yourself and your partner. Protect yourself.

- Let your partner know of any injuries you have that would prevent you from doing certain movements.

- If something hurts, stop doing it. Come out of any position slowly and smoothly. Even if it hurts, do not jerk or change quickly.

- Communicate with each other.

- Always be aware of what your partner is doing.

- Take care of each other: move slowly and carefully at first, allow yourselves time to adjust

to each movement or shift of weight, protect yourself and your partner in unexpected falls or in surprising changes, and don't take your partner where he doesn't want to go.

- Do not try lifting your partner overhead.

4. Explain that partners can balance by leaning on each other or pulling in opposition while maintaining equal distribution of weight, or by holding or supporting parts or all of the partner's body. Guide Players through a few partnering exercises to demonstrate these basic partnering techniques.

- Leaning back to back, partners lower themselves until they are sitting on the floor, then stand up in the same way.

- Partners hold both hands and pull in opposition as they lower to a sitting position and stand.

- One partner balances his weight on his hands and knees. The other partner lays forward over his back (close to his hips), then alternates lifting his arms and legs off the floor. Challenge Players to lift arms and legs off the floor to strike a flying Superman pose.

5. Give partners time to explore new and unusual ways to balance and support each other.

6. As they become more comfortable working with each other and supporting each other, direct partners to improvise a series of poses and movements in which they are always in contact and supporting each other's weight. Tell them to try not to preplan the next move, but to let the actions determine what happens next.

Variations

Choreography Have partners choreograph a series of movements in which they alternate contacting and separating from each other, or keep moving continuously while remaining in contact with each other.

Group Partnering When partners are working safely, giving consistent care and attention to each other, try having Players work in larger groups. Experiment with gymnastic tricks and group balancing challenges.

Examples:
- Do a somersault that ends with a balance action by two or more people.
- Make a human pyramid and transform into another configuration.

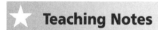

Teaching Notes

Management Tips

Prerequisites Balancing Act may not be an appropriate activity for all groups. Players should already be able to trust one another and work together before attempting to partner each other. You may wish to have them try some of the trust exercises in Chapter 10, Short Takes, before playing this game.

Safety Tips If possible, have Players work on a cushioned surface, such as large gymnastic mats. Outside, a grass field would be better than a blacktop area. Make sure that the area is clear of objects and debris. Each couple will need enough

space to experiment freely—at least an eight-foot square area. If your space will not safely accommodate all Players at once, divide them into several groups. If movement partnering is new to the Players, it would be a good idea to match partners by size and weight to minimize the risk of injury.

Partner Demonstrations As Players are experimenting with balancing movements, look for partners who are working particularly well together. Ask the partners to demonstrate for other Players. As they are demonstrating, point out their good use of safety and balancing techniques.

Connections

Dance Bring in some dance books or videos for students to study partnering poses and movements. Encourage students to watch dance performances on public television channels, on video, or in the theater and to take notes on the balancing and partnering techniques they observed.

Art Study the concept of balance and compare its uses in other fields, such as painting, sculpture, and architecture.

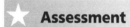

Assessment

Teacher Observations

Keep a close eye on how Players are interacting with each other. Do not hesitate to intervene if you

notice any potentially dangerous situations, such as Players who are trying to lift too much weight, moving too quickly, or disregarding their partner's feelings or actions. Use the following questions to assess their ability to participate in this activity.

- Are Players following the safety rules? (See step 3 of Directions.)
- Do partners' movements depend on a supportive relationship?
- Do partners seem to trust each other? Are they working cooperatively and in a relaxed manner?
- How imaginative and adventurous are the partners? Are their explorations taking them into some interesting movements? Are partners moving freely from movement to movement, allowing the dynamics of their actions to determine what they will do next?

Group Discussion

Have Players discuss what they learned during their partnering explorations. What worked, and what didn't work?

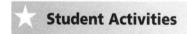

Book

page 13 (Background Reading)

Journal

Ask Players to write about the importance of practicing trust and following safety precautions when performing a balancing act.

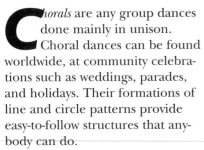

Choral Dances

Chorals are any group dances done mainly in unison. Choral dances can be found worldwide, at community celebrations such as weddings, parades, and holidays. Their formations of line and circle patterns provide easy-to-follow structures that anybody can do.

Choral line dance patterns may take the shape of curves, triangles, parallel rows, or reflect the edges of the dance space. They can be designed as a path or route to follow. The form of simple choral dances is reflected in their names: a line dance is performed in a line and a circle dance is performed in a circle.

Equality is implicit in choral dance forms because there is no dominant position, except when it's necessary to have a Leader or Caller of step sequences. When there is a Leader, she can be thought of as a master of ceremonies who sets the tempo and often calls what steps the dancers are to do next.

Within the choral structure there are no hard and fast rules. Choral dances may be performed holding hands or not; with a Leader or not. They may be simple or complicated, using only one pattern or a combination of patterns, such as circles, straight lines, spirals, double circles, figure eights, and serpentine formations. It is possible for both line and circle patterns to occur within one dance. A single line dance may turn into a contra line dance (two lines facing each other). Rhythm may change within the dance. Solos or duets can occur within the basic unison structure (as in American square dances).

★ Directions

1. Before creating a choral dance, decide how you want to organize the group. Work in one large group, or divide the Players into teams. Depending on the individual talents in your group and the complexity of your choral dance steps and patterns, you may decide to use a Leader(s).

- Choose one Leader who remains Leader throughout the dance.
- Changing Leaders: Agree upon a cueing system to decide when or where to switch Leaders.
- Alternating Leaders: Players at the head and tail positions can be designated as alternating Leaders, depending on the direction calls of the dance.

2. Select formations for your choral dance. Following are some suggestions and examples for line dances and circle dances.

Line Dances Arrange groups or teams in one or more lines which maintain a consistent spatial relationship to one another. Mass formations can be created using two or more columns of Players. To make a line formation, Players may stand side by side or front to back. They may also stand in several lines, forming columns (parallel lines facing the same direction) or in a contra dance formation (two lines facing each other).

Example of how to make a new contra dance:

(As inspired by Jerome Robbins's choreography in the musical *West Side Story,* a modern version of Shakespeare's *Romeo and Juliet.* The feuding Montague and Capulet families are transformed into two New York City rival gangs, the Jets and the Sharks. Their antagonism is theatricalised by using the contra dance form.)

- Divide the group into two teams.
- Teams face each other in parallel lines, leaving a large open space between the teams.
- Each team selects its first Leader. Leaders stand in the middle slightly forward of their teams so that everyone can see them easily.
- The Leader of one team performs a simple repeatable rhythm and action pattern. (For example: Four two-count jumping jacks, followed by a low spin that lasts for four beats and ends in a frieze of four beats.)

Skills

- ★ Creating a choral dance by cooperatively selecting formations, floor patterns, and steps
- ★ Memorizing and performing complex movement steps, patterns, and sequences
- ★ (Optional) Exploring the history of choral dances in different cultures

Time

30 minutes to an hour

Space

Adaptable to any large open space, indoors or outdoors

Materials

Live or recorded music or rhythmic sounds are useful.

- Decide how many times the pattern should be repeated. (Six or seven repeats will give the team members enough time to learn and practice the routine).
- Both teams copy the Leader's action as exactly as possible. The opposite team mirrors the spatial pattern of the performing team. (If performers go right, the opposite team goes left; if they go forward, the opposite team goes backward.)
- The opposite team's first Leader starts the next action pattern.
- When a Leader has completed his pattern, he goes to the end of his line.
- Alternate team challenges until everyone has performed as Leader.
- Once the teams understand the structure of this competition contra dance, they can begin to refine their performance, with both teams understanding that they are making one piece together.

Example of how to make a single line dance in cheerleading style:
- Work as one large group or in teams.
- Choose a repeatable rhythmic sound pattern such as a song or chant, or sounds made by clapping, stamping, or doing the hambone.
- Add unison dance movements that create line formations and are set to the rhythmic patterns.
- Have cheerleaders perform the group's choreography and rhythms.

Circle Dances Circle dance formations can be made by having the Players stand in one, two, or more circles that are placed concentrically, cross paths, weave in and out, or function separately. Following are descriptions of some well-known circle dances.

- **Hokey Pokey** Players stand in a single circle performing the actions they sing about: "You put your right foot in, you put your right foot out, put your right foot in and you shake it all about; you do the Hokey Pokey and you turn yourself around; that's what it's all about." This chant is repeated using different parts of the body, such as the head, hips, and arms. The last chant, which is usually, "put your whole body in, put your whole body out..." ends with participants bowing or bending at the waist while shaking their hands and raising and lowering their arms, singing: "You do the Hoooookey Pokey, you do the Hooookey Pokey; that's what it's all about! *(clap, clap).*
- **Xoros Choros** An ancient Greek circle dance that led to the development of the use of rhythmic dances performed by the chorus in ancient Greek drama. There is no exact description available, but reconstructions can be made by studying vases, sculptures, or friezes from ancient Greece.
- **Hora** A popular linked circle dance of Rumanian origin performed on special occasions, such as weddings and coming of age parties. This dance was made famous by its inclusion in the Broadway show and movie, *Fiddler on the Roof.*
- **Ring Around the Rosie** A traditional children's circle dance and chant. It originated as a charm against medieval plagues.
- **Native American Pow-Wow, Opening Ceremonies** A turn of the century Native American tradition that developed after the federal government banned traditional dances on the reservations. The opening ceremonies are performed by all the participating tribes. They circle the performing arena, dancing to drum rhythms and chants. After this opening ceremony, competitions in

individual dance categories begin, such as the Shawl Dance, the Fancy Dance, and the Hoop Dance.
- **Cakewalk** This African-American dance was first performed by slaves on big Southern plantations. It is a circle dance in which dancers "strutted their stuff," tilting their bodies backward and kicking high as they circled the prize cake. The best dancer and highest kicker received the prize. Special clubs were formed where competitions were held. The best men performers received a champion belt and the women received a diamond ring as prizes. Later, this became a popular entertainment that was performed on the vaudeville circuits.
- **Maypole (or Ribbon) Dances** This circle dance originated in medieval rural dances celebrating springtime on the first day of May. In earliest times, these dances were done around a living tree that later was substituted by a pole. It wasn't until the nineteenth century that ribbons were attached to the top of a pole and incorporated as part of the dance. The dancers circle the pole and weave in and out, plaiting the ribbons. These dances were found in several European countries and in Mexico. Today, Maypole dances are still danced with various standard figures (steps) that have evolved.

3. Decide on a route for the dancers to follow. (Players could also have the option of not predetermining their floor patterns, but rather to improvise how and where they move through the space.) Players could design a floor pattern using geometric patterns such as a serpentine, spirals, triangles, squares, perpendicular lines, or concentric circles. Following are some suggestions for ways to do this.

Use Existing Markers in the Space
Follow the placement of objects or markers, such as a rope or stair banister, or take advantage of existing lines already marked on a floor for games such as basketball, hopscotch and shuffleboard. Many cultures have used floor markings to guide the dancers as they travel from one place to another. Such dances were sometimes called labyrinth or maze dances. Traces of ancient sacred dance patterns have been discovered in writings and drawings in Scandinavia, Persia, Tibet, Egypt, Crete, and Britain.

Use Points of Reference If there are no pre-existing objects or floor markers, use points of reference such as doors, walls, furniture, or people placed in the space to maintain the pattern of the floor dance.

Design a Map Using any of the above methods, draw a floor pattern on a piece of paper that dancers can follow. Use a key to indicate where specific shapes or steps are to be done. On the map, include other points of reference in the performing space, such as doors, windows, or columns.

4. Finally, choose the steps and movement patterns for the choral dance.

Learn Existing Dances Research folk, social dance, or other choral dances from library books or participation in community arts or recreation facility classes.

- **Quadrille or Cotillion** Originally a French dance for an even number of couples in square formation that became a popular ballroom dance by the nineteenth century.

- **Chain Dances** (such as the *allemande* and *farandole,* which were the first recorded social dances that spread throughout Europe in the fourteenth and fifteenth centuries) A procession of couples either circles the hall or moves down the center of the room and turns to go back to the starting point. Sometimes partners separate, men to the left and women to the right, and meet at the end of the room to come up the center, hand in hand. Americans are most familiar with this form in the Virginia Reel.

- **Sword Dances** (such as the morris dance) Preparation dances for war performed either before, during, or after phases of conflict.

- **Square Dance** An American folk dance that became popular starting in the nineteenth century. Square dances are derivative of old round and chain dances, such as the European quadrilles and cotillions. There are four couples (eight dancers) and a caller, who instructs the dancers by shouting out or singing the steps to follow.

- **London Bridge** A children's song and dance that combines a tag game with a reel and is repeated over and over again: "London Bridge is falling down, falling down, falling down. London Bridge is falling down, my fair lady. Take a key and lock her up, lock her up, lock her up. Take a key and lock her up, my fair lady." As with other children's rhyming games, there is some historical event that influences the style and words of the chant and game.

- **Line Dances** Conga, bunny hop, electric slide, military parade displays

- **Circular (Round) Dances** Maypole dance, reels, kolos, sarabandes

Create New Dance Steps and Patterns Create new dances from any movement activity. Form small groups or have the whole group work simultaneously on solos that they share with one another. The group decides what solos or parts of solos will be used to create the group dance. Following are some ideas to help Players get started

creating steps. Select the most successful patterns for the whole group to learn and perform. Perform as a unison line or circle dance.

- **Social Dance Forms** Ask everyone to perform any social dance steps they already know. Select a series of steps from those being demonstrated and combine them into phrases. Decide how many times to repeat phrases or steps before going on to the next phrase or step.

- **Locomotors** Identify the seven locomotors: walking, running, skipping, jumping, leaping, sliding, hopping. Have each Player create a repeatable pattern using at least three locomotors. If the whole group is performing in unison, choose which series of locomotor patterns will be performed. If Players are working in small groups, two or more teams can teach each other their patterns and put them together to make a longer unison series that all can perform.

- **Daily Life Actions** Have participants create a series of three or four actions that can be combined into a repeatable pattern. For example, ask everyone to choose at least two daily life actions (waving hello, shivering, pointing to a direction) and one or two other sound or movement qualities (turning, leaning, clapping). Have participants teach one another their patterns. Combine several patterns into a series.

Performance Suggestions

Music Choose music that reflects the culture or period of the choral dance steps. Records and tapes can be borrowed from public libraries. Ask for volunteers or the school band or chorus to provide live music. Percussion instruments, fiddles, songs, chants, hand-clapping, and stamping are all ways to help participants move in the same rhythm.

Costumes If you want to emphasize the unison look of the group, have everyone decide on a color scheme to follow, such as blue or black jeans and white shirts; earth colors; or any kind of red, white, or black tops, bottoms, and accessories.

 Teaching Notes

Management Tips

Setting Up a Circle Have everyone make a circle formation by standing with both arms extended so that only fingertips touch from person to person. That way, everyone will have enough room to move comfortably and they create the shape of the circle. If you need a smaller or larger circle, ask everyone to step forward or backward two steps. Sometimes, placing the dancers on markers, such as a circle painted on a gymnasium floor, will help the dancers maintain their shape and position.

Working Together Cooperatively Circle dances that require holding hands need everyone to move with equal energy. Holding hands might bring up behaviors of giggling and teasing. Discourage yanking or hanging on others. If these problems occur, have Players work for awhile without holding hands, asking them to maintain their spatial relationships. Then go back to holding hands again.

Simplifying the Activity For beginners, choose existing dances with simple step patterns that do not require extensive drill, such as the hokey pokey, the bunny hop, or the grapevine. Or, have the participants supply their own steps that they feel comfortable doing. Young adults love to supply their own steps and music and may enjoy the disciplined drill required to perform intricate steps in unison.

Following Patterns Begin by practicing simple walking steps before moving on to more elaborate step variations. Identify the dance patterns by name as students learn the form.

Stimulating Choreographic Ideas Use daily life experiences to recall events that involved forming lines or circles. Try them out or recreate them as a way to begin thinking and improvising a choral dance score.

Connections

Cite choral dance concepts, such as use of shape and pattern, and compare them to their uses in another discipline.

Social Studies Choose dances that come from the culture, historical period, or place that is being studied in history or literature classes. Compare folk or social dances of different cultures. Make cross-cultural connections. Study how dance forms change through time and place, adapting from urban to rural, religious to secular, peasant to court settings. Make connections between contemporary choral dances that the students may be doing, such as the electric slide, and compare them with similar historical dances, such as the Samba parade dances in Carnival.

Science According to dance historians and anthropologists such as Curt Sachs, the earliest dance forms may have been learned from watching animals move in lines and circles. Various animals have been observed using circle and line formations with regularity, including bird-mating displays, bee flight patterns, and games that apes play. Make a study of ritual animal behavior and either recreate the animal dances or find similarities to existing dances.

Special Needs

- Choreograph wheelchair dances using the same basic rules to find spatial patterns and variations.

- For Players who may experience difficulty learning complicated steps, create choral processionals that use a unison path and individual interpretation in choice of steps. For example, everyone can be asked to walk a zigzag pattern from Stage Right to Stage Left. The walks use each person's personal style.

  - Work as one large group or in teams.

  - Select or create a path or route to follow.

  - Using a follow-the-leader format, Players follow the path or route from beginning to end at least one time. (Mountainsides, garden pathways, mazes, gymnasium floors with painted markings, or inlaid floors with large geometric patterns offer good pathways to follow.)

  - The route or path maintains the unison organization. The steps may or may not be in unison, eliminating the pressure to be exactly together in performance.

Background Notes

Because choral dances are so universal, there are infinite and complex variations to the forms. Chorals have been called by hundreds of names, including *ronde* and *route* (French), *riad* (Russian), *kolo* or *korlo* (Balkan), *chakram* or *rahda* (Indian), *rune* (Scandinavian), *reel* (Scottish), and *sarabande* (Persian/Spanish). The roots of these various names for the dances refers to choral dances as they are known in their countries of origin, and might also suggest times and places of ceremony.

Historical descriptions of the dances described in this activity are based on entries in the *Dictionary of the Dance* by W. G. Raffe and *World History of the Dance* by Curt Sachs.

 Assessment

Teacher Observations

- Do Players demonstrate an ability to work cooperatively in small groups?

- Do Players demonstrate concentration and focus in performing movement skills?

- Can Players memorize and reproduce movement sequences?

- Can Players accurately transfer a spatial pattern from the visual to the kinesthetic? Can they transfer rhythmic patterns from the aural to the kinesthetic?

Group Discussion

- What did you like about creating and performing a choral dance?

- How and why do you think choral dance got started?

- What examples of circle and line dances have you seen?

Student Activities

Book

pages 14–18 (Background Reading)

Journal

Have Players write about the kinds of dances they most like to perform, and those they like to watch being performed. Tell them to explain their preferences.

Acting Skills

The activities in this chapter will give Players opportunities to practice the life skills of communication, self-presentation, and teamwork. They also help Players develop their powers of observation, focus, creative problem solving, organization and follow-through, and self-discipline. As they practice these acting skills, Players will gain confidence to develop and express a personal voice and a world view.

There are many different schools or styles of acting:

Stanislavsky and method acting, Brecht, Kabuki, Chinese opera, pantomime, clowning, and theater sports, to name a few. You will find that all of these methods can be adapted to serve curriculum needs, or be useful for individual projects. Look for games and activities that will train in the techniques that promote solutions specific to your project goal.

Ask Players to keep exploring new information so that they will remain open in their responses and grounded in the present. An open mind is especially valuable in the acting games and activities that require collaborations, which by their very nature challenge Players to deal with unpredictable changes and various points of view.

Some of the most basic and necessary acting tools are included in this chapter's games and activities. Audience/Performer lets both you and the Players find out what each person likes to perform, and what Players think performance is all about. Enter/Exit helps Players become aware of their actions on stage. It also helps performers learn the language of the theater, so they have experience using the vocabulary for parts of the stage and stage positions. Tug of War and Operator give Players movement experiences that also involve working together as an ensemble. Tug of War provides practice in pantomime, and

Operator teaches the importance of clear communication, even over great distances. Relationships to a Chair, Clichés, and Doubles offer improvisational structures that help Players think through characterization, use of vocal expression in monologues and dialogues, script analysis, use of props, and staging performances.

Other activities that concentrate on acting skills can be found in Chapter 1, Orientation Games, and Chapter 10, Short Takes. These chapters contain many warm-up and rehearsal exercises and games that develop concentration through listening and focus and build ensemble spirit through cooperation and trust.

Audience/Performer

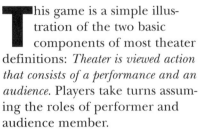

This game is a simple illustration of the two basic components of most theater definitions: *Theater is viewed action that consists of a performance and an audience.* Players take turns assuming the roles of performer and audience member.

Audience/Performer serves as a dramatically clear introduction to the power of theater, since the performer must decide what a performance is by choosing what to perform, then perform it in front of an audience. It also serves as a guide for Leaders, showing them what each member of the group believes is a performance.

Skills

★ Taking turns assuming the roles of performer and audience member

★ Entering the stage and performing spontaneously

★ Discussing the meaning of the terms *audience, performer,* and *performance*

Time

10 to 20 minutes. The activity may last longer, depending on the size and interest of the group.

Space

A stage is preferable, but the game is adaptable to any space.

Materials

You may allow Players to use small hand props or to wear costumes.

 Directions

1. Clearly designate two areas within the workspace: a stage/performance area and a house/audience area. Since the performance begins or ends when an actor enters or exits the stage area, its boundaries should be clearly established. Explain to the Players that they are onstage the moment they enter the boundaries of the stage area and are offstage the moment they exit the boundaries of the stage area. The game begins with everyone sitting in the *house,* as the audience space is traditionally called.

2. Explain that each Player is to assume the roles of audience member and performer. Ask everyone to complete the following cycle at least one time:

> Be an audience member.
> Be a performer.
> Be an audience member.

3. Tell Players that they are to go to the stage one at a time to perform something. After ending a performance, the performer returns to the house area and becomes part of the audience.

4. The game can end after everyone has performed at least one time. Players may repeat the cycle any number of times.

Variations

Simultaneous Solos Have several Players perform their solos onstage at the same time.

Duets, Trios, Quartets Organize Players in small groups. Allow groups time to work together to create a performance.

Enter from Stage Right Designate the offstage or backstage area to the right and left of the performing space as the points of entry and exit. This gives performers practice in entering and exiting from the offstage area rather than from the house. Ask half of the group to serve as the audience while the other half of the group performs. This setup will encourage Players to observe and learn from one another.

Changing Spaces Have the group perform this game in different kinds of spaces: outdoor, indoor, formal stage area, entranceway, stairway, and so on. Discuss with the group how different spaces influenced performance qualities and their perceptions as audience members.

 Teaching Notes

Management Tips

Marking Stage Boundaries To clearly demarcate the boundaries of the stage or performing area, walk the edges of the performance area and mark them with tape, chairs, ropes, or by some other means.

Encouraging Performers To engage shy performers, try any of the following:

• Call out a person's name or tap him on the shoulder when it is his turn to perform.

- Have each returning performer choose someone who has not yet performed.

- Have Players begin on the stage but not within the boundaries of the performing area. After they perform, Players join you in the house as audience members. There are a couple of reasons why this change of beginning position overcomes performance fears and shyness. One is that the stage can look formidable when viewed from the audience's perspective, and the distance that has to be crossed to get to the stage can seem overwhelming. It is also not so intimidating to begin as a group, even though each performance is still done as a solo.

- It is at your discretion to allow some Players never to perform, or to suggest specific ways to perform, such as offering jokes, singing a song, playing a musical instrument, doing magic or gymnastic tricks. You can also model ways to participate by performing a simple bow, greeting, or sneeze. This can happen whenever you feel a great hesitation by Players.

Building Empathy Encourage Players to participate as audience members by watching and staying in focus on the Players onstage and supporting one another with applause. Make sure Players know that they have to take turns and respect one another, both as audience members and performers.

Defining Audience Point of View Remind Players that as long as a performer is seen, she is performing. "If you can see the audience, the audience can see you." Therefore, the performance begins with the entrance and ends after the exit.

Breaking the Fourth Wall If you are playing this game on a stage, discussion may arise regarding a theater convention known as the *fourth wall*. This refers to an imaginary glass wall that separates the audience from the performance, allowing the audience to see what is happening on stage. If a performer goes through that imaginary wall rather than using the side or back wall entrances and exits, it is referred to as "breaking the fourth wall." It can be used as an effective piece of stage business but should be used consciously and sparingly. The stage seems to lose some of its magic and power if the fourth wall is broken too often as a quick and convenient solution to getting on and off.

Special Needs

If some Players are using wheelchairs, set up a playing area that is easily accessible. If some Players are deaf, situate the interpreter so that Players can see him and so that the interpreter can see everything on stage. This might be on the fourth wall line, or curtain line, stage right or stage left. Invite any assistants, including specialists and aides, to take part in the performance of the Player.

 Assessment

Teacher Observations

- Did students demonstrate proper audience etiquette while watching other Players perform?

- How readily did Players take their turns performing? Did their performances demonstrate that they understood where the stage boundaries were and the fact that a performance starts when crossing the stage boundary and doesn't end until crossing it on the way offstage?

- What kinds of things did Players choose to perform? Was there a wide variety? Did students concentrate on verbal, movement, or pantomime performances?

- In the follow-up discussion, did Players understand the meanings of the terms *performer, performance,* and *audience?*

Group Discussion

Discuss the meaning of the words *performer, performance,* and *audience.* Then ask the following questions.

- What do you think it takes to make a performance?

- What is the job of the audience?

- Does the audience have a responsibility to the performers, and vice versa? What are these responsibilities?

- Can a performance happen when nobody is viewing it? Can you think of any examples of performances that could happen without an audience?

- Why is there a *fourth wall?* (See Management Tip, Breaking the Fourth Wall.)

 Student Activities

Book

pages 19–20 (Overview)

pages 21–23 (Vocabulary)

pages 24–28 (Rules for audience and performers)

Journal

Ask Players to write about what they learned when they took the roles of performer and audience member. Have them explain why audience etiquette is so important to a performer's success.

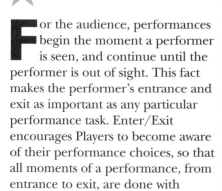

Enter/Exit

For the audience, performances begin the moment a performer is seen, and continue until the performer is out of sight. This fact makes the performer's entrance and exit as important as any particular performance task. Enter/Exit encourages Players to become aware of their performance choices, so that all moments of a performance, from entrance to exit, are done with awareness and intention.

The game Enter/Exit begins when each Player enters the performing space, and ends with the Player's exit. The Leader assigns a task for each Player to accomplish

Skills

★ Identifying stage boundaries and stage directions
★ Practicing preset stage entrances and exits
★ Interpreting and performing an assigned performance task
★ Analyzing the performance task by breaking it down into separate ideas

Time

15 to 30 minutes performing time, depending on the size of the group and whether the game is done in teams or individually. Evaluation time could range from 1 to 30 minutes of analysis and discussion.

Space

Enter/Exit can be adapted to any available space. It can be played on a formal stage, in a classroom, or in any open space.

Materials

Small hand props, costumes, set pieces, and sound environment can be added as needed.

from entrance to exit. A complete performance will consist of three steps: Enter, Perform a Task, Exit.

This is a good game to use in introductory classes. Since its rules are easily understood, Enter/Exit can be explained and played quickly. Using improvisation, Players can simply react to cues that the Leader calls out as they prepare to enter. The game works well with beginners and advanced performers.

Enter/Exit has proven to be a reliable, enjoyable, and expandable game structure. Basic theater skills, such as clear presentation and focus and use of standard theater vocabulary, can be introduced and developed using this simple and direct structure. The game can be used to develop scripts for autobiographical, biographical, and historical scenes. It can also be used to help participants develop communication and self-presentation skills necessary for interviewing and public speaking, such as maintaining poise, using gestures effectively, projecting the voice clearly, and improvising answers to questions.

★ Directions

1. Describe the rules of Enter/Exit to the Players: Each Player will enter the "stage," perform an assigned task, then exit.

2. Explain the location of the "stage" boundaries, entrance/exit points, and the audience. If you are using a classroom or large open area, the audience location will help you determine the type of stage you are using. First locate where the audience will be. Then set

the boundaries of the playing area, such as the front of the classroom, a section of hallway, or half of a basketball court. Tell Players whether the stage area will correspond to those in proscenium theaters or those in a theater in the round or open theater setting (with an audience on all sides). Let them know if any offstage or wing areas are provided. There may be some convenient furniture or barrier that can function as a line or offstage wing. If not, these boundaries have special significance, because there will be no place for the performers to hide from the audience as they can in the wings of a proscenium stage.

Set the entrance and exit points according to standard Stage Right and Stage Left orientation: When performers face the audience, Stage Right is to their right; Stage Left is to their left. If you are using a proscenium stage, entrances and exits should be from either offstage area. Everyone has to agree exactly where the enter and exit points will be. For example, in a classroom where students sit at desks, it could be decided that the moment a performer stands, he enters the playing area, and the moment he returns to his chair to sit, he exits. Or performers could stand behind a line that, when crossed, indicates an entrance or an exit.

3. Indicate where performers should wait to enter: from Stage Right or Stage Left (see diagram, page 48), Area #1 or Area #3, South or North (see diagram, page 49), the house/audience, against a back wall, or sitting in classroom chairs. This place may also function as the exit point. There should always be an audience, even if it is only you.

Standard Names for the Proscenium Stage (6–9 Playing Areas)

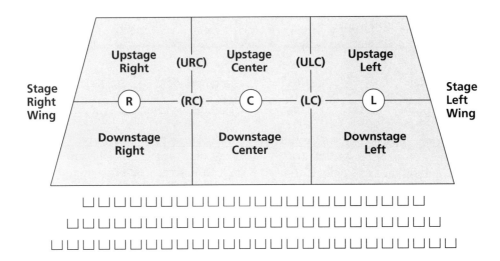

4. Assign everyone a performance task, leaving the interpretation of how to do it up to each individual. The task can be assigned when a performer is about to enter the performing space, or earlier. You may assign the same task to everyone (encourage Players to find different solutions) or assign different tasks.

Tasks should be simple and presented in easily understood directions. Following are examples of simple performance tasks that are to be combined with an entrance and exit direction. They are grouped in three major categories of directions: action tasks, motivation tasks, and monologue/interview tasks.

Action Tasks
- Perform something.
- Move as quickly/slowly as possible.
- Laugh.
- Fall.
- Perform an amazing feat that concludes with a verbal "Ta Dah!"
- Perform a verbal or gestural cliché.
    Examples:
    verbal clichés: O.K., you know, no way, yeah, What's up?
    gesture clichés: thumbs up/down, arms across chest, hand to forehead

- Use a small hand prop in some way that is different from its usual function.
- Pantomime using an imaginary tool or other object.

Motivation Tasks
- Do something to make us notice you.
- Characterization: You are a character, such as a relative, a friend, a creature from outer space, or a real historical figure.
- You are being followed by a speeding car.
- You have lost your keys.
- You are looking for a friend.
- You are expecting to see _____ (friend/enemy /family, festivity, tragedy, dinner on the table, a snake, an angel, a fire engine).
- You are lost in the desert/ forest/Arctic.

Monologue/Interview Tasks
Ask performers to give specific information, answer questions, finish incomplete sentences, or tell a short story. Have performers speak as themselves or as characters. The Leader can ask Players to answer one command or a list of several to encourage memorization skills.

- Introduce yourself.
- Tell something nobody knows about you.
- Describe: family position; jobs worked; places lived; places traveled; places you wish to travel; your favorite _____.
    The person who influenced me the most is/was _____.
    I am unique to the world because _____.
    I wish _____.
- Complete the sentence: My wish for the world is
    _____.
    I spend my money on
    _____.
    I want to become a leader of _____ because
    _____.
    An event that changed my way of thinking was _____.

Dialogue Tasks
Select two Players to stand and improvise a conversation while using at least two of the standard acting positions, as illustrated in the diagram on page 50. After their improv, ask Players which positions most effectively communicated the content of their conversation.

5. Play until each Player has had at least one turn to enter, perform a task, then exit.

Typical Playing Area Designations for Theater in the Round, or Open Theater

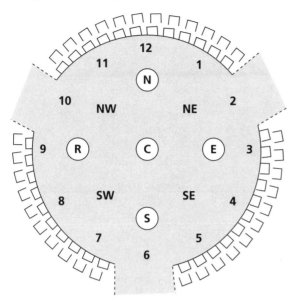

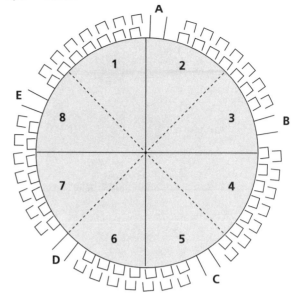

⭐ Teaching Notes

Management Tips

Intention and Awareness If Players are having difficulty thinking of something to do during their entrance and exit, tell them that even a simple walk can be a solution. Remind Players that the important lesson is working with intention and awareness: the goal is to be aware of what is done in every moment and to do everything with intention.

Have Players practice different ways to focus, so that their performance can be shared with an audience in both a proscenium theater and a theater in the round (open theater) setting.

Performance Groupings The entrances and exits can be performed as solos, duets, trios, or in teams. This decision may be influenced by the size of the group, the type of space, and the readiness of Players to perform. If many Players are experiencing hesitation or reticence in going onstage, try directing them to overlap one another's performances so that more than one Player is on the stage at any moment. Or group Players into small teams to perform. Being part of a group will relieve some of the performance anxiety.

Theater Terminology Help performers learn theater terminology by giving them task directions that include specific stage directions and identify parts of the stage.

Examples:
- Enter Upstage Right and arrive at Downstage Left with a take, then exit Upstage Left.
- Stand in the Stage Right wing, enter to Downstage Center, remain there for 10 beats, then exit to Stage Left wing.
- Enter Area #1 and arrive in Area #4; exit from Area #6.
- Enter the South stage area; go to the East stage area; exit from the West stage area.
- (Work in pairs.) One partner enter from Center Stage Right, and one partner enter from Center Stage Left. Meet Downstage Center and have a conversation that begins in Cheating positions and ends in Full Back positions. Exit from the same area as you entered.

- Enter the stage from the house through the fourth wall, walk Upstage to the back wall or *cyc,* do some bit of stage business, then exit to the Stage Left wing.

Connections

When tasks are related to a specific academic discipline, you will be able to observe how much students have absorbed from classroom reading and discussion. This game can be used as another way of testing what students have learned.

Language Arts Tie this game to speech and debate objectives by assigning performance tasks such as giving a speech (made-up or memorized); answering questions to practice job interviewing techniques; or recounting a personal experience, using voice and gesture to add to the emotional impact.

Standard Positions Performers Use to Share Scenes

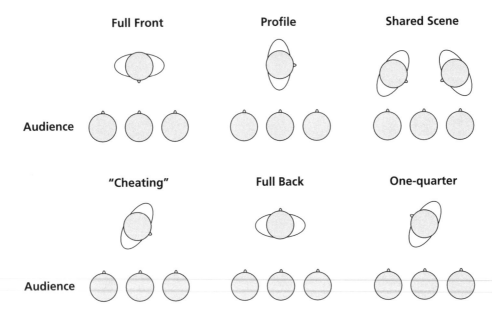

Full Front   Profile   Shared Scene

Audience

"Cheating"   Full Back   One-quarter

Audience

★ Assessment

Teacher Observations

In giving an open-ended task for Players to perform, you can observe what each performer believes is a performance. Solutions reveal each student's individual style and interests. These strengths can be capitalized on in future performance work.

Group Discussion

To increase Players' stage awareness, ask them to analyze what they have performed. By breaking down the three-step structure of Enter/Exit into performance tasks, or ideas, participants will learn to attend to every detail of their performance. Did they perform one continuous idea/intent from their entrance to their exit? For example, did they enter with a "hello" that continued, unchanged, until the exit? This is an example of a one-idea solution. Did they perform two, three, or more ideas, such as a walk on and a dance off (two ideas) or an entrance with a "hello," a monologue, a bow, and an exit walk (four ideas)? Ask Players to describe what they did in each section (Enter/Perform/Exit) and see if others in the group agree with each Player's analysis.

★ Student Activities

Book

pages 29–30 (Theater and Stage Terms)

Journal

Ask Players to write about what they learned in this exercise.

- What did you learn about the relationship of acting positions to acting?

- Did you find it easy or difficult to follow specific stage directions while performing? Explain.

- What did you learn about yourself as a performer?

Operator

Operator is similar to the traditional children's game called *Operator* or *Telephone*, in which a message is whispered from ear to ear, down a line of players, until the message arrives at the end of the line. The last person to receive the message repeats it out loud. The first person then reveals the original message. Often, the difference between the beginning and ending messages causes everyone to collapse into laughter.

To play this version of Operator, the messages are not whispered. Instead, the messages are shared with the audience, passed across a large space from Player to Player. There are infinite types of messages Players may choose to send. A verbal message can serve many different functions. It can introduce the group, introduce the title or describe the content of a performance piece, or make a political statement. It can be nonsense, tell a story, or be pure sounds, rather than words. A message may even be purely physical, consisting of action only, unaccompanied by sound.

★ Directions

1. Initiate a discussion about the traditional game, Operator. Explain that in this version of the game, the messages can include physical action and will be passed across a large space. Help the group to select the type of message they are going to send.

2. You may wish to have the group practice sending messages in a line. The first person in line initiates a message. The message travels from Player to Player in order, from the first to the last person in line. The last person in line sends her message to the first person in line. Allow everyone to take a turn at starting a message.

3. Once Players are comfortable sending and receiving messages, try the game in a scattered formation. Have Players count off, or assign each Player a number. These numbers represent the order in which the Players will send their messages. Tell Players to scatter throughout the space, selecting a spot or station where they will remain throughout the game. (With younger Players, you may wish to position Players, rather than allowing them to select spots randomly.) It is not necessary for all the Players to see each other. They only need to see a sender, the person with the number preceding theirs, and a receiver, the person with the number following theirs.

4. Player 1 becomes the first Leader. The Leader initiates the message, which is then passed from Player to Player in numerical order. If time permits, give everyone a turn to be the message initiator. Try one or all of the Performance Suggestions for greater challenge.

Skills

★ Initiating, sending, receiving, and interpreting verbal and physical messages

★ Following a prearranged order when passing messages

★ Observing, listening, and communicating effectively to pass verbal and physical messages across large spaces

★ Analyzing what kinds of messages communicated most effectively

Time

15 minutes to several 1-hour sessions

Space

Adaptable to any space, including balconies, stairways, hallways, aisles, and so on

Materials

In performance, the Players could be in uniforms that identify them to their audience.

Performance Suggestions

Overlap Messages The Leader begins a new message after only two or three people have received the previous message. Several messages may be traveling through the Players at the same time.

Improvise Messages The Leader makes a new sound and/or action message each time the piece is performed. The message and action will be a surprise to the other Players.

Memorize Messages This can be done through rehearsing the preset sounds and actions, until everyone has memorized them. This variation will not lead to surprises. It is useful in performances viewed by audiences when you want to impart a message that will help the audience feel welcome, introduce the Players, or explain the piece.

Record Messages Players draw and/or write their ideas on index cards. The cards are shuffled into a performance order. One person reads the contents of each card to the Leader. For example, "Jump twice and say 'Hi.'" The Leader then performs an interpretation of that card and passes the message down the line. This system avoids memorization.

 Teaching Notes

Management Tips

Start Simply When first playing the game or working with learning disabled Players, keep messages and formations simple. For example, set a limit of one action or three words per message. With practice, this limit can be increased. Work within a small space and organize Players into teams of four to eight people. As the Players become more comfortable with the game's structure and their expertise increases, try forming longer lines, sending longer messages, and

arranging scattered formations around the room. The next challenge would be to send messages over a greater distance.

Performance Order Double-check that all Players not only know their own performance order, but also know which Players have the numbers directly preceding and following theirs. This is necessary so that everyone knows who will be sending them a message (the sender) and who will be receiving their message (the receiver). Remind Players to make sure that when they have chosen their scattered positions they can be seen by both their sender and their receiver.

Body Language In scattered formation, the Players will probably need to turn their bodies toward their sender, then their receiver, in order to receive and send their messages. After sending their message, direct Players to always turn to face the Player who will send them the next message.

Connections

The content of the messages can be connected to any subject that the Players are studying. The game can be used to help them memorize important facts, learn and explore imagery in poems, or practice foreign languages.

Special Needs

- This is a very adaptable activity. The messages could be designed to accommodate Players in wheelchairs, leg braces, or with other physical limitations.

- For deaf Players, signing could be enlarged past the standard space used in conversation to accommodate visibility in a large performing arena.

- For blind Players, Operator could be played as a calling game, or the calls could be descriptions of movement cues. To hold a sequential pattern when passing

messages, blind Players would have to use either voice identification or a number system that is called out as part of the sender's message. Or have blind Players stand in a line formation with a Leader reading aloud a series of preset messages written in Braille. After each message is read it is passed sequentially down the line. The Braille message cards could also be sent down the line so that each Player can read and perform the messages.

 Assessment

Teacher Observations

After the group discussion, you may wish to have Players try Operator again. Observe whether Players incorporate the points they discussed earlier. Have the types of messages changed to those that communicate most effectively?

Group Discussion

After Players have each had a chance to initiate a message, use the following questions to lead them in a discussion about how effectively their messages were being sent:

- Did the messages change as they passed from first to last Player?

- What kinds of actions and words communicated most effectively from Player to Player?

- What kinds of actions and words communicated most effectively across a large space?

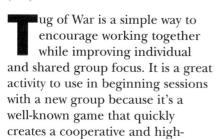

Tug of War

Tug of War is a simple way to encourage working together while improving individual and shared group focus. It is a great activity to use in beginning sessions with a new group because it's a well-known game that quickly creates a cooperative and high-energy atmosphere.

The traditional game of Tug of War requires the use of a rope. Playing Tug of War without a rope is a pantomime exercise. When the game is played as intensely as Tug of War with a rope, the Players should feel the same kind of energy.

Skills

★ Working in teams to play Tug of War
★ Observing details in order to replicate movements and dynamics
★ Focusing attention on the actions of other Players to create a unison pantomime of Tug of War without a rope

Time

10 to 20 minutes

Space

Adaptable to any open space. Clear the space of any sharp or unnecessary objects such as furniture or backpacks on the floor.

Materials

A strong rope, at least eight feet long. You will need two to three feet of rope per player.

★ Directions

Tug of War with a Rope

1. Place a rope on the ground and set a center line (with masking tape, or chalk) that will become the marker for winning or losing the game.

2. Divide the group into two teams of equal strength. Have teams position themselves at either end of the rope. Players should stand single file along the rope, facing the opposing team.

3. Tell Players to pick up the rope with both hands. At a signal from you, both teams try to pull the opposite team toward their side, across the center line. The team that succeeds, wins. If teams reach a standstill for more than a couple of minutes, you may decide to call "time."

Tug of War without a Rope

1. Keeping the same two teams, tell Players to play Tug of War with an imaginary rope. Explain that an observer should be able to "see" the same rope being pulled by all the Players at the same time. The technique that creates the illusion of one rope is for each Player to focus his/her eyes on the hands of the Player in front of him/her.

2. If Players are having difficulty miming Tug of War, have them repeat playing with a real rope. Instruct Players to notice how they perform important details such as where and how they place their hands on the rope, how their body weight is balanced through their legs and feet, and the way their weight shifts as they pull and are tugged.

Variation

Two Players play, both with and without a rope.

 Teaching Notes

Management Tips

Safety Tips Following are some tips for avoiding injuries during play.

- Reiterate the basic rule that all Players are responsible for taking care of themselves and each other.

- To prevent rope burns, have each Player make a slipknot in the rope to hold onto.

- Use padded flooring or athletic mats, when available.

- Intervene as a referee, if necessary. When a potentially dangerous situation, such as yanking too hard on the rope, appears to be happening, try changing dynamics by asking Players to

work in slow motion or by calling "Freeze" and suggesting ways that Players can adjust their body stances and hand positions on the rope to alter the push and pull tensions.

Special Needs

Players unable to participate in the game for physical reasons could take on the role of referee. Otherwise, they could be observers. One of the observers' jobs would be to call out or signal in some way (such as using a whistle or hand sign) when the imaginary rope can no longer be seen. Another job would be to contribute to the group's evaluation discussion.

 Assessment

Teacher Observations

- Did Players play Tug of War with a Rope safely and responsibly?

- How effective were Players' pantomimes as they played Tug of War without a Rope? Were team members working together to pull the imaginary rope? Were the two teams aware of each other? Did they appear to be playing the same game?

Group Discussion

You may wish to break the group up into several teams so that Players can observe and critique one another's pantomimes. Use the following questions to stimulate a discussion that will give Players useful ideas for trying this game again.

- Did everyone appear to be using the same rope?

- Did both teams appear to be in agreement as to which side was gaining ground and which was losing ground?

- Where did you focus your eyes as you played the game?

- Did you use your sense memory in the pantomime as recalled from playing Tug of War with a real rope?

 Student Activities

Journal

Ask Players to write about how they can apply skills learned in this game to other activities, either for performing purposes or in their daily lives.

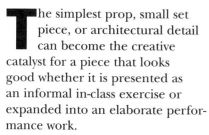

Relationships to a Chair

The simplest prop, small set piece, or architectural detail can become the creative catalyst for a piece that looks good whether it is presented as an informal in-class exercise or expanded into an elaborate performance work.

Relationships to a Chair offers this kind of reliable game structure. Perhaps this game's success rate is based in the simplicity and familiarity of the given task. As performers focus on the game's simple rule of choosing a series of positions in relationship to a familiar object, in this case a chair, they relax and use personal style while presenting with formal awareness. This

activity is useful in introductory or orientation sessions and could also be developed into a class performance project.

 Directions

1. It might be useful to begin with a brainstorming session. Ask Players to list possible spatial relationships a person could have to a chair. For example, beside, behind, in front of, beneath, sitting on, standing on. Place the list where Players can refer to it during the activity.

2. Have everyone get a chair. Ask the Players to place themselves in a specific spatial relationship to the chair.

3. Once everyone has chosen one spatial relationship to the chair, ask them to choose three others. Then direct them to arrange the four relationships in a specific order.

4. Ask Players to repeat their series of four relationships at least four times, until they are certain of the order. Explain that the details of how each relationship is performed can be set, or changed each time the series is performed.

5. Allow Players to show one another their Relationship to a Chair series. If the group is large, divide it in half or form smaller groups for this sharing time.

Skills

★ Working with a prop
★ Exploring spatial relationships with an object
★ Creating, rehearsing, and presenting a performance based on a series of spatial relationships to a chair
★ Analyzing a performance from an audience's point of view

Time

30 minutes or longer. The time it takes to complete the series of relationships can vary greatly according to the age and special needs of a group.

Space

This activity can be adapted to any space.

Materials

Sturdy chairs, one per participant, if possible. A variety of sound environments can provide a frame and change of dynamics for the actions.

Variations

Relationships to Different Objects Any other appropriate object or architectural detail can be substituted for a chair, such as a table, sculpture, wall, picture frame, ladder, plastic pipe, and so on. When using an object other than a chair, a different list of relationships may apply. For example, when using a wall, relationships might include the following: touch the wall, lean against the wall, slide down the wall, push against the wall, "spread eagle" on the wall, mime climbing up the wall. Note that the operant word is now a verb, rather than a preposition.

Relationships to a Person Substitute a person or persons for the object, and perform the series of actions. (This can be especially interesting, fun, and evocative when the original object is a wall.)

Locomotor Transitions Between each relationship, the performers could be asked to walk, run, or use another locomotor to move away from and then return to the object.

Relationship Scores Have each participant create a score by selecting a particular object or architectural detail and providing four to six relationships to it. Players can create solo performances from their scores or direct other Players to perform their scores.

Performance Suggestions

Transitions If the study is going to be presented to an audience, then the transitions between relationships becomes an important element of the piece. As performers move from relationship to relationship, tell them to notice how they are making transitions—how they move from position to position. With this awareness, the transitions become as important as each spatial relationship. The transitions can be set, meaning the Players determine exactly how to move from the first relationship to the second relationship, or they can change with each performance.

Varying the Performance Once the Players have set a series of relationships, they can be performed many ways and for any number of repetitions. Try any of the following variations or combinations of variations:

- Vary the tempo: normal, fast, slow, variable, etc.

- Have Players perform the series in slow motion.

- Set the performance to a specific rhythm. Different kinds of sounds can be supplied to provide a set rhythm, or make a droning beat on a drum or other rhythm instrument. Let performers decide how many beats to allow for each relationship.

- Set a time limit. For example, you might instruct performers to take one minute to complete the performance of each position, thirty seconds to complete each transition.

- Have Players add a frieze as each relationship in the series is accomplished.

- Have Players speak a monologue while they perform the relationship series. Either supply the subject of the monologue or give Players open choice.

- Ask Players to sing while performing the relationship series.

- Have the whole group perform their solos concurrently. Ask Players to freeze when they have completed their series, so that the piece ends when all are in a frieze together.

- Have Players teach their series to a partner to make a longer series that both perform as a duet. Or create trios, quartets, or a whole group unison series based on an individual Player's series. If everybody has learned one series, this series can be performed as a round or a canon. Divide Players into groups and decide when each group begins the series and how many times each group should repeat the series before ending in a frieze.

 Teaching Notes

Management Tips

Progressions Depending on the time available, you may want to do the basic rule on one day and then try some of the variations and performance suggestions on another day. Or, this could all be done within one session. Each series will build on the energy of the preceding variation, and going through the progression can increase the impact of the experience.

Props Ideally, there should be enough chairs to equal the number of participants so that all Players can work at the same time. If there are not enough sturdy chairs available, divide the group into teams and have one team perform while the other teams observe, until all teams have played the game.

Safety Use your judgment regarding the *standing on* spatial relationship. Collapsible chairs, especially the common metal folding ones, can be very dangerous. If you feel it's safe to include the *standing on* relationship and have to use folding chairs, advise Players to stand toward the front of the chair's seat.

Connections

Language Arts This activity is very useful for teaching parts of speech in English and other languages—especially prepositions, prepositional phrases, and verb forms. The monologue performance suggestion provides a playful way to practice conversing in other languages.

Special Needs

- This game could make some wonderful wheelchair activities.

- Some adaptations for particular physical disabilities may have to be made. Take into consideration whether Players can accomplish tasks such as grasping an object to move it or changing body position in the allotted time.

- If you have Players who have difficulty, it would be better to concentrate on the physical challenge and to ignore the verbal element introduced in the Performance Suggestions.

Background Notes

Chairs, because they are pervasive and available (and can be inexpensive) in our environments, have long been popular props to use in performance works. Sometimes one chair is used, sometimes many; sometimes chair pieces are solo works, sometimes group works. Chair dances have appeared in Broadway shows, in movies, and in experimental performance works. Choreographers David Gordon, Pina Bausch, Beverly Blossom, Anne Teresa de Keersmaeker, and Yvonne Rainer have all made chair pieces that are considered among their major works.

 ## Assessment

Teacher Observations

- Were Players able to list different spatial relationships that a person could have to a chair?

- What kind of spatial relationships did Players form with their chairs?

- Were Players able to memorize and repeat a series of spatial relationships?

- In discussion, were Players able to analyze the pieces from an audience's point of view? Did they give one another constructive criticism and advice?

Group Discussion

Have the group analyze the pieces from an audience's point of view. Encourage participants to discuss what works and what doesn't and to suggest changes that might create more dynamic images or potent relationships to the chair.

 ## Student Activities

Journal

- Suggest that Players keep a log of interesting spatial relationships they notice between themselves or other people around them. A few days after completing this game, ask Players to describe how it made them more aware of their spatial relationships to people and objects in their environment.

- Encourage Players to research and write about a performer who uses a chair in his or her performances.

Clichés

Clichés are popular sayings or catchy phrases or ideas that, by virtue of long use and repetition, become truisms or familiar ideas. The term *clichés* may also refer to gestures and facial expressions that have taken on specific meanings.

By asking for examples of clichés from a group of participants, you can tap into verbal and physical expressions of communication that are powerful by virtue of their strong meaning to that particular group.

Clichés can reveal much information about differences of experiences between generations, cultures, and genders. The game can even be used to make a kind of anthropological or sociological comparison study of these differences.

Skills
★ Performing and exploring the meanings of commonly used verbal expressions, physical gestures, and facial expressions
★ Experimenting with intonation, timing, and body language to change the meaning of words and gestures

Time
30 to 60 minutes

Space
Adaptable to any space

Materials
Writing materials for listing clichés

★ Directions

1. To begin the game, present the term *cliché* to the group and, depending on participants' familiarity with the term, either develop a definition with the group or provide a definition.

2. Ask for examples of verbal clichés that are used or recognized by the group. Record a list of clichés so that Players can easily refer back to it.

3. Have each Player choose a series of three to five verbal clichés to perform for the group.

4. Repeat the same process with physical clichés (gestures, facial expressions).

5. Have each Player select a single verbal or gestural cliché to perform three to five times. Direct Players to change intonation, timing, and body placement with each repetition to communicate different meanings and feelings.

6. Follow each Player's performance with a discussion of the different meanings or feelings that the observers perceived. (See Assessment.)

Variations

Cliché Monologues Players combine a series of verbal and/or gestural clichés, which they repeat three to five times, communicating different meanings and feelings with each repetition.

Characterization Players perform a series of verbal and/or gestural clichés as a specific character.

Duets Have Players pair up. Each Player chooses one verbal and/or gestural clichés. Partners engage in a dialogue, using only their chosen cliché. Changes in intonation, timing, and body placement will communicate the subtext, or meaning, behind the conversation.

Group Dialogues Divide Players into small groups. Each Player chooses a series of three to five verbal and/or gestural clichés. Players have a conversation with one another using only their selected clichés.

★ Teaching Notes

Management Tips

Interpreting Clichés When Players share examples of familiar clichés, discuss their meanings. Compare individual interpretations of the cliché, reminding participants that there are no right or wrong answers. If your classroom has students from many cultures, ask everyone to share a cliché from his or her own background.

Connections

Social Studies Compare popular clichés across several cultures. For example, in the United States, a hand gesture meaning "Come here" is done by inclining the hand, palm up, toward the body. In Italy, the same meaning is conveyed by the opposite gesture: "Come here" looks more like our wave "Good-bye." In some places in the world, a verbal "Good-bye" is never said—it's considered bad luck or bad manners. Even within the United States there are many variations of the

same cliché. Meanings differ from region to region, generation to generation, and culture to culture. Show old television shows, newsreels, or movies to spark a discussion of how clichés have changed over time.

Language Arts Compare more than one video or audio version of a Shakespearean play. If possible, find two very different interpretations of the same play, such as one designed in contemporary style and one in Elizabethan style. Select a particular scene or speech to analyze. Discuss any differences in meaning between the two productions, and how these differences were projected. Besides differences in the delivery of dialogue, Players should be aware of the influence of design elements such as setting, color palette, and background music. The same exercise can be done with works by other playwrights, such as Tennessee Williams and Eugene O'Neill, or with a number of movies and songs.

★ Assessment

Teacher Observations

• Did Players understand the meaning of the term *clichés?*

Were they able to offer examples of verbal and physical clichés?

• Were Players able to use intonation, timing, and body placement to communicate different meanings or feelings?

• Were Players able to interpret different meanings in others' performances?

Group Discussion

After each Player's performance, ask the audience what meanings or feelings they understood the performer to be projecting; then ask the performer to respond as to whether these observations agree with what was intended. Encourage Players to discuss what details of voice and body language help project specific meanings. For example, a flat tone of voice might indicate a lack of interest. If possible, videotape cliché monologues, duets, or group dialogues for Players to watch and analyze.

★ Student Activities

Journal

Ask Players to think about other kinds of clichés and their meanings besides verbal, gestural, and facial expressions. For example, musical clichés, such as trumpet fanfares announcing the arrival of someone or something important. Tell them to choose one cliché and describe how it is used and what it means.

Suggest that Players keep a running list of verbal and physical clichés they notice in their daily lives. At the end of the term, they might enjoy sharing their lists.

Doubles

Doubles is a term used to describe a theatrical concept called "internal action." As taught around the turn of the twentieth century by Konstantin Stanislavsky and still used by many contemporary actors, it asks the performer to prepare for a role by trying to understand what motivates the character, such as feelings of fear or love, circumstances, wishes or goals, then selecting external actions, such as gestures, timing, style of speaking (including tone of voice) that reflect the character's internal state.

This method of portraying several realities in one character or situation has also been referred to either as *text* and *subtext* or *shadow* and *substance*. Often what the audience sees and hears is the text; what the Player is thinking and feeling is the *subtext*.

Skills

★ Analyzing character motivations
★ Creating characterizations by selecting external actions that reveal the character's internal state
★ Performing scripted or improvised scenes as invented characters

Time

20 to 30 minutes

Space

Adaptable to any space

Materials

Costumes, small hand props, set pieces, and music may be used to create mood and enhance images. Special lighting effects can be employed to highlight the character, put the character's shadow in a shadow, or to create a shadow play.

In the game Doubles, Players try different readings of scenes or scores by experimenting with how the *text,* what is spoken, is influenced by the *subtext,* what is thought or felt. Players are asked to communicate text and subtext through words, tone of voice, action, or a combination of these elements.

The two realities may also be communicated to the audience by using two actors in the roles of *substance* (text) and *shadow* (subtext). The performers actually make two images, or doubles, of the same character. One Player performs the text, while the other shadows the first Player to relay the subtext. Any number of performers can be added as shadows of the character.

★ Directions

1. Divide the group into pairs or small teams.

2. Choose to work on a scene from an existing script (see Student Book, Chapter 12), or direct Players to improvise a scene from a short story, real-life situation, historical event, or other source material.

3. Assign or allow Players to choose one of the following methods to perform their scene.

- **Monologue** Working in pairs, one performer says a line and the other says or does what the first performer is really thinking.

Example:

Player 1 (Substance): *Talks about how she is sure to become famous while posturing in front of a mirror.*

Player 2 (Shadow): *Talks about her doubts of achieving fame. Could be done in mirror image, with subtle differences, or standing behind and shadowing Player 1.*

- **Dialogue** Partners work together. One speaks (text) and one shadows (subtext).

Examples:

Text (1st Substance): Hello.
Subtext (1st Shadow): Oh no, not him again.

Text (2nd Substance): Hello.
Subtext (2nd Shadow): Finally, we meet.

Text (1st Substance): How are you?
Subtext (1st Shadow): I don't really care.

- **Movement Shadows** Players work with a partner. One Player moves and the other Player stands in relationship to him (behind or to the side), offering a different movement interpretation.

Examples:

Substance: *Waves hello.*

Shadow: *Shrugs shoulders, with a critical face.*

Substance: *Makes "angelic" images/ actions.*

Shadow: *Makes "devilish" images/ actions.*

4. Have partners or teams perform their Doubles scenes for the group. Decide whether performers should improvise their scenes instantaneously or discuss and practice their scenes before performing for the group.

Variations

Across Time Doubles perform the same character at different ages.

Across Dimensions Doubles perform the same character as a dead spirit and a live person.

Personality Traits Doubles perform the same character using masks to portray different aspects of the same character.

Different Mediums Doubles use different techniques of performance to portray different aspects of the same character, such as one speaking and one singing, one dancing and one acting, or one acting and one playing a musical instrument.

Solo Doubles Monologue One Player performs a monologue that contains both the text and subtext of one character.

 Teaching Notes

Management Tips

Character Interviews After the Players have been working on their Doubles scenes for awhile, conduct interviews of each character. Interviews can be conducted by the Leader and/or other Players. Have each Player become her character to answer the questions. Ask questions that would clarify how Players see their characters through events and circumstances, real or imaginary, that may have affected the character's life. Following are examples of interview questions:

- What year is it and how old are you?

- Who are you (name, citizenship, cultural identity)?
- What do you look like?
  - Describe your physical characteristics and style.
  - What are you wearing?
  - Do you have any physical mannerisms, such as a tic or nervous fidgeting?
- What is your family background?
  - Are you an only child, or one of many?
  - Are you rich or poor?
  - Where have you lived?
- Who/what do you love and hate?
- What kind of work do you do?
- What are your goals and ambitions?
- What is your favorite music, food, etc?
- What worries you?
- What world events have shaped your life?
- Who is in your family?
- What makes you angry/happy?

All the biographical information Players have considered will strengthen their identification with their characters, although the audience may never be aware that this process took place. Generally, accept how a Player conceives the character unless it is truly inconsistent with the text and scene.

Verify Characters' Relationships Check to see if Players have figured out their characters in relationship to other characters and their stage situation. For example, see if Players playing members of the same family, business associates, or characters in some other ongoing stage relationship agree upon mutually shared facts and experiences.

Set Entrance/Exit Locations Ask Players where (what imaginary place) their characters are coming from when they enter the stage and where (what imaginary place) they are going to when they exit the stage. Answers should make sense in terms of the text and how they see their characters.

Connections

Language Arts/Social Studies/History

Ask Players to write biographies of their characters. (See Student Book.) The biography should be based on any information given in the text or the scene that would be consistent with the historical, social, political, or familial circumstances of that character. If students are enacting a historical scene or portraying an actual person, encourage them to research historical records, literature, photographs, music of a particular period, or other sources to help them create their biographies. If possible, Players could interview the real character or someone who knows about the character and/or his circumstances.

Background Notes

This system of reading between the lines of the text was emphasized by Konstantin Stanislavsky (1865–1938), the Russian actor, director, and teacher, as part of his training of actors. His concepts continue to have a profound influence on twentieth century performance style throughout the world. In the United States, where his work continues to be taught under the label *method acting*, it is well-known through the work of film and stage personalities, including actors Marlon Brando, Paul Newman, Joanne Woodward, Ellen Burstyn, Montgomery Clift, Robert DeNiro, Dustin Hoffman, Karl Malden, Marilyn Monroe, Rita Moreno, Jack Nicholson, Al Pacino, Martin Sheen, Kim Stanley, Maureen Stapleton, Rod Steiger; and directors Lee Strasberg, Sidney Lumet, Elia Kazan, Joshua Logan, Harold Prince, Jose Quintero, Francis Ford Coppola, and numerous others.

Choreographer and dancer Martha Graham frequently employed Doubles by having more than one dancer play the same character, revealing different times (ages) or thoughts in the same person. In many of her dances she was trying to "objectify in physical form" or "reveal the inner man." *Letter to the World*, premiered in 1941, is based on the life and poetry of Emily Dickinson. There are two Emilys, both dressed in white. One Emily (text/substance), called "One Who Speaks," is the observer and commentator who says, "I'm nobody! Who are you? Are you nobody, too? Then there's a pair of us." The other Emily (subtext/shadow), "One Who Dances," interprets her commentaries with dance action. Sometimes the two Emilys dance together, acknowledging each other's presence, and sometimes they share the same stage picture while appearing to be in their own separate worlds.

Writer/director David Gordon's *The Mysteries and What's So Funny*, 1991, represents text and subtext by having actors represent various stages in the life of the same characters. He casts both Young Sam and Old Sam, and Sam's wife, Young Rose and Old Rose. At various key points the characters are shadowed by their other ages, and by the actions of Anger I and Anger II, who reveal the subtext. For example, the Old Sam and Old Rose speak to each other with pent-up anger while the Young Sam and Young Rose enact their moment of falling in love. While a middle-aged couple, called Mr. Him and Mrs. Her, politely fight a verbal battle about who is going to get what for breakfast, their shadows, Anger I and Anger II, manipulate the couple from behind, beating on them and flinging them about to reveal the characters' true depth of feeling.

In the National Theater of the Deaf's staging of *Ophelia*, the character called Ophelia signs her text. Another actor, who sometimes is her shadow, verbally translates what Ophelia has signed. In addition, the shadow sometimes speaks and signs a subtext to reveal what Ophelia really means or is thinking.

Recently in California, a young actors' performing company created a play based on their versions of fairy tales, called *Happily Ever After . . . Not!* One character, Princess, speaks her wishes in the traditional fairy tale mode, while Princess Alter Ego gives back a piece of her mind through a subtext that uses contemporary language and values.

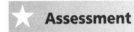

★ Assessment

Teacher Observations

- Did Players understand the concept of doubles? Were they able to create and perform doubles scenes in which characters revealed both text and subtext?

- How adept were students at analyzing and portraying character motivations? Were they able to reveal their characters' inner feelings?

Group Discussion

Ask the group to share examples and analyze the use of text and subtext in everyday life.

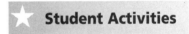

★ Student Activities

Book

pages 31–32 (Background Reading)
pages 33–34 (Performance Models)

Journal

Have Players look for and record examples of instances in which people's words and feelings don't seem to match.

CHAPTER 4

Improvisational Techniques

Throughout this book, games and activities employ improvisation to explore ways to perform. This chapter looks more closely at how to use improvisational techniques. Quick thinking, brainstorming, free association, spontaneity, and reacting in response to a changing situation are all life skills that also describe improvisation.

Improvisation is a spontaneous creative process done with no preparation, an exercise in "thinking on your feet." The performer simultaneously creates and performs his or her solution, responding to a structure and to variables of the performance, including the space, sounds, props, or other performers. Improvisation can be used as a training, rehearsal, or performance technique.

Open Improvisation is a term that refers to completely unrehearsed improvisations.

Predetermined Improvisation refers to a performance that uses a well-rehearsed structure, within which the improvisation happens.

 Improvisational Structures

The choice of any improvisational structure, the device that guides the Players' choices, depends on your objectives and goals—the ones you start with and those that emerge during the creative process. Therefore, each project's structure will be unique.

Over the centuries, many devices have been developed to structure improvisations, including the following.

Game Structure

Players agree to use the rules from an existing game or they make up their own game rules. The rules provide structure to an improvisation in the same way that rules organize any sport. The game is played by solving how to interpret the rules.

Plot Outline, Scenario, or Script

Players create, listen to, or read a skeleton plot of a story that they then perform, improvising details of dialogue and action. (See Scenarios, page 96.) Following are two ways to start this kind of improvisation.

Daily Life Situation Players select a particular situation, then decide on either some or all of the following elements:

- Who (the characters)
- What (the problem or event that happens)
- Where (the place or setting)
- When (the time the event occurs)
- Why (the characters' motivation for doing what they do)

Stock Character Types Players select characters from the repertory of recognizable character types: villain, hero, ingenue (young innocent female), soubrette (female flirt), foolish teacher or doctor, wise fool (clown), wise servant. Then Players decide the *What, Where, When,* and *Why* for each character to make a plot outline for each scene. (See Stock Characters, page 175.)

Score

A score is a performance structure. (See Chapter 6, Scores.)

Series of Tasks, Actions, or Events Make a list of tasks to do, verbs, historical or imaginary happenings, or other things that can be performed in a random collage or arranged into an order.

Interpreting Images Players select one or more visual images, either imaginary or from photographs, paintings, drawings, or other sources. Images can be arranged randomly or ordered into a score. The score can direct Players to perform the images by imitating them, by reacting to or interpreting them, or by using them as inspiration for the setting or plot of a story line. (See Living Pictures, page 125.)

Borrowing Musical Forms Adapt musical composition ideas for a performance structure. (See Chapter 7, Musical Forms.)

Site-Specific Projects

(See Chapter 8, Site-Specific Projects.)

Using an Existing Site Players choose a site, examine and analyze its properties, and design performance activities that can occur only within the site boundaries.

Creating an Installation Players choose a site that can be designed as a set or environment (a corner in the classroom could be the site). They add objects, sculpture, performance, video, light, sound, or any other elements to the site to create an installation. The audience may be included as part of the installation.

Relocation to a Different Site Players adapt a set and activities designed for one site to fit in another. The original site design may have been based on imagination, a memory, a historical site, or a public space that cannot be accessed for performance. (See Relocations, page 167.)

 Directing Advice

Direct Players to improvise the unknown details of the structure. In an improvisation, details of dialogue, story line, action, or stage business are moment-to-moment developments. Surprises often happen. It doesn't matter exactly what happens, as long as Players deal with what is happening, stay in the present, and keep trying new things.

Examples:

- Direct Players to improvise a scene depicting a family at breakfast time. Improvised details that might set off a chain of events within this daily life scenario could be an announcement that someone is leaving home, actions indicating that someone is late for school or work, a dialogue in which someone expresses hatred or love for someone else, and so on.
- Direct Players to improvise from a score. They have many choices of how to interpret the score. For example, Players can choose to perform events or actions in the score in random order, or use various chance systems to arrange a sequential order, or create a map that directs Players along paths or tells them what to do in specific areas of the performing space.

Ensemble Building

To help your group learn to work together, present games with rules that emphasize teamwork or ensemble values of cooperation. Stress that everyone shares the same goal of working together to solve the interpretation of the structure. Play these games with the understanding that everyone's ideas, impulses, and actions are to be encouraged, included, and supported. Do not allow Players to become directors of each other. They have to find a way to help one another within the improvisation, and to solve problems through improvisation.

Directing Devices

Huddle After the structure is chosen, you can give Players a few minutes to think over their solution to the improvisational structure. Direct teams to "huddle" together in conference, in the same way a football team huddles to decide the next play. The ending of a huddle can be punctuated with a team handshake, call, or some other spirited expression of their readiness to perform together. Huddles can also be called within games, to change their course of direction. It's a good idea to set a time limit of one to two minutes for each huddle.

Whispered Instructions Whisper instructions to individual Players to inform them about at least one of the following elements of their parts in the improvisation: the *Who* (character), *What* (action or event), or *Why* (motivation) of what to play. The other Players should not hear what is whispered. You can continue to influence events during the course of the improvisation by using the same device.

Challenges You, the Players, or the audience can challenge performers to top one another's personal best by asking them to solve instant skits, do physical tasks, or respond to audience or director's commands or suggestions.

Add a Competitive Element Players challenge themselves and each other, thereby teaching each other. They practice one-upmanship of their own or each other's feats or wit.

- Play games where Players are called out of the improvisation if they don't follow the rules. The game is over when there is only one Player—the winner—standing. (See Musical Chairs, page 220; Audience-Suggested Skits, page 76.)

- Teaching by competition is a regular part of tap dancing, break dancing, the hacky-sack game, or stand-up comedy. Use critical analysis to make Players aware of how they make judgments to decide what is better.

Coaching Suggestions to Keep the Action Going

- Tell Players to be alert and in the moment, as they will need to know all information that is given at any time in the improvisation. Remind them to react to everything and to allow the unexpected. For example, if someone throws a ball, another Player has to catch it or acknowledge it in some way.

- Coach Players to show, rather than tell, something that has happened or will happen. Tell them to keep the action onstage so the audience can see what happens. It is not as interesting to have the action happen offstage, revealed to the audience by a description of another time or place.

- Coach Players to keep the action happening between them by not canceling or erasing the story set up by a teammate.

- Encourage free association of ideas. Ask Players to try not to edit while performing and to allow things to happen without judgment. If you decide to continue working on a scene, editing can happen after a lot of ideas have been explored.

- If you observe that Players feel lost or don't know where to go to get to the end of a scene, coach them to reincorporate or reintroduce material rather than to go forward into unknown territory. Suggest that they reuse information that was already offered through actions, characters, or events. This can help Players make connections that will lead to an ending.

- Change the action by interrupting its present course. Use devices such as Rescue Squad, Transformation, Wild Card, or Joker, as described in the following section.

Devices for Changing the Onstage Action

There are various devices to keep improvisations from floundering or stalling. One, generally known as Transformations, and another, called Rescue Squad, probably originated in the theater games workshops of Viola Spolin and were further developed by Joe Chaiken in his work with the Open Theater.

Transformations

A *transformation* is a fundamental change in any element of the performance: the *Who, Where, When, What, How,* or the style. A change of any one of these elements from within the scene, by any of the Players, will result in a change in the scene. Then the story continues in the transformation, at least until another transformation is made. Sometimes it's fun to call for a "rewind," and reverse through a whole series of transformations back to the original scene. For example, a classroom transforms into a forest; a grocery store line transforms into a bread line from the 1930s; a husband and wife transform into two machines.

Rescue Squad

This variation of Transformations can be used to energize a scene. A Rescue Squad can be initiated by any Player or team not presently onstage. Players may, at any point in the improvisation, join the onstage action. Sometimes, a call of "Stop!" or "Freeze!" is used to initiate a Rescue Squad cue. The onstage action freezes until someone from the rescue squad enters to replace a Player. That Player then exits, or stays and works within the change or transformation. New characters can be added who bring new information to the scene, or a Rescue Squad can call for a transformation. The improvisation continues. This could happen many times within one scene.

Wild Card

Wild Card is the title given to a person who is asked to join the action as a new character, who either changes the course of action or embellishes the existing situation. The Wild Card listens to a team planning its improvisation, but does not participate. Sometime after the improvisation has begun, when the characters are clear, Wild Card can go in and out of the scene, according to what he thinks will help the improvisation. The Wild Card can be chosen by you, the team, or the director of the scene.

Joker

Joker is the title of a facilitator, the person who leads discussion between the audience and the performers. The Joker device was invented by Brazilian director Augusto Boal, who suggests using the joker as a referee or agent of change. The Joker may be the Leader or one of the Players. She comments on the action, or freezes the action to allow for audience discussion concerning what is right or wrong with the way problems are being resolved onstage. The Players then incorporate this information into their improvisation by changing their characters' actions or circumstances; or the Joker could direct members of the audience to replace Players (as in Rescue Squad), so that new Players could create a change in how actions should, could, or do happen.

★ Chance Systems

Sometimes artists look for ways to free themselves from habitual ways of gathering, ordering, or interpreting information or performance materials. To do this, they use many kinds of systems that involve the element of chance and agree to follow a structure that has been determined, at least in part, by random selection. Following are suggestions for how to use various kinds of chance systems.

Direction Calls

You and/or the Players make a list of tasks to do, actions to perform, or texts to speak. Someone (you or a Player) acts as director who gives commands to the performers; commands are based on the lists. The director calls out directions that tell performers what to perform, where to perform, how to travel (forward, backward, to the right, to the left), the number of repetitions, and so on.

Chart of Correspondences

Ask Players to make a grid or chart and to make two lists. The lists will consist of various categories of information, such as numbers, parts of speech, colors, or parts of the body. Write in items from one list along the horizontal edge of the grid; place items from the second list along the vertical edge. (It may be more convenient to assign each item on one list a letter, and each item on the other list a number.) In order to make a score, choose a way to make the two lists of information connect. This can be done by throwing dice or other objects, and interpreting the way they fall as a way to perform. Or the lists can be programmed into a computer to provide as many combinations as possible or needed. Or create some other system to connect the information. Players perform in a random or numbered order. (Dancer/choreographer Merce Cunningham popularized this system.)

Object Toss

Use coins, dice, beans, sticks, or other small objects to determine a performance order.

- List and number any actions, text, images, or other performance materials. Throw the dice and record the number that faces up. Match the number on the dice to the corresponding item on the list of performance materials. That is the item that will be performed first. Continue throwing the dice until you have a performance order for all of the actions, text, or images on the list. Decide if repetitions are to happen, and record these as part of the performance score.

- Choose several small objects and number them. Toss each object onto an image, action, or color. Players perform their images, actions, or colors according to the order in which the objects have landed.

- Using one object, toss it over the images. Perform the images in the order in which they are selected by the toss.

- Think about what implications could be found from a toss that falls high or low on an image, in a curve or diagonal, to the left or right, and so on. Use that information in the performance of the image.

Deck of Cards

Ask Players or teams to make a deck of cards out of original or copied images. Decide how to deal the cards, to teams or individuals, who are then asked to perform their interpretation or imitation of the images.

- Assign an arbitrary order to the cards, and perform as ordered.

- Develop a game that creates a new arrangement each time it is played.

- Use the images to create a story that has a beginning, middle, and end.

Paper Bag

Inside a paper bag, you or the Players place images, objects, or file cards on which have been written action verbs, adjectives, names of colors, quotations, and so forth. Players draw a designated number of images, objects, or cards out of the bag. What is drawn will be the basis for their score or script. (See Paper Bag Dramatics, page 74.)

Computer Program

Research one or more ideas and program all related information into a computer. Customize the information into minimenus that can be accessed to make timelines, graphs, charts, or scripts that will serve as a blueprint for a performance structure.

- Folklorist and anthropologist Alan Lomax has developed a computer program called "Global Jukebox" that uses interactive compact and video disks to demonstrate thousands of music and dance performance styles. This program can call up information for cross-cultural comparisons. It can also search for historical roots.

- "LifeForms," a computer program developed at Simon Fraser University, near Vancouver, is being used by Merce Cunningham to create choreography electronically. According to a *New York Times* article:

The program uses a computer screen with three visual elements:
- a sequence editor, which allows the user to build, edit, and customize body stances or movement and to store them in minimenus for future use (more than 200 motifs, from lying prone and walking to leaps and pirouettes, are available for instant viewing on miniscreens);
- a stage, which can be tilted and turned to allow any vantage point and on which any number of figures can be placed;
- a timeline strip, which provides a visual summary of the body positions chosen for each figure.

. . . The choreographer selects a sequence of movements for each character and strings them together inside the timeline frame. The figure is then assigned a position on the stage, and on command performs the selected sequence. Theoretically, any number of dancers can perform simultaneously, and the relationships of the figures both in space . . . and time . . . can be infinitely varied. ("This Computer Loves to Dance," by Max Wyman, *New York Times,* 27 June 1993)

Background Notes

Improvisation has been used in many performing arts disciplines, including theater, dance, film, and music. A list of names of performing artists and companies who use improvisation could go on endlessly. Following is an incomplete list, categorized by discipline.

Theater

Contemporary improvisational theater groups often find inspiration by combining the styles of Renaissance commedia dell'arte acting troupes with the late nineteenth- and early twentieth-century European political cabaret theater styles.

Another major influence on contemporary improvisatory theater methods are Viola Spolin's theater games, which she began constructing in the 1930s, while working with children and adults in neighborhood-based Work Progress Administration (WPA) theater programs. (See Living Newspaper, page 208, for a related history of WPA theater projects.) Spolin wanted to find ways to train people that would allow them to feel free to act as themselves, without telling them "do this" or "do that." She felt that by playing theater games, people could solve how to create together, through the rules of the game. Her book, *Improvisation for the Theater,* originally published in 1963, has become a classic reference for actors, directors, teachers, and group leaders.

Since the 1950s, there have been many comic actors who work together using improvisation. Renowned associations included the Compass Players and Second City, both originally from Chicago (Paul Sills, Viola Spolin's son, was a major participant and organizer, as were Mike Nichols and Elaine May); the Committee of San Francisco; and the television show "Saturday Night Live," which hired a lot of alumni from these companies. The work of these companies strives to be immediately accessible and interesting to audiences, fast-paced, and never the same twice. The actors often perform without formal scripts, basing their improvisations on scenarios, game structures, and in response to audience suggestions. Many well-known actors trained in this manner, including David Shepherd, Severn Darden, Barbara Harris, Shelley Berman, Anne Meara, Jerry Stiller, Alan Arkin, Paul Masursky, Joan Rivers, Alan Alda, David Steinberg, Gilda Radner, John Belushi, Dan Aykroyd, Shelley Long, Steve Martin, Martin Short, Sandra Bernhard, Robin Williams, and Whoopi Goldberg.

In New York City, starting in the 1960s, the Living Theater, directed by Julian Beck and Judith Malina, and Open Theater, directed by Joe Chaikin, further developed improvisational theater for both the rehearsal and the performance process. Beginning in the 1970s, Mabou Mines, the Wooster Group, and the Performance Garage were among other theater companies that continued working in this tradition, often creating original collaborative ensemble works by building up layers of improvisation.

In the 1980s, English director and writer Keith Johnston created the concept of theater sports, which set up a competitive system for judging Players and added many new games to the literature of improvisation. Beginning in Canada and spreading to the United States, a whole network of Players has grown up around theater sports. It has been adopted by many college theater training programs and in many cities there are theaters that provide at least one night a week for anyone to participate in theater sports, either as audience or performers.

Many international directors regularly use improvisation to develop communal scripts out of exploratory work with the actors, including Jerzy Grotowski in Poland, Peter Brook in Paris, Augusto Boal in Brazil, Tadashi Suzuki in Japan, and Richard Foreman and Peter Sellars in the United States.

Dance

Twentieth-century dancers have mined improvisation as both a source of invention and performance work. Isadora Duncan, Merce Cunningham, Anna Halprin, Simone Forti, Trisha Brown, Suzushi Hanayagi, Steve Paxton, Deborah Hay, Kei Takei, Molissa Fenley, Blondell Cummings, and Andy de Groat are a few examples of the many improvisational practitioners from the world of dance. Many choreographers, including Pina Bausch and Martha Clarke, build their dances from layers of improvisations by company members.

Performance Art

A combination of performing and visual arts improvisatory forms can be seen in what is termed *performance art*. The Fluxus artists, early practitioners of this multidisciplinary form, include visual artists Robert Rauschenberg, Claes Oldenburg, Nam June Paik, Joseph Beuys, and Adrian Piper. Theater artists Allan Kaprow, Peter Schumann, Spalding Gray, George Coates, Rachel Rosenthal, Diamonda Galas, and the Kipper Kids all develop their work through improvisation, even though the work may eventually become set into a repeated form.

Music

Composers and musicians from various periods and styles have used improvisation in performance. Throughout the world there are musical traditions in which musicians improvise on chord structures, rhythmic patterns, melodic themes, scales, or other formal devices. Many contemporary Western musicians have studied classical music traditions from India, Africa, and Latin America to change their ways of thinking. In the United States, jazz music's stock in trade is improvisation. Some well-known American musicians who use improvisation in performance include John Cage, Cecil Taylor, Ornette Coleman, Charlie Parker, Dizzy Gillepsie, Sun Ra, La Monte Young, and Miles Davis.

Film

The film industry also has a long tradition of using improvisation. Many of the early silent movies, including those of Charles Chaplin, Buster Keaton, and Harold Lloyd, were made by shooting improvisations rather than strictly adhering to written scripts. After multiple takes, the film was edited into the final cut. Contemporary directors such as Federico Fellini, Robert Altman, and Rob Reiner have also used improvisational process to make their films.

Lists

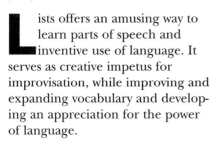

Lists offers an amusing way to learn parts of speech and inventive use of language. It serves as creative impetus for improvisation, while improving and expanding vocabulary and developing an appreciation for the power of language.

Players make two or more word lists. One will be a list of colors, which will be combined with other lists made of nouns, verbs, adjectives, or adverbs. Then Players experiment with ways to express their combinations of words, such as a *slow black* or a *pink punch*, in sound and action.

Skills

★ Categorizing: creating word lists of colors and specific parts of speech
★ Combining words from different lists to create descriptive phrases
★ Experimenting with expressive use of body and voice to convey meaning of word combinations

Time

Allow for 15 minutes to discuss and make the lists and 30 minutes or more to experiment with movement ideas.

Space

Lists can be made in the classroom. Use any large, open space to experiment with finding ways to physically and vocally express word combinations.

Materials

Paper and writing materials to record lists

Note: This idea was first introduced to us in the 1970s by Crystal Samuels Miller, an arts education consultant for school districts throughout the country in programs sponsored by the National Endowment for the Arts.

★ Directions

1. Ask Players to make at least two lists of words. One list will contain the names of colors. The other lists will each contain words from one part of speech such as adjectives, adverbs, nouns, or verbs.

Examples:

colors	adverbs	adjectives
red	slowly	gorgeous
black	effortlessly	slow
magenta	swiftly	hot
yellow	shortly	tremendous
purple	slyly	vibrant

nouns	verbs
car	punch
train	rock
tree	flow
rain	fidget
sun	stomp

Record the lists on the blackboard or overhead projector, or ask each team or individual to record their own.

2. Have Players make combinations of words by choosing a color and linking it with one of the words from the parts of speech lists.

3. Allow some time for Players to experiment with ways to make their word combinations into a performance of sound and action.

4. Have Players perform their combinations. This may be done as solos, in teams, or as one group. For example, choosing words from the list above might result in a performance of a *hot red*, a *slow black*, a *gorgeous magenta*, a *yellow punch*, and a *vibrant purple* car.

Variations

Descriptive Phrases Ask for a specific kind of descriptive word that will further challenge Players' movement ideas.

- **Time words** speedily, slowly, suspended, fractured
- **Space words** thin, between, huge, wide, encompassing, expansive, spreading, gaping, spanning
- **Direction words** zigzag, spiral, down, across, bearing, heading, tack, drift, path
- **Texture words** wet words such as squishy, sopping, drenched, humid, damp, or sloppily; dry words such as arid, seared, thirsty, crisply or crunchy; rough words such as coarse, jagged, stony, harsh; smooth words such as even, flat, constant, level

Create Sentences Have Players combine words from more than two lists to create short sentences. For example: The red, hot car flew down the street. Ask Players to perform the sentences.

Create Skits or Dances As a group or in teams, have Players combine several phrases or sentences to create a short skit or dance. For example: The red, hot car flew down the street and ran into a crisp, yellow sun that went spiraling toward the gaping, black universe.

Combine Players' Phrases Have individual Players teach one another their word and movement phrases. The phrases can be combined into one skit or dance that is performed as solos, duets, teams, or a group piece.

Add Music If you have student musicians who want to create original music, have them improvise in response to the chosen phrases.

 Teaching Notes

Management Tips

Creating Lists and Phrases Allow for flexible interpretations of the lists. Encourage use of surprising, weird, and unusual combinations. Have a dictionary on hand to explore synonyms. Have Players make word lists individually. For added fun they can exchange lists with one another. You can put all the lists in a paper bag, from which teams or individual Players each draw one.

Connections

ESL and Foreign Languages Make the lists using either bilingual words or words from the language being studied.

Language Arts Read and/or write poetry and prose that explores colorful use of language.

Special Needs

- For students who have difficulty learning the parts of speech, this game provides support through experiential learning.

- For students who have trouble building vocabulary, Lists is a playful way to expand their vocabulary and use of words.

- Some students may have difficulty tracking word combinations across the columns of several lists. Try color coding each combination that is selected. The color names could be written in the color of the word. After a word from another category is chosen, it could be underlined or highlighted in the same color.

- For students who have difficulty reading, make the lists visual by using felt boards and felt cutouts.

- Write the lists in Braille so that visually impaired students can read and respond to them.

 Assessment

Teacher Observations

- Were students able to produce ideas for the lists?

- Were students sensitive to the descriptive potential of their lists?

- Did students respond to their phrases with creative and expressive movement and sound solutions?

Group Discussion

Have Players observe and discuss one another's performances. Focus the discussion on the meaning the performer's movements and/or sounds conveyed to the audience. Encourage performers to share their thought processes: What did their chosen word combinations mean to them? How did they decide to express this meaning in sound and action?

 Student Activities

Book

pages 35–36 (Overview)

pages 37–38 (Vocabulary)

pages 39–41 (Background Reading)

pages 42–43 (Rules of Improvisation)

Journal

Ask Players to write about their experience of making combinations of words and then acting or dancing them out.

Paper Bag Dramatics

In Paper Bag Dramatics, the Leader fills paper bags with a collection of pictures, words, symbols, and objects. Each team of Players receives a paper bag and improvises a skit using all the items it contains. The items in the bag can be seen, used, or heard within the improvisation. The paper bag items serve as catalysts and prompters, giving Players information to build a structure on which to improvise. By organizing the items into a playing order, Players create a performance score. If they decide to improvise a story line, Players can use the items to organize a scenario, or skeleton plot. As is essential to all improvisations, details of dialogue and action are left to the moment of performance, when teams perform their improvisations for one another.

★ Directions

1. Gather items to fill the paper bags, or ask Players to collect them. The items can include small objects found in the environment or scavenged from home or the classroom (toys, leaves, rocks, twigs, hardware, articles of clothing, utensils, etc.); words, symbols, or phrases written on small pieces of paper or cut from newspapers or magazines; and pictures or photographs of people, places, objects, or events. Choose one type of item, or use a mixture.

2. Divide the group into teams of three to five Players. Fill one paper bag for each team, placing the same number and type of items in each bag (five to ten items works well). Another option is to place all the items in one large paper bag, and direct each Player to draw out a specific number of items. Direct each team to use all of the items in the bag—words, pictures, or objects—to improvise a skit.

3. Give teams time to explore their paper bag items and to plan how they will use them in a skit. Tell them that a good way to get started is to organize the items into a performance order. Following are some suggestions for how to organize the items into a performance.

- Use the items to inspire a performance of a series of unrelated events. This kind of improvisation could end up looking similar to vaudeville blackout routines: a joke, followed by a chase, followed by a dance, and so on.

- Use the items to create a story line. This could be done by using a script outlining technique called *scenario*, also known as a treatment or a skeleton plot. To figure out a *scenario*, Players must get together and agree on all or some of the basic *W* questions: *Who* are the characters? *Where* are they? *What* are they doing? *When* is the action happening? The *Why* and *How* are solved during the improvisation, based on the team's *Who, Where, What,* and *When* choices.

4. Have the teams perform their paper bag improvisations for one another. A guessing game could follow each skit, in which observers try to guess all of the items (objects, words, or pictures) with which the team started.

Skills

★ Improvising ensemble skits that are structured on the use of a random collection of pictures, words, symbols, and/or objects

Time

30 minutes to an hour. It's helpful to set a time limit both for preparing and performing the improvisations.

Space

There must be sufficient space for several teams of Players to plan their improvisations. A stage or large room cleared at one end would work best for the performances.

Materials

Paper bags; index cards or scraps of paper with words or symbols written on them; small, scavenged objects (cans, rocks, pencils, leaves, sticks, balls, coins, pieces of fruit, knickknacks, scarves, dishes, toys, etc.); photographs or pictures cut or copied from newspapers, books, or magazines

Teaching Notes

Management Tips

Leaving Details for Improvisation
During the planning session, Players should not script their dialogue or decide on specific stage business, or action. It is much more exciting to add these details as they come up in the improvisation. This element of surprise will encourage Players to think quickly and to play their skit as a team by responding to the immediacy of each item with no preconceived ideas. Paper Bag Dramatics will take the Players into unexpected twists and turns of direction that could not be anticipated in the planning.

Connections

Language Arts Ask Players to fill the paper bags with words that have been cut from newspapers or magazines, or that have been written on index cards. Use words from all parts of speech, or specify only one or two. Encourage the use of words that have strong descriptive qualities; they are good catalysts for action. For example, *slip* instead of *go, spy* rather than *look, snob* rather

than *person*. One way to expand Players' vocabularies is to ask them to search for synonyms for the words they have chosen. Players can choose to use the words by turning them into actions, speaking them as part of their dialogue, or both acting and speaking them within the context of the improvisation. Verbs translate into actions, nouns translate into characters or objects in the setting, adjectives and adverbs give ways to understand qualities of character, actions, or setting. Teams can experiment with ordering their words to come up with different improvisations.

Assessment

Teacher Observations

- Were Players able to work together within their teams to plan and perform a skit?

- How adept were Players at improvising? Did they truly act in the moment, or were too many details scripted? Were they able to think on their feet, or did they freeze or flounder when faced with unexpected situations?

Group Discussion

After each team has performed its skit, invite viewing Players to share their observations. Can they name the paper bag items used in the skit? What did they like best about the skit? Ask performing Players to describe how they decided to structure their skit and use their paper bag items. Then ask them to discuss the details that "just happened" during the improvisation.

Student Activities

Book

pages 44–47 (Background Reading)

Journal

Ask Players to write their feelings about improvising in performance. As the skit progressed, did they become more relaxed and confident?

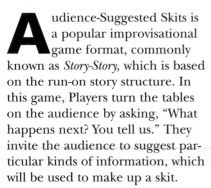

Audience-Suggested Skits

Audience-Suggested Skits is a popular improvisational game format, commonly known as *Story-Story*, which is based on the run-on story structure. In this game, Players turn the tables on the audience by asking, "What happens next? You tell us." They invite the audience to suggest particular kinds of information, which will be used to make up a skit.

Audience-suggested skits are a sure-fire way to build an ensemble, since the Players must rely on one another to solve whatever the audience throws their way. The skits are also exciting for the audience, because the outcome is unknown and everyone understands what a great risk the Players are taking.

Skills

★ Improvising stories and scenes based on audience suggestions of style, setting, character, etc.
★ Directing improvised run-on stories by soliciting suggestions from audience and cueing Players
★ Practicing acting skills: vocal expression; expressive movement, including pantomime; inventing characters that interact in an ensemble

Time

15 minutes or more

Space

Adaptable to any space

Materials

A box of small hand props and costumes can be useful to inspire character or bits of stage business.

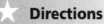
Directions

1. Divide the group into at least two teams. Teams will alternate taking turns at being audience and being performers.

2. Have each team choose a Director. This is the person who will explain the rules of the game to the audience and then ask them for suggestions. In addition to the frequently requested categories of style and title, the Director can ask the audience to provide other kinds of information.

Examples:
- Situation
- Character types or names
- Object
- Place
- Time
- Occupations
- Experiences of the most embarrassing kind
- First line and last line (The Players have to create the middle of the story to connect the beginning and ending lines.)
- Combination of any of the above

The Director also has the job of keeping the improvisation moving along by going back to the audience for more suggestions when the improvisation needs an infusion of energy.

3. To begin the improvisation, have the performing team stand in a line or semicircle. Their Director asks the audience to suggest a story title and a performance style in which to tell the story. (*Style* refers to any literary or performance form, such as romantic comedy or tragedy.

See Performing Suggestions for a list and descriptions of performance styles.)

4. Once the title and style are chosen, ask the Director to point to one of the Players to cue her to begin telling the story. The Director can decide when another Player should take over the story. After receiving a cue from the Director, each Player picks up where the previous Player left off.

5. This process continues until the Director decides that the story is complete. Then the Director points to a Player and calls out, "And the moral of this story is…" and that Player supplies a moral that summarizes the tale.

6. Have the teams rotate being audience and performers.

Variations

End with a Limerick and a Dance
Instead of a moral, the Director asks for an ending summary in the form of a limerick, and asks the audience to supply a dance style, such as tango, boogie woogie, ballet, or minuet, that a Player must perform while saying the limerick.

Acting Out the Story Instead of simply standing and telling the story, the team performs the story as it is told, with Players becoming the characters and objects in the story. In this case, the Director coaches from the sidelines (see the Joker and Wild Card suggestions in this chapter's introduction) and continues the job of getting information from the audience.

Competition Add a competitive element, by letting the audience act as critics or umpires. Give them permission to call Players "out" if they do not perform according to certain criteria. To avoid being called out, Players must:

- Avoid repetition
- Avoid overly long pauses
- Maintain proper grammar
- Be logical
- Correctly spell any word on demand from the audience

The Player who breaks a rule and is called out takes over as Director. He may ask the audience for a change of style or a new piece of information before directing Players to continue with the story. When the next Player is called out, the current Director sits down. The last Player standing is the winner, and may be directed by the audience to do a moral or limerick wrap-up of the story.

Limit Players' Story Contributions
The Leader or Director can limit Players to saying only one word, or one sentence, parts of sentences, or syllables of words.

Performance Suggestions

Performance Style Vary performance style by specifying one of the following particular styles.

- **Elizabethan Theater** 1600s English theater. Plays were written in verse as in the works of Shakespeare, Marlowe, and Ben Jonson.
- **Guerilla Theater** Street theater that takes the audience by surprise.
- **Cabaret** An intimate style of theater performed in clubs and coffee shops, consisting of a series of skits, songs, and other variety acts, often involving political satire.

- **Vaudeville** Popular entertainments performed in music halls or theater settings, involving a series of skits, jokes, mimes, songs, and dances, etc.
- **Soap Opera/Melodrama** Daily life problem plays, as seen on television and in movies, involving stock characters and situations.
- **Mock Opera** Scripts that are sung in the style of an opera with recitative and arias.
- **Operetta** A light opera using a mixture of talking and singing.

- **Medieval Mysteries** European medieval allegorical plays representing moral or religious ideals. Performed to celebrate special occasions.
- **Thrillers** Who-done-its.

Scripted Audience Participation
Audience participation is built into the script of Alvan Colón Lespier's play *The Caravan*, on pages 203–213 of the Student Book. Throughout this one-act play, the audience participates in the role of audience, for a community festival performance by a band of traveling Players. Twice,

the Players invite the audience to suggest solutions to the problems of their characters. The actors are expected to deal with the audience's responses to their questions, finding a way to resolve their improvisation and continue onto the conclusion of the script.

Teaching Notes

Management Tips

Team Size Keep teams small. Allow no more than four to eight Players per team.

Model the Director Role You can model the first turn as Director to show Players how the role is to be played.

Alternate Directors You could keep changing Directors within each skit, even without adding the Competition variation. Every time a Player gets stuck in trying to move the story forward, that Player takes over as the new Director.

Planning Huddle If the audience suggestions seem to need some planning, allow the Players to go into a huddle where they decide the *Who, What,* and *Where* questions. They do not need a complete plot or scenario; they just need to know the answers to the three *W* questions. They may also want to decide how to begin. Set a time limit for the huddle (one or two minutes), and have music that the audience can listen to while the huddle is in progress.

Players Provide Style Choices Players can prepare a set of cards on which they have written the names of various literary or performance styles. The Director can show the audience these cards, asking them to choose one, or the Director can select one for the performers to use in their skit.

Connections

Language Arts/Social Studies Ask that any suggestions of style or other content be related to current curriculum. Or limit the choices to other specific topics such as current events, a particular novel, or a specific place or time.

Foreign Languages Play the game in a language other than English or a combination of languages.

Background Notes

According to Janet Coleman in her book, *The Compass,* the run-on story format of this audience-suggested game is based on a set of rules first suggested by Larry Arrick for the 1950s Chicago-based improvisational company known as the Compass. The classic game title is *Story-Story.* Arrick devised it because "the company had gotten so good the audience didn't believe they were improvising." *Story-Story* has taken on many variations over the years, as it has been played in improvisational theaters throughout the country, including the television game show "You Don't Say."

Assessment

Teacher Observations

- Did Players listen to one another and use information given by others to add to the story?

- Did Players improvise a story that had a beginning, middle, and end? Was the story imaginative and logical?

- If they acted out the story, did Players develop characterizations that used body and voice to express motivations?

- Were Players comfortable and competent in the Director's role? Did the Directors manage to keep the improvisation moving?

- Were audience members attentive and quick to offer suggestions?

Group Discussion

After all teams have finished their improvised stories, ask Players to discuss the process and the final products of this game.

- What effect did the audience participation have on the improvisation experience?

- How well did team members follow one another's leads to create a story that made sense? As an audience member, could you follow the stories?

- Was the Director role essential in this game? How? If you were a Director, what did you discover about directing an improvisation?

Student Activities

Book

pages 48–50 (Performance Model)

Journal

Ask Players to address the following questions in their journals:

- How did it feel to have to improvise on the spot?

- What helped you to move ahead?

Inventing New Games

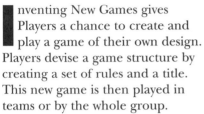

Inventing New Games gives Players a chance to create and play a game of their own design. Players devise a game structure by creating a set of rules and a title. This new game is then played in teams or by the whole group.

For the Players, Inventing New Games offers the challenge of figuring out what makes an interesting game, encourages independent thinking, and allows for inclusion of Players' current interests, styles, and tastes. Playing one another's original games honors everyone's ideas.

For Leaders, this activity offers a window into the tastes, interests, and styles of a group. (It is also interesting to see how frequently the "new" game structures are a recycling of traditional game structures.)

Inventing New Games can be used as a final exam. In either written or oral form, the original games furnish an accurate tool to measure participants' understanding of how to create performance games with rules that provide sufficient guidance to direct and focus the Players, while at the same time allowing space for individual freedom of interpretation. When the new games are taught to and played by other Players, you can observe how they have progressed in their development of communication, focus, leadership, and ensemble skills.

★ Directions

1. Introduce the project by generating a group discussion about what ingredients are needed to play any game. Depending on the nature of the game, the list of ingredients might include the following items:

- A list of rules that provide structure to the game

- A description of how participants will be organized to play the game (as a group, in teams, pairs, or individually), including the roles they are to play

- A statement of space requirements

- A list of materials or equipment, as needed

- A decision to have either a cooperative or competitive focus

- A time limit

- A title

2. Organize the Players. Have them work together as a group, in teams, or individually to invent new games, play the games, or both.

Teams should contain about three to eight Players.

3. Assign each Player, team, or the whole group to invent a new game. This assignment can require an oral presentation in class, or it can be given as a writing assignment to be done either in class or at home. Decide whether you want to leave the assignment completely open-ended or whether you want Players to create a specific kind of game. For example, you might ask for reinterpretations of well-known games, such as follow the leader, baseball, tag, or relay races. Or you could assign Players to create a scenario, or skeleton plot structure, to be used for a scene. If you want Players to create rules for an improvisation, ask them to provide evocative bits of information to structure an improvisation, including news topics or articles and famous quotations.

4. When Players have completed their new game inventions, allow the authors to present their games to the entire group, one team, or several teams. Players listen to

Skills

★ Understanding and analyzing game structures

★ Inventing new games and presenting them orally or in writing

★ Directing others or working collaboratively to interpret and play a game

Time

One hour or more. It could take a few sessions to give everyone a turn at directing her game.

Space

Adaptable to any space

Materials

You may wish to make available objects such as a parachute, a large ball, ropes, and poles, which Players might incorporate into their game plans.

the presentation of each game, then discuss it until they understand and agree to the rules. As in the general practice of playing performance games, or performing any improvisations, once everyone is in agreement about the game's basic rules or structure, they allow other decisions to be made while they are playing the game. If the game involves a plot and characters, as in a scenario structure, the Players need only establish the *Who*, *What*, and *Where* before they begin to play the game. Detailed decisions involving dialogue and story line should be left as moment-to-moment developments.

5. Choose one of the following methods for directing Players while they play the new games.

- Authors direct other Players through their games.

- Teams direct themselves. They may be interpreting another team's set of rules, an individual author's set of written rules, or they may have made up their own game. Give teams a few minutes to huddle to review the rules and discuss how to play the game.

6. Have Players perform the new games for one another. Teams can watch other teams, or the whole group can be divided in half to play the same or different games. Continue playing the games until all the new games have been tried.

Variations

Audience Input Someone, either you, the author, or an appointed Player, can be a Director who asks for audience input. The Director can ask the audience to call out information that the Players have to incorporate as they play the game. Requests can be for a change

of rules or actions; addition of characters, props, and costumes; or a change of time or place.

Replacing Players Members of the audience can replace Players by calling out "Stop!" When the Players hear this call they freeze until the audience member who called out "Stop!" replaces a Player. Then the improvisation continues with the new Player.

Teaching Notes

Management Tips

Organizing Players Your decision about whether to have individuals, teams, or the whole group invent new games will depend on the size of the group and the amount of time you wish to spend on this activity. If your group is small (fewer than ten Players) and you have two or three sessions available, by all means allow each Player to invent and direct his own game.

Exchanging Games Have Players exchange oral ideas or written assignments so that all games are played by a team that does not include the author. This will emphasize the importance of clear communication and will facilitate freedom of interpretation.

Using Improvisational Devices Decide whether to allow the group to use improvisational devices such as Rescue Squad, Transformations, Wild Card, or Joker, as described in this chapter's introduction.

Alternating Roles Keep alternating the roles of the teams, so that everyone gets a chance to be watchers and Players within any one session.

Connections

ESL/Foreign Languages Conduct this game in either a combination of English and the language being used or studied, or only in the language being studied.

 Assessment

Teacher Observations

- In discussion, did Players seem to have a clear understanding of what information is necessary to play any game?

- Did their invented games demonstrate this understanding?

- Were Players able to clearly present their games to others?

- Did Players demonstrate leadership and teamwork skills as they worked to interpret and play new games?

Group Discussion

After Players have played a new game, ask them to review the game, using the following questions as a guide.

- Did this game work? Why?

- Were there enough rules given to support the Players?

- What further information or revision of the rules might make this game more easily understood or more fun to play?

 Student Activities

Book

page 51 (Background Reading)

Journal

Ask Players to invent their own new game.

Scriptwriting

A *script* is the name given to the written text in plays and other performance works. Today, the word *text* refers to all written speech, action, movement, design, sound, and visual cues that the audience will see and hear. Film scripts also routinely include camera angles, shot distances, and the number of shots. All of these elements are considered to have equal importance. Scripts may also include a cast list of characters (sometimes including descriptions of the characters), a list of scenes, a suggested prop list, and set design notes.

Theater scripts come from both written and oral sources. Sometimes a narrative, or story line, is sung or chanted while dancers, puppets, or actors embody the tale. This is true in the Hawaiian hula dance plays, south Indian masked *Kathakali* dance plays, Javanese *Wayang Kulit* (shadow puppet plays), Chinese opera, and Japanese *Noh* plays and *Bunraku* puppet plays. In the tradition of classical ballet, dancers mime the important events of the story, adding decorative dance scenes that embellish the tale. Many theater styles have developed sign language vocabularies, using gestures and facial expressions and characteristic masks and costumes to help communicate the tale.

There are many models on which to structure scripts, including solo narratives, collages of related or unrelated events, and ring compositions, which repeat the beginning at the end. For a long time, Western theater emphasized the model set forth in *Poetics,* a treatise on tragedy by the Greek philosopher, Aristotle (834–322 B.C.). According to Aristotle, the whole must encompass a three-part structure that includes a beginning, middle, and end. A parallel concept, called *Jo-ha-kyu,* is discussed by the founder of the Japanese Noh play form, Ze-ami (1363–1443), in his theoretical treatise, *Kadensho. Jo-ha-kyu* means

Chapter 5

Scriptwriting 81

introduction, development, and resolution. This structure was used for both the internal construction of plays and the planning of an entire day's program. The activity Boy Meets Girl will give students practice in using this three-part structure.

In this chapter, you will find various kinds of activities that will help your students write original scripts. Conventions of Scriptwriting discusses the mechanics of scriptwriting. In the activity Living History, you can assign specific topics to research for scripts. Storytelling suggests many ways to tell or write monologues or dialogues that start from an imaginary source, or come from oral and written literary traditions. Scenarios shows how to make scenes through structured improvisations, or how to create improvisations based on adaptations from literature, updates of existing plays and films, or popular forms such as soap operas, jokes, and advertisement jingles. Surveys and Fill in the Blanks take familiar structures from sources outside theater and adapt them to theatrical uses.

Writing original scripts solves the problem of finding a play that will fit the particular configuration of your group. When the participants write the play it saves you from long searches for a script that meets your needs. It will have enough roles for everyone, divided into the correct number of male and female parts, and it will be appropriate for Players' ages and interests. The length and ambition of the project will be tailor-made, and you can even add a part for the new student who arrives in your class two weeks before the premiere.

If you do not want to start from scratch, there is always the possibility of mounting a production from an existing script for a one- to three-act play. Or you can choose to do scenes excerpted from plays. If you choose excerpted material, you run the risk that because performers will not experience the entire play, they may not understand the whole vision of the work or the motivations of their characters. Therefore, when you choose to do excerpted scenes, have the performers read the entire text. Excerpted scenes work best for training Players in audition skills.

★ Choosing Text for a Script

If you decide to direct a performance project that involves a written script, the following questions might be helpful when thinking through what choice to make. These questions apply to selecting either a topic for an original script, or choosing among existing scripts.

- Can this idea or text be brought to life? Is it theatrical?

- Is it appropriate material for this group?

- Can I enjoy and feel comfortable with this work?

- Who will be the audience? Will it be interesting for them?

- Will it give everyone a creative experience and allow everyone to participate in some way, either as actors, designers, or technicians?

- Does it have enough parts to accommodate this group? Do the male and female role assignments reflect the makeup of my group?

- Can the technical effects be solved within the givens of my group, the performing space, my resources, and available budget?

- Is it structured well enough or written well enough to remain interesting through in-depth analysis and rehearsal time?

- Will this project be fun to work on? Will we gain new experiences from doing it?

★ Developing an Original Script

Script development in commercial theater commonly begins with scenarios and treatments. When the writer finds someone interested in the treatment, it is developed into a script, which is showcased in public readings. The next stage is a workshop phase, leading to a production of the play, usually in a small regional theater. Script revisions continue, often in response to audience reactions, until a final draft evolves. A few plays are revised again for a larger production, such as those slated for Broadway.

If you think you might want to expand a classroom lesson into a performance project, keep a record of all work sessions to remind yourself of information that could become part of the script. This might include improvised action and dialogue, ideas for organizing the plot structure, characterizations, and any other details, including production ideas, that surfaced during improvisations and discussions. Record these materials on audiotape or videotape for later transcription, or take written notes during or immediately after each session.

If you know that, at some future date, you are going to be responsible for preparing a performance on a particular subject, you might enjoy preparing the way some writers do. Over a period of time, collect news articles or other materials and ideas on a specific subject. Keep this information in a box or file to be organized at a later time. For example, if the subject is Thanksgiving, ask students to bring in any information they find on this topic, including foods and their preparation, regional celebrations, harvest practices, news articles, costumes, and so on.

When you feel you have gathered enough information, draft a preliminary performance order. Affix your ideas to a series of pages, one large sheet of paper or cardboard, or a bulletin board. You can choose one of several organizational methods. This can be done by you and/or a committee of students.

- **Cut and Paste** Cut and paste selected dialogue and action into a running order. Pieces of dialogue can be reordered under topic headings, each topic on a separate piece of paper.

- **File Cards or Sticky Notes** Another organization method that will help you find structure is to record important events, actions, scenes, entrances/exits, and transitions on file cards or sticky notes (it is not necessary to put dialogue on these cards or notes).

- **Storyboard** If you prefer working visually, use a storyboard to show the events of your script idea (See Scenarios, page 96.) Images could be drawings (stick figures work fine), cutouts, tracings, or photocopies. Sequence the images to create your running order.

When you script the dialogue in, follow the sequence that you organized in your cut and paste or storyboard.

You could practice these methods on a small scale in the game Paper Bag Dramatics (page 74). If you want to adapt a literary work, try Jingles (page 20).

It is standard practice to take revisions into a rehearsal process because what is written on the page does not always work well on stage, and each new script goes through several revisions to work out problems. Sometimes one or more students will offer to write a script that becomes the basis for a class performance project. They will need to understand that their script will go through many revisions and changes and that this is part of the process and not a reflection on their contribution. You and your students will experience the differences between writing a script for live performance and performing it. What works on the page may not work in live theater. Even published scripts get revised to fit a change of actors, times, places, or form, such as going from stage to film or from film to stage.

Keep revising the script until you find a running order that feels right. This usually takes two or three drafts before you work out the final version.

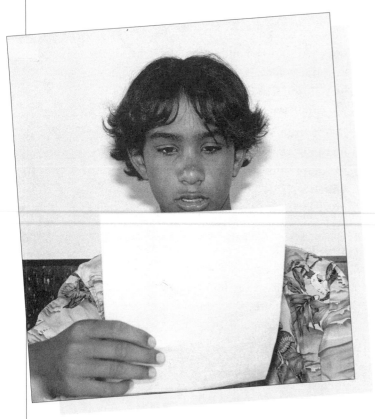

Sometimes "the final version" is determined by a time crunch. When dress rehearsal is upon you, it's time to stop revising!

★ Working with a Script

Once a script is written or chosen, there are some standard practices that make the rehearsal process run more smoothly.

Sit-down Reading

Ask the group to sit together in a circle, close enough so that everyone sees and hears each other easily. Read the script together, at least two times.

- **First Reading** Go through the text, reading section by section. Stop for any necessary explanations of pronunciation, definitions of words, corrections of typographical errors, or other general questions from the group. (If there are many words that need to be defined, you might want to provide a glossary.)

- **Second Reading** Read the text together, nonstop, so that everyone hears the flow of the words.

Discuss the Text

Decide the given circumstances: the *Who, Where, When, What,* and *Why* of the work.

- **Who** List the characters and provide short biographies describing them by name, age, work, likes and dislikes, relationships to other characters, and so on.

- **Where and When** Name the setting—the specific locations and times given in the text.

- **What** What happens? What is the problem, conflict, and mood?

- **Why** What is the meaning or message of the story, poem, speech?

Identify the Theme

After the group is familiar with the text, ask them to summarize the story in a word, phrase, or sentence. This could be done as a writing assignment that is then shared with the group. Or just have a group discussion, where everyone shares their ideas. Choose the one idea that can serve as a theme to focus the performance.

★ Assigning Roles

You can make these decisions yourself, based on your experiences with your students, or you can run an audition. If the production will involve design and technical crew jobs, include them in the list of possible assignments. That way everyone understands that backstage, design, choreography, and music jobs are valued as much as any acting assignment. You could also audition other performing jobs, such as dancers, singers, and musicians. Players may want to prepare scenes, songs, or dances with another Player in the group.

An audition does generate a lot of excitement. As they prepare for the audition, Players start investing time and commitment to the project. You could ask Players to prepare for at least two, or maybe even three roles, that interest them. Suggest they read the play through many times on their own and pick out a monologue or scene to prepare for the audition. You can also avoid the audition issue by finding ways to perform in teams or as a unison group.

An audition could consist of everyone presenting his or her choices. Sometimes you may need to ask Players to read for roles they did not prepare, just because you have a hunch they will fit the part, or because no one has chosen to audition for that role and you need to see some possibilities. The auditioning process may take more than one session.

Ask each Player to give you a list of three characters he or she would like to play, in order of preference. Then make a large grid, listing the names of all the characters across the top of the grid, and the Players' names down the left-hand margin of the grid. By each Player's name, log in his part or job preferences. After you fill in the chart with everyone's preferences, decide how to assign roles by balancing all the variables of Players' wishes, what jobs have to be filled, and your instincts for what will serve the play and the Players the best. Generally, giving people the parts they want works out well.

 Management Tips

Keeping Scripts Suggest Players put their scripts into a portfolio or loose-leaf notebook, so they stay organized and in one place.

Highlighting the Script After the parts are given out, have each Player highlight every line she speaks. She should also highlight any indications of entrances and exits for her character, or any other cues and stage business that involve her character.

Recording Rehearsal Changes Remind Players to bring their scripts to every rehearsal, even after they have memorized their lines. When they record changes directly in their scripts they will be organized to study any changes of blocking or line revisions that might occur during the rehearsal. (If you have a large group, and can spare a Player, make one job assignment be Assistant Director, Script Editor, or Stage Manager. That person's job includes keeping an up-to-date record of rehearsal changes for all parts.)

Revising the Script If the script has gone through significant rewrites, give everyone a new version that includes all line and cue changes. Tell the Players to highlight their lines and cues, again, in the revised script. This will also help members of the tech crew, who have to run their cues off of a final script.

Conventions of Scriptwriting

Conventions of Scriptwriting introduces students to the mechanics of standard scriptwriting style by having them examine how an actual performance script is written and read. It also introduces a discussion of the function of dialogue, comparing scripted and narrative texts.

There are many ways to set up a script. This exercise is designed to acquaint students with the standard scriptwriting format. In this activity, students learn to identify and use standard print mechanics for conversations intended to be read in a narrative text, and conversations intended to be spoken in a play. Through class discussion and comparison of narrative and script samples, students become aware of how scriptwriting conventions make

it easier for a performer to identify who is speaking.

Players record conversations in both narrative and scripted formats. The conversations can be designed as interviews. They can also function as an exploratory exercise to begin writing an original script.

★ Directions

1. Show students two print samples that include dialogue, one in narrative form (from a short story or novel) and one in script form (from a play). Discuss the differences in punctuation and layout used to identify speakers and their speeches or conversations.

- Compare punctuation and page setup.
  Narrative
  Discuss how conversations are written in paragraph form, calling attention to the following usage rules.
  – The use of designators, words or tags used to indicate the speaker and, perhaps, the tone of speech, as in *he said happily,* or *she shouted*
  – The use of quotation marks to set off the words of each speaker
  – The use of paragraph indentations to signal a shift in speaker
  – The use of basic punctuation, such as placement of periods within quotes and the use of commas to indicate speaker and mood or parenthetical expressions

Script
Have students look for ways in which the script form differs from narrative form, calling attention to the following conventions in scriptwriting.
– In a script, every speech is separated by space. Each speaker is identified by name, which is placed in the left margin, sometimes followed by a colon. The speech is printed to the right of the name.
Example:
HAMLET: To be or not to be, that is the question.

Sometimes, the speaker's name is centered above his speech.

HAMLET
To be or not to be, that is the question.

– Quotation marks are not used to set off dialogue in scripts.
– To increase readability, script-writers often capitalize every letter of each character's name.
– Within scripts, directing notes, design ideas, or any other information that is not to be spoken by the performers should be placed in italics or within parentheses, or both.

- Analyze the function of dialogue.
  Narrative
  Discuss how dialogue can be used to present or explain what characters are thinking and reveal their relationships with one another. In fiction, a narrator can report or present facts and descriptions that show how the character speaks and acts, and interior monologues can be used to reveal the thoughts of characters.

Skills

★ Analyzing and comparing the format and functions of dialogue in narratives and scripts
★ Engaging in impromptu dialogues
★ Recording and performing from dialogues written in script and narrative forms

Time

One or two sessions lasting 30 minutes to an hour and a half

Space

Adaptable to any space

Materials

Paper and pencils or pens. If available, audio or video recording equipment can be used to document the conversations and help Players who have reading or writing difficulties.

Script

Discuss how in theater, information is communicated through what the characters say and do. The scriptwriter can take advantage of the fact that the audience will see how the characters look and act. Actors and directors will add details of tone, gesture, and motivation. In theater, the dialogue has to show what is happening, rather than tell.

2. Divide the group into teams of four or six Players. Ask each team to divide in half.

3. Explain that half of the team will engage in a short conversation, while the other half listens and records the conversation (in writing and, if possible, on tape). Then direct team halves to reverse roles.

4. Give Players time in class to rewrite the notes they made of the overheard conversation in two writing styles: narrative form and script form. (This step could become a homework assignment.)

5. Have Players read their narrative conversations out loud for their teams. Then have them perform

their scripts. Or, have teams exchange their work, then read or perform for one another.

6. Discuss the experience of reading from a text in narrative form and a text in script form.

Variations

Specify Conversation Topic Specify a particular topic for the conversations, so that the writing assignment can become the beginning of a script for a performance project.

Write the Script as Sides *Sides* are a form of script in which each actor's script shows only his full speeches and cues from the preceding speech, which include only the ending word or phrase. Stage directions are limited to the most necessary action or dialogue delivery suggestions. To create sides, have each listener record the words of only one speaker. To complete the sides with the preceding cues, recorders share and collate their recordings of individual speakers. Players could perform their own sides, the sides they recorded, or swap with another team.

Conduct Interviews Have Players prepare a list of interview questions, then have them interview one another. Compare differences and similarities in the answers to the questions. This variation could be structured as another script development device for a performance project, similar to Surveys (page 104), one of the activities in this chapter, or it could address another need, such as a discussion of current events or other topical issues in your classroom.

★ Teaching Notes

Management Tips

Setup Have teams work in clusters, scattered in different parts of the room, so that conversations can be clearly heard within each team.

Accurate Recording Ask Players to speak slowly enough for their teammates to be able to accurately write down what is said. Alternatively, provide each team with a tape recorder to tape the conversations. Suggest that Players read back

their notes on the conversation, to check with the speakers and other recorders for accuracy, and to add missed details.

Time Limit Keep the writing task brief by setting a time limit for each conversation—for example, no more than three minutes—so that the writing sample will not become such an ambitious undertaking.

Recording and Using Sides There are many advantages to using sides. Because they do not have the entire script before them, actors have to listen to each other to know what is happening. This gets them working together from the beginning rehearsals, concentrating on each other rather than focusing on the page. Using sides also helps eliminate the temptation to mouth other characters' lines, a problem for many young performers.

Conduct Connections

Language Arts Use this exercise to give Players practice in using the mechanics of punctuation in written dialogues, and to teach them the differences of layout and punctuation in narrative and script forms.

Foreign Languages/ESL Conduct conversations in a language other than English, or speak and record conversations bilingually.

History Have Players converse as characters who lived in a particular time, place, or situation, or who have a particular occupation. The characters could be famous or anonymous people.

Special Needs

- Have interpreters available so that deaf students can participate with hearing students, or non-English speaking students can participate with students who only speak English.

- Assign scribes for students who have difficulty with writing, or use tape recorders so that they can transcribe the conversation later on, at their own pace.

 Assessment

Teacher Observations

- Were students able to engage in spontaneous dialogue?

- Were students able to accurately record the conversations of others?

- Did students correctly employ the differences in mechanics for dialogues written in narrative form and script form?

- Did students appear to grasp the differences in the function of dialogue in scripts and narratives?

- Were students able to perform from scripted dialogue?

Group Discussion

- Explain the differences between narrative and script print styles.

- Which would be the easier way to learn a part if you were acting, reading from script or narrative format?

- What dramatic purpose could be served by your dialogue? Does it reveal the nature of the characters and their intentions? Does it affect another character or characters? What is that effect?

 Student Activities

Book

pages 53–54 (Overview)

pages 55–56 (Vocabulary)

pages 57–63 (Background Reading)

Journal

Ask students to record an overheard conversation as a script, or to write an original script.

For example, you could start a study of scriptwriting by reading and discussing the script, *Tricky Tales,* pages 230–260 in the Student Book. Then ask your students to write their own tricky tale, one that they make up, or one based on an existing tale.

To do the latter, you could direct students to break down the story into a series of actions, or make a plot summary in paragraph form. Use rehearsal improvisations to develop dialogue and stage business, and then select dialogue and actions from the students' improvisations to make the script.

If you choose to perform the play *Tricky Tales* using your class's tale, other additions to the script will help it play smoothly. If your new tale involves characters not mentioned in the existing script, you will need students to write the new characters' introductions into the beginning "doughnut" section, change or add transitions between tales, and add the new characters into the ending scene. You could further reorganize or adapt portions of the *Tricky Tales* script to better fit the size and interests of your group, by deleting one scene here or there, or by adding more than one new tale.

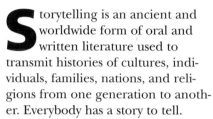

Storytelling

Storytelling is an ancient and worldwide form of oral and written literature used to transmit histories of cultures, individuals, families, nations, and religions from one generation to another. Everybody has a story to tell.

Storytelling can be presented as an oral or written project, or both. A story can be presented simply by one speaker telling the tale on a bare stage, or it can be embellished by adding several speakers, music, puppets, dance plays, slide shows, or any other elaboration possible to imagine.

Skills

★ Selecting stories to perform
★ Deciding, as a group, how to dramatize a story, including details of script interpretation, characterization, and design elements
★ Writing a script based on literature
★ Acting in improvised and scripted scenes
★ Exploring stories, legends, themes, and styles from a variety of cultures

Time

This could be a one-session experience, lasting from 30 minutes to an hour and one-half, or it could be extended over several sessions.

Space

Adaptable to any space

Materials

(Optional) Books, newspapers, and magazines; costumes, small hand props, and set pieces; live or recorded music to enhance the telling of the tale

★ Directions

1. Choose a story. One way for the group to begin is to ask Players to suggest favorite stories that they would like to perform together. Ask them to recall favorite stories from their childhood, or to pick favorites from the year's reading assignments. List the suggested stories on the blackboard or on chart paper. Then use one of the following suggestions to decide on a story to perform.

• As a group, decide by majority vote which story to act out.

• Divide your group into teams. Allow each team to choose the story they want to work on and to solve how they will perform it.

If there is enough time and interest, try as many stories as possible.

2. Decide on the storytelling format.

• **As Written** Using a storybook, read the story aloud.

• **As Remembered** Ask volunteers to tell the story aloud from memory or have each Player write down his version. Discuss and decide which remembered versions or parts of remembered versions will make up the story to be told in performance.

• **Leader as Narrator/Storyteller** You direct the group through your own telling of the story.

• **Fractured** Retell the tale in a new way.
  – From a different character's point of view, such as the Witch's or the Wolf's point of view in *Little Red Riding Hood.*

  – Update the traditional version to contemporary time, place, and language.
  – Change the place, change the ending, add new characters, etc.

3. Decide how the story will be performed.

• **Solo** Perform as a solo. Add visuals, music, costumes, and props to help support the sense of character and place.

• **Group** Select one of the following ways to divide roles.
  – All Players perform everything in the story, simultaneously.
  – Let Players play the parts they want to play. Have everyone participate by allowing more than one person to play a single character. Try to get Players to volunteer for whatever characters are left over, or have everyone do that part in addition to the one they have chosen.
  – Assign parts, remembering to cast everything in the story, inanimate and animate. Work together to perform the story.
  – Have different teams choose and perform the same or different stories. Each team can decide how to divide up the parts.

4. Decide how Players will work out performance details. Following are some ideas.

- **Personification** Personify every noun in the story. Performers become doors, tables, trees, houses, mountains, the sun, people, animals.

- **Pantomime** Physicalize every action in the story. Performers act out every action mentioned in the story, such as opening the door, creeping up the stairs, jumping back and screaming, eating the dinner, falling asleep.

- **Characterization** As a group, set characteristic ways to walk, talk, and gesture for each character. Begin by asking Players, "How would you walk and talk if you were a wolf? Or a witch? Or a prince?" Then ask everyone to become a wolf, witch, or prince. Observe Players' characterizations, then choose a few people to demonstrate for the group. Or play follow the leader, allowing each Player to take a turn as the Leader, moving and talking in the style of a character. Have everyone imitate each demonstration of style. Choose one style for each character, selecting those that the group looks good doing. Remind everyone to use the chosen style of voice and movement whenever that character appears in the story.

- **Call and Response** You (or a Player) say one line, then the group imitates or echoes it, mimicking your vocal tones and actions.

- **Repetition** Emphasize important actions and lines in the story by repeating them more than once, changing speaking volume, the rhythm of speech, and the size of actions. Repetition helps both audience and performers by highlighting important moments or information in the story line. The Leader/Narrator can call for repetitions, or the Players can discuss where repetition should occur.

- **Reverse Order** Tell Players to pay careful attention to all the details of each action in the script. Direct Players to play the actions forward and backward, similar to running a film forward and backward. The whole story, or parts of the story, could be done in reverse.

  Example (from *Sleeping Beauty*): Open the secret door, climb up the twisting and turning castle stairs while brushing away the cobwebs, go through the creaking door, and arrive at the bell tower. In order to leave the secret room in the bell tower, do everything in reverse.

- **Group Endings** Have everyone come together at the story's end in one of the following ways:
  - Celebration party/ dance/parade
  - Escape chase/run-around
  - Happily ever after
  - Unhappily ever after
  - Bows

5. Decide if the final narrative of the story should be recorded in writing and/or audiotaped or videotaped.

Variations

Original Story Create an original story. The story can be told in writing or orally.

Story Based on Fact Choose a subject related to your curriculum or current events. Using facts as a starting point, make up a story.

Story Based on Exaggerations Have Players try creating a tall tale, a legend, an outrageous lie, or a boast.

- **Tall tales** is a folklorists' term for stories based on a little truth and a lot of legend. The truth is stretched, exaggerated, and embellished to the furthest possible extent. In the tall tale spirit, a storyteller might swear that grasshoppers are big enough to drive a plow; bedbugs grow so huge that when they are driven from a bed they jump up on chandeliers and bark at people; and pet snakes can be used to brake the front and back wheels of a stagecoach when it's going downhill. In the telling, there is some semblance of fact. The storyteller often places the tale in the location where it is being told; the place names and characters may change from locale to locale, but the basic narrative stays the same.

- **Lies** Have everyone tell an outrageous lie that has a grain of truth.

- **Boasts** Have everyone tell a fanciful and impressive boast. Boasts could take the following simple form: "I am the most

  _____ (synonym of *terrific*, *wonderful*, *great*, *super*, etc.) _____."

Legends Some famous legends are based on fact but take the form of tall tales. They evolved around a particular region or profession. Whaling, mining, exploring, hunting, cowboy trades, or even the land itself can be featured in the tales. Some familiar American tall tales appear to be based on the lives of real people, including the stories of Pecos Bill, John Henry, Molly McGuire, Frankie and Johnnie, and Johnny Appleseed. According to folklorists, a story like Paul Bunyan does not properly qualify as a tall tale because it is derived from written, rather than oral, tradition. (Paul Bunyan was the creation of writers and public relations men for the lumber companies.)

- As a group, read a variety of folk legends. Or assign each person to choose a few tales to read. Have everyone choose one legend from their reading. Share orally. Or have Players retell the tale, adding details of place and character that link the tale to their lives.

- Write a scenario based on a legend. Read the scenario to the group and have them improvise dialogue and actions.

Management Tips

Encourage Players' Strengths Jobs can be assigned in a group project, so that people who like to write can be the recorders, and people who like to speak can be the actors. Adding set and costume designers, composers, and musicians to this endeavor will provide additional ways to encourage the strengths of all students.

Story Resources Invite local storytellers to perform for or work on a storytelling project with your class. Use your local library for field trips or to borrow recordings or videotapes of stories. Another resource would be to ask family members to share stories from their heritage, bringing their historical and cultural perspectives to the students.

Connections

Language Arts This activity will teach students how to tell and listen to a story. It can also be used to study specific types of stories, such as legends or tall tales. Challenge students to research and compare interpretations or different versions of a story or legend to make their own interpretations.

Social Studies Help Players learn about other cultures by having them read and perform their stories. Identify one theme and ask students to find out if it appears in the stories of more than one culture. Contrast the different points of view of the different stories.

Foreign Languages Listen to and/ or tell the stories in their language of origin.

Special Needs

- Include stories that exist only in the deaf world. Discuss with your class the differences between languages of the deaf and hearing world. Discuss the structural and content differences. There are many excellent stories on videotape performed by and for the deaf community that may be available in your local library.

- Storytelling can help Players who experience distress when called upon to either speak or write. If individual projects are assigned, Players who have trouble writing down their stories can speak their story, assisted by Players who act as their scribes. Or, their oral stories can be recorded on audiotape or videotape. The reverse is also true. Those who love to write but have difficulty presenting their work can write their stories to be told by those who love to speak.

Background Notes

Recently, there has been a resurgence in the art of storytelling. Many performers are using the form. They may speak autobiographically in the first person; or they may construct character portraits, speaking as each character. The piece may be about the character or experiences of the person, function as the expression of a witness or chronicler of a time and place, or look like an MTV high-tech, stand-up comedy act. Some of the most prominent storytelling practitioners include Bill Cosby, Lily Tomlin, Whoopi Goldberg, Spalding Gray, Laurie Anderson, Eric Bogasian, Margaret Cho, Anne Deveare Smith, and Garrison Keillor.

Perhaps one reason the form has risen in popularity is that the solo storyteller on a bare stage offers a practical solution to production problems in the diminished resources of today's theater world. Another reason is the intimacy of the form, the way it establishes connections between the audience and the performer, and its relationship to our affection for talk shows, celebrity watching, and popular therapy. Storytellers affirm our sense of place and history. Besides the solo performers of high visibility, there are also regional storytelling societies throughout the United States, which have established a network of national associations and conventions.

 Assessment

Teacher Observations

- Were Players able to work together to dramatize a story?

- Did Players use their bodies and voices expressively to make characters and situations come alive in performance?

- Did Players write a final script they were proud of?

Group Discussion

Encourage Players to discuss and evaluate their storytelling experiences.

- Did the story you selected work well in performance?

- Were you happy with the way the story was dramatized? Which details did you like the best?

- How does a written story differ from a told or performed story?

 Student Activities

Book

pages 63–64 (Background Reading)

Journal

Ask Players to imagine and write the story of their lives in another time.

Boy Meets Girl

Boy Meets Girl represents one of the most fundamental script formulas. This formula, familiar to everyone, consists of a three-step progression: a beginning, a middle, and an end. Basically, the three-step progression functions as a way to make a work hang together, a way to plot the course of the action.

Beginning The beginning defines the situation by sharing information of setting, introducing characters, and stating the problem to be solved or the objective of the work.

Skills

★ Understanding and identifying the three-step progression (beginning, middle, end) of standard script plots
★ Writing three-step script formulas
★ Planning improvisations by selecting details of character, setting, and action
★ Performing improvised scenes based on three-step scripts

Time

If used as an exercise, allow 30 minutes or an hour. This activity can be extended over several sessions if you want Players to experiment with various solutions or if you decide to turn it into a major performance project.

Space

Adaptable to any space

Materials

Chalkboard, light board, or individual writing materials. Hand props, costumes, and set pieces can be added to enhance the work if it is taken into performance.

Middle The middle contains all of the obstacles or complications that get in the way and lead to a crisis, or turning point.

End The end reveals the crisis, resolves the conflict, and/or finds a resulting outcome, resolution, or conclusion. The outcome could appear as a surprise, as in *deus ex machina,* a device of a miraculous or mysterious nature, or it can be the result of a logical progression.

The most familiar expression of this three-step progression is:

1. BOY MEETS GIRL
2. BOY LOSES GIRL
3. BOY GETS GIRL

Directors and choreographers often use this formula as a springboard to structure new projects. By simply substituting different characters and action verbs for those in the standard progression, it is possible to imagine an infinite variety of instant scripts. A very different course of action is implied with the following substitution of characters:

1. MONSTER MEETS PERSON
2. MONSTER LOSES PERSON
3. MONSTER GETS PERSON

This activity is useful either as an exercise in scriptwriting and plot development, or to develop a script for a performance project.

 Directions

1. Begin by introducing three-part (beginning, middle, end) plot formulas, explaining the function of each step. Write the classic Boy-Meets-Girl formula (see introduction) on the blackboard and ask Players to discuss examples of stories, movies, or television shows that use this plot progression. Suggest that by substituting different characters (or objects) and verbs in the standard formula, Players could create an infinite variety of plots. Work with the group to create a few examples.

2. Divide Players into small groups to come up with variations on the Boy-Meets-Girl formula. Ask groups to record their plot formulas, then to choose one to act out.

3. Direct groups to decide how to improvise on their formulas by deciding the *Who* (characters), *When* and *Where* (setting), and *What* (action). Allow time for the groups to practice their improvisations. Remind Players that in improvisations, details of dialogue and action that solve the *How* and *Why,* can be changed during each performance.

4. Have groups perform their improvisations for one another.

5. (Optional) Have groups record their improvisations to use as the basis of a written script or choreographed score.

Management Tips

Practicing Solutions Have teams use different areas of the work space, so they can maintain focus. Besides talking the improvisation through, encourage teams to practice their solution at least once before showing it to the rest of the group. Try to check in with each team at least once before it performs to make sure Players understand the directions and that everyone is being included in the process.

Recording Improvisations Each time an improvisation is performed, give students time to record their improvisation in writing. Or designate one member of each team or certain members of the class to be scribes or technicians who record the improvisations on audiotape or videotape. The tapes can be transcribed into script form at a later date. See the introduction to this chapter for suggestions of ways to turn an improvisation into a performance script.

Connections

Language Arts Boy Meets Girl provides an easy-to-understand and amusing formula for students to write well-made plays that contain a beginning, middle, and end. The Boy-Meets-Girl formula is also an excellent tool for illustrating sentence structure:

    SUBJECT VERB OBJECT

History You may want to analyze a subject from material the class is studying in history. The class can analyze an event within the context of a three-part structure.

Example:

1. BRITAIN RULES AMERICA
2. AMERICA FIGHTS BRITAIN
3. BRITAIN LOSES AMERICA

 Assessment

Teacher Observations

- Were Players able to create unique variations on the three-step formula?
- Did their improvisations clearly reflect plots containing a beginning, middle, and end?
- Were Players able to identify the three-part structure in one another's improvisations?

Group Discussion

Discuss with your students what makes a beginning, middle, and ending in a plot. After each team performs its improvisation, ask the audience to try to guess the formula used. Have the Players discuss the three-part formula as performed by each team.

 Student Activities

Book

pages 65–66 (Writing model)

Journal

Have Players practice writing three-step plot formulas in their journals. Have them write three formulas: one from their lives, one from a historical event that interests them, and one from a work of literature that they have read this semester.

Fill in the Blanks

Fill in the Blanks starts with a script that is missing words. The blanks are filled in, then the completed script is performed. Within the script, there may be specific instructions about the kind of information to put in each blank. For example, one blank may require a verb, an adverb, or a noun; another blank may ask for an exclamation or a silly word; and a third blank may call for a body part or an animal.

A fill-in-the-blanks script is a convenient device when you need an instant performance. It can be structured as a "who-done-it," a historical reconstruction, a fable, a commercial, a radio show, or a television situation comedy.

Skills
★ Writing original fill-in-the-blanks scripts
★ Choosing how to fill in missing details of other's scripts

Time
At least 30 minutes. Depending on how you want to use the project, it can be a one- or two-session activity or take several sessions to prepare a performance.

Space
Adaptable to any space

Materials
Writing materials such as paper and pens or pencils; chalkboard; overhead projector

★ Directions

1. Introduce the idea of fill-in-the-blanks scripts by asking the group to fill in the blanks in the following example.

If I were ruler of the world I would

_____.

And then everybody would

_____.

And then _____.

2. Then offer the following fill-in-the-blank activity. Point out that in this example, there are directions in parentheses beneath the blanks. The blanks are to be filled in with specific information: answers to the questions *Who, What, Where,* and *Why.*

Three things happened on the way to _____.
                                        (where)
I lost _____.
                        (what/who)
I found _____.
                    (what/where/who)
I tricked _____.
                        (who/what/why).
And then _____.

Explain that other kinds of directions can also be used in writing a fill-in-the-blank script. For example, instructions for each blank may ask for a specific part of speech, such as a noun, verb, adjective, or adverb. (See the first Variation for an example.) Directions may be even more specific, asking for a color, an exclamation, an animal, or a mode of transportation. (See the third Variation for an example.)

3. Divide the Players into small teams (four to six Players). Ask teams to each write an original fill-in-the-blanks script. Remind them to decide whether or not to provide directions for how to fill in the blanks. You may wish to specify a certain kind of fill-in-the-blanks script, such as one of those listed in the Variations. (Also see the assignment on pages 66–68 of the Student Book.)

4. Have teams exchange their scripts. Provide time for Players to read and fill in the blanks in the scripts.

5. Have teams share their completed scripts by reading them aloud for the group. If time allows, have Players perform their fill-in-the-blanks scripts for one another, using improvisations.

Variations

Adapting Literature An existing poem, fable, or short story can provide the structure for a fill-in-the-blanks script. Players read the story, and decide which words to delete. They identify the type of answer they want readers to fill in for the deleted words. They may ask for words that are parts of speech, such as nouns (N), verbs (V), adjectives (ADJ), adverbs (ADV), and prepositions (P). You can also choose to adapt a news article (movie reviews, current events, an advice column), advertisement copy, or song lyrics in this way. The following example is a fill-in-the-blanks adaptation of an Aesop's fable with instructions that call for blanks to be filled in with specific parts of speech.

A _____ (N1), _____ (N2), and _____ (N3) decided to start a business together. The _____ (N1) borrowed _____ (N) to finance their business; the _____ (N2) brought _____ (ADJ) _____ (N); and the _____ (N3) brought _____ (ADJ) _____ (N). When the three of them went _____ (P) the _____ (N) to _____ (V) _____ (ADV) to sell their _____ (N), they lost their _____ (N), just escaping with their _____ (N). Since then, the _____ (N1) never _____ (V) at night for fear of _____ (N). And _____ (N2) thinks that their lost _____ (N) was stolen by their _____ (N) so he _____ (V) watching them. The _____ (N3) explores every _____ (N) and _____ (N) and believes _____ (N) will return of its own accord. Moral: A _____ (N) who has been _____ (V) by a _____ (N) will _____ (V) it forever.

Same Script, Different Solutions

Have the whole group write one script, then divide Players into teams to fill in the blanks and perform. Players will enjoy hearing and seeing different perspectives.

Character Biographies

The following structure can lead to a biography of a character.

I am _____ .
　　　　　Name

(Create a sound and movement to go with this name.)

This is what I can do _____ .
　　　　　　　　　　Power

(Describe your special strength, trick, or magic power.)

I have a big problem: _____ .
　　　　　　　　　　Problem

(Describe your problem.)

I can solve it by _____ .
　　　　　　　　　Solution

(Give your solution to the problem.)

However, there's a new problem: _____ !
　New Problem

(Describe the new problem.)

Note: This devising of new problems and solutions can go on, problem after problem.

 Teaching Notes

Management Tips

Present Scripts If your time is limited, or if you have a specific type of script in mind, you can provide Players with a formula fill-in-the-blank script. The script can be set up to provide parts equaling the number of performers in the group and to work with limitations of place, time, and subject.

Collaborations Arrange to involve other teachers in the project. Have each class write fill-in-the-blank scripts. Classes exchange and then solve and perform the scripts for one another.

Connections

Language Arts Fill in the Blanks provides an amusing way to learn language skills. It can be used to teach the parts of speech; to practice using and answering journalistic questions—*Who? What? Where? When? Why?* and *How?*—and to teach how to better communicate the main ideas of a topic.

History/Social Studies Set up a fill-in-the-blanks script that requires students to fill in names, dates, places, and people in a specific topic of study. This exercise could be used as a research project, a review of material learned in class, or as an exam.

Special Needs

For Players who are sight impaired, provide text in Braille, or assign a student helper to read the script to them and record their answers.

 Assessment

Teacher Observations

- Were Players able to fill in missing details in fill-in-the-blanks scripts? Did they follow directions to do so?
- Were Players able to work collaboratively to write a fill-in-the-blanks script?

Group Discussion

Have Players discuss ways in which a fill-in-the-blanks script could be written for a performance.

- What kind of script plot would you choose?
- What kinds of information would you ask for in the blanks?
- Who would fill in the blanks? How?
- What details would you set, and what would you improvise?

Student Activities

Book

pages 66–68 (Writing Model)

Journal

Ask Players to create a fill-in-the-blanks story to share with the class.

Scenarios

A *scenario* is a plot outline or summary of actions for a vignette or entire play; the terms *skeleton plot* and *treatment* are synonyms, although treatment can infer a more extended synopsis that is used in film and television scriptwriting. Scenarios generally contain no dialogue and are improvised by an ensemble of actors. (See Background Notes for more information about scenarios.)

There are basically two steps for working with scenarios: writing a scenario, and creating the performance through improvisation. This lesson offers many different structures to create scenarios that can be improvised into scenes. It is also possible to use scenarios to make full scripts. If you intend to do this, be sure to record or take notes on the workshop improvisations, highlighting actions and dialogue that worked in the scene.

Scenarios offer opportunities for participants to contribute in a variety of ways. They can function as writers, actors, directors, technicians, or designers. They can also document script development by recording, editing, and revising the script as it evolves.

★ Directions

1. Decide how to organize your group to write the scenarios and then to improvise on them. Scenarios can be individual writing assignments, or they can be written by teams or the whole group. The project could be one scenario that everybody works on; either each team finds its own solution or the whole group finds a solution. Or each team could write its own scenario and perform it. Or teams could exchange scenarios to perform.

2. Select a scenario format from the following list.

List of Actions or Events To begin the skit, provide or ask Players to provide a first sentence that states an action or event. Then have Players list four to ten steps that move the scene to its end.

For example: *He/She slammed the door quickly.*

Example: The following ten-step scenario was written by an eighth-grader.

1. Several children find a bright shiny object.

2. Children argue about what it is. A younger one wants to tell parents; older one threatens the kid; one suggests they hide it; one thinks that because it doesn't do anything it is broken.

3. Two pick up object arguing over who should take it.

4. Drop object while arguing, and it breaks open.

5. Find small alien animal inside looking sick.

6. Children spend next few days nursing it back to health.

7. Children consider "it" as a friend/pet/family member.

8. Alien disappears.

9. Youngest tells parents whole story.

10. Parents cannot understand why children would lie like that.

(When Players improvised this scenario, the Alien was a film canister that happened to be in the room. Players added another step to the scenario: they became "infected" into aliens whenever they put their finger inside the canister.)

Skills

★ Writing an original scenario (plot outline) for a short play
★ Improvising on a scenario structure in performance
★ Directing a performance of a scenario

Time

This activity could take place in a series of sessions of at least 30 minutes. The first session could be used to introduce scenario form, or to present an existing text that will be the basis of a scenario project. In following sessions, the group could write their scenarios, experiment with improvisation solutions, and perform for one another.

Space

Adaptable to any space

Materials

Writing materials. Costumes, hand props, set pieces, and music can be added to enhance the performance.

Open-ended Group Treatments The group writes a treatment by setting up a situation in eight to fifteen steps, leaving the ending open to be solved during improvisation. (This format could be done as a mystery. All teams are given the same circumstances, then each team is asked to solve the mystery through improvisation.)

Beginning and Ending Ask Players to suggest a first and last sentence that state actions to begin and end a skit. Have the group improvise the middle.

Scene-by-Scene Summaries In paragraph form, Players summarize the *Who, What, Where, When, Why,* and *How.* They may include any important props, costumes, and music, and possibly some crucial lines of dialogue.

Plot Summary Players write a one-paragraph summary of the plot.

Example:

One socially elite family gives a masked costume ball. Among the party guests is the son of another socially elite family, enemies of the host family. The host's daughter and the enemy's son meet while dancing and fall in love. Confrontations arise. Factions form. The party breaks up, and later that night, the couple meets secretly and pledges to marry. They secretly marry. The family feud continues. The groom is exiled. To avoid marrying her parents' choice of a husband, the bride appears to die. The groom returns and, believing his bride to be dead, kills himself. Will the bride join her husband in death? Will the families continue to sacrifice their children, or reconcile their differences?

Specific Real-life Subject Plot Players choose a specific subject and outline a plot based on that subject. They then improvise dialogue and actions for that plot. The plot could be based on historical events, current events, or topical subjects.

Adapt Existing Literature Players write a skeleton plot based on the text of a myth, novel, short story, play, opera, or fairy tale. They improvise dialogue and actions in performance. The plot could be performed in the spirit of the original text, or it could be changed. For example, a tragedy could become a comedy, a story could be presented from a different character's point of view, or the whole work could be looked at from a contemporary viewpoint. When a fairy tale is told from the performers' viewpoint, in a modern telling of the tale, it is referred to as a *fractured fairy tale.*

You could also give Players a scenario of a well-known story or play without disclosing the name of the original story, and see if they can figure out its source.

Example 1:
Ask Players to guess the source of the following scenario (*The Ugly Duckling*).

A newcomer is shunned and teased by the group because they think that he/she looks and sounds different. Newcomer learns to be alone, separate from the group. As time passes, newcomer's appearance and vocal sounds change, so that it is clear to the newcomer that he/she really is different from this group. By chance, he/she finds a group like her/himself. Does he/she join this new group?

Example 2:
La Quida, an eight-step scenario in list form, written by tenth-graders. This is a contemporary treatment of *Cinderella.*

1. Once upon a time there was a house in the middle of a ghetto.

2. There was a fine girl who lived in it and she had an ugly step-mama and two ugly stepsisters.

3. Her stepmom made her serve her.

4. One day she went out to the mall and met a guy who was having a house party and he asked her to go to the party.

5. She snuck out and went to the party and lost her Fila shoe.

6. Da (sic) Player drove her home in his '64 Impala. His hydraulics accidentally shot her out the window.

7. Prince José Charming came on his low-rider bicycle and picked her up.

8. She got on the handlebars, they rode into the sunset, and lived happily ever after.

Example 3:
This scenario, written by a ninth-grade student, is a fractured fairy tale, *The Three Bears,* told from the Bears' point of view.

1. Goldie goes on nature walk.

2. Three Bears are out looking for food because they are hungry.

3. Bears sneak into Goldie's house.

4. Bears eat all of Goldie's food.

5. Bears break Goldie's chairs and bed.

6. Goldie comes home, notices broken chairs, and screams.

7. Bears hear scream and come downstairs to Goldie.

8. Goldie gets scared by Bears and runs off.

9. Bears go back to sleep.

Select Characters Ask each performer to chose a character *(Who)*, which could be a stock character. Players improvise together, in character, to find the plot's *What, When, Where,* and *How.*

Enter/Exit Scenario List entrances and exits of characters in order. Establish time and place for each entrance and exit, and characters' actions and motivations. You could also include in the scenario a prop list and a few lines of important dialogue.

Storyboard Scenario Sequence a series of visual images, showing the events of the scenario. Images could be drawings (stick figures are fine) or cutouts of picture tracings or copies.

3. Allow Players time to experiment with their scenarios by improvising on the structures.

4. Have Players perform their scenario improvisations for one another.

5. Record the improvisations in writing or on videotape or audiotape. These recordings can serve as the basis for future development of the improvisations if you wish for Players to turn them into more ambitious improvisation projects or to write a complete performance script from the scenario and improvisations.

★ Teaching Notes

Management Tips

Time Constraints Decide how much time you want to allow for this assignment. If your time is limited, do not ask each Player to write a scenario, since it will take a lot of time to perform each one. Instead, have Players work in teams or as a group to write and improvise on the scenarios.

Choosing a Director Allow the group or each team to choose their director, who may or may not perform. If that director proves to be ineffective, Players can choose to replace him.

Different Directors/Same Scenario Have different people direct the same scenario. Ask Players to discuss differences in directors' interpretations and leadership style.

Connections

Technology Encourage Players to explore the capabilities of electronic media in storyboard format. Add music, sound effects, and special effects for a multimedia production.

Language Arts Turn the study of required literature into experiential learning by having students adapt it into scenario format and an improvised performance. Ask students to research the historical or cultural background of the text to better understand the literature being performed.

Social Studies Have students research the cultural and historical background of a period and create scenarios consistent with their research.

• Outline the important moments of a historical event. Choose characters and improvise dialogue and actions. Dialogue could be based upon actual quotes. (See Living History, page 101.)

- Ask Players to select a newspaper article and write a skeleton plot based on the events in the article. Assign parts, including any characters in the story, and a reporter or commentator on the action. Players should improvise dialogue and actions. (Players can include direct quotations, headlines, or any other information in their performance, including photographs.)

Special Needs

Use the storyboard technique to make scenarios with students who have reading or writing problems. This could be done in cartoon or comic book form. Words connected to the images could be added to facilitate reading and writing skills.

Background Notes

The term *scenario* comes originally from the skeleton plots used by actors in the Italian commedia dell'arte (1550–1750) to improvise dialogue in comedies rather than perform set scripts. There were hundreds of scenarios but, as they were not intended as literature, most have disappeared. All that was generally written down was the plot outline, the cast of characters, some stage directions, a prop list, and maybe a few set lines of dialogue.

In the early commedia dell'arte, scenarios took the form of charts that were used by the prompter to keep a list of properties and cues for actors' entrances and exits. Later, scenarios also became scene-by-scene summaries of the action, which were posted backstage to be used by the actors as a memory aid. These charts and summaries served as the jumping off place for the actors' onstage improvisations.

The actors had no rehearsals; they came onstage, following their list of entrance cues, and performed through improvisation. They knew how to cue the beginnings and endings of scenes or topics, had stock business and stock

dialogues to work into or out of any situation, and relied upon traditional gestures and costumes the audience would identify with each stock character.

Commedia utilized many popular plot devices that are recognizable today because they carried over into the plays of Shakespeare, Lope de Vega, and Molière. Such plot devices included mistaken identity; a young woman dressing as a man; disguised characters; young characters who discover they are related and royalty; friends torn between love and loyalty; lovers posing as servants and vice versa, often to save them from marrying a rich, old person; the servant who is smarter than the master; and the use of twins or multiple twins.

Assessment

Teacher Observations

- Did Players write scenarios in which the action progressed from a beginning to an ending?

- Were Players able to interpret and dramatize a scenario?

- Were Players able to improvise and perform scenes based on a plot outline?

- Were Players able to use their voices and bodies expressively to bring characters and situations to life?

- Did Players demonstrate that they have acquired basic acting techniques?

Group Discussion

Discuss with your students how treatments and scenarios are used in film, video, and television today. Check *TV Guide* for a source list of scenarios and stock characters of sitcoms at the beginning of each fall season. Magazines and newspapers regularly publish soap opera plots, and they can be used as other references for this discussion.

Student Activities

Book

pages 69–70 (Writing Models)

Journal

Ask Players to write a soap opera plot scenario.

Scriptwriting Model

In the business of television writing today, treatments are the standard format for the first development stage of a pilot project. Once a project is approved, a script is written based on this initial treatment. The following process can be adapted to the making of any script that begins as a scenario or treatment.

Creating a Scenario

Writer Ishmael Reed worked with a group of middle and high school students in Berkeley, California, to create a one-act play. First he read and discussed an African animal folktale with the group. Together, they devised the following scenario/treatment in plot summary form, centered around a main character and an event.

> Poppa Buzzard (the main character) decides to invite all the animals in the forest to a potluck dinner to celebrate the ending of death (the event). The guests do not know that Poppa Buzzard intends to make them his meal. Once they realize his intention, the other animals have to find a way to save themselves.

Initial Scriptwriting

This scenario became the basis for a performance script. To make the script, each student was asked to choose an animal character to play in the scenario. During the initial scriptwriting phase of the project, students were given four writing assignments. Each assignment was to be written in first person, from the point of view of the animal character.

Assignment 1 Write a monologue that will introduce your animal character. State your character's name and describe your power, reveal what your character thinks about Poppa Buzzard's invitation, and tell what food you will bring if you do attend the potluck.

Assignment 2 Describe why (motivation) your character will participate in the potluck.

Assignment 3 State a problem your character has with some other character at the event, your fears of the event, and why.

Assignment 4 Describe the most unforgettable incident in the life of your character.

Improvising, Developing the Plot

Assignments 1 and 4 became monologues that were inserted into the script. Assignments 2 and 3 were used as the basis for improvisations of actions and further dialogue that took place. For example, in the potluck scene, all the characters improvised dialogue and action based on their characters' choices of alignments and conflicts with other characters. They also discussed what they thought about the potluck food and Poppa Buzzard. At the dinner table, conversation moved between this improvisational material and monologues about each character's most unforgettable incident (Assignment 4).

Details of plot development went through many revisions as the Players noticed inconsistencies and found new business. As the group began to better understand who they were and what their relationship was to the event and one another, the problems of plot were solved.

This was the final version of the skeleton plot.

- Poppa Buzzard sends letters to all the animals in the forest, inviting them to come to his potluck dinner to celebrate the ending of death.
- With his henchmen, Turkey and Crow, he intends to kill the invited animals, to make his own dinner.
- Animals discover Poppa Buzzard's plot.
- Animals save themselves by tricking Poppa Buzzard.
- Animals force Poppa Buzzard to take a vegetarian oath.
- Animals disperse, before Poppa Buzzard can go back on his oath.

Finalizing the Script

During rehearsals, the improvisations were recorded in writing. Some of the improvised lines were incorporated into the final script. This final cut-and-paste script included the skeleton plot, each character's original monologues, directions for improvised dialogues and actions, additional pieces of memorized dialogue written to smooth out the progress of the plot, and stage notes that indicated where improvisation was to occur as part of the performance.

Designing the Production

In performance, the production involved the use of taped music, animal masks, and costumes chosen from the participants' wardrobes. Actors used a few hand props, but most objects were indicated through pantomime. The set was minimal and used existing objects that were available in the performing space. A table, covered with an oil cloth, was transformed into an oven by reversing its cloth to reveal a hand-painted oven. No chairs were used, so the animals knelt around the table. A rug completed the stage picture.

Choosing a Performing Space

This piece needed an intimate setting. Fortunately, a room in the school with stained glass windows, wrought iron casements and chandelier, arched corners, and a marble fireplace was available. The grand manner style of the room cast an appropriate mood for Poppa Buzzard's feast. The audience sat on either side of the performing area, a setup popular in medieval and renaissance theaters.

Living History

To play Living History, each student writes and performs a monologue based on the life of a particular person. Living History offers an opportunity to help students actively participate in studies of people from the present or past. By combining research with a performance, students learn more about their subject and feel more involved with the learning process. The familiar tasks of reading and writing take on an importance and immediacy when the student actually becomes the person she has studied. Living History projects can be individual or team assignments. They are applicable to language arts, social studies, science, and history classes.

 Directions

1. Ask each Player to choose a person to become in a monologue performance. Depending on your objectives, the chosen person can be any of the following.

- A historical character who is either an actual, famous person or a fictional, anonymous person who can represent a time or event

- A family member or friend, either living or deceased

- An imaginary person from another place and/or time

2. Assign Players to research their chosen person. Share these directions with them.

- If a person is deceased or if for some reason it is not possible to interview him or her, gather information through research using books, film, newspapers, and other communication media. If possible, interview someone who knew the person or lived during the time of that person's life.

- If the person is living, and available, set up an in-person or a telephone interview.

  – Prepare interview questions ahead of time.

  – Interview the individual.

  – Take notes and/or tape record the information.

3. Have each Player use information he gathered during his research to write a monologue about the character that he will later deliver in front of the group, taking the part of the character. (See the assignment on pages 71–72 of the Student Book.) Following are some directions for writing the monologues. You may wish to write them on the board or copy them in a handout.

- Monologues should be written and spoken in first person; the character is speaking.

- Portray an event or a moment in time from the life of the chosen character.

- Consider the character's point of view. What is the character's age at the time of the event? How does the character feel about the event?

- Choose whether the person is talking in the past, present, or future tense in her relationship to this event or moment of her life.

Skills

★ Researching a chosen person through a variety of print materials, other media, and interviews

★ Writing a monologue about the chosen person

★ Preparing to become the chosen person by exploring and selecting details of appearance, movement, and manner of speaking

★ Performing, observing, and evaluating living history monologues

Time

This is a project that could take several sessions. Allow 30 minutes to an hour in the first session, during which time you can teach students how to research and gather information about their characters. One hour or more in succeeding sessions might be needed to improvise and refine

characterization (this could be a take home assignment) and to share performances.

Space

As a monologue or dialogue, adaptable to any space. As a living history play, a suitable performing area should be chosen.

Materials

Ask Players to provide their own tools for research, such as tape recorders with microphone for interviewing, library books, and writing materials. For performances, you may require students to provide a hand prop or indication of costume to create the look and setting of the character. A living history play can easily become an elaborate extravaganza with set and costume possibilities.

- **Present Tense** Character is speaking at the moment of the event or during the event.

   Scientist: "I can hear your voice, Dr. Watson."

   Explorer: "I am on the moon. I can see Earth."

   Politician: "I am fighting to make the world safe for democracy."

- **Past Tense** Character is speaking after the event has happened.

   Scientist: "I won the battle against the polio virus."

   Explorer: "I found the Northwest Territory."

   Politician: "I helped women get the right to vote."

- **Future Tense** Character is speaking before the event has happened. The character might be hoping for, dreaming about, or fearing the future event.

   Scientist: "I will try to find the vaccine that will end polio forever."

   Explorer: "What will happen if I fall off the edge of the earth?"

   Politician: "I believe that all people are created equal and should have equal rights."

- Whenever possible use words the person actually wrote or spoke about this event or moment. When this is not possible, make up what you think he or she might have said in this event or moment.

4. Allow Players time to prepare for a performance of their monologues. Explain that each Player will become the person (character) she has researched, incorporating details of her subject's gestures, style, and manner of speaking. Suggest that Players might want to use a hand prop and/or indication of costume to help create the look and setting of their characters. (Assembling, preparing, and using props and costumes helps performers to focus on their characters.)

5. Have Players share their monologues with the group.

Variations

Dialogues Have partners write and perform dialogues by pairing up various characters.

Examples:
- Two Benjamin Franklins of different ages converse.
- Stephen Douglas debates Abraham Lincoln.

Living History Plays Have the whole group work together to research a particular time in history or group of people. The research should be divided among Players. Collate and organize the research into script form. The resulting play becomes a living history of this group of people or time, with the whole class participating as characters in the drama.

 Teaching Notes

Management Tips

Content of Interview Questions
Students may need help with learning how to do research and ask interview questions that will glean enough information to form a characterization. Tell them to think about the interview in terms of what is important in their own lives, for example, important milestones; personal style (gestures, ways of moving, speaking, and dressing); interests, hobbies, talents, beliefs; family ties; favorite music, foods, or reading materials.

Performing Monologues
Monologues and dialogues can be delivered with script in hand, or from memory. This will depend upon the level of commitment you want to give to performance. It can be as simple or as complicated as you like.

Connections

Social Studies/History

- **Mock Trial** Players learn the jobs and take the roles of lawyers, witnesses, jurors, judges, reporters, and defendants. They choose a real or imaginary event to make the basis of a trial.

   Example:
   One Syracuse, New York, middle school class staged State v. Dorothy Gale. Dorothy Gale was put on trial for killing two witches in Oz. Witnesses from the Land of Oz took the stand. Her defense: "The Wizard made me do it."

- **Mock Election** Players stage an election. They could base their performance and take their roles from a current local or national campaign, or make up an imaginary situation. They could follow the process from the primary level to the inauguration ceremony for the winner.

- **Historical Recreations** After doing the appropriate research, students recreate a famous event or time.

   Examples:
   - Salem, Massachusetts, witch trials
   - 1960s Civil Rights sit-ins
   - The forced migration of the Cherokee Indians along the Trail of Tears

Special Needs

Allow Players with speech problems or language problems to solve the characterization performance using pantomime.

Assessment

Teacher Observations

- Were Players able to use their research to write about their characters?

- Did Players understand how to use past, present, and future tense? Did they apply this information to their performances?

- Could Players interpret their characters dramatically using basic acting skills and expressive use of body and voice?

- Were Players able to create original dialogue for their characters?

Group Discussion

Discuss what Players learned about their characters by planning and performing a monologue. How did they like learning about characters by watching living performances, rather than reading or hearing about the characters?

Student Activities

Book

pages 71–72 (Writing Model)

pages 73–74 (Background Reading)

Journal

Ask Players to imagine the life of a relative, real or imaginary, from three or four generations past. Have each Player write a monologue about some part of that relative's life. Remind Players to decide if they will write about the present, past, or future in their relative's lives.

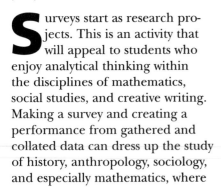

Surveys

Surveys start as research projects. This is an activity that will appeal to students who enjoy analytical thinking within the disciplines of mathematics, social studies, and creative writing. Making a survey and creating a performance from gathered and collated data can dress up the study of history, anthropology, sociology, and especially mathematics, where students are learning to make graphs, figure percentages, and compile statistics.

Skills

★ Selecting a survey topic, format, and targeted population
★ Writing survey questions
★ Collecting and collating responses to a survey
★ Writing a script based on survey responses
★ Planning, rehearsing, and performing a production of a survey script

Time

Allow for several sessions that last from 30 minutes to an hour. A survey project could take anywhere from one to several weeks, beginning with the formulation of survey questions and ending with a performance based, at least in part, on the information obtained from the survey.

Space

Adaptable to any space

Materials

Writing materials to make the survey questionnaire and record data. Audio or videotape recording equipment would be useful during interviews. Props, stage sets, costumes, lights, and musical instruments or tapes can be added later if the Director and Players decide to develop the survey information into a performance.

★ Directions

1. Decide whether you want the survey to be done individually or as a group research project. Have the group (or each individual) select the type of survey they wish to conduct. Following are some suggestions.

Factual, personal information that can be quantified

• Age/birth date
• Family position
• Schools attended/grade level achieved
• Jobs held
• Number of places lived in
• Places visited/traveled
• Ways to relax
• Pets

Personal beliefs and feelings

• Likes/dislikes
• My favorite _____
• Wishes/hopes
• Qualities of a friend/enemy
• What makes an adult/child
• What makes me angry/happy
• I spend my money on _____

Opinions on current topics of interest

• Drugs
• War/peace
• Sexuality
• Homework/office work
• Old age
• Money/wealth
• Politics
• Health care

2. Help the group choose a targeted population, which could be based on a specific age, job, school, community, or interest group.

3. Ask Players to write questions to accumulate data. The questions could be written as a handout or questionnaire, which is to be completed by the targeted population, or in the form of interview questions.

4. Direct Players to collect data. Responses can be gathered through individual interviews or filled in directly on a questionnaire. Audio or video equipment can also be used to record data. If surveys are conducted within the classroom, answers can be logged on the blackboard or recorded by each individual.

5. Help the group collate the responses, using the method most appropriate to the data: making line or bar graphs, figuring percentages, or simply listing answers.

6. Work with the group to develop a script from the collated data. Order the data, then set up a structure that unifies the information. For structures, try setting the information into the form of a poem, news report, advertisement jingle, editorial essay, rap, or song.

7. Guide the Players through rehearsal and performance of their script. The script may be performed as dialogue or monologue; be spoken or sung in chorus; or be used as a background sound environment to accompany visual images, dances, or shadow plays.

Performance Suggestions

Following are three examples of how students turned their survey data into a performance.

Example 1:
Students surveyed daily-life school events and recorded them in video news magazine format, as though they were the world events of that day. Station identification and advertisements (related to a consumer products question on their survey) of imaginary products important to the performers were interspersed between the news items. (This method would work equally well as a radio broadcast or in live performance.)

Example 2:
Working with a math teacher, a statistical analysis of the student population at a girls' school in California was developed. The data gathered concerned the students' and their families' histories, work choices, educational experiences, and living patterns. The collated information became part of a script that was spoken by a chorus and accompanied by a shadow play about the immigration history of California women. Parts of the performance became very humorous when spoken text about the number and type of pets, ways of spending time and money, and future plans of the entire student body was juxtaposed against shadow images of film goddesses, working women, and daily-life activities of present-day California women.

Example 3:
Students made lists of their likes and dislikes on the subjects of foods, sports, animals, ways to relax, and their wishes for the future. The teacher collated the information and set it into a rhyming rhythm structure which the students chanted as they danced. Following are a few verses of the script:

Chorus

So so so so so said all the girls

So so so so so said all the boys

Dancing in the school

Learning by the rules

Sooooooooooo.........

I like rock-n-roll radio, movies and TV (repeat 3 times)

So show me Karate Kid, The Jedi, The Dark Crystal and E.T.

Chorus (repeat)

I hate dishwashing, bedtime, cleaning my room, and sewing

Poison ivy, blood, volcanoes, hospitals, and dying

Seafood, pig feet, eggplant, peas, parsley, and bacon

Madonna, Michael Jackson, The Beach Boys, and Voltron

Chorus (repeat)

I like my family, my friends, Fat Boys, Fly Girls

Holidays and birthdays, vacations, and curls

I like the day better than the night

I like to learn about the world and life

Chorus (repeat)

 Teaching Notes

Management Tips

Devising Surveys With students, discuss the kinds of information they could use for a performance script, and the type of survey that would generate this information. Allow Players to decide what questions to ask and how to ask them. In order to make collating the answers easier, figure out a survey format that students can easily use, such as fill-in-the-blanks, or questionnaires containing enough space for answers to be written on the form.

Publishing Survey Results If the survey is related to the school community or would be of interest to them, publish the results of the survey in the school paper. If it is used as part of a performance script, include it in the program handed out to the audience.

Interdisciplinary Collaboration Arrange to involve math, social science and language arts teachers in the project. The social studies classes can design the questionnaire and conduct the interviews or decide how to collate the data on survey forms; the math classes can decide how to represent the answers in percentages, fractions, and graphs; and the language arts classes can use the data to write the scripts.

Connections

Mathematics Total the answers; decide how they can be categorized to compute responses into percentages or fractions for each category; analyze percentages or fractions by grade, gender, positive or negative response, or any other way you would like to do it. Present this data in a graph or in another organized format.

Social Studies Suggest survey questions and format the questions for discovering responses based on cultural, gender, or age-related issues. Classes can design the questionnaire, conduct the interviews, and decide how to collate the data on survey forms.

Language Arts Could be used to learn interviewing techniques and to practice communication skills. Study the questionnaire answers together, to think about how to use them for script purposes. Students can then divide the information according to categories, to facilitate organizing the information they want.

Special Needs

Use Braille and interpreters to include sight and hearing disabled students in the data collection and interviewing process.

 Assessment

Teacher Observations

- Were students able to collaborate to choose a survey topic, format, and target population and to write survey questions?
- Did students follow through by gathering survey responses and collating them in a useful format?
- Were students able to plan and write a performance script with minimal help?
- Did the final script/performance show an understanding of the survey material and the production process?
- Did students address production and design elements when planning for performance? How elaborate were the final results?

Group Discussion

Ask students to discuss the following question: How did this activity illustrate the idea that theater is a reflection of life in particular times, places, and cultures?

 Student Activities

Book

pages 75–76 (Writing Model)

Journal

Ask Players to describe a survey topic they would like to develop into a performance script.

Survey Model

This script was developed as a coda to a production of *Our Town*, a three-act play by Thornton Wilder about the lives of people in a small New England town around 1911. The coda was added to update the material, and to tell the audience how the performers felt about their lives in a northern California town of the 1990s. In order to write the script, students surveyed the student body at their high school. Some of the survey questions became part of the coda.

Stage Manager (narrator): And the survey asks, "Who are you?"

(offstage voice answers): I don't know

  : I am the person answering this question

  : a friend

  : Superman (don't tell anyone)

  : no one special

  (and so on)

(actor enters): You probably know who I am by now.

Stage Manager: *(continues reading the questionnaire)* What/who were you in your past life?

(Two actors enter and, standing back to back, say the following)

  : a bad child

  : Probably some traveler. I absolutely love to travel.

  : I was the Ugly Duckling.

  : I was a woman who struggled for 60 years.

  : I was an Egyptian prince.

  (and so on)

Stage Manager: *(Continues reading)* What is your outlook on life?

(Three speakers)

  : Life is nothing till you die.

  : Life is pretty cool. Sometimes it's a drag, though.

  : Don't worry too much.

  : Live for today.

  : It's hard. I just plow through.

  : Hard, but amazing to be in!

  (and so on)

Stage Manager: *(Continues reading)* What do you hate?

(Four speakers enter USC and walk DS on their first line, and sit together in a clump)

  : I hate questions.

  : I hate stupid people who do certain activities to impress other people; or people who feel sorry for themselves.

  : Greed

  : Racism

: I hate nothing and no one. I believe you should give all things great and small a chance to improve.

All: Not

: Whale killing

: Heavy metal

: School

: Homework

: Those little crusty things on your eyes when you wake up after you have slept

(and so on)

(Speakers exit DSR and DSL)

Stage Manager: *(Continues reading)* What issues are important to you?

: My life is important to me.

: Sports

: Peace, love, friends

: Makin' money and being employed

: Equality in every sense

: AIDS

: The homeless

(and so on)

Stage Manager: *(continues reading)* What do you look for in friends?

(Four performers enter to CS, and fool around with each other, in a friendly way)

: Hugs

: People who don't judge unnecessarily and are easy to talk to

: I like to be able to trust people. I feel comfortable knowing that they won't lie or steal from me.

: A true friendship

: Nothing really

Stage Manager: *(Continues reading)* How do you see yourself ten years from now?

(All performers enter from DSL wing and cross to DSR, where they join each other, cheering each other on or commiserating, as appropriate to the prediction)

: 10 years older

: A beach bum

: Living in New York, on stage eight times a week

: With a job I enjoy

(and so on)

Stage Manager: Thank you, ladies and gentlemen, thank you, scholars.
(Then the play went back into the Stage Manager's closing speech of Our Town.*)*

Scores

Artists are always looking for new ways to work with materials and to free themselves to think of new and different relationships to their art. Harold Rosenberg, art critic and poet, called this the "tradition of the new."

Performance artists frequently break out of the confines of any one performing form—such as dance, music, theater, or poetry—to work in multidisciplinary ways. In doing so, they also need to find innovative methods to record their ideas for rehearsal and

archival purposes. Scholars and artists began referring to these new recording systems as scores.

A *score* is a structure, an arrangement, or a recording system for a series of actions to be performed.
Scores can take many forms: a scenario; a series of
dance or mime actions that are recorded in a shorthand of symbols or descriptive words; a collection of
photos, drawings, or words; a series of verbal cues, or
rules; a map; and so on. Similar in function to a
musical score, which is read by a group of musicians
so that they can play together, a performance score,
which is read and interpreted by performers, provides directions and guidance for what to do or how
to approach an idea.

At the core of every performing project is structure. Scores are like safety nets; they allow experimentation while providing a certain amount of organization for the creative process. In the same way
that a skeleton supports the body, a score supports
the ideas the performers want to communicate.

Examples:
- A score indicates that performers are to move
  from points A to B to C to D. Performers improvise the details of how they move to each point.
- A score shows a map of a circular path, a rectan-
  gular path, and a zigzag path. Performers follow

the map, improvising details, such as type of
movement used and the order in which they
follow the various paths.
- A score consists of a series of photographic
  images. Performers decide whether and how to
  imitate, animate, or react to the photos.

Different systems of scoring offer built-in possibilities for improvisation. They may be either open or
predetermined. *Open improvisations* are spontaneous
performances without preplanning. Everything is
performed differently every time the score is read.
Predetermined improvisations entail a rehearsed performance structure. During the course of rehearsals,
the performers agree to an order of rules or actions
upon which the improvisation is built. Details remain
open to change.

Horse Ballet, Traveling Lines, Clock Pattern,
Compass Points, and Gifts contain ideas for scores
to structure various elements, including movement,
text, and spatial design, in playful formats. The
activities Cut and Paste, Living Pictures, and Live
Movie suggest ways to assemble materials into
scores. They offer fresh ways to approach creative
problem solving.

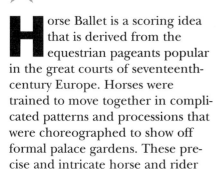

Horse Ballet

Horse Ballet is a scoring idea that is derived from the equestrian pageants popular in the great courts of seventeenth-century Europe. Horses were trained to move together in complicated patterns and processions that were choreographed to show off formal palace gardens. These precise and intricate horse and rider

spectacles survive today in the famous displays of the Royal Lippizaners of Austria and the Royal Canadian Mounted Police.

As in the historical model, Players will make a horse ballet by designing and sequencing their own series of changing floor patterns, formations, routes, and actions. This will be the score they perform in teams or as a whole group.

★ Directions

The following directions are flexible; you may want to rearrange the sequence of these suggestions to better fit your resources, time, and the needs of your group.

1. Introduce your group to the historical background and diagrams of standard patterns of horse ballets. (See diagrams, next page, and Background Notes.) Explain that they are going to make their own version of a horse ballet by designing floor patterns and choosing actions and sounds to perform while moving through the patterns.

2. Organize Players into teams. Direct each team to select a floor pattern, an action, and a sound (optional). Following are some ideas that you may wish to share with the teams.

- **Floor Patterns** Borrow from the classic horse ballet patterns: cloverleaf, spirals, serpentines, squares, triangles, parallel lines, figure eight, stars. Or make up your own.

- **Actions** Use any locomotor: walking, running, hopping, leaping, jumping, skipping, or galloping. Or choreograph your own phrases of movement combination.

- **Sounds** Talking, singing, clapping, playing percussion or other musical instruments

3. Give teams time to rehearse their ideas for floor patterns or figures and locomotor actions. Then have them show their ideas to the whole group.

4. Have the whole group devise a method to record these ideas. After they have recorded each team's ideas, have them create a score in which they determine the sequence of the floor patterns and combine all of the teams' floor patterns and actions into one horse ballet. Tell them to record the score by using diagrams and/or lists of names for each formation and action.

5. Have Players decide how to perform their horse ballet score. To do this, they must determine the sequence of floor patterns, transitional routes between figures, and how teams perform.

- Teams perform the sequence of floor patterns one after the other, following the same route.

- Teams perform simultaneously, each starting from a different beginning point. The score should indicate how each team follows its own route.

Skills

★ Designing floor patterns and choreographing actions

★ Developing spatial awareness and body control

★ Recording formations and actions in a score

★ Deciding how to perform a movement score

★ Learning about the history of horse ballets and exploring how their formations and pageantry are still used in current entertainments

Time

Horse Ballet will take at least one hour-long session to introduce the concept and have teams design a floor pattern and an action. It will take another session or two for the group to combine the teams' ideas into a single score and to decide how to perform the score. If you plan to perform Horse Ballet for an audience, it may well take additional sessions to rehearse the formations.

Space

Adaptable to any large, open space

Materials

A sound environment may be added.

Horse Ballet Formations

Dome 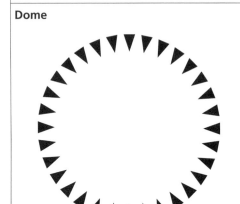	**Cloverleaf** 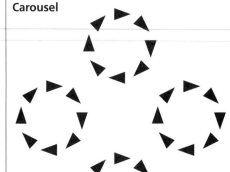	**The X** 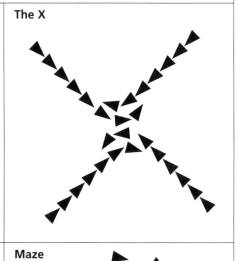
Diamond 	**Carousel**	**Maze** 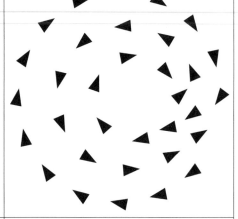

Variations

Tempo Change the tempo within a formation, such as going from fast to slow, or slow to fast.

Follow the Leader Rather than preset the action to be done in each formation, have Players select a Leader, who makes movement choices that everyone imitates.

Reverse Players reverse the order in which they perform the formations.

Interweaving Lines Ask teams to figure out how to cross through other teams. One way is to always pass right shoulders, as in square dancing; another is to always pass upstage.

Team Scores Each team makes up its own score. Teams can perform their own scores, or exchange scores to perform.

★ Teaching Notes

Management Tips

Warm-up Game Have Players practice walking a large figure-eight floor pattern, filling up the entire space. Start by asking Players to stand so that, as a group, they form a figure-eight shape. Their task is to maintain the shape as they walk, making sure that only one person is crossing the center at any one time. Once Players have become adept at walking at a normal pace, ask them to speed up or slow down while still maintaining the figure-eight formation.

Choosing Patterns The environment of the performing space might predetermine the appropriate floor patterns, for example, a gymnasium floor with basketball markings, a Louis XIV-style formal garden, or a shopping mall.

Team Size The number and size of teams can vary according to the size of the performing space, the amount of rehearsal time you have, and the willingness of your group to practice teamwork. If teams are small, it's easier to maintain focus and to stay together.

Rehearsal To do a horse ballet, the performers will need to drill the routines many times in order to perfect the patterns. Remind Players about the amount of rehearsal time that cheerleaders and marching bands have to put into their routines to make them clean and sharp.

Focus Players need to be aware of one another in order to avoid collisions. They need to look ahead and not look at the floor, and to use their peripheral vision.

Color Coding The scores could include color-coded diagrams, so that Players can more easily visualize their routes, especially when they overlap. Teams could also wear color-coded costumes to differentiate them.

Connections

Mathematics Ask students to use different geometric patterns in their scores.

History Study the similarities, cultural significance, and functions of court pageant forms and architectural design in the European Renaissance palace styles. Compare these to Asian, African, or Latin American court ceremonial customs and palace architecture.

Special Needs

If students have trouble moving in unison, have them concentrate on maintaining the floor patterns, allowing them to solve how they do their actions individually.

Background Notes

Dressage, the guiding of a horse through a series of complex maneuvers involving turning, walking, and fancy stepping, is still used in horsemanship training today. The classic groupings of ballet dancers, the *corps de ballet,* are direct descendants of this equestrian form. Similar mass groupings and changes of floor pattern are used in the precision dancing formations of the Radio City Music Hall Rockettes, marching band and dance squad half-time events at football games, Busby Berkeley's movie musicals, and water ballets.

 Assessment

Teacher Observations

- Were Players able to work together in their teams to design a floor pattern and choreograph an action to perform while traveling through the pattern?

- Were Players able to devise a method to record their floor patterns and actions? Were they able to agree on a sequence of the floor patterns and actions to make a group performance score?

- Were Players able to design a score that utilized their space?

- Were Players able to create a performance based on their score? Were they able to vary details with each performance?

- Did Players understand how the formations of historical horse ballets have survived in present-day entertainments?

Group Discussion

Discuss with Players how horse ballet formations continue to influence popular entertainments of the twentieth century, such as marching band and cheerleader routines at football halftimes, parades at the Olympic Games, social dance floor patterns, and water ballet routines.

 Student Activities

Book

pages 77–78 (Overview)

pages 79–80 (Vocabulary)

pages 81–82 (Performance Model)

Journal

- Suggest that Players keep a log of interesting floor patterns and movement ideas for future performances.

- Encourage Players to create their own performance score for a Horse Ballet. (See Student Book, pages 81–82.)

Traveling Lines

Traveling Lines is a walking dance that celebrates the infinite variety of personal walking styles. It was inspired by choreographer Steve Paxton's score for *Satisfyin' Lover,* 1967. Anyone who can walk can play this game; it can also be played in wheelchairs. The Players travel through parallel channels, following a series of visual and timing cues, which are included in the score along with the spatial organization of the boundaries and channels.

★ Directions

1. Define the boundaries of a large, open playing area. Designate start and finish lines that provide for the longest possible playing distance. Tell Players to imagine that parallel

Skills

★ Learning, remembering, and following written or verbal cues
★ Judging spatial concepts such as distance and relative measurements
★ Maintaining awareness of relationship to others

Time

At least three 30-minute sessions: one to set the cues, one to practice, and one to perform and discuss

Space

Adaptable to any large, open space. A gymnasium, playing field or empty stage would be ideal.

Materials

None

channels run between the start and finish lines. Explain that Players will travel along these imaginary channels much like runners and swimmers race in parallel lanes.

2. Decide whether you want Players to work in solo, duet, or team configurations. Assign each Player, duet, or team a number and have them line up in numerical order on the start line. Each number is assigned an imaginary channel. Make sure Players know how wide their channels are.

3. Give each Player or team a set of verbal or written time and action cues that tell them when to begin and the manner in which they are to travel. Explain that it is essential for Players to pay attention to their cues because some of the cues are dependent on the movements of other soloists or teams.

Examples of timing and movement cues:
- Walk a straight line in your channel, across the performance space, without stopping.
- Assign one or more stops (pauses) between start and finish. For example, assign Players to walk across a fraction of the space (one-half, one-quarter, two-thirds), stop for a specific number of seconds, then continue walking to the finish.
- Cue Players to sit, stand, or kneel for a specified number of seconds during the stop.
- Set the beginning or stop cues in relation to another Player's stop position.

4. Tell Players that walking is the locomotor they will use to travel the parallel channels. Ask them to

begin and end in stillness. When you give the start signal, Players follow their preassigned cues. The game ends when all have reached the finish point.

Variations

Group Movement Have all Players perform the same set of time and movement cues, simultaneously.

Change of Pace Have players speed up or slow down the timing of the entire piece or parts of the piece so that the Players are walking in slow motion or running instead of walking at a normal pace.

Change of Locomotor Ask Players to use locomotors other than walking to perform their cues.

Traveling on Wheels If you are performing in an outdoor site, consider having all Players on wheels, using wheelchairs, skateboards, roller skates, roller blades, or bicycles.

Performance Suggestions

Preparation You may wish to decide ahead of time the number of channels and write out a cue sheet that lists time and action cues for a corresponding number of Players or teams. Each performer could be handed a copy of the cue sheet.

Setting Start and End Points

- Begin and/or end outside of the audience's view.
- Begin and/or end within the audience's view.

Varying the Cue Sequence

- The whole sequence of cues may be repeated more than once.

- Reverse the sequence of cues.
- Make a loop from the end point back to the beginning point again. The loop can occur outside of the boundaries of the playing area, or at the beginning and end of each channel.

Example of a Cued Sequence:

Player 1

1. Walk straight across the performing space from beginning to end without stopping.

2. Stand still until all Players have arrived at the finish line.

Player 2

1. Begin walking when Player 1 passes the halfway point of the performing space.

2. When you reach the three-fourths mark, sit for thirty seconds.

3. Continue walking to the finish line.

4. Stand still until all Players have arrived at the finish line.

Players 3 and 6

1. Begin walking when Player 1 crosses one-third of the performing space.

2. When you have crossed one-quarter of the performing space, stop and stand still for twenty seconds.

3. Continue walking. When you have crossed two-thirds of the performing space, stop and sit for fifteen seconds.

4. Continue walking to the finish line, then stand still until all Players have reached the finish line.

Players 4 and 5

1. Begin walking when Player 2 sits at the three-quarter point.

2. When you reach the halfway point of the performing space, kneel for fifteen seconds.

3. Continue walking to the finish line. Stand still until all Players have arrived at the finish line.

Teaching Notes

Management Tips

Setting Boundaries and Markers
Set the boundaries and markers of the performing area, so that everyone can identify the start, one-fourth, half, three-fourths, and finish points. Chairs, masking tape, or any other available material can serve this purpose. During rehearsals, it may be useful to place markers on these points. Or suggest Players find details in the space, such as marks on walls, windows, and doors to help identify and remember each fractional division in their cues.

Rehearsing It is helpful to have Players try out their cues on their own at first. Then have everyone rehearse together.

Sharing Space To manage a large group, divide Players into teams. Team Players share cues and can then move together, as a clump. Be sure to allow enough space in each channel to accommodate the teams.

In solos, duets, and trios, you could also stagger the cues to help with traffic control, so that only a few Players move at any one time.

Assigning Players You may want to give Players their team assignments. Put Players with leadership skills on each team, or create a buddy system so Players can help each other remember their cues.

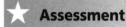 Assessment

Teacher Observations

- Were Players able to figure out and execute their cues?
- Were Players able to stay on task while working within a team? Were they able to cooperate?
- Could Players see the larger picture of several individuals or teams working together?

Group Discussion

Ask Players to discuss the ease or difficulty they experienced in putting the following skills into practice: remembering written cues, using other Players' movements as visual cues, maintaining a consistent time perspective, judging spatial distances.

Student Activities

Book

page 83 (Performance Model)

Journal

- Ask Players to write their own set of cues for a performance of Traveling Lines. (See Student Book, page 83.)
- Ask Players to describe two or three different styles of walking that they observed during this activity.

Clock Pattern

The score for this activity takes the form of the face of a clock and a set of rules to follow. Players are directed to move around the clock face, performing activities that occur during each time. Clock Pattern was inspired by a 1964 work by choreographer Sally Gross. It is a game that can be used to teach spatial awareness, time concepts, teamwork, and focus.

Skills

★ Performing on a real or imaginary clock face
★ Miming daily activities that correspond to time
★ Following cues to change positions

Time

This activity could be played in one or two sessions of 30 minutes to an hour. It could be developed into a larger performance work with additional rehearsal time.

Space

Adaptable to any open space

Materials

Masking tape or chalk to draw a clock face on the floor; sturdy pieces of paper to write times on; a musical instrument, bell, buzzer, or timer to use for sound cues

Preparation

Before playing the game, preset a large outline of a circle on the floor, using masking tape or chalk. Write the numbers 1 through 12 on pieces of paper and place them inside the circle, where they would be located on a clock face.

★ Directions

1. Assign each Player a time, such as eight o'clock or ten o'clock, or have everyone choose a time. Start the game by asking all Players to go to the position on the clock that corresponds to their assigned or selected times.

2. Tell Players to act out an activity appropriate to the time of day. For example, a Player standing at twelve o'clock might pretend to be eating lunch.

3. Explain that when you (or a selected Player) call out "change time" or give a sound cue, such as ringing a bell or buzzer, everyone should move to a new time location and begin a new action appropriate to that time of day. Players continue acting out their activities until a new cue is called.

4. The process is repeated until the changed time cue has been given at least eleven times. Ask Players to choose a different time position after each cue.

5. Ask Players to create a score for performing this game. The score could include one or all of the following variables.

• A set amount of time for each activity at each location
• A cueing system for changing positions on the clock
• A set activity for each time
• A pattern for changing positions
• Changes in other performance variables such as tempo, level, and dynamic. Direct Players to use two or more changes during the course of the game.

Variations

Limiting Times Players choose or are given four to six times of the day to perform. When a cue is sounded, Players change to one of their times.

Providing Time Choices Call out several time choices at a time, giving Players a choice of which time they will act out.

Using a Spinner Let the choice of time be determined by a spinner. (You can make a spinner out of sturdy cardboard. Draw the numbers of a clock on a circle on the board. Affix a pointer to the board with a brass fastener.) All Players move near the time indicated by the spinner and act out the same or different activities that occur at that time of day.

Playing without a Clock Pattern Play the game without a clock pattern on the floor. Designate a playing area in which the Players will perform various times of the day called out by the Leader. Players act out their interpretation of the call anywhere within the playing area.

Miming a Day Eliminate the clock face. Ask Players to stand anywhere in the playing area. When the caller calls out a time, Players mime whatever they do at that time of day. The calls could go through a twenty-four-hour cycle, allowing a minute or two per call. You could specify if this is a school-day or a weekend day, or leave this up to the Players.

Performance Suggestions

Taking Positions Have Players begin outside the playing area and enter either the circle or the playing area to begin their performance. If there is a circle, Players can perform either outside, inside, or on the circle in the area of a specific time period.

Transitions Transitions from one time to another could be performed in many styles.

- Players move in unison by using some agreed-upon rhythm (such as the ticking of a clock) or action to get from one time to another. Pure dance movement such as a current social dance could also be used.

- Players mime an action such as riding a bicycle, motorcycle, boat, skateboard, bus, car, train, or subway to get from one time to another.

- Players use various locomotors, such as skipping, hopping, or sliding, to get from one time to another.

 Teaching Notes

Management Tips

Spatial Adjustments Make the clock face as large as possible within the dimensions of your playing area. A larger circle can accommodate more Players at one time. (If you think of the clock face as slices of pie, Players can stand anywhere within each slice that represents the number called.) A smaller area may necessitate playing the game in teams, with teams taking turns as performers and audience.

Transitions Create an arbitrary system for Players to move from one time to another.

Examples:

- Always move clockwise, hour by hour.
- Always exit the circle at the old time and re-enter at the new time.
- Use a numerical order by performing only odd or even numbers.
- Perform both the A.M. and P.M. times before leaving a time location.
- Direct Players to go back two hours or move forward three hours.

Connections

Social Studies Discuss how living by natural daylight and darkness might be different than living with mechanical clocks (which were invented around the thirteenth century) and electricity. Discuss how contemporary time values may differ from those in the past or from those in which electricity is not available.

Geography Discuss time zones and how they are established throughout the world. Ask Players to use one specific location as a reference point and figure out what time it is at other places on the globe. For example, have each Player choose a place in the world she would like to visit. Ask her to figure out the difference between her own time zone and that of another location. When the Leader calls out the local time, each Player goes to her corresponding time zone equivalent.

 Assessment

Teacher Observations

- Were Players able to perform on a clock face pattern?
- Were Players able to follow cues to change positions?
- Were Players' mimes of daily activities clearly performed? Did their activities correspond to the times Players were standing on?
- Were Players able to work together within a limited space or set?

Group Discussion

Use a performance of daily life activities to illustrate how people spend their time. Discuss similarities and patterns. Discuss how much of this is free choice and how much is structured by someone or something else, such as chores, school, commuting, homework, and so on.

Student Activities

Journal

Have Players keep a journal of a single day's activities, recording them hourly.

Compass Points

In this activity, Players use the cardinal directions as a design structure from which to create a score. Crossroad paths, oriented to the cardinal points, provide a floor pattern to travel, and a way to make connections with various types of conceptual information. Players could be asked to select actions that relate to influences of climate, place, time, or culture. For example, Players might travel in the correct direction to reach the Andes or the Himalayan Mountains, while performing actions they associate with the place to which they are traveling. Players could also decide to use symbolically the compass design of two crossed lines to build a score based on concepts of opposites, such as moving from positive to negative, from high to low, or from fast to slow. In Compass Points, Players learn to apply space and time concepts to fit the design and objectives of a particular project.

Skills

★ Understanding directional concepts and using the four cardinal directions to guide stage movement
★ Selecting details of character, motivation, setting, and action based on directional concepts and associations
★ Creating performances depicting journeys from one location to another

Time

This activity could be done informally, in one or two sessions of 30 minutes to an hour, or it could be developed into a more ambitious performance project.

Space

Adaptable to any open space

Materials

Masking tape, rope, or chalk, paper, and markers to make floor compass. Add costumes, props, and sound as needed.

Directions

1. Teach Players how to locate the four cardinal directions (North, South, East, and West) on a compass. Make connections to any study of geography, maps, or social studies curriculum.

2. Help Players transfer this knowledge of direction to the playing area. Define the boundaries of the performing space by marking the circumference of a circle on the floor with masking tape or chalk. Indicate the four cardinal points with paper labels, which you place on the floor or the walls just outside the playing area. (The placement of each direction could correspond to the actual North, South, East, and West directions of your performing space.)

3. Divide Players into four teams: the North team, the South team, the East team, and the West team. Explain that each team is going to create a performance that depicts a journey from their direction of origin. (For example, the North team will be coming from somewhere in the North.) Decide ahead of time what the playing area represents— a city, state, nation, continent, the world, or the universe. Tell teams to choose a starting point and a destination point within this designated area for their journey. (For example, if the playing area represents the United States, the North team might decide to travel from Minnesota to Texas.)

4. After teams have chosen their routes, tell them to decide on a scenario for their performance. Within their teams, they must agree on details of character, setting (historical and geographical), and motivation. Advise them to ask and answer questions such as these:

• Who are we?
• Where are we traveling from and where are we going?
• How will we get there? What mode of transportation will we use?
• Why are we going?
• What will we do once we get to our destination?

5. Give teams time to plan their performance and to choose and practice actions that portray their scenarios.

6. Have teams share their Compass Points performances with one another.

Variations

Compass Spinner Have Players spread out in the playing area. Make a compass spinner (see page 119) to call out directional cues for Players. If the spinner lands on South, Players must either turn and face South, move due south from their current position, or travel toward the South label in their playing area. Allow Players to choose actions that remind them of each cardinal direction, or add an action to your call: "Go North through an ice storm." Tell Players that when they arrive at their destination, they should stop their action and stand still and silent until the next direction is called. The stop could be a frieze that is consistent with the action and direction.

To make a compass spinner, draw a circle on a piece of cardboard and label the cardinal directions. (Add Northeast, Northwest, Southeast, and Southwest to increase choices and add to the challenge.) Attach a pointer to the center of the circle with a brass fastener.

Group Friezes Players are assigned positions on a real or imaginary floor compass. Players create friezes that reflect qualities of each geographical direction. Ideas for the friezes can be generated before playing the game by having Players make lists of adjectives that describe essential qualities that they associate with each direction.

Unison Actions Players agree on actions to perform in unison on the compass points. The actions could be related to a history or geography lesson or be a pure movement idea. Players could perform the same action to all directions or agree on a particular action for each direction.

Opposites Mark two paths—one between North and South, the other between East and West—on the floor compass. Encourage Players to think of opposites that they can portray while traveling across the paths. For example, starting out slow in the East and speeding up as they move West.

Performance Suggestions

Outline for Making a Compass Points Score

1. Make a connection—historical, emotional, visual, or other—to the locations of the compass points.

Relate the subject matter to curriculum or assembly theme.

2. Find or create a text, actions, and/or a sound environment, based on this connection. Poetry, newspaper articles, historical records, and folk songs and dances are great resources. Actions to perform could be mimes and movements inspired by place, character, occupation, hobbies, traditional songs and dances, or historical events.

3. Establish cues within the text and/or sound environment, make a performance order, and rehearse.

Entrances

- Players enter the playing area and scatter randomly within its boundaries.

- Players go to preassigned beginning positions inside or outside the boundaries of the playing area.

- Assign each Player a number. These numbers will be used by the Leader (you or a Player), who calls out one or more numbers in combination with a direction. The call cues Players when and how to travel on the floor compass.

Preparing the Space Players could look into traditional ceremonial forms to begin the performance. Many Native American dancing and singing ceremonies prepare the performing area by honoring the spirits of the four compass points, or the winds, by walking toward each direction and bowing or calling out to the East, West, North and South. Other actions, present in many religious or community functions in Asian and African cultures, include sweeping the performing areas with brooms, or marking the boundaries with sprinkled cornmeal, flower petals, or colored sand.

Adding Design Elements For a more elaborate project, add details such as music, costumes, character, small hand props, text, and additional actions.

Floor Maps Make floor maps using two long strips of butcher block paper and painting the outlines of Players' hands and feet along the length of the strips. Then lay the papers on the stage floor in an X-shaped or +-shaped grid, labeling the ends of each strip by their directional names (North, South, East, and West). In performance, this floor map can be helpful as a focusing tool and stage direction guide, as well as adding a festive design element.

 Teaching Notes

Management Tips

Scriptwriting The text can be written by you, and refined through watching rehearsals. It can also be written by someone in the group, or built up through group improvisations.

Rehearsal Set If using paper paths, make two sets, one for rehearsal and one for performance. It is likely that one set will be destroyed in the enthusiasm of practicing. This is especially important if you have added drawings of hands and feet to your paths.

Connections

Geography Make calls and actions relate to geographical information such as place names, climates, and geological configurations. Players could also study and discuss various transportation systems or work related to natural resources to inform their actions. For example, camels vs. skiing as a mode of transportation; oil or mineral excavations vs. farming rice or herding cattle.

History and Social Studies Make calls and actions relate to particular times, people, or events. If connecting this game to a study of cultural heritage, Players could be asked to interview their families. This oral history information could give Players ideas for actions and characters to play.

Language Arts Make calls and actions relate to literary characters and plots; study poetry from various places to use as a basis for text, to be spoken by narrators or Players as they travel from point to point.

Special Needs

Sometimes it is helpful to map the stage directions so that everyone can visualize the paths and positions they are to follow.

Assessment

Teacher Observations

- Were Players able to use the four cardinal directions to guide their stage movement?
- Did Players create and perform scenarios that correctly and imaginatively utilized directional associations?

Group Discussion

Discuss stereotypes associated with direction or place that Players used in their scenarios. How did these stereotypes arise? Discuss how place or location influences culture.

Student Activities

Journal

Ask Players to describe other ways that compass points could be used to organize a performance score.

Compass Points Model

The content of this piece came about as a result of an elementary class's responsibility to participate in a Thanksgiving assembly. We, as directors, wrote the text. We started with a search through Native American texts, looking for a connection to the Thanksgiving theme. A fragment of a Native American praise song, "The people came from all over. . ." became the inspiration. The project took into consideration a major curriculum focus for the term, which was to teach concepts of opposites and relationships. The opposites, North and South, East and West, were connected to relationships, both directional and generational.

Two paths of two lengths of white paper were made and placed in an X-shaped pattern that extended from the upstage right to downstage left and upstage left to downstage right diagonals. These paths helped organize Players.

The class was divided into four teams. Each team was assigned the name of one of the cardinal direction points: North, South, East, or West. The team names corresponded to their beginning position on the compass points.

Each Player chose and assembled a costume for her own character—a real or imagined ancestor. Some dressed in full regalia from their countries of origin: Korea, Nigeria, Amsterdam, and Japan; others dressed as urban cowboys or fairy tale royalty; one came as a monster.

To begin, each team stood at the outside edge of its assigned compass point in a "family photograph" pose. When they heard their cues, teams knew it was their turn to cross to the opposite compass point. Players walked on top of the paths, making up their own movements that related to their costume character. When they arrived at their destinations, they assumed friezes in character.

The text was performed in a call and response style. In beginning rehearsals, the Caller was usually a Leader. Later on, this role was given to a student. Following is the performance script.

North team

West team   East team

South team

After a few beats of performing "family photographs," the Narrator cues all teams with a call from the text.

Narrator: They came from all over.

All: They came from all over.

Narrator: They came from the North.

North team: We came from the North. (*North team travels their path, walking in character, to the opposite side—South—where they join the South team and freeze in a new "family photograph."*)

Narrator: They came from all over.

All: They came from all over.

Narrator: They came from the West.

West team: We came from the West. (*West team travels their path, walking in character to the opposite side—East—where they join the East team and freeze in a new "family photograph."*)

Narrator calls, and South and East teams respond with the same text and action as above.

Narrator: They came from all over.

All: (*All teams walk to center stage in character to form a group family photograph.*) We came from all over.

Gifts

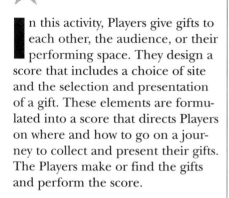

In this activity, Players give gifts to each other, the audience, or their performing space. They design a score that includes a choice of site and the selection and presentation of a gift. These elements are formulated into a score that directs Players on where and how to go on a journey to collect and present their gifts. The Players make or find the gifts and perform the score.

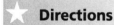
★ Directions

1. Have Players find or make a gift to give. The gift may be a real object, a symbolic representation of an object, a verbal expression, or something imaginary.

Skills

★ Making or finding a gift to give and deciding how to present it

★ Creating a performance score by designing a route, travel method, and purpose that suits the chosen performance site

★ Following a score in performance

Time

This activity could take a single one-hour session, or be done in depth over several sessions. Figure planning time, collecting time, rehearsal and discussion time, and performance.

Space

Adaptable to any indoor or outdoor space

Materials

Found objects; various art supplies to make gifts, such as tape, string, nylon fishing line, writing pens, strips of cloth or plastic

Examples:
- Ask Players to bring to class an item from their lives.
- Ask the group to make gifts, either in class or as a homework assignment.
- Take Players on a walk through any outdoor or indoor space, looking for "found gifts" that can be exchanged or given to others.
- Have Players find or make items that can be used to build a group gift, such as a mound, a sculpture, or a collage.
- Ask Players for intangible gift ideas, such as wishes for the future, the world, the group activity, or whatever is applicable to the situation.

2. To begin creating a score, find a site and designate a path or paths that everyone will travel, or direct Players to do this as an individual, team, or group assignment. Use architectural and natural details in the space to help design paths and actions. For example, Players can walk or run between trees, fountains, stairs, or other markers.

3. (Optional) Formalize the score by mapping the space and the route. Give everyone a copy of the map. For example, a map locates the center of a large circle and indicates that everyone begins by standing around the circumference. Players are shown a path to travel that takes them in progressively smaller concentric circles, until they arrive at the center to exchange gifts.

4. Have Players perform the score, starting at the beginning point and traveling to the ending point.

- Choose a beginning point, which could be out of sight of the audience, if there is one.
- Choose a locomotor, or series of locomotors, that everyone uses to travel the path.
- Choreograph a series of movements that will allow Players to continue traveling through the space. The movement series can be repeated from the beginning to the end of the path.
- Move in a straight line, circle, or zigzag path, depending on what best fits the space.

5. Direct Players to present their gifts at the ending point.

- Ask Players to decide where and how to give the gifts. It could be a silent ceremony, or a written or improvised presentation.
- Ask Players to decide who receives the gifts. Are they exchanged with each other or presented to the audience? Are they left in the space, as offerings to a tree, a house, a park, or the wind?

Variations

Wishes Have Players write their wishes on uniform lengths of cloth, plastic, or paper strips to be displayed by tying the strips to a tree, pole, string sculpture, or bulletin board.

Treasure Hunt Make lists of objects that could be preset within a designated area, or that could be found there. Divide Players into teams, or have them work individually. With lists, Players go on a hike to find objects that can be used as gifts.

Performance Suggestions

Adapting to the Audience Players move toward the audience, stopping in front of them to perform the gift exchange.

Statement of Purpose Add a statement to the gift-giving ceremony.

Examples:

I wish that _____.

My wish for the world is

_____.

This gift is for _____

because _____.

 Teaching Notes

Management Tips

Ecology Caution Players to try not to damage or significantly alter the space in their search for gifts.

Observation To help Players understand the full impact of this score, divide the group in half and have them observe one another rehearsing.

Connections

Science Direct students to select gifts from the environment that connect to their studies, such as gathering natural objects like stones, bugs, or leaves. Students could identify these findings by their geological and biological names. They could even make a collage of these gifts. Or have Players collect trash items from the environment. The collection of these gifts would help clean up the environment, which is a gift in itself.

Social Studies Have students study and replicate various forms of gift giving in other cultures and times.

Special Needs

Pair students, so that they can help each other gather gifts.

 Assessment

Teacher Observations

- Did Players find or make appropriate gifts, according to directions?
- Were Players able to design and follow a score that included beginning and ending points, a clearly defined route, movements to perform along the route, and a concluding gift presentation?
- Did Players maintain a proper performance attitude as they traveled the route and exchanged gifts?

Group Discussion

Ask Players to discuss whether or not this activity expanded their idea of what constitutes a gift. Did the ceremony of the gift exchange add to the value of the gift? How?

 Student Activities

Journal

Ask Players to describe a gift they would like to give and a gift they would like to receive.

Gifts Model

Following is a description of a nighttime performance of Gifts that was created by teenagers camping in California's Sierra Mountains.

The directors chose a wide sloping path through a wooded area as the performing space and asked Players to find a gift, real or intangible, from the environment. The Players, holding flashlights shaped like *Star Wars* laser beams, started unseen, at the top of the hill. The audience stood at the foot of the hill. At an agreed-upon signal, all Players appeared and turned on their flashlights, then began "spirit writing" any message, drawing the letters of their messages as largely as possible. The flashlights remained on throughout the rest of the performance.

On a second signal, Players zigzagged down the path, hid behind bushes and trees, stopping and starting at will. Whenever they stopped, they could spirit write again. When Players reached the end of the route, they waited in stillness until everyone had arrived. Then, one by one, they offered their gifts to either the audience or the space, placing them at the audience's feet. As each Player presented his gift, he said, "I give _____ (this gift) because _____."

Cut and Paste

Cut and Paste asks Players to make a performance score by employing the technique of collecting many ideas, from verbal or visual sources or both, and combining them into a new work. Cut and Paste is a terrific game for people who may have trouble initiating ideas, or who think they are not creative. They will find themselves responding to ideas in collected materials and, before they know it, will be creating new ideas of their own.

Skills

★ Researching a subject to collect ideas and materials

★ Using a cut-and-paste technique to organize bits and pieces of collected texts and visuals into a performance score

★ Improvising on found materials and experimenting with order to refine the score

★ Making a final script or score and performing it, publishing it, or displaying it

Time

This activity can be done in several sessions of 30 minutes to an hour. The first session could be spent gathering materials, and subsequent sessions could be used for experimentation and organization of material.

Space

Adaptable to any space

Materials

Magazines, newspapers, literature books, art books; scissors; tape, paste, or glue; paper (butcher block, typing, paper bags, cardboard, etc.); copy machine; costumes, hand props, and set pieces as needed

Directions

1. **Choose a Subject** Work with Players to choose a subject or idea as a starting point for collecting materials, or decide to make a random selection of materials.

2. **Research** Assign Players to research their chosen subject and to collect appropriate texts and images. The collected texts may be borrowed from such diverse sources as poetry, fiction, biographies, essays, newspaper articles, and brochures or other forms of advertising. Images can be taken from photographs, paintings, drawings, and postcards. Tell Players to gather together bits and pieces of text and/or images that catch their eyes, until the group decides there is enough information with which to work.

3. **Preliminary Cut** Tell the group to sort through the collected materials and to select the pieces that are relevant to their project.

4. **Preliminary Paste** Ask Players to improvise on the found materials and assemble them into a preliminary order, or vice versa, to make a script or score that will serve as a guide for further rehearsal improvisations.

5. **Edit** Encourage Players to experiment with relationships between their bits and pieces by assembling, collaging, combining, and recombining them. Keep refining the script or score as rehearsals progress, editing until it settles into a playable form.

6. **Final Paste** Once Players have edited or organized the materials into a final performance order, have them literally paste the bits and pieces into the final script or score.

7. **Share** Have Players perform the script or score, display it in your school, or publish it in a school magazine or newspaper so that the group may share their work in some way.

Teaching Notes

Management Tips

Research Research can be done as a homework assignment, or the group could use a library and research information together.

Copy Materials Tell students to copy or trace all information so that it can be cut and pasted without causing damage to the original materials.

Connections

Language Arts Take bits and pieces of various poems and characters, situations, or scenes from various stories, and create a new work.

History Choose a subject connected to curriculum content for research and development. Speeches and documents can be excerpted or used in totality for text.

Journalism Publish the cut-and-paste script in your school newsletter, journal, or yearbook.

Visual Arts Collaborate with the language arts, history, or social science teacher for topics to use. Introduce students to collage and assemblage techniques. Exhibit the assemblage or collage score.

Special Needs

Have students with reading difficulties collect visual images during their research. Discuss the content and significance of their images prior to the preliminary cut.

Background Notes

There are many techniques related to cut and paste. Collage was used extensively by the dadaists and surrealist artists of the 1920s and 1930s. In the 1950s, writer Byron Gysin coined the term *cut and paste* for his writing process of taking bits and pieces of text from various sources to create a whole new work.

Assemblage, a term coined in the 1950s by the French painter Jean Dubuffet, is another visual art technique that juxtaposes objects from the environment and combines them into paintings, sculptures, and new environments. *Deconstruction* and *postmodernism* are more recent terms that refer to similar art processes. Architectural examples of this art process are seen in public buildings constructed since the 1980s. These buildings borrow bits and pieces from various periods of architecture and recombine them into new juxtapositions. With the advent of word processing and computers, the terms *cut* and *paste* have evolved into new connotations, uses, and technologies designed for writers, filmmakers, composers, choreographers, and visual artists.

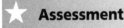 **Assessment**

Teacher Observations

- Were Players able to stick to their subject while researching, collecting, cutting, and pasting their materials?
- Were Players able to work together cooperatively and come to consensus over cutting and pasting decisions?

Group Discussion

Throughout the process of experimentation, focus on their experience of working with the collected materials. Ask them to express what they want to accomplish with the whole work, and if changing the order of images makes any difference in their understanding and feelings about individual images pieces of text or the work as a whole.

 Student Activities

Book

page 84 (Background Reading)

Journal

Ask Players to write a detailed description or to make up a story about one of the images they have selected for the score.

Cut and Paste Model

We directed a group of young teens in a vaudeville-style play, called *joE,* which was created using cut and paste.

Choose a Subject The title, *joE,* came first, at the inspiration of one student who just "felt it was right," including the eccentric capitalization. Nobody had a clue as to what it meant or how it would become a play.

Research We researched the title word, *joE*—its meanings, history, and people who had borne the name. *Joe* turned out to be a synonym for the words *joke* and *clown.* Materials collected for *joE* included jokes, historical monologues about *Joes,* well-known sayings including the word *joe,* clown routines, vaudeville shticks, quotes, and mimes. It seemed inevitable that our play was to become a series of bits and pieces, running gags, and routines, similar to a vaudeville show, ending with a spoof of a trial of Joes.

Preliminary Cut Players selected information to make various bits and pieces.

- **Routines** Clown, commedia dell'arte, and vaudeville routines that used physical jokes, such as lines and chases and shadow boxing
- **Text** Slogans and sayings about Joe used as punch lines in the script; gags from joke books or originals; commercial advertisement formats; quotes including the word *Joe;* monologues by rulers named Joe; a trial scene consisting of a jury of Joes who hear the fictitious cases of the Joe defendants before the Joe lawyers, bailiff, and judge

Preliminary Paste We assembled the found materials into a preliminary order and improvised on the rough score.

- Players tested out jokes.
- Players improvised choreography for lines and chases.
- Players improvised monologues. The "History of joE" became the spoken text for the lines and chases.
- Players improvised dialogue using famous quotations that incorporated the word joe, such as, "Say it ain't so, *Joe,*" "Joe-Blow," "He's a good Joe," "a real Joe," and "a Joe from Cocomo." These quotations inspired them to create more rhymes.
- Players sang and danced songs composed with the help of a guest composer.

Edit Players experimented with and reordered information.

Final Paste Players organized the information into a set performance order. Choreography, songs, and lines of the skits were also set. The lines and chases became the glue, or transitions, that connected the skits of narrative text.

Performance Costumes, props, lighting, and set design completed the process.

Living Pictures

Projects such as Living Pictures offer an alternative to learning by the spoken and written word, and address learning needs of people who think and communicate visually. In Living Pictures, Players choose one or more visual images, which serve the function of a score, and decide whether to imitate, react to, or recreate the images in performance.

A Living Picture score does not look like traditional play scripts because the visual information replaces verbal language as text. Its purpose is more related to a musical score, in which musicians read notes to play. In Living Pictures, the images are the notes, and the actors play the images

to create a scene. The images serve as a catalyst for nonverbal or verbal responses, or both.

Any literature, history, art, or communications lesson can be connected to this project. Living Pictures encourages cultural understanding by introducing participants to one another's interests through the visual information that they bring to the project. As a group project, it will take advantage of various people's strengths as they work together as a team.

★ Directions

1. Ask each Player to select one or more visual images. The choice of image can be limited to a particular subject or design element, or may simply be a random selection of interesting images.

Sources:
- Photocopies of artworks from books (paintings, sketches, sculptures, photography)
- Tear-outs of photographs or illustrations from magazines and newspapers
- Photographs
- Original drawings or paintings made by the participants
- Drawings, tracings, or rubbings from existing source materials

Subject matter:
- Famous artworks
- Popular advertisements
- Family, friends, pets
- Places
- Current events
- Historical figure, place, time, or event
- Pure geometric shapes, colors

2. Explain how the images will be used to make a score that will serve the function of a script.

3. Direct Players to study the images, observing all details of shape, emotion, relationships, and so on. Discuss how they might perform the images, to make them come alive. This can be achieved in many ways.

- **Imitate the Images** Performers assume the shape, feeling, emotion, or task as shown in the image.

- **React to the Image** Performers portray emotions and actions that the images elicit.

- **Recreate the Image** Performers gather costumes, props, and set pieces similar to those in the image, then visually recreate the scene.

4. Help Players organize the images into a score. Encourage them to play with the images, rearranging them until relationships become clear.

Suggested ways to organize/arrange images:
- **Chronological Sequence** Real or imaginary time sequence
- **Collage** Overlapping relationships
- **Random** No specific pattern or system
- **Story Plot** Organize images into a story line with a beginning, middle, and end. Create a realistic story from current events, personal experiences, or oral histories. Create an imaginary story from advertisements, paintings, photos, and so on.

Skills
★ Selecting images and organizing them into a performance score
★ Analyzing visual images and deciding how to perform them
★ Creating a performance based on a score made up of visual images

Time
Plan to take at least two one-hour sessions to prepare the group, select images, and try out scoring ideas. Further investment of time will vary greatly, according to the ambitions of your project.

Space
Adaptable to any open space

Materials
Could involve use of old magazines, newspapers, photos, art books; notebooks; butcher block paper, writing materials, tracing paper, scissors, glue, tape, or staples

- **Categories** Group images by category or subject matter. When working on specific subjects, group each topic. For example, if the subject is the Civil War, the topics might include Jefferson Davis, Abraham Lincoln, the Union, the Confederacy, and battles. Or, if the subject is the family, topics might include holidays, vacations, traditions, parents, children, grandparents, and pets. Arrange the images in parallel columns according to topics within the subject matter. To perform each image in the progression you have arranged, start at the top and go through to the bottom of each column, before moving on to the next column.

- **Mathematical Progressions** Number the images and perform in order. Or number the images and perform sequentially or create a mathematical progression in which to perform the images. Images may be performed more than once, according to the progression. For example, have one team perform the odd numbers and the other team perform even numbers. Or perform in multiples of twos, threes, or fours.

- **Chance Systems** Use a chance system to free the Players from their usual ways of ordering information. (See pages 67–69 in Chapter 4, Improvisational Techniques.)

5. Have Players create a visual score that they can use during rehearsals and performance.

- Place images in a notebook, one image per page, ordered sequentially. During performance the notebook can serve as a tool to cue Players about what comes next. After each image is performed, the page can be turned to the next image.

- Affix images to a long piece of paper that can be easily made from cut paper bags, butcher block paper, or newspaper. Arrange images in a linear path, in parallel columns, or in circular patterns.

Place the score where it can be easily seen, either onstage or offstage on the floor, a wall, or a table. Wherever it is placed, the Players will have a quick reference tool to consult as needed during rehearsals and performance. Each new reading of the score can serve to remind the Players of the source of their original interpretation of the images and could elicit another point of view.

6. Help the Players use their score to create a performance. Following are some performance suggestions.

Nonlinear Structure (does not follow a story line)

- Repeat the order more than once.

- Assign a number of repetitions to each image, category, or series of images. Perform the number of repetitions decided upon for each image, category, or series of images.

- Arrange the images in a path, either on the floor or on the walls. Have the Players follow the path from beginning to end, performing each image at its location.

Story Line Structure

- As a group, tell the story by performing the images as organized in the score.

- As soloists, each performer constructs a character and story line from the arranged images.

- Perform as solos.

- Two or more simultaneous solos (designate playing area for each solo)

- Two or more performers whose solos interact with each other

Multiple Scenes Have Players create simultaneous scenes within one playing area by sharing the stage space. Actors can shift the audience's focus from one scene to another by having everyone, except featured performers, go into a complete freeze; by having all conversations become inaudible except for that of the featured performers; or through use of a spotlight that draws the audience's attention to the featured stage area.

Examples:

- A restaurant scene in which the audience overhears conversations from each table, one at a time.

- A scene of a gallery of statues or paintings that come to life, one at a time.

Performance Suggestions

Adding Design Elements

- Use one object to suggest a room, such as a rug, a bed, a table, or a chair.

- Use light, pathways, or roped-off areas to define or divide each scene within the playing area.

- Suggest character or style with props or costumes.

- Add hand props such as a cane, sword, torch, or a basket. Sometimes these objects can be mimed by the performers to create an effect as real as the actual object.

- Add full costume or a suggestion of one, such as a hat, vest, apron, or cape.

- Use puppets to suggest other people or animals, or small handheld flats made from cutouts of cardboard or Styrofoam to suggest place and time with such images as clouds, mountains, the sun, or the moon.

Teaching Notes

Management Tips

Introduction Before class discussion, give a homework assignment to your group to bring in images of anything that catches their eye from newspapers, magazines, postcards, or other sources. Or ask them to bring photos from their family albums. Use these images as the basis of your introduction to the activity.

Choosing Images The visual images can be chosen by Players as a group or individually. To decide which images to actually use in the score, the group could vote on all choices or choose one from each Player. The total number of images will depend on how complicated you wish to make the score and performance.

Try Different Score Arrangements After Players have arranged a preliminary score, keep changing the order of the images for awhile, perhaps even trying different approaches. For example, one day arrange and perform them in a story plot sequence, and on another day arrange them in an arbitrary order. In this way, Players will learn more about the images and their feelings about them, and will begin to discover what type of score works best for them.

Connections

Art Ask Players to choose images of artworks from a specific period or that are representative of a certain style. Or have Players analyze the artistic elements (shape, line, form, space, color, texture) or principles (repetition, movement, contrast, balance) in all of the images in their score.

History/Social Studies Choose images related to curriculum content.

Special Needs

Assign someone to describe the images to blind or visually impaired students.

Assessment

Teacher Observations

- Were Players able to work together to select and organize images?

- How did Players choose to organize their images into a score? Did they experiment with different arrangements before selecting one?

- Did Players understand how a collection of images could be a script?

- How did Players respond to the images? Did their analysis and performance show a thoughtful understanding of individual images?

Group Discussion

Discuss with your students how they felt using a script made of visual images rather than text. Which do they like better? Why?

Student Activities

Book

page 85 (Performance Model)

Journal

Have Players write a response to each image in the group score.

Live Movie

We have all become familiar with the visual effects available through video and film. Images recorded through the eye of a camera can be edited into any sequence and manipulated into any appearance. Live performances, however, can only happen in real time, as seen through the eyes of the director, performers, and audience.

Live Movie provides a way to create a live performance employing visual and editing techniques

Skills
★ Learning about filming and editing techniques and applying them to live theater
★ Creating scenes to fit chosen sites
★ Planning a live performance as if it were being recorded through a camera lens
★ Editing and revising individual scenes and arranging them into a final performance order

Time
This score will require one session of one to two hours for introduction, and at least three others to plan, rehearse, and perform the score. If you decide to expand this project into a larger performance, it will require more time.

Space
Adaptable to any space. Look for spaces that offer multiple qualities of shape, content, level, and color.

Materials
Paper, pens (to draw the map); sound environment or music, small hand props, and costumes as appropriate or needed

normally associated with film and video formats. The director and Players are asked to conceptualize, perform, and edit their ideas from the perspective of a filmmaker or videographer. Instead of the camera framing the image, the performers direct their voice and body focus and manipulate the stage picture to capture the audience's attention. The performers' focus creates a positive and negative effect, meaning that what the audience is directed to see is the positive, and what they are led to ignore is the negative. For example, when creating transitions between live theater scenes, performers could stage their blocking to imitate the film editing technique of cross fades by having one scene move backward, upstage, into darkness; as the other scene moves forward, downstage, into light.

Play this game with students who have been working in the performing arts and are interested in furthering their skills.

★ Directions

Following is an overview of considerations that might come up when making a Live Movie. Depending on your group and your project, you will find that issues of design and planning can be considered at any time in the process. You might want to arrange the sequence of these suggestions to better fit your resources, time, and needs.

1. Have Players watch a short film and analyze it by noticing how the director has used the camera to select images and how the images have been edited. Tell Players to watch for the following filming and editing devices.

Filming Techniques:
• **Zoom** The camera eye comes in close, to zero in on details.
• **Pan** The camera eye moves across huge spaces.
• **Close-Up** The camera eye frames a detail and excludes the background, as in a head shot.
• **Long Shot** The camera records from a distance, as in a full body shot or a panoramic view of a scene.
• **Medium Shot** The camera records a distance that is somewhere between a long shot and a close-up, such as a view of the body from the waist up.
• **Single Shot** The camera focuses on only one character.
• **Two-shot/2S** The camera focuses on two characters.
• **Three-shot/3S** The camera focuses on three characters.

Editing Techniques:
Editing provides transitions, changes of angle, or sequencing.
• **Dissolve** One image cross-fades by overlapping with another image
• **Fade** One image disappears (fade-out), to be replaced by another (fade-in).
• **Cut** To jump the action from scene to scene or angle to angle

- **Rearrangement of Time**
  - **Fast Forward** Speeding up time
  - **Slow Motion** Lengthening of time
  - **Flashback** Going backward in time, temporarily
  - **Flash Forward** Going forward in time, temporarily
  - **Rewind** Reversed order of the images, going backward toward the beginning
  - **Freeze Frame** Stopping action by holding a single frame still, as in a photograph
  - **Jump Cut** A transitional device to communicate that time has passed, achieved by splicing two or more similar images taken at different times

2. Discuss how film techniques can be adapted to create a live performance. Following is a list of acting and directing techniques that apply film techniques within live performance scenes or transitions between scenes.

- Players gesture or move within the confines of the area that they want the audience to notice. For example, if a Player wants the audience to focus on his face, as in a close-up shot, he keeps all movement to a minimum except for facial expressions, gesturing only within the width of the head and shoulder area. Or, to direct the audience to look toward a specific part of the playing area, Players move only in that area.

- Players freeze any part of the body or do not move into playing areas that they do not want the audience to notice.

- Players get the audience to focus on another performer or on an object or place by directing their attention toward the object, place, or person.

- Use lighting to focus the audience's attention on what you want to be seen. For example, lower the intensity of light (fade-out) or turn it off (blackout) on what you don't want seen. Or use changes of color and light angles to signify a change of time and place.

- Players increase the size of their actions and the volume of their voices or music to call attention to the incoming scene, and vice versa, cueing the audience to change focus to a new scene.

- Players move from downstage to upstage areas on an exit (fade-out), and vice versa (fade-in), to cue the audience of a changing scene. If the two happen simultaneously, you will achieve a cross-fade effect.

3. Choose an indoor or outdoor space, or a combination of spaces, having site-specific qualities appropriate to the images or story line. Players' solutions should be totally integrated and dependent on the design and qualities of this space; their events should be able to exist only inside this space. Choose one of the following ways to work on scenes in the space.

- Have the group work together, in one space, on one idea.

- Divide the group into teams to work in one space. Combine all the scenes to create the final work.

- Divide the group into teams and also divide the space into playing areas equal to the number of teams. Have each group choose the area they would like to work in, or assign groups a place in which to work. Assigned areas will be used as sets for events in the Live Movie. Divide a rectangle or square into equal areas; divide a circle into triangles, as you would cut a pie; or set the boundaries in any other configuration, as appropriate to the space. For example, one team could work on a grassy hill, another on a cement area in front of the hill, and still another on a path leading to the cement area. Direct each team to make a scene for its space. Teams may work on the same idea, or different ideas. Have all Players work together to order and edit the scenes into one score.

It may be useful to have Players make a drawing of the performing space, a map that clearly shows the playing space, indicating borders and details of landscape or architecture, and the division of space. Remind Players to decide where the audience will be placed. If you will be using more than one area, try to make it possible for the audience to see all scenes from one location, or decide how the audience can move from area to area.

4. As a group, start to plan a performance that designs every moment as though it were being recorded through the lens of a camera. Think of images that have the potential to create stage effects equivalent to filming and editing devices. Solutions could take the form of a narrative in scenario/treatment or storyboard form relating to the environment, mood, or history of the place; or be nonlinear, with no story.

5. Have Players improvise on their score, working out scenes and images to find material. Have them view one another's improvisations and record the images that work. Have everyone decide where to edit the group or team events. Ask viewing Players to describe what they recall from each team's ideas.

6. Help Players revise the initial scenario/treatment, storyboard, or nonlinear series of images based on their improvisations and discussions. Make editing decisions by using all or parts of each team's events.

- **Call the Shots** In the editing process for film or video, every time the image changes or the camera angle or lens changes, it is called a shot, and it requires an edit or cut.

- **Order the Shots** Make a preliminary performance order of the shots, indicating the beginning and ending of each image or shot.

- **Edit the Shots** Establish how the edits happen for each shot, by employing freeze frames, cross fades, dissolves, or other devices to move from edit to edit.

7. Ask Players to perform their solutions. To make a performance that uses all the group or team spaces, put together the events from each section. Discuss how to put the edits (the relationships of all team events) into a final performance order.

Examples:
- Events from one group can be juxtaposed against events from another.
- Freeze frames can stop the action of one section as another takes over. Define the beginning and ending shot of each team's scene, so that Players know when to go into freeze frame.
- Use cross-fades and dissolves to overlap the beginning and ending of sections.
- The ending could rewind so that every detail of the action reverses in order back to the beginning of the piece.

8. Have Players perform their Live Movie so that the images are created through the effects of the scripted shots and edits.

Variation

Make a Video or Film Turn the Live Movie performance into a video or film. This will require additional planning and experimentation for each shot and edit. Or make a video or film simultaneously with the live performance.

Performance Suggestions

Freeze Frame When working in teams, teams that are not in the shot remain onstage, in freeze frame.

Sound Effects Teams that are not performing in a scene help the performing team by adding sound effects or appropriate verbal and musical responses to the event.

★ Teaching Notes

Management Tips

Use these warm-up activities to illustrate how to simulate film effects in live performance, and to help focus the audience on where you want them to look at any one moment.

Giving and Taking Focus Divide the group into four teams. Two teams watch while two teams simultaneously improvise scenes, side by side. Performing teams take turns at giving and taking focus. This means that while one team is talking and moving (taking focus), the other team is nearly silent and still (giving focus). Cue the teams when it is their turn to be in focus by directing a flashlight toward their area, or having a Player focus a pretend or real camera toward their playing area. Alternate the focus, until the Players understand the concept. Have all teams switch, so that those in the audience get to be performers, and vice versa.

Close-Ups Have Players create one-minute monologues or mimes. Direct them to perform their monologues or mimes using only their

faces and voices. Any hand gestures should move only within the range of the head and shoulder areas.

Connections

Language Arts Use literature from the curriculum as the basis for scriptwriting or structuring scenarios. Have Players compare a film script to a play script, noticing how screenwriters include camera shots, angles, and point of view.

History, Social Studies, and Current Events Create scenes and use a space that evokes a time or place related to course work.

Background Notes

Ellis Island, a film that Meredith Monk directed, composed music for, and choreographed, is an excellent example of how an artist can create a site-specific work using multidisciplinary forms. The film's location is Ellis Island, the infamous point of entry for all immigrants arriving in the United States through New York harbor from the 1800s until the 1950s. *Ellis Island* would not look the same if it were performed live or performed in another space.

Through her choices of images, Monk reveals the history of the place and the memory of what it was to be an immigrant. The site she chose was the main building and its surrounding grounds before renovation. The camera eye records close-ups of artifacts such as baskets, valises, and medical instruments; and long shots of spaces such as hallways, views from windows, and immigrants seated on benches in the large central hall. Monk also used time-lapse photography so that in one minute or so, the viewer sees day pass to night and again to day on Ellis Island; and freeze frames, so that single frames appear to be documentary photographs from the period. (This illusion is broken by one performer's intimate action of brushing the lint off of the coat of a family member.)

Costumes call up past times. Actions include performers dancing, running frantically until they stop suddenly in a rising cloud of dust, and passively standing or sitting. Music combines folk and classical traditions with traces of sounds from Europe, Asia, Africa, and Latin America.

 Assessment

Teacher Observations

- Were Players able to understand and apply the techniques of one art form (filmmaking) to another (live theater)?

- Did Players use filmmaking vocabulary during rehearsals and in their scores?

- Were Players' scenes site-specific?

- Were Players able to manipulate the audience's focus? Did they take the audience into account when staging the performance?

- Were Players able to plan a performance as if it were being recorded through a camera lens, and to carry out this plan as they improvised, edited, and revised individual scenes?

Group Discussion

Use the following questions to engage students in a discussion about how film and video can manipulate what is seen and felt by the observer.

- How can the camera trick the eye?

- How can a live performer manipulate what you see?

 Student Activities

Book

pages 86–88 (Background Reading)

Journal

Ask Players to write a movie review, discussing the film's use of filming, editing, and special effects techniques and how they manipulated what they saw.

Musical Forms

Many artists like to borrow from other art forms to change how they think about and create their own art form. This chapter looks at how music can be used as a model to inspire new ways to think about performance structures. Since music has been defined as organized sound, it is easy to understand why musical forms can be transferred into organizational structures for artists of other disciplines.

There are four structural models presented in this chapter. All adapt easily to dance and theater performance. *Canons* and *rounds* are musical forms;

part forms and *call and response* have been used extensively in both music and literature.

Canons A melody repeated by one or more voices, overlapping in time in the same or a related key.

Rounds A melody for two or more voices that is repeated by one or more voices at equal time intervals, continuing until all voices have joined in and completed at least one cycle.

Call and Response A repeating pattern of one voice's statement (call) is answered by another voice or group of voices (response).

Part Forms A way to analyze a work by breaking it down into its component parts. This can be done through a breakdown of the rhyme or rhythmic patterns, or verse and chorus patterns.

In the same way that these four representative types of musical forms have been broken down in this chapter, you could choose any musical, rhythmic, or poetic structure to analyze and adapt to another discipline.

Artists frequently borrow, imitate, or improvise on musical structures to organize their images, words, ideas, or actions. Following are some suggestions for doing this.

- **Imitate the melodic line of the music.** Use a theme and variation structure, as found in canons and fugues; use a back and forth pattern, as in call and response; copy rhythm patterns into movement and/or vocal expression, as in part forms.

- **Use the music's mood.** Adopt the dramatic and emotional effects inherent in the music and make it visual. Or use music to evoke a mood, as it is used in film sound tracks.

- **Work in counterpoint.** Combine, in a parallel relationship, two or more melodic lines of the music. For instance, in a party scene, one group dances to the music, while another group argues over a card game. Visually and aurally, one group appears to be smooth and continuous in a legato rhythm, while the other is angry and jarring in a staccato rhythm.

- **Work in contrast to the music.** Juxtapose actions to create contrast, such as in performing a party scene with dangerous sounding music, as a way to portend a future event.

- **Add repetition.** Extend the length of a work through repetition of parts, as is done in rounds and canons.

- **Improvise.** Respond to the melodic line, the rhythmic patterns, chord patterns, or basic structure of the parts of a musical work. Players could respond with an improvised variation on each call, in call and response; or improvise on the structure of a part form.

Listed below are examples of dance and theater performances built on musical forms. Many can be found in video format, or in photographs in dance and theater anthologies.

Examples of using music to create dramatic and emotional effects:

- Story ballets such as *Swan Lake*, *The Sleeping Beauty,* and *The Nutcracker* (music composed by Peter Illych Tchaikovsky); *Petrushka,* and *The Rites of Spring* (music composed by Igor Stravinsky); and modern dance choreographer José Limon's adaptation of Shakespeare's *Othello* in his 1949 work, *The Moor's Pavane* (music composed by Henry Purcell, arranged by Simon Sadoff)

Examples of call and response:

- Alvin Ailey's choreography to gospel music in his signature piece, *Revelations*
- Lee Breuer and Bob Telson's opera, *Gospel at Colonus,* a modern combination of the call and response techniques found in Greek classical theater and American gospel music

Examples of choreographers who use musical structures to inspire movement:

- Doris Humphrey's *Passacaglia,* where she expressed Bach's theme and variation structure through her mass groupings of dancers

- Twyla Tharp's *The Fugue,* with twenty variations on a twenty-count theme from an idea she heard in Bach's *Musical Offering*
- George Balanchine's abstractions of musical forms as exemplified in his ballets to Tchaikovsky's *Theme and Variations* and Bizet's *Symphony in C*

Example of cross-disciplinary use of music, poetry, and dance:

- Mark Morris physically expresses the unity of the language of text and music in *L'Allegro and Il Penseroso,* his choreography for George Frederic Handel's musical setting of John Milton's poetry.

Call and Response

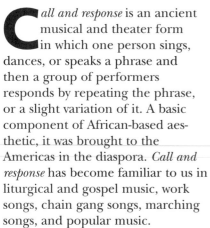

Call and response is an ancient musical and theater form in which one person sings, dances, or speaks a phrase and then a group of performers responds by repeating the phrase, or a slight variation of it. A basic component of African-based aesthetic, it was brought to the Americas in the diaspora. *Call and response* has become familiar to us in liturgical and gospel music, work songs, chain gang songs, marching songs, and popular music.

Performers who want to involve audiences often use call and response. Religious leaders of various faiths have long used call and response to include their congregations in the service. Choreographer Alvin Ailey used his childhood memories of Southern church forms of call and response in his signature suite of dances, *Revelations*, which includes the songs "Oh, A-Rock-A My Soul" and "Didn't My Lord Deliver Daniel?"

Skills

★ Improvising and selecting actions to correspond to lyrics
★ Rehearsing and performing a call and response work

Time

30 minutes to an hour

Space

Adaptable to any space

Materials

Source materials for listening or reading; a drum or other percussion instrument to help keep the rhythm

★ Directions

1. Choose an existing call and response song to perform.

Examples:

- Sailing/Work songs: "Blow the Man Down," "Haul Away Joe," "Lowlands," "One More Day," "Go Down Ol' Hannah"
- Marching songs: "Caissons Go Rolling Along," "Sucking Cider Through a Straw," "Sound Off (one, two, three, four)"
- Spirituals/Carols: "Swing Low, Sweet Chariot," "I Ain't Gonna Grieve My Lord No More," "One More River," "Ezekiel Saw a Wheel a Rollin'," "Rise Up Shepherd, Follow"

2. As a group, decide on actions to correspond to each call and response. One approach is to ask everyone to improvise actions for a line of text. Volunteers can demonstrate their solutions, then the group selects which actions to use.

Examples:

Slave Work Song

Call: *Foller de drinkin' gourd* + peg leg walk to the right

Response: *Foller de drinkin' gourd* + peg leg walk to the left

Call: *For de ol' man is a waitin' for to carry you to freedom* + peg leg walk to the right

Response: *Foller de drinkin' gourd* + peg leg walk to the center with eyes scanning the sky

(**Note:** *Foller (follow) de drinkin' gourd* was a code in the form of a song. It signaled slaves that an opportunity to escape to freedom was at hand. According to an account in J. Mason Brewer's

American Negro Folklore, this song talks about a conductor, on what was known as the underground railroad, who was a sailor with a peg leg. He would leave signs for slaves to let them know he was in the area: trail markers made by his natural left foot and the round hole of peg leg. Other code words in the song refer to the "drinkin' gourd," which is the Big Dipper, and the "gre' big un," or the Ohio River, which would have to be crossed on the way North.)

Marching Drill

Call: *Sound off* + marching (one step per word)

Response: *One, two* + marching

Call: *Sound off* + marching

Response: *Three, four* + marching

Call: *Cadence call: one, two, three, four* + marching

Response: *Three, four* + halt and freeze (at attention)

3. Choose a caller (the Leader, a volunteer, or someone assigned by the Leader).

4. Practice the call and response words and actions.

5. Have Players perform the call and response work.

Variations

Make Up Your Own Call and Response Text

1. The basis of the call and response could be a speech, poem, dance, song or a litany of any topic. Choose a topic, such as creating a cheerleading call for the next school game, writing an

editorial on school issues or current events, or some topic of great interest to the Players.

2. Write a text and/or choreograph actions. Decide where to break the text for the patterns of the calls and responses. Decide if responses will be exact repetitions of the calls, or whether responses will be stated as a chorus/refrain like those used in songs and poems. The response could also be an echo of the call that repeats many times, changes in detail with the repetition, or modulates from loud to soft.

3. Decide how to structure the performance of your call and response.

- **Solo + Group** One Player is the caller and everyone else is part of the response. Or, vice versa.

- **Group Leader + Group** Leader is always involved in both the call and the response, acting as conductor of both the callers and the responders.

- **Two Groups** Each group has a Leader. One group is assigned to do the calls, the other does the responses.

- **Group vs. Group** Call and response used as a competition or question and answer form. For example, composer Leonard Bernstein and choreographer Jerome Robbins used a form of call and response as a kind of competition between two gangs, called the Jets and the Sharks, in the rumble scene from their 1957 musical (1961 film), *West Side Story* (their adaptation from Shakespeare's *Romeo and Juliet*).

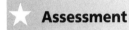

Teaching Notes

Management Tips

Team Solutions You may wish to divide the Players into teams. Ask each team to create its own performance solution to the same call and response text. Have teams share their solutions with one another.

A discussion following the presentations can highlight the unique qualities of each solution, illustrating how there can be many interpretations of the same source material.

Leadership Often, a Leader emerges naturally from the group. Acknowledge that person's initiative and formalize the role. If this does not happen and the group is having difficulty collaborating, play follow the leader games (see Traditional Games, page 219) in which everyone takes a turn as Leader and the group can practice following a Leader's cues and listening to one another. You may want to assign someone to be Leader.

Accompaniment A drum or other percussion instrument or a recording of the song can help to keep the group together rhythmically.

Connections

Music/Language Arts Have Players analyze the musical and textual structure of the call and response songs they use or create. For example, the following are popular verse or stanza patterns used in call and response, which may or may not involve rhyming:

- Four-line verse with a repeating fourth line: AAAB, CCCB, DDDB, and so forth.
  - Call: repeats phrase for three lines
  - Response: fourth line (refrain that repeats with every verse)

- Four-line verse with alternating pattern: ABAB, CBCB, DBDB, and so forth.
  - Call: first and third line repeat phrase
  - Response: second and fourth line (refrain that repeats with every verse)

- Four-line verse with the last line always changing: AAAB, AAAC, AAAD, AAAE, and so forth.
  - Call: repeats phrase for three lines
  - Response: fourth line phrase changes with every verse

- Three-line verse: ABC, DEC, FGC, HIC
  - Call: first and second line develop an idea, each sets a different phrase
  - Response: third line repeats like a refrain, using the same or almost the same words

Social Studies Challenge Players to research and find examples of call and response patterns in the music, songs, poems, sermons, speeches, or dances of a specific culture, perhaps from their own cultural heritage.

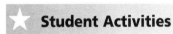

Assessment

Teacher Observations

Did the Players work well together? Were they able to collaborate effectively to create and select actions? Was a Leader necessary?

Group Discussion

Discuss with Players how the patterns of repetition in call and response can be used as a tool for communicating a message and increasing a group's energy. Ask them to think of other ways in which repetition is used to get their attention or influence their lives. Refer to advertising, media, popular music, and sports.

Student Activities

Book

pages 89–90 (Overview)

page 91 (Vocabulary)

page 92–93 (Background Reading)

Rounds

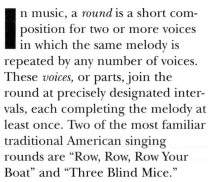

In music, a *round* is a short composition for two or more voices in which the same melody is repeated by any number of voices. These *voices,* or parts, join the round at precisely designated intervals, each completing the melody at least once. Two of the most familiar traditional American singing rounds are "Row, Row, Row Your Boat" and "Three Blind Mice."

The round structure can be adapted for use in any style of performance by two or more soloists or teams. It conforms easily to spoken text, any kind of physical action, including dance, and of course, musical expression. For example, Players could perform a monologue using the round structure by repeating the same lines of text in overlapping solos by several different actors or teams (raps lend themselves easily to this). Or Players could create a sequence of actions or dance movements that are repeated as overlapping solos by different Players or teams. Use this musical structure to take any informal class study into a performance piece.

★ Directions

1. Make sure that Players understand what a round structure is. Either listen to a musical example, sing a simple round that can be learned quickly, such as "Row, Row, Row Your Boat" and "Three Blind Mice," or create a clapping pattern that can be overlapped at designated intervals. Divide the group up into two or more voices/parts. You can act as the conductor to cue when each voice should enter the round.

2. Divide the group into teams or have Players work individually. Give each team or individual a number.

3. Have each team or individual create a short vocal or action phrase. Round phrases can be made from texts either borrowed or created, daily life actions, dance movements, songs, random sounds, or any combination of the above elements.

4. Sequence the phrases into a repeatable order, which everyone learns.

5. Players decide the number of times the sequence is to be repeated and the point in the sequence at which the next "voice" begins. Have each part complete the sequence at least one time.

6. Have each team or individual begin the sequence in the designated number order. The parts will overlap as each voice begins and completes the sequence for the agreed-upon number of times. The first group to begin will finish first; the last group to begin will finish last.

Performance Suggestions

Beginnings and Endings There are many choices for beginnings and endings, which will be influenced by your performing space.

- Players maintain a frieze until their part begins and after it ends. They remain in the frieze until the last part/voice has ended. This is a strong performance device for any age, and young Players can do it well. Instruct them to hold their frieze positions as in a photograph.

- Players face upstage until their part begins and after it ends, until the last part has ended. They turn to face downstage to perform their part.

- Players enter when their part begins, and exit when it ends.

Performance Preparation Rounds need to be rehearsed in order for the parts to be clear. Repetition is the best way to learn and polish a Round into a performance piece. If the Players continue to have difficulty, have the conductor become part of the performance.

Skills

★ Identifying a round structure
★ Creating short vocal or action phrases
★ Memorizing and repeating a sequence of phrases
★ Dividing into multiple "voices" to perform a round in overlapping order, following cues

Time

15 minutes to an hour, depending on the length and complexity of the round and the scope of the project

Space

Adaptable to any space

Materials

Drums, electronic keyboard, wooden blocks, and other musical instruments can add texture, a rhythmic structure, and even provide another voice. The performance can be accompanied by live singing or recorded music.

Management Tips

Timing Either you or one of the Players could perform as a conductor to help each team or soloist to enter on cue. If rhythm is essential to the performance, then the conductor can also keep a steady beat for the Players. Consider using a drum or other percussion instruments to accompany the Players and help them with their timing.

Leadership/Teamwork If teams are having trouble with cues and working together, assign one Player on each team to be the Leader, who will be responsible for the cues.(Sometimes this occurs naturally, and it's useful to acknowledge when this happens.) Instruct the Players to follow the cues of their Leader, even if the Leader makes a mistake. This will be a good lesson in teamwork and the responsibility of leadership.

Connections

Art Analyze the use of repetition and overlapping in visual arts design, including architecture.

 Assessment

Teacher Observations

- Did students understand round structure?

- Were students able to create vocal or action phrases? Were they able to order the phrases in a sequence, then memorize it?

- Were students able to set and follow cues?

Group Discussion

Discuss how the round structure helped Players organize a performance piece, and how it impacted their ideas.

- What role does repetition play in helping to communicate ideas? Does repetition make work seem bigger, clearer, more complex, or boring?

- How does putting words and action into a rhythmic structure influence the message?

Canons

3

A canon is a musical form that has been popular in Western music since around the year 1200. The word *canon* means "rule" in Greek. *Sumer is icumen in,* set for four voices, is one of the earliest canons ever written. Canons contain a melodic line that is performed by two or more voices. The first voice makes a statement that is joined at different intervals by succeeding voices. Canons are similar to rounds, with the main difference being that a canon is a more complicated form with many possibilities of variations. Whereas rounds are an imitative, follow-the-leader form of composition, sometimes called a "perpetual canon," canons have many forms and types with variations based on changes such as differences of pitch, increase or decrease in volume, or reversals or inversions of the thematic phrases.

Johann Sebastian Bach's *Musical Offering* and *The Goldberg Variations* and Wolfgang Amadeus Mozart's Serenade in C Minor are classic examples of canon structure from the Baroque period. Romantic composers Mendelssohn, Schumann, Schubert, and Grieg all wrote compositions in canon form. In the twentieth century, Schoenberg, Webern, Bartok, Hindemith, Messiaen, and Berg have all composed canons.

★ Directions

1. Discuss the basic structure of a canon (see introduction). Play an example of the musical form. Then talk about how to translate the music's structure into another artistic form, using physical (dance), verbal (monologues), and/or visual (set design) language.

2. Ask individuals or teams to create thematic phrases of movement, language, sound, or visual design.

- **Movement** Design a thematic phrase of hand gestures, locomotors, social dance steps, or daily life mimes.

- **Language** Write an original or choose an existing monologue or speech to be the thematic statement.

- **Sound** Compose an original thematic phrase of music, use an existing musical phrase, or create combinations of existing musical phrases. Or use other sources of sound:

  - **Body Music** Players make sounds that use their bodies as instruments, such as clapping, stamping, clicking, snapping, or beating on the chest or thighs.

  - **Found Items** Use everyday items, such as trash cans, spoons, or pots and pans as musical instruments.

  - **Musical Instruments** Use available percussion or other musical instruments.

3. Have Players share their thematic phrases with the group. Direct the group to select one thematic phrase to use in creating a canon. (Players may decide to connect two or more phrases.)

4. As a group, Players devise variations of the chosen thematic phrase. Variations on the phrase can include using opposite qualities, such as going forwards and backwards, traveling or remaining stationary, changing emotional content from happy to sad, or using all male and all female teams. Variations can also include altering the volume, rhythm, dynamics or number of Players performing one voice.

5. Direct Players to incorporate their variations into a canon structure. Some of the things they must decide include the number of voices (and the number of Players performing each voice); the number of repetitions; timing of phrase

Skills

★ Analyzing the structure of a canon

★ Creating thematic phrases of movement, sound, language, or visual design

★ Working in a group to explore and select variations of thematic phrases

★ Utilizing the structure of a canon to organize a performance piece

Time

At least 30 minutes

Space

Adaptable to any space. A large, cleared space is preferable, especially if thematic phrases are movement oriented.

Materials

A pitch pipe or musical instruments such as guitar, piano, electronic keyboard, autoharp, drums, and woodblocks will add texture and can even provide another voice.

overlaps; spatial design, including stage placement and floor patterns; and accompaniment.

6. Have Players set up the performance sequence of their canon. Give a number to each soloist or team that corresponds to the order in which they begin their part of the canon. Set all entrance and exit places and cues. Give Players time to practice.

7. Have Players perform their canon.

Variations

Double Canon Create a canon with two themes. This will require at least four voices.

Retrograde Canon Make a phrase. First voice performs phrase as made. Second voice performs phrase in reverse.

Augmented and Diminished Canon Make a phrase. Make it appear bigger or louder, smaller or softer, by adding or subtracting the number of Players in each voice. For example, four performers jumping is visually bigger and louder than two performers walking.

Performance Suggestions

Monologues One speech, delivered by three or four voices (each voice can be performed as a solo or chorus). Performers arrive at or are placed in different parts of the stage, stand shoulder to shoulder, or are constantly moving on a path.

Movement A phrase of movement is performed by three or four solo voices or teams. Explore variations of the phrase by performing movements clockwise and counterclockwise, forward and backward, or repeating them twice as fast and/or twice as slow.

Sound Use a rhythm or melody that can be repeated by several voices. Make variations by performing loud and soft, using different tempos, changing accents, or changing

octaves. Perform as an orchestra, in one place, or scatter Players throughout the performance space.

Combinations Combine any of the above.

 Teaching Notes

Connections

Language Arts Have Players create a canon performance based on a monologue. Choose a monologue from existing plays, or have Players write their own.

Music Challenge Players to analyze the structure of different forms and to create or plan a performance work that incorporates the same structures.

 Assessment

Teacher Observations

- Were Players able to understand musical canon structure and discuss how to translate that structure to another art form?

- Were Players able to create thematic phrases? Were they able to work together to devise variations of a thematic structure?

- Were Players able to create a canon structure performance?

Group Discussion

If possible, videotape the Players' performance and have them watch it several times. Otherwise, have them perform the piece in two groups, so that all Players will have the opportunity to watch it. Use the following questions to help Players assess their completed canon piece.

- How is your piece similar to the musical canon we listened to?

- Is the original thematic phrase clear in the work as a whole?

- Did all of the variations have a recognizable connection to the original phrase?

- What kind of emotional and/or visual impact did the canon structure give to your piece?

 Student Activities

Journal

Ask Players to explain how they would improve the group's canon piece.

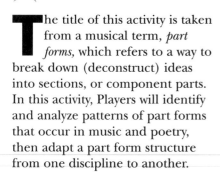

Part Forms

The title of this activity is taken from a musical term, *part forms*, which refers to a way to break down (deconstruct) ideas into sections, or component parts. In this activity, Players will identify and analyze patterns of part forms that occur in music and poetry, then adapt a part form structure from one discipline to another.

Skills

★ Analyzing structure in music and poetry by identifying parts and patterns

★ Transferring structural patterns from one discipline to another

★ Creating, rehearsing, performing, and evaluating original works that reflect or imitate part form structures

Time

30 minutes or more, depending on how much time is needed to listen to and discuss the source or reference materials

Space

Preparation work could be done in a classroom; performance work adaptable to any space

Materials

Audio equipment and recordings of music or poetry (see suggested selections in Background Notes); copies of poems or access to source books for poetry selections; writing materials for planning ideas. If Players choose to perform live music, use drums, electronic keyboard, wood blocks, or any other musical instruments available.

★ Directions

1. Play recordings of music or poetry readings, or pass out copies of poems, that are good examples of different part forms (see examples in Background Notes). Ask Players to try to identify where each part begins and ends and what patterns exist. In order to analyze the structure, discuss what to listen for in music or poetry, and what to look for in a written poem (see information in Background Notes).

2. Decide whether you would like Players to work individually, with partners, or in teams. Explain that Players are going to create a cross-disciplinary work that uses part forms. Have each individual, pair, or team choose a work of music or poetry based on a specific part form structure to be the model for an adaptation into another discipline. Models could be chosen from discussion examples or Players can find or create their own musical or poetic example of a part form structure. For example, a Player might choose or write a sonnet, then write music or choreograph a dance that imitates or reflects the sonnet's structure. In like manner, Players could adopt the structure from a piece of music and express it in a dance, text, or visual art.

3. Tell Players to first be certain that they have identified the structure of the model. Then suggest that they transfer the pattern, one part at a time. For example, if the model is a popular song with the

pattern *abab,* and Players are transferring this structure to a dance, then they can first choreograph an *a* phrase, then a *b* phrase, then repeat (exactly or slightly varied) the two phrases to reflect the *abab* pattern.

4. Once Players have created their adaptations, allow time for them to practice their part form combinations until they are memorized and can be repeated.

5. Have Players show one another their part form pieces. Ask observing Players to identify the part form pattern of each piece.

★ Teaching Notes

Management Tips

Check in with the Players at the beginning of the activity to make sure that they have correctly analyzed the structure of their models. Circulate to keep them on track as they work on transferring their model part form patterns to create their cross-disciplinary part form works.

Connections

Language Arts This activity can be used to help students learn the function of theme and how to identify themes and variations in larger works. It is an ideal activity to use for students studying poetic forms, rhyming patterns, and meter.

Music Use this activity to explore musical form and to analyze how various works are structured.

Background Notes

In music, it is rare for a composition to contain only one idea, or theme. It is more usual for the first musical idea, or *part,* (A) to be followed by a second idea (B), which either ends the composition or continues to a third idea, which is either a new idea (C) or a repeat of the first idea (A). Parts can be added indefinitely, but it is rare to have more than five parts in a musical composition.

This organization of musical ideas into a part form structure has parallel uses in literature. The most popular part form in both music and literature is the three-part form or theme, referred to as the ABA form.

Part 1 (A) contains statement of the theme

Part 2 (B) is a departure from the theme

Part 3 (A) is a return to the theme

The return to the theme in Part 3, or the restatement of A, may be exact or it may start with just the opening measures of the first idea, then continue with somewhat different material developing.

Examples of part forms in classical music:

- **Two-part forms** Bartok's *Mikrokosmos* Nos. 126 and 139; Beethoven's Bagatelles Op. 119, No. 8; Brahms's Waltzes Op. 39, Nos. 5 and 6
- **Three-part forms** Haydn's Sonatas, No. 11 in G, No. 30 in D, No. 31 in D; some of Chopin's Mazurkas, such as Op. 6, No. 4; No. 7, No. 5 (Intro); Prokofieff's Classical Symphony, Op. 15
- **Four-part forms** Bernstein's *Five Anniversaries,* No. 2 (codettas); Scriabin's Etude Op. 8, No. 10
- **Five-part forms** Schumann's *Album for the Young,* Op. 68, Nos. 18 and 33; Mozart's Sonata in C (K.545), II (codetta)

In poetry, forms such as sonnets, sestinas, ballads, and villanelles are created based on variations of the metrical structure and rhyming patterns. Breaking down and identifying poems by their rhyming patterns is done similarly to breaking down music into idea or part forms. The four forms discussed below indicate the wide variety of rhyming schemes used in poetry.

Quatrain Form This four-line form is the most common stanza form in European poetry, and possibly the world. It was popular by the Middle Ages. The quatrain form generally followed is a cross rhyme pattern of *abab* or *xbyb* (in which *x* and *y* represent unrhymed lines). The lyrics of most hymns and popular music of today are written in this formal pattern. Two other quatrain rhyming patterns, which are frequently used in sonnets, are *abba* and *aabb.*

Sonnet Form The sonnet is perhaps the most popular and widely used poetic form in English language poetry since its introduction in the 1530s. It is a fourteen-line poem, usually written in iambic pentameter, that may employ various rhyming schemes.

- The Italian sonnet pattern is divided into two sections: an *octave* (eight-line form with rhyme scheme of *abba abba*) plus a *sestet* (six-line form consisting of either a quatrain and a couplet, *cdcdee;* an alternation of two rhymes, *cdcdcd,* or three rhymes, *cdecde*).
- The English pattern generally contains three quatrains and a couplet.
  - The Spenserian pattern goes: *abab bcbc cdcd ee;*
  - The Shakespearean pattern goes: *abab cdcd efef gg.*

Examples of sonnets and sonnet authors:

  - **English Renaissance** William Shakespeare's "Shall I compare thee to a summer's day?" "No longer mourn for me when I am dead," "Let me not to the marriage of true minds." Sonnets by John Donne, Ben Jonson, John Milton, and Edmund Spenser
  - **Nineteenth Century** E. B. Browning's *Sonnets from the Portuguese;* Sonnets by John Keats, William Wordsworth, Samuel Taylor Coleridge, Lord Byron, George Eliot, and Christina Rossetti
  - **Twentieth Century** Dylan Thomas's *When All My Five and Country Senses See;* June Jordan's *Sunflower Sonnet Number One, Sunflower Sonnet Number Two;* Adrienne Rich's *The Insusceptibles;* Gwendolyn Brooks's *What Shall I Give My Children?* Sonnets by W. H. Auden, Claude McKay, Muriel Rukeyser, Robert Frost, Robert Lowell, Stephen Spender, e. e. cummings, and Margaret Walker

Qasida Form A lyric poem that can address mystical or philosophical themes, satire, or elegies. The qasida form uses a rhyme scheme of *aa bb cc,* etc., that can run to over one hundred lines. It was common to Arabic, Persian, Turkish, and Urdu literature starting around the eighth or ninth century. It was employed for various uses: in courtly poems praising a patron, in praise poems for a tribe or curse poems for enemies, or in love poems.

Ballad Form A *ballad* is a short narrative song that has its origins in oral traditions. A story is told, often in first person, with plot as the central element and little detail to inhibit the quick delivery of a single line of action. Well-known folk song examples include: "Barbara Allen," "Springfield Mountain," "Frankie and Johnny," "Tom Dooley," "John Henry," "Molly Malone," "Jessie James," and "The Streets of Laredo." The ballad form uses six-, eight-, or ten-line stanzas with rhyming patterns of *abaBbcbC,* or three eight-line stanzas with a rhyming pattern *ababbcbC*. The use of a capital letter indicates the last line of the first stanza, which serves as the refrain, being repeated as the last line of each stanza and the "envoi," or a closing stanza of 4 (*bcbC*) or 5 to 7 lines that often serves as a dedication to an important person or a summary of the whole poem. Many poets, including Keats, Coleridge, Yeats, and Heine, have also used this form.

 Assessment

Teacher Observations

Use the following questions to assess Players' ability to analyze and utilize part form structures in works of art.

- Were Players able to identify distinct parts and overall patterns in recordings of music and poetry?

- How successfully did Players transfer structural patterns from a model to a new discipline (music to dance, poetry to visual, etc.)?

- Were part form patterns clear in Players' presentations? Were observing Players able to identify patterns?

Group Discussion

Ask Players to discuss their experience of working with part form patterns.

- How easy or difficult was it to transfer a structural pattern from your model to another discipline?

- Which was easier: to create a piece based on a part form pattern, or to recognize patterns in other Players' works? Explain.

 Student Activities

Book

pages 94–97 (Performance Models)

Journal

Ask Players to describe how they made critical choices.

- Why did you select the model you used?

- How did you decide what disciplines to put together?

- How did you choose the material that represented the *a, b, c, d* phrases?

Site-Specific Projects

The term *site-specific projects* refers to artworks that are conceived for, installed in, and/or performed in a particular space.

One intent of Site-Specific Projects is to expand the participant's perception of art and the art experience into the environment. These projects open the possibilities for participants to manipulate, respond to, or create environments. Even the most ordinary sites are rich sources for the creation of art. The interconnectedness of life and art is addressed in this chapter's projects.

Numerous environments have performance potential: the school playground, hallways, city streets, a beach, a park's trail system, a grouping of trees or sculptures, or a building exterior. Once you become aware of environments as source material and look at them as performing spaces, your perception of public spaces and places will change. You will begin to understand how they have been designed to create special effects and influence people's use of space.

Site-specific projects can be infinitely varied in their creative use of space. A site-specific environment might include both audience and performer, or arrange a separation of the audience from the performance. The environment might be preset, or created during the course of the event.

Site-specific projects offer design opportunities that expand thinking beyond traditional set design. Whatever exists or is found in the space can become material for the project. In addition to the performer's actions and scored or scripted material, this creative process encourages the perception and use of such things as rocks, trees, ladders, walls, escalators, and revolving doors as part of the performance and/or set. It may involve sounds that occur naturally in an environment, such as waterfalls, bird calls,

or honking horns; ambient lighting, such as street-lights, moonlight, shadow patterns, or lightning; and other visual design elements, such as paving patterns, trees, and stair rhythms and shapes.

All the activities in this chapter have the Players' relationship to the environment or performance site at the core of their structures. They suggest at least one of the following basic approaches to conceptualizing the Players' relationship to space and the environment.

Existing Space Players use a particular space exactly as it is found.

- Players analyze the space and decide how to use it.

- Players diagram the space, describing its limits, its characteristics, and the objects in it, including natural features, architectural details, or other constructions.

- Players indicate on the map actions to be performed in the space.

- Players adapt and perform within the space scores that were created elsewhere.

- Players use the map as a score for performance.

Installation Players create a new environment that changes an existing space.

- Players add natural or man-made objects to a space.

- Players rearrange objects found in the environment.

- Players use the space in an unusual way.

- Players create a score/map/script of the installation and describe how to perform in it.

  Examples:

  - Many artists are using video and slide installations to create environments for museums and galleries, sometimes including the observer as part of the installation.

- Dan Flavin's rooms of fluorescent light.

- Maya Lin's Vietnam Memorial in Washington, D.C., is designed to give the spectator an illusion of walking into the earth, while his image is reflected on top of names of the dead etched into the polished stone surface.

Relocation Players recreate a particular space that they have observed, researched, or imagined. The relocation is based on a remembered space, a space from another place or time, or an imagined space. Players make a map/score/script to perform in the original site. They then relocate the original site to a new performing space. This recreated space may not be visually apparent to the audience and may only exist in the mind of the performers. Players move within the performing space as though in the imagined or remembered space. Props and/or a stage set may be used to suggest or recreate the space, or the space may be left empty.

Examples:

- Abstract a street of tall and short buildings by fitting a space with tall and short ladders.

- Observe a bus stop over a period of time and then recreate the scene in your work area.

★ Background Notes

People have been making art in relation to environments for centuries. Some precedents for site-specific creations include the prehistoric sculpted earth pyramids of North America, Stonehenge, archaic earth drawings of the Nazca Pompa Ingenio in Peru, American Indian petroglyphs on rock outcroppings, Japanese rock gardens, kachina ceremonies that travel from the surrounding hills into the living areas of the Hopi communities, cleansing ceremonies on the steps leading into the Ganges River in India, outdoor mazes, medieval mummers' plays in town squares, European Renaissance promenades, and pageants that recreate historical events at their sites.

In the 1960s, many artists experimented with presenting their work in alternative, nontraditional spaces. During this period, dancers and theater artists frequently conceived of works where space was one of the motivating factors. Dance and theater happened on city streets, walls, rooftops, and in church naves, galleries and museums, laundromats, and parking lots.

Many visual artists worked outside the limits of the standard venues of galleries and museums and the standard materials of paint and canvas. Natural elements such as earth, water, the sky, and plants became their materials. They also collaborated with scientists and computer experts to invent new mediums of expression. These collaborations of art and technology have become familiar. Famous institutional sites that continue to encourage artists' collaborations with science are the participatory exhibits at San Francisco's Exploratorium and the holographic events at Disneyland and Walt Disney World.

Examples of contemporary visual artwork that are site-specific and often employ natural materials and the processes of nature as their medium include Andy Goldsworthy's "collaborations with nature," sculptures of stone, ice, moss, and wood that exist in their natural environment; Robert Smithson's *Spiral Jetty* in Utah, made of black rock, salt crystals, earth, red water, and algae; Patricia Johanson's highway gardens; Nancy Holt's *Sun Tunnels* in the Great Salt Lake of Utah, made of crossing concrete sewer pipes; Allen Gussow's outlines of figures on a beach—using found stone, twigs, seaweed, and other debris—that last only as long as the next tide; Walter De Maria's *Lightning Field,* a one-mile grid of poles in the New Mexico desert that attract lightning displays; Douglas Hollis's *Sound Garden* of wind pipes in Seattle; *Cadillac Ranch,* an art installation in Texas consisting of a row of half-submerged, upended Cadillacs by a group called Ant Farm, and Christo's *Running Fence* in Sonoma County, California, and his wrapping of Germany's Reischstag.

Site-related works such as these, and those in the following games, can be permanent or impermanent, can engage the viewer as part of the work, and can unite ordinary life and art. In each case, a specific relationship with a site and its environs is established as an integral part of the artwork.

Wall

In Wall, Players design their relationship to a wall. The wall may be real or imaginary. Players choose a pattern of action, such as moving in unison in a line along the wall, closely parallel to or touching it. Wall was one of the games developed by The Children's Troupe as part of their site-specific performance piece, *Horse Ballet*.

Skills

★ Analyzing the spatial and visual elements of a real or imaginary wall as the impetus for a performance piece

★ Creating and memorizing actions to perform while traveling along a wall

★ Directing others in a performance

Time

Allow 30 minutes for introductory session; can be developed over several sessions

Space

Any available wall, indoors or outdoors. If the performers decide to try an imaginary wall, use any large, open space. In choosing the wall, consider different types of walls: a wall of windows, a cyclone fence, a hedge, the side of a building, or a freestanding divider such as a sports backboard. Ideally, the wall should be free of pictures, furniture, or stored objects that would be in the way of Players.

Materials

In performance, Players could wear a uniform that will help the audience see them as members of a performing ensemble.

★ Directions

1. Help Players choose and get acquainted with a real or an imaginary wall. Lead the Players in a discussion of the wall's visual elements (line, color, texture, space).

- If using a real wall, Players may chose any large flat or curved vertical surface. (See suggestions in Space note.)

- If using an imaginary wall, the illusion can be created within any large open space. Agree upon the placement, length, height, width, and shape of the imaginary wall.

2. Decide whether Players will create solo Wall performances, or work in pairs or teams.

3. Tell Players to decide where their Wall performances will begin and end.

Examples:
- **Wall + Space** Begin at one end of the wall and continue beyond the other end of the wall into the space, extending the line established by the wall.
- **Freestanding Wall** Using a freestanding flat or other structure that is approximately twelve to fifteen feet wide, move along both sides of the wall, appearing and disappearing from the audience's view.
- **Changing Wall** If the wall is imaginary, the Players may choose to change the shape and height of the wall. If working in a team, Players must decide where the changes are to happen so that all Players can maintain the illusion of the same wall.

4. Players create and memorize a simple action or series of actions to perform repeatedly as they travel along the wall, from the beginning to the end point. If Players are working in teams, they must decide whether they will perform the actions as an ensemble or one at a time.

Examples:
- **Wall Dance** Choose a simple movement or a series of movements that can be performed in unison, against the wall.
- **Locomotors + Wall** Ask Players to experiment with walking, running or using other locomotors to go away from and then return to the Wall. Have them choreograph a series of four to ten locomotors and set the number of repetitions the series is to be performed.
- **Wall + Time** Performance tempo of the action changes from slow to fast, or vice versa. Set the series of movements on a rhythm. Try various rhythms, such as 3/4, 4/4, 5/4, and 6/8.

5. If time allows, have Players direct one another in their Wall pieces. For example, soloists could pair up to create duets, one team could direct another team, or a single Player could direct the whole group.

Variations

Magnetic Wall Players choose a spot at some distance from the wall. This is their beginning position. They imagine the wall as an extremely powerful magnet. The Players are also "magnets," and are attracted to the wall. The Players can choose to freeze when they contact the wall, pass along the wall "magnetized," or pull away from the wall with the "magnetic" force creating resistance.

Relationships to a Wall Ask each Player to choreograph four to six relationships to a wall. (See Relationships to a Chair, page 55, for further ideas of how to lead this variation.)

Locomotors and Relationships Ask each Player to design four to six relationships to a wall. Then have them create four to six locomotor phrases that take the Player toward and away from the wall, to be used as transitions. Suggest to Players that the four to six relationships be against or near the wall, to contrast with the traveling locomotors.

Relocation Repeat any of the above ideas using a variety of walls. Try to find walls that have different textures, qualities of space, color, and so forth. Ask Players to describe how these differences affect their performance experience.

Performance Suggestions

Establish a "Backstage" Area If the site has no place to be out of the audience's view, a decision should be made about the manner in which the Players will wait to begin and end. You could ask them to stand quietly to the side of the performing space, even asking

them to stand with their backs to the audience as a signal that the work has either not begun or has ended.

 Teaching Notes

Management Tips

Art Use this activity to help students learn how to recognize various architectural styles and design elements. Select a variety of building or architectural designs that are examples of particular places or period styles, such as Classical Greek and Roman, Middle Eastern, Federal, Post Modern, or Arts and Crafts. Discuss how design elements might influence an individual's experience in the space.

 Assessment

Teacher Observations

- Did Players use the space creatively?
- Did they use the visual elements in the space in determining their selection of actions? Was the wall integral to their performance?
- Were they able to memorize and repeat movement patterns?

Group Discussion

- How did your wall choice influence your movement choices? Did its size, shape, color, or texture affect your performance?
- Do you think this activity might make you look at public spaces in a new way? How might architectural design influence the way people use a space?

 Student Activities

Book

Gallery

This activity presents another way to design and display activities within the boundaries of a space. A gallery is assembled by using image cues, such as photographs, drawings or symbols, or word and phrase cues. Just as architects and landscape designers provide structural cues and path systems to guide people on how to use a space, this game asks Players to react to visual images or language cues that they have placed throughout the space.

Skills

★ Interpreting and responding to visual and textual cues with creative and expressive movement, including pantomime
★ Developing sensory and emotional awareness
★ Experimenting with production design: mapping stage movement, order

Time

30 minutes or more. The first session may be devoted to gathering the information and materials. Subsequent sessions can experiment with placing the materials in several arrangements throughout the space and performing these different versions.

Space

Any large, open space, indoors or outdoors

Materials

Paper and drawing supplies, glue, tape, scissors, thumbtacks

★ Directions

1. Ask Players to gather entries for their gallery.

Suggestions for gallery entries:
- **Images** Find or make drawings, photographs, paintings, cartoons, or other visual source materials.
- **Symbols** Find or draw familiar symbols, such as editing marks, mathematics or scientific symbols, corporate logos, emblems, or symbols found on road signs, instructions, or maps. Symbols could also be made up to stand for agreed-upon actions or text; in which case they should be referenced in a key.
- **Words** Cut and paste or write words on paper to cue Players as to how they are to use areas or travel pathways in a space.
  - Action verbs (slide, fall, wait, spin)
  - Adjectives that elicit mood (excited, elated, uptight, joyful, fuming, disinterested) or atmosphere (expansive, contained, tranquil)
  - Descriptive terms or phrases (straight as a rod, wallowing in it, drag your feet, two-faced, head in the clouds, smelling like a rose)

2. Ask Players to make performance cue sheets by pasting, drawing, or writing selected gallery entries (images, symbols, or words) on large sheets of paper, one image, symbol, word, or phrase per sheet. They will function as commands to be interpreted by Players as they perform.

3. Establish the boundaries of the playing area. Have Players place or scatter the cue sheets within the playing area, either on walls or the floor. The placement of the cue sheets establishes where each symbol, image, or word is to be performed. (These cues could also be indicated on a map of the performing space. See Performance Map, page 159.)

4. Ask Players to decide how they will travel through the playing area to perform their gallery.

- Players could design an order or path to follow that connects them to each cue sheet.

- Players could travel anywhere within the boundaries of the playing area, choosing where, when, what, and how long to do each cue.

5. Direct Players to perform their gallery of images, symbols, and/ or words. Players will imitate, interpret, or react to the content of each cue.

★ Teaching Notes

Management Tips

Teams Divide the group into teams. Ask each team to make a set of cues for a space that the whole group has agreed upon, and design where the cues are to be placed. You or the group could decide upon a limit for the number of cues that each team provides; six cues is a comfortable number with which to begin. Teams can exchange cues and perform those of another team, or every team could take a turn performing all the sets of cues.

Connections

The visual images and language cues can be connected to various curriculum study areas.

Language Arts Use word cues that focus on specific parts of speech or phrases containing metaphors and similes.

History and Social Studies Address current events by using news photographs, headlines, and copy. Use famous historical quotes and photographs.

Foreign Languages Use bilingual word cues or cues only in the language being studied.

Special Needs

- ESL: Write bilingual word cues.
- Use Braille or audiotaped cues for Players who are visually impaired, or have them travel through the cues with a seeing partner.
- If necessary, arrange the space to accommodate wheelchairs.

 Assessment

Teacher Observations

- Were Players able to conceptualize, design, and produce a gallery environment?
- Did Players respond to image cues with creative and expressive movement solutions?

Group Discussion

- Do you think that the visual and verbal cues created a gallery environment? Why or why not?
- How do you think professional designers manipulate space to cue people on how to use the space? Give some examples.

 Student Activities

Journal

Ask Players to respond to the gallery performance experience.

Sculpture Garden

This game uses an indoor or outdoor environment as the inspiration for the creation of a sculpture garden. Working individually, in teams, or in one large group, Players become sculptures that reflect or react to the chosen space. For inspiration, Players may relate to the shape of architectural details and natural or human-made objects, such as a rock garden or piece of furniture. Players then share their sculpture poses and work together as a group to organize a sculpture garden performance.

★ Directions

1. Define the boundaries of the playing area, the area that will be referred to as the "garden." Explain

Skills

★ Observing and responding to the environment
★ Working in a group to organize and perform a sculpture garden

Time

30 minutes or more

Space

Any indoor or outdoor open space

Materials

Music can be added to create a sound environment. Art supplies, if maps are being drawn. Small hand props, bits of costume, and cloth could be made available to add to the sculptures. If you are planning a public performance, a uniform costume for the Players will distinguish them from other people in the environment.

that Players are going to create a sculpture garden by becoming sculptures that in some way reflect or relate to the garden space. In a discussion call Players' attention to details in the environment that might be useful in making their sculptures, such as architectural details or any specific natural or man-made objects.

2. Have Players work individually, in teams, or in one large group. Tell Players to choose and go to a spot in the playing area where they will become a sculpture. Encourage them to experiment with how to relate or react to that spot. Players could use their bodies to copy, become part of, or work in opposition to the details they choose in the space. Another approach would be to create a sculpture that infers a daily life relationship to these details.

Examples:

- **Copy a Shape**
  - Freeze as a copy of a pillar, tree, or rock next to that pillar, tree, or rock.
  - Copy the pose of a mannequin in a store window.
  - Shape your body into a right angle that reflects an architectural design element.

- **Become Part of a Shape**
  - Stand on a pedestal (piece of rock, stair) to become a neoclassical-style sculpture.
  - Become a decoration on the door jamb.

- **Opposition to a Shape**
  - Stand vertically next to a horizontal architectural line.
  - Lie down in a row of straight lines, dissecting a circle or oval-shaped playing field.

- **Daily Life Relationship**
  - Place your hand on the doorknob and in a position of someone about to open or close the door.
  - Pose on a bench, reading an imaginary book.
  - Become a person looking into a display window of a store.
  - Freeze in a position that reflects how someone could work in the space, such as a carpenter, an electrician, a gardener, or a teacher.

3. Give Players time to improvise sculpture poses in several places. Then have them share with each other some of their favorite solutions.

4. Ask Players to design a sculpture garden performance piece by selecting the ideas that work well in the space and with each other. Suggest that Players can become more than one sculpture by remaining in place, changing from pose to pose, or by moving from place to place, always assuming a new pose in each new location.

5. Decide how long the performance will last. Allow Players to decide how and when to change their sculpture poses within the time limit. For example, if the performance lasts fifteen minutes and each Player has five poses, they may perform their poses in equal or unequal time segments.

6. Perform the sculpture garden.

Variations

Design a Garden Have Players draw a map of the selected garden indicating boundaries and any significant details of the spatial environment. Players then indicate the placement of sculptures on their maps. Players could even draw the actual sculpture poses on the map. After Players have designed the sculpture garden, have them bring it to life.

Document a Garden Have Players draw their live sculpture garden either from memory or as quick sketches that are done on site.

Guided Tours Have some Players become docents who guide a tour through the sculpture garden, pointing out the historical and artistic relevance of each work.

Soap Box Create a sculpture garden to which monologues or dialogues will be added. Predetermine a cueing system so that Players know when to speak and when to be silent. Speeches could be performed in English or another language.

Monologues Each sculpture comes to life with a monologue. It can be a manifesto (a declaration about something that the statue wants changed in life) or a lecture. Topics can relate to curriculum or be open choice. Remind Players that the monologues are to be presented in the character of their sculptures, whether they are mythic gods, ordinary people, rocks, or right angles.

Dialogues Have statues converse or debate with one another. Remind Players to maintain their characters throughout the discussion.

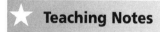
★ Teaching Notes

Management Tips

Warm-Up If you anticipate that your group may have difficulty relating to the environment with poses, begin with the following simple exercise. Ask all Players to find a shape in the environment to copy, such as a vertical, horizontal, or curved line. Then ask them to do

something that is the opposite of that shape.

Safe Poses Ask Players to pick poses that are safe for the space, themselves, and others. Tell Players that each person is to take responsibility for himself by supporting his own weight and maintaining his own balance, even when it may appear that several Players are depending on each other in a pose.

Group Poses For large group poses, Players could be given numbers and could join the sculpture pose one by one.

Connections

Art History Sculpture Garden could be a great art or history project. Existing works of art could be brought to life, or historical tableaux (see Living Pictures, page 126) could reflect a historical event or period. By using the Guided Tour variation, you could enhance learning about other cultures and integrate the use of different languages.

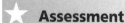
★ Assessment

Teacher Observations

- Were Players able to describe what they observed?

- Did Players' sculptures relate to the environment? Did Players copy shapes, become part of them, or infer daily life relationships in their poses?

- Were Players able to work cooperatively to select poses and organize a performance work of their sculpture garden?

Group Discussion

- How did Sculpture Garden help you become more aware of the environment and your relationship to it?

- Did you notice anything about the space you hadn't noticed before?

- Did you feel a part of the environment when you were posing as a sculpture?

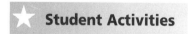
★ Student Activities

Book

page 106 (Performance Model)

Journal

Ask Players to describe a space or environment they think would make a good site for a sculpture garden.

Junk Pieces

Junk Pieces offers ways to make installations that function as set designs. An installation may create an environment that completely changes the entire performing space, or only slightly modifies it. It requires gathering together many objects ("junk") and then playing with them. Players may decide ways to preset the junk in a space, or leave it randomly scattered about. The objects may be used in ways related to their usual functions, or in ways that are entirely unrelated.

Junk Pieces can show how one person's junk is another person's treasure. From a lack of budgetary or material resources, you may find that "necessity is the mother of invention." Finding and manip-

ulating the objects can be an impetus into new explorations and experiences.

Junk Pieces can also be used to illustrate how recycled objects can be used to create something new and useful, which may last for only a few minutes or could become a permanent installation.

★ Directions

1. Divide the Players into teams. Have the teams divide up the junk you have previously gathered.

2. Choose a space where you will design the junk pieces. Each team may use the whole space or only a portion of it.

3. Direct Players to work with the junk until a design or performance idea that is dependent on the junk starts to form. You may wish to share some of the following ideas to get the Players started.

- **Create Junk Environments**
  - Make a landscape of objects, randomly scattered about the space. To perform, constantly move throughout the space while changing the configuration of the junk.
  - Design a junk set. Use the junk for a particular concept. For example, build a home out of plastic pipes and parachutes; use large pieces of cardboard cutouts or paper bags to create a forest of trees; use chairs to create a train.

- **Use Junk as Props and Costumes**
  For example, turn bamboo poles into a hand-held fence; use strips of mylar secured to a dowel rod to represent rain; use a large cooking spoon as a wand; turn paper bags into masks or tunics; use cotton mop heads for wigs.

4. Tell teams to plan and rehearse their junk pieces. Suggest that Players keep a record of their experimentations with the junk, through drawings or words, to help them plan their final junk pieces. You may wish to share the following planning ideas.

- Design your junk piece set concept. Make two-dimensional drawings that show how you want the junk set to look, or create a three-dimensional mock-up of your design.

Skills
★ Creating set designs and environments using miscellaneous objects
★ Working in a team to explore, plan, and perform a junk piece

Time
The introductory session can run from 30 minutes to an hour and a half. This activity can be developed over a series of sessions.

Space
Any large open space, indoors or outdoors

Materials
This project may require scavenging supplies. Investigate local resources. Some communities have free distribution centers for educators and community groups. Visit recycling centers. Try sending out "wish list" letters to parents and local merchants in your com-

munity. Sometimes you can get donations from your local sporting goods or department stores. If this project becomes a public performance, you can offer them program credit or free advertising space.

Suggestions:

Man-made objects, such as parachutes, tires, ladders, rope, lengths of elastic, large sheets of plastic, bolts of fabric, balls, plastic pipes, orange cone-shaped markers, benches, chairs, tables, umbrellas, buckets, paper bags, and cardboard boxes. Natural objects found in the environment, such as tree branches or trunks, bamboo poles, shells, and rocks

Preparation
Prior to playing Junk Pieces, gather together miscellaneous large and small pieces of junk, such as those listed in the Materials section.

- Select one of the following formats to help Players remember their performance tasks.
  - **Game** Create a series of rules, which Players interpret to play the game.
  - **Score** Devise a system for arranging or recording a series of performance actions. Your score can be drawings, photos, a list of tasks, or a map that shows how the junk is arranged and includes locations and descriptions of performers' actions.
  - **Scenario** Write an outline or plot of actions to which the performers improvise details of dialogue and actions.
  - **Skit** Establish a scene by choosing *Who, What,* and *Where,* from which the performers improvise.

6. Have the teams perform their junk pieces for one another.

Variations

Follow the Leader Have Players perform in teams of three to four Players. Each team lines up in the traditional follow-the-leader fashion. All teams interact with the environment at the same time. Each team works independently of the other teams. Sometimes teams may interact when their paths cross, affecting one another's activities. Examples of team interaction include one team leapfrogging over another team; one team moving objects into or out of the pathway of another team; one team giving another team a "high five" salute as they pass by.

(**Historical Note:** This variation was the basic idea of a work by choreographer Yvonne Rainer and sculptor Charles Ross, called *Room Service,* which premiered in 1963 at Judson Memorial Church, New York City. Three teams of three Players each roamed about the large sanctuary of the church, which was full of randomly scattered objects, such as large welded pipe sculptures, bed mattresses, springs, tires, and loads of other assorted junk.)

Tableaux Vivants Using the junk to construct an environmental set, Players create a vision, a slice of life, where they live in a frieze or series of friezes. *Tableaux Vivants* can be presented on a proscenium or open stage, or it can be on trucks or wagons in a large open space, where the audience moves from *tableau* to *tableau* (as in the presentations of medieval mystery plays). To help audiences understand the *tableaux,* a written description can be supplied. Use posters that function like subtitles in a film or supertitles in an opera (the words of text that are projected above the proscenium), or have text available for the audience to read at each *tableau,* explaining the story.

(**Historical Note:** This variation is similar to those designed by Peter Schumann's Bread and Puppet Theater in the Resurrection Circuses they put on during the 1980s in Vermont.)

Journey In this variation, the junk environment is seen and used as a landscape through which the Players take a journey. The objects may be arranged to form pathways, be used as a cueing device for direction changes, or the performers may improvise how they climb over, under, around, and through the junk.

Performance Suggestions

Preset and Strike The junk can be preset, or introduced as part of the entrance and removed as part of the exit.

Sound Let Players decide whether they want to include any of these sound ideas in their environment.

- Try "playing" the junk by banging on it, or brushing it with another object to see what kinds of sounds it may produce. (The 1990s show, *Stomp,* uses this method of creating rhythms for the performers; steel drum bands make their instruments by recycling steel oil drums.)
- Have a wandering musician improvise during performance (use any instruments that interest your Players).
- Play recorded sound effects.
- Use existing musical scores or create your own.

Costumes Make costumes out of junk by using scraps of fabric, plastic, newspapers, boxes, and paper bags. Another choice would be to wear team uniforms.

Program Order When working with teams, arrange a program order that the teams rehearse, so that one team's use of the environment segues into the next. Use the rearrangement of the junk as transitions, assigning jobs to Players to make it go smoothly, safely, and quickly.

Management Tips

Safety Discuss and demonstrate how to move the junk safely. Have Players work cooperatively to carry large objects so that no one's back is strained. You may want to assign a Traffic Manager, whose job is to help make sure that no collisions occur. If this is to be a large project, ask parents or aides to supervise and work with each team.

Storing Junk Objects Sometimes, people get very attached to their junk. Find a safe place to store it so that it cannot be easily taken and it will not interfere with other uses of the space.

Connections

Science and Social Studies Use this project as part of a unit on garbage, recycling, or environmental reclamation. Include objects that are being recycled presently, such as tires and plastics, or work in environments that are being "recycled," such as garbage dumps turned into parks or vacant lots recycled as gardens.

Language Arts Have students write scripts that can be performed using a junk environment, short stories that describe what is going on in the junk piece, poems or news accounts of the junk piece, or a press release to attract an audience for your project.

Teacher Observations

- Did Players find new ways to move in space and use objects in space?
- Were Players able to respond and adapt to a constantly changing spatial design?
- Were Players able to discuss, record, or notate their theater production concepts and execute them in a two-dimensional or three-dimensional set design, or a script, game, or score?

Group Discussion

- What is your definition of an environment? Has it changed since you did this piece? Why?
- Do you think the junk created an environment?
- Were you able to use the junk to change how the space felt or appeared?
- Did the junk appear to change when its use in the space changed?

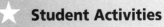

Book

page 107 (Performance Model)

Journal

Have Players note what they learned about theater productions (set design, building sets, using props, etc.) during the activity.

Floor Map

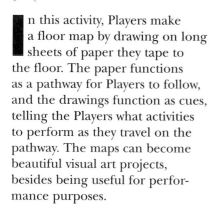

In this activity, Players make a floor map by drawing on long sheets of paper they tape to the floor. The paper functions as a pathway for Players to follow, and the drawings function as cues, telling the Players what activities to perform as they travel on the pathway. The maps can become beautiful visual art projects, besides being useful for performance purposes.

★ Directions

1. Decide whether Players will make their floor maps by working individually, as one group, or divided into teams.

2. Provide long rolls of butcher block paper, or smaller sheets of paper that Players can tape together into long strips. Explain to Players that they are going to make a floor map out of the paper, which will be placed on the floor like a path.

3. Discuss with Players the kinds of activities they could perform along the floor map. After they have chosen their activities, have them draw symbols, pictures, or words on the paper to represent these activities. Players could also add word and symbol cues to signal direction changes or draw pictures showing facial expression to indicate mood or character changes along the path. Or they could assign numbers to specific actions and place the numbers on the floor map to cue Players. If this method is used, be sure Players make a key for other performers to follow.

4. Direct Players to place their maps on the floor. Maps can be affixed to the floor with tape, or be held down by the performers or their assistants. (You may wish to have Players reverse the order of steps 3 and 4, so that they first tape their paper path to the floor, then draw on it.) Placement of the floor maps can follow any floor pattern.

Examples of floor patterns:
- Series of parallel lines
- Zigzag progression
- Crossing paths
- Geometric shapes such as triangles, squares, or diamonds

5. Have Players perform their floor maps for one another.

- Perform as solos or in teams.

- Traveling can occur on or next to the floor map, progressing from the beginning point to the ending point.

Performance Suggestions

Hands/Feet Pattern Participants travel the pathway decorated with patterns made from the outlines of their hands and feet. They may actually fit their hands and feet into the outlines on the path, or decide on a different way to travel the path.

Cardinal Points Use the floor map to suggest performance ideas based on connections to the four cardinal directions (North, South, East, and West). Place two long strips of paper on the floor in the shape of a crossroads path, with the four ends oriented to the four directions. Ask students to relate their activities to geography, travel, climate, geology, politics, or culture. For example, ask Players to go on a journey from North to South. As they journey, Players call out where they are starting from and where they are going. A script can be written, or borrowed from existing poems or quotations, that is connected to the places and people being represented by each group of travelers. (See Compass Points, page 119, which uses the floor map in this manner.)

Skills

★ Selecting activities to perform, and drawing activity cues on a floor map

★ Blocking stage movement by making a floor map

Time

This activity can be divided into at least two sessions. The design part of the project can be discussed and executed over one or two sessions of 40 minutes to an hour. The performance solution to the project can take place in another session of similar length. If developed into performance, rehearsal sessions will be needed.

Space

Adaptable to any open space, indoors or outdoors

Materials

Long strips of paper such as butcher block paper, colored markers or fabric paints, tape to secure the ends of the paper. Besides taking the form of one long strip of paper, a floor map could also be created by using long strips of cloth, rope, or tape. If using cloth strips, dowel rods can be stapled or sewn at either end, to help anchor the strips. Activity cues can be drawn on separate pieces of paper that are placed beside the path.

Teaching Notes

Management Tips

Rehearsal Suggestions Use one of these ideas to protect the floor map during rehearsals:

- Have Players work in their socks.
- Have Players travel next to the floor map, rather than on top of it.
- Duplicate the map. Use the copy during rehearsal, saving the original for performance.

Sound Try out different sound environments, if Players have not thought about this design aspect. Sound can organize the performance by providing a unifying rhythm; sound can also energize the performers.

Connections

History Make a timeline on the floor map that relates to historical events, places, or periods being studied. Have Players perform appropriate actions for each item on the timeline.

Language Arts Have Players include spoken text in their floor map performances. They could improvise monologues and dialogues, or read or memorize existing literature to recite while traveling the map.

Visual Arts Make the maps reflect the decorative art style of a period or place being studied. Besides drawing, use other techniques, such as wood block printing and stenciling.

Special Needs

- This activity works well with students who have difficulty with memorization, because the floor map actually contains all of the cues. If their problem is related to tracking, the pathway will keep them on task.
- For students who have difficulty with reading, use symbols and other visuals as cues.
- For students with focus and attention problems, this game helps develop those skills by providing support through experiential learning.

 Assessment

Teacher Observations

- Were Players able to devise and follow activity cues on the floor map?
- Did Players explore a variety of solutions in constructing their floor maps and selecting activities? Did they incorporate elements of dance, music, and the visual arts into their compositions?
- Did the map's floor pattern seem to aid Players' focus and spatial perception?

Group Discussion

- Did you find it helpful to have the blocking (floor pattern) made visual? How?
- What kinds of cues were easiest to follow?

 Student Activities

Journal

Have Players describe spaces that include designs similar in function to their floor maps.

Performance Map

6

To make a performance map, Players first choose a site and draw a physical map of it, indicating its distinguishing physical characteristics and establishing its boundaries. Players then add their concept of how performers are to use the space. For example, they may include on the performance map what actions will happen, where these actions will be located in the space, and the order in which they will be performed.

This performance map serves as a guide for performers. The resulting piece, a site-specific project, is completely dependent on the particulars of the chosen space. When a piece has to undergo major revisions in order to be relocated to another site, then you know that you have succeeded in being site-specific.

★ Directions

1. Choose a performing space, or allow Players to agree on one. Choices could include a garden, a gymnasium, a classroom, a hallway, or a street scene. If possible, visit the space and call attention to its boundaries and physical characteristics, including natural features, architectural details, or other objects.

2. Have each Player draft a diagram of the space while they are in it, to be refined later. Alternatively, you could have all Players participate in the creation of one map, or direct them to work in teams, with each team making a team map. On their maps, Players should indicate the spatial characteristics, such as boundaries, edges, or limits, and locate significant physical details

that break up the space. For example, a map of an indoor space might include walls, doorways, windows, furniture, and other architectural or design details. A map of an outdoor space might show the placement of trees, hills, pathways, buildings, and courtyards.

3. Ask Players to think about what kinds of activities and events they might want to perform in the space and where they might want to do them. Suggest that Players record their ideas. Other performance elements they could consider include sound, script, lighting, and costumes. This conceptualizing could happen in the space itself or occur later, in the classroom.

4. After they have made a final decision about what to perform, have Players decide where to locate these activities in the performing space. If planning to perform before an audience, Players must also decide where to place them, if and how the audience should move with the performance, or if they should be asked to become part of the performance. These design problems can be solved many ways. Following are some suggestions.

- Divide the space into areas. Decide what activities or events are to take place in the space at specific locations, or stations.

- Create a route to follow and specify activities to take place along the route. Designate entrance and exit points.

- To add to the performance challenge, decide what happens in the transitions between events, when the performers travel from station to station.

Skills

★ Analyzing and diagramming the physical characteristics of a performance site

★ Conceptualizing and refining a site-specific production

★ Designing stage action and blocking stage movement

★ Recording performance activities and their location and order on a performance map

Time

The introductory session, in which Players choose and map a specific site, will take at least 30 minutes. Performance Map can evolve into a major project. Sessions will need to be divided into limited objectives: choose and analyze a space; locate the

boundaries of the space; teach students how to map the space. In following sessions, you could discuss what to do in the space; experiment with working in the environment and designing activities for the environment; have students locate their choices of activities on their maps; and try performing the maps for each other.

Space

Adaptable to any space, indoors or outdoors

Materials

Materials for making maps: paper, pencils, crayons, markers, butcher block or other kind of paper, and tape. Costumes, small hand props, and set pieces may be added later if appropriate for the project.

5. Advise Players to think about the order in which they want the activities to be performed. They may choose random order, allowing for each individual performer's choice. However, if they wish to predetermine the order of activities for performance, Players must indicate this on their maps. This could be done simply by numbering activities or stations.

6. Tell Players to add these activities/events and their location and order to their maps. Following are some suggestions for accomplishing this.

- Draw the space divisions, route, and/or stations on the map.

- Assign a symbol or number to each activity.

- Locate the symbols or numbers on the map where the activities are to take place.

- Make a key of the symbols and numbers so anyone may read and interpret the map to understand what to do and where to do it.

7. Decide how you want the group to perform the performance maps. Players can:

- give solo performances of their own maps.

- perform solos of their own maps, simultaneously, in small groups, or with the whole group.

- exchange maps and perform another Player's map.

- select one Player's map, and perform simultaneously, with interpretations left up to each individual.

- select one Player's map and have all perform in unison.

- form teams to perform a selected map. This can be done simultaneously with other teams, or one team at a time.

- use a number system to perform a selected map. Assign each member of the group a number and designate one Player as caller. As the caller calls out a number or numbers, those assigned the numbers perform the map. Decide how the number system is to be connected to the reading of each map. For example, the caller directs Players 2, 4, 7, and 10 to go to the jumping area in the left-hand corner by the door, or to the pink area in the center, or to follow the zigzag path.

Variations

Audience Participation When an audience is to be part of the performance, decide if they are to be stationary (watchers within the environment) or if they are to participate. If the former, rope off an area for the audience to use, or have guides to direct them to an observation area. If you want the audience to participate in the performance, how will they know what to do? One possibility is to divide the audience into groups, which are led by Players. Each Leader knows the activities to ask his group to do. Leaders may carry a flag or play an instrument, to identify them as Leaders and to keep their groups together. In this way, the audience learns how to participate in the environment as any Player would. Another possibility is to give the audience copies of the maps and ask them to interpret and perform the maps individually.

Perform in Character Have Players create a real or imaginary, human or nonhuman character or characters who might use the space or have a connection to the space. For example, Players could go through "a day in the life of. . ." create a narrative, or place scenes along the route or within various specified areas.

Transitions A performance map could include transitions that take Players to various particular points of arrival (stations), or to gathering places as performers travel their path.

- Station 1 (top landing of a stairway): Sit at the landing for ten seconds.
- Transition 1: Run down the stairs to Station 2.
- Station 2 (doorway): Stop in a frieze for twenty seconds.
- Transition 2: Laugh as you move down the hall to Station 3.
- Station 3 (classroom doorway): Line up.
- Transition 3: Walk silently into the room.

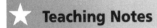 **Teaching Notes**

Management Tips

Post the Maps Place the maps in an easily accessible area, so that performers can consult them when necessary.

Interpreting Performance Maps Allow for flexible interpretations of directions. Different readers may come up with different solutions to the same diagram.

Rehearsal Suggestion Have performers walk the space with map in hand to orient themselves to the space and to understand the directions given on the map. They should also rehearse the activities that are to happen along the route or in the stations.

Performance Tip Have performers memorize the route, directions, and areas for performance.

Connections

History Choose a space that is connected to a historical event or period, and have the map reflect research on events or ways of life of that time.

Language Arts Have Players include text in their concept. For example, certain parts of the site could be designated as areas in which to improvise monologues and dialogues or give a literature reading.

 Assessment

Teacher Observations

- Were Players able to draw physical maps of their chosen sites?
- Did Players design activities that responded to the environment?

- Did Players use their maps as a method to design and record production ideas?
- Were Players able to follow the directions recorded on their performance maps?

Group Discussion

- Did you find a performance map a useful tool in designing, recording, and performing a production? How?
- Did you learn to see space in a new way? How did particular details in the space influence your selection of actions and their locations?

 Student Activities

Book

pages 108–109 (Writing Model)

Journal

Ask Players to give examples of what they learned about designing a performance for a particular space.

Mapping a Remembered Space

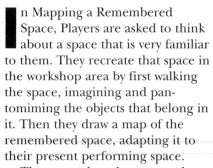

In Mapping a Remembered Space, Players are asked to think about a space that is very familiar to them. They recreate that space in the workshop area by first walking the space, imagining and pantomiming the objects that belong in it. Then they draw a map of the remembered space, adapting it to their present performing space.

The remembered space can be invoked many ways through performance. Pantomime can communicate the spatial design and any objects that belong to the remembered place; or sets, sound, lighting, props, and costumes can recreate the remembered site. The Players could also write a script. Whatever is done in performance should be appropriate to the remembered space, and any characters portrayed should be connected to it.

★ Directions

1. Ask Players to close their eyes and visualize a space that is very important to them, and that they know extremely well. It could be their own room, a room in their grandparent's or best friend's home, a park, a store.

2. Direct the Players to walk around the rehearsal space as though they were in the remembered space. Tell them to decide how to orient the remembered space in the rehearsal space. For example, they could decide the location of doors, windows, furniture, and anything else that belongs in the space.

3. Help Players recall all of the important details of their remembered spaces.

- Ask everyone using an indoor space to enter through the doorway of their remembered space, open and close the windows, and use the furniture and objects in the room.

- Ask everyone using an outdoor space to walk to the main focal point of the space and use the space in ways that show the characteristics of the space.

4. Ask each Player to draw a map of the remembered space, placing it within the boundaries of the real performing area. The map should indicate boundaries, architectural/landscape details, and furnishings. If possible, have Players draw the map during class time. If given as a homework assignment, ask them to draw only from memory, not while they are actually in the remembered space.

5. Have Players perform their remembered spaces for one another. After each Player's performance, the other Players could discuss their impressions of where and what the space was and what was happening in it.

Performance Suggestions

Monologue Have each Player improvise a monologue, playing himself or another character. To work on character development, ask Players to think of one word or phrase and one action that they associate with that person. Then suggest that they try as many ways as possible to repeat the action and phrase, doing them in different places. Finally, have them add more words and actions to build out the character. Ask Players to explain the

Skills
★ Visualizing and re-creating a place through sensory recall
★ Drawing a map from memory
★ Using pantomime
★ Creating an environment that functions as a set

Time
Multiple sessions lasting 30 minutes or more, with each session targeting a limited objective. The first session could involve choosing a remembered site and deciding how to make it conform to the limits of the workspace. Making a map of the space could be assigned as homework. In following sessions, Players could create an imaginary set, design and construct a real set, gather or make props, improvise ways to perform, and finally add characters' actions, and text.

Space
Theoretically, adaptable to any space

Materials
This project could be done with nothing, leaving everything to the imagination. It could be done with a bare minimum of drawing supplies, and perhaps some masking tape to mark entrances, furniture, windows, or other important details that belong to the space. Or it could be done with whatever materials can be gathered to recreate a set as elaborate as you and your students wish to make it.

reason for, or the story behind, their word and action choices. This explanation could become the monologue, or be added to what was being done originally.

Dialogue Have Players improvise a dialogue between two or three characters.

- One character could be the performer. All characters could be performed by the same Player, or a different Player could portray each character.

- Two monologues could be reworked as a dialogue that takes place within one space or two spaces (as in a telephone conversation).

Players Become the Set Have each Player direct other Players to create her set by becoming the set pieces. In other words, Players take on the shape of tables, doors, lamps, and other objects in a remembered space.

Abstract Set Every object in a room can be represented by chairs or tables. For example, a line of four chairs can be a bed or bench. Two chairs with backs facing the audience can stand for a lunch counter.

Time Cues Tell Players to imagine that they are in their remembered spaces. Call out various times of day, asking everyone to pantomime whatever they do at that time in their space. (Tell Players to exit the playing area when they are not ordinarily in their space, and to enter and remain in the remembered space when they are usually there.)

 Teaching Notes

Management Tips

Visualization Exercises To prepare students to visualize a space in great detail, lead them in sense memory exercises for a week or so before they begin this project.

Examples:
- Ask Players to visualize how they left their bedrooms that morning. Were the shades drawn or open? What clothes were on the floor? Were their beds made? Tell them to check their bedrooms when they go home to see if their memories were correct.
- Ask Players to visualize how they came to school. What did they see as they rode or walked? Have them list five to ten things they saw and share them with one another.
- Have Players observe what happens on the playground or during lunch break. Ask them to list five to ten things they heard, smelled, tasted, or saw.

Marking the Space Call specific directions that everyone does simultaneously.

Examples:
- Walk the edges of your remembered space, making it the actual size, if the workshop area allows.
- Stand at the entrance to the space.
- Walk the edges of large objects in the space, such as beds, sofas, desks, and chests.

Recall and Pantomime Have everyone visualize the same kind of space. For example, ask everyone to remember the place where they sleep at night, or the space they feel is "theirs." Ask them to pantomime any activities they do in their space, and in doing so, to reveal the appearance, size, and details of the space.

Peer Evaluation Throughout the course of working on the project, have Players observe one another's pieces and provide feedback about what is being communicated about the remembered space.

Connections

Visual Arts Encourage Players to make two-dimensional drawings, and/or three-dimensional models of their remembered spaces.

Social Studies If the remembered site is connected to family, friends, or a local area, connect this activity to an oral history project. Tell students to interview people who have memories related to the space. The information gathered in the interviews can then be used to write a narrative, which is included in the performance.

Language Arts

- Have Players write an autobiographical story, poem, or essay.

- Have Players write a script and develop characterizations that suggest place and time.

Assessment

Teacher Observations

Look for consistency in how Players use the objects in the space. Make sure that the door is always in the same place, and that it opens and closes in the same direction, that tables and other objects remain consistent in their placement and size.

- Does the performance reflect the map that was drawn?

- Did students use pantomime effectively to indicate the objects in and characteristics of the space they were presenting?

- Did students create characters through their use of the space and its objects?

Group Discussion

- Could you really see the remembered space throughout the activity? Did you feel you were actually in the space as you performed?

- What helped you maintain the focus needed to be consistent in communicating the physical details of the space?

- What senses did you find were most useful in helping you recall and visualize the space and the people connected to it?

 Student Activities

Journal

Encourage Players to enter selected observations of places or people, including bits of overheard conversations. These observations could become source material to be used for designing sets, writing scripts, or creating a character.

Mapping an Imaginary Space

In Mapping an Imaginary Space, Players get a chance to indulge in complete fantasy, or to make the style of another time and place their own. They create a drawing of an imaginary place, then make a map in which they adapt their vision to fit into the performing space. Then they decide how to perform in the imagined space so as to communicate its properties and the activities that occur there. The performances could be done in a minimal style, using pantomime to communicate objects and character, or they could involve full production elements, such as a script, a set, sound, lighting, props, makeup, and costumes.

★ Directions

1. Ask each Player to create a drawing of an imaginary place. It can be from any place in time or space, including a completely original concept. It can be based on a literary or historical setting.

2. Have the Players translate their drawings into a map that fits the imaginary space within the boundaries of the real performing space. The map should indicate boundaries and important architectural or landscape details and furnishings. If there is to be a set, base the design upon the map.

3. Have Players improvise in their imaginary spaces. Help them explore the sensory characteristics of their imaginary spaces by asking them leading questions about the spaces and suggesting ways to manipulate objects.

Examples:
- *You want them to clarify the boundaries of their space:* Walk the edges of your space. Where does the space begin and end?

- *You want them to react to imaginary stimuli of sounds, smells,* *sights, and touches:* What do objects in the space feel like? What can you hear? Is the temperature hot or cold? What can you see in the space? What can you see in the distance?

- *You want them to convey differences of weight, size, volume:* Is that object heavy or light? Is that wall rough or smooth to the touch? How high it? How far do you have to reach across the table?

4. After the Players have established a firm idea of the imaginary space through exploratory improvisations, tell them to decide what they will perform in the space. What characters will they portray? What happens to the character? Allow time for the Players to improvise to select essential qualities of movement to express character and story line. If they seem to need additional help, cue them with questions such as the following.

- Who lives in this space? Is anyone with you?

- What do you do all day long in this space? What is the usual routine?

- What unusual events could happen?

5. Allow Players to share their pieces as works in progress.

Skills
- ★ Visualizing an imaginary space
- ★ Mapping out an imaginary space and recreating it in the performance space
- ★ Improvising a performance based on a set design
- ★ Using voice and pantomime to portray character and plot

Time
Several sessions, each lasting at least 30 minutes. In the first session, ask Players to imagine a space and make a drawing of it. Then, have them translate their drawings into maps that fit inside the available performing space. In following sessions, they could experiment with designing and constructing a set or improvise ways to perform in the environment, selecting actions and words to create character and plot. If the set is to remain imaginary, have performers work out the placement of their imaginary set.

Space
Theoretically, adaptable to any space

Materials
This project could be done with nothing, leaving everything to the imagination, or it could be as elaborate as you and your students wish to make it. If you take the latter route, it may require scavenging supplies for building sets.

Teaching Notes

Management Tips

Realizing Design Visions If you and your Players want to see their imaginary space ideas become performance pieces, discuss how they might want to do it. Students often have great and grand ideas that have been honed by big-budget Hollywood and television special effects. As with all artists in realizing their visions, they will be faced by realistic limitations of budget, space, and time. Can a great vision be brought to life within these limitations? Yes! A vision of a golden staircase can be accomplished with a painted stepladder or stack

of boxes. A vision of a castle with gargoyles and a moat can be formed by people. Encourage Players to use their imaginations; sometimes, it is more effective to create an environment using nothing but the imaginary images evoked through pantomime and, perhaps, sound and lighting effects.

Connections

Art Have Players study the drawings of artists—such as Leonardo da Vinci's flying machines—to discover that artists often record ideas that they never expect to become a reality, or that they are not sure how to make a reality.

History If the imaginary space is related to a particular historical period or event, encourage Players to research written sources such as speeches, journals, newspapers, recorded dialogues, and existing plays and include excerpts of the text in their performances.

Language Arts Have each Player write a script, using a narrative play structure, that has as its setting an imaginary space.

★ Assessment

Teacher Observations

- Were Players able to use the available materials to realize their design and production ideas?
- Did they create environments—real or imaginary—that functioned as a set?
- Did their movements and words help make the set come alive?

Group Discussion

- What did you like about creating a set from your imagination? If you had the chance to do this project again, would you choose the same imaginary space? What made this choice so satisfying to work with?
- Which part of the activity did you like best? Why?
- Was it difficult to recreate your imaginary space in the performance area? Explain.

★ Student Activities

Journal

Ask Players to describe another imaginary space they would like to create, knowing what they know now about creating a performance environment. Have them explain how they would go about constructing a set for performance.

Relocations

What do you do when you love a site but can't perform in it? Relocate the site! For example, you would love to perform on the span of a bridge, but can't get legal clearance; you want the drama of rush hour at a major subway station, but it is not safe for your group of performers to be there at that time; you want your class to do a project related to a recent field trip to a historical or cultural site.

To relocate the site to its new home, first visit your chosen site or study photographs, drawings, and any written descriptions of that site. Then record your observations, feelings, and reactions to the space, making them primary source material for a performance work. Finally, adapt your observations of the original site to a new location, using the primary site as inspiration and model.

Skills

★ Recognizing that theater can be a reflection of life in particular times, places, and cultures
★ Analyzing an environment to develop performance ideas
★ Working collaboratively and safely to select and create elements of set, lighting, and sound to signify environments and costume and makeup to suggest character
★ Designing a set based on an actual place

Time

Sessions can last 30 or more minutes and be divided into sessions that each target one or two steps of the directions. A field trip to the chosen site could take a half a day.

Space

Adapt any site to your work or performing space.

Materials

Art and writing supplies for making maps. Research materials, including books, films, and videos, may be helpful. Hand props, costumes, and set pieces can be added to the environment. Materials can be as simple or elaborate as time, money, interest, and availability will allow.

★ Directions

1. Choose and visit a specific site to make observations. Direct Players to closely observe the site and the people or objects in it. Cue Players to notice smells, sounds, dialogue overheard, personal thoughts while in the space, actions done in the space by themselves or others, and natural elements, such as the wind and rain. Suggest that Players make mental or written notes while in the space to refer to later.

2. If possible, have Players improvise in the space, sensing the qualities that are particular to that place, time, and the inhabitants of the space. Ask them to try imitating or mirroring objects and people that inhabit the space.

Example:
Watch a person sitting on a bench feeding pigeons. Sit on another bench, at a distance so that the person is not aware of what you are doing, and mirror her actions.

3. Have Players translate the observed site into a rough map of the site, either while they are at the site, or after you return to your workspace.

4. To create a relocation, take Players to their performing space and have them adapt the original site's map to this space.

5. Have Players collaborate to create a performance. To make a performance that uses the relocated site, Players can try recreating exactly what they saw, or they can create a new vision that is inspired by what they saw, heard, and felt in the original site. Share the following ideas with the Players to help them get started.

• Build structures or create suggestions of elements found at the original site. Ladders could become buildings and bridges; a parachute or sheets of plastic could become a lake; tables and chairs could be stacked to represent a mountain; flashlights could be used to recreate lightning; a length of rope can serve as a path; pieces of a sheet could be clouds under the performers' feet.

• Become a person or object that you observed, imagined, or researched within the original site.

• Improvise, trying different orders of actions until a performance score evolves.

• Create problems to solve, or actions to perform, that are appropriate to ordinary life in the space.

Example:

Four people agree to meet each other at the entrance to a subway station at a certain time. Each must solve how to get there on a route different from everyone else's. When they meet, they all decide what to do next.

Variations

Site Research Research a site you can't visit. Collect visual data. Study films, videos, photographs, paintings, graphics, or maps. Find written descriptions in diaries, journals, books, and news reports.

 Teaching Notes

Management Tips

Working in Teams If you have a large group, divide it into teams. Team members can be assigned or can volunteer for tasks.

Production Jobs If your group decides to turn their Relocation piece into a full-scale production, assign specific jobs to certain individuals or teams. (See descriptions of production jobs in Chapter 11, Showtime! pages 235–238.)

- **Writing a Script or Score** One person keeps a record of improvisational material to be used in writing the script. Another collates the information into a performance order. Another types the final draft.

- **Director** Each team could assign one of their Players to be their director.

- **Designing the Environment** Someone may design the set, another the sound, another the lighting, and another the costumes. Or all Players share this responsibility.

- **Technical Crew** Someone is stage manager, who coordinates all the Players and supervises the crew. Other Players can be the crew who run the lights and sound, maintain props, gather and maintain costumes, set up and strike the set.

Connections

Relate the choice of site to what the class is studying in history, social studies, literature, or science.

Science Visit a nature museum that has an exhibit of a live bee colony and ask Players to map the colony's patterns.

History and Social Studies Visit n historical restoration site and divide up Players to map different areas of the site.

Language Arts Visit a local site that inspired the setting of a poem, story, or novel. For example, visit Monterey, California, to see Cannery Row, where John Steinbeck's novel of the same name was located; the Hill District of Pittsburgh, the setting of many plays by August Wilson; or the Albuquerque, New Mexico, landscapes and Indo-Hispanic culture of Rudolfo Anaya's novels.

 Assessment

Teacher Observations

- Were Players able to concentrate on making observations of a site?

- Were Players able to translate their observations to a map?

- How did Players create their Relocations performances? Did they manage to convey the original site?

Group Discussion

Lead a discussion about how theater can reflect life in particular times, places, and cultures. Ask students what they enjoyed about relocating a site from one place to another. Did they feel that their relocation performances really evoked the original space and its inhabitants?

 Student Activities

Book

page 110 (Performance Model)

Journal

- Have Players describe a site that they would like to recreate in a stage set.

- Ask Players to go to a site and record their observations and feelings about the site.

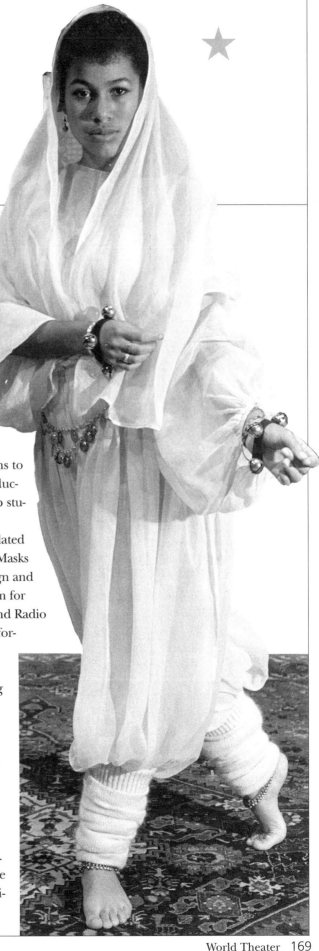

World Theater

This chapter is a resource of theatrical forms. As such, it does not lend itself to the lesson plan format previously used. It is intended as an opportunity to familiarize the teacher and students with world theater genres and provide explorations of the forms from a variety of perspectives, such as performance experimentation, historical research, critical reviewing, video and live theater exposure, biographical reading, set/costume design, and advertising projects.

Many of the forms include examples from various traditions, cultures, and times, and suggest resources for research projects and audience viewing. For hands-on experiences, there are warm-up games and activities, and directing suggestions to help introduce skills and methods. If you decide to make a production using these genres, you will find suggestions on how to help students create their own versions of the forms.

Clowning and Stock Characters address performance issues related to finding and developing character. Shadow Plays and Puppets, Masks and Masquerades, and Radio Theater give opportunities for design and technical production experiences, besides providing a fresh forum for scriptwriting. Melodrama, Living Newspaper, Readers' Theater, and Radio Theater refer to scripted forms that lend themselves easily to performances that do not require long preparations, memorization of lines, and special performing techniques. Tableaux Vivants and Entr'Actes show you how to take quick studies and, by structuring them into a sequence, create a cohesive event.

All of these popular theatrical forms can be mixed and matched to make an event that suits the needs of your students and curriculum, and the time available. If used for performance purposes, World Theater activities can be combined with other activities in this book, be complete events in themselves, or be used as structures or techniques to solve parts of an event.

These interdisciplinary forms exemplify the axiom that theater reflects the life of particular times, places, and cultures. They are vivid, attractive vehicles to illustrate how arts influence and reflect culture and history; and to provide audience experiences that develop students' aesthetic appreciation.

Clowns and Clowning

What is funny? This is the central question to consider in order to be a clown. The answer will always be personal, because every clown is unique.

A clown cannot perform a joke, as though he knows it is a joke. In order for a bit to play as funny, a clown needs to set up his or her actions in completely serious situations, using the same kinds of theatrical questions and preparation that are used to find any character. Every slip, chase, fall, or last-minute rescue must have a justification that answers the *Who, Where, What,* and *Why* questions. For instance, if a clown falls, the manner in which he falls can be the result of a banana peel in his path, how the curtain opens, or the excessive energy he uses to bow.

Clowns explore the possibilities of each situation looking for the surprise that will earn a laugh from the audience. Most clowns deal with actions that are unexpected, that catch the audience unaware, that may be a little dangerous, scary, or violent. They make jokes about what we are afraid of, angry about, or shocked by, giving us the safety valve of laughter to deal with our feelings.

Clowning is a form of theater requiring years of training to master. Much clowning depends on physical comedy, so would-be clowns study dance, mime, acting, and acrobatics. They often master unusual skills to create specialty acts, becoming a contortionist, fire eater, trapeze artist, juggler, magician, or slack or tightrope gymnast. Many clowns study music as well.

Clowns and Clowning gives Players many ways to think about clowning and how to discover a clown character. They can research historical precedents, analyze their own and others' perceptions of humor, experiment with designing costumes and/or masks to express character, and improvise comic bits or routines.

⭐ Researching the Form

According to Eric Partridge's etymological dictionary, *Origins,* the word *clown* comes from the word *clew,* meaning *lump* or *lumpish,* and refers to a person who is a buffoon or clumsy boor, a farm worker who seemed funny to townspeople. *Clown* eventually came to mean a funny fellow, a jester.

Sometimes known as a *trickster,* as in African and Native American cultures, and sometimes thought of as a fool or jester, the clown's roots go back to prehistoric times, where foolishness might have played a part in lightening the awesome nature of ritual ceremonies. We can still see relics of clowning traditions in the whirlwind appearances and disappearances of the Yoruban trickster *Egungun,* who transforms from human to snake to man to woman to baboon, and who makes fun of foreigners, in contrast to the mysteries and beauties of the other *Egungun* masks; and in the New Mexican Hopi Indian clowns, who, in mud-smeared faces and rabbit-fur wigs, ride their horses and shoot their bows and arrows backward, mocking the serious kachina dances with their wild interruptions. Clowns are given a similar role in China, Bali, and India, where they are allowed to improvise interruptions at very sacred theatrical presentations.

European clowning origins can still be seen in traditional folk drama and holiday celebrations. One example, still found in English country villages, are the fools, wearing charcoal blackened faces, foxtails on their heads, and costumes of paper ribbons attached to their clothes. Their job is to clear the performance space at festivals. The *Wilde Manns* of Basel have a related task, at Carnival time, when they sweep tree branches at children who try to grab the apples attached to their skirts of leaves.

In medieval and Renaissance times, the traditions of jesters and fools developed from those of the

Materials

You can do a lot of wonderful clown work without anything. However, it is fun to be able to offer a grab bag of hand props, including juggling clubs, balls, ropes, hula hoops, buckets, mops, and bits and pieces of costumes, especially all kinds of hats. If you decide to teach makeup skills, you will need to supply students with the necessary tools and equipment, or ask them to supply their own. (See Chapter 11, Showtime! and the Student Book for makeup suggestions. You will need acrobatic mats to practice gymnastic stunts.)

traveling troubadours or minstrels. They were singers whose songs conveyed the political and social gossip before the days of newspapers. Jesters, or fools, became powerful in the courts, influencing policy decisions through their jokes and banter.

The origin of Western theatrical clowning has its roots in the masked theatrical performances of Greece and Rome. These traditions relied greatly on grotesque masks and distorted movement. The farces required so much mime and dance that performers had to be skilled acrobats. Their plots and stock characterizations fed directly into the masked comedies of the commedia dell'arte, where they flourished, passing on a rich heritage of even more stock character types and stock stage business. These traditions continue today, passed down through twentieth-century clowns of radio, film, and television comedy: Charlie Chaplin, W. C. Fields, Mae West, Max Sennett, the Marx Brothers, Laurel and Hardy, Jack Benny, Bert Lahr, Steppin Fetchit, Lucille Ball, Cheech and Chong, Robin Williams, Eddie Murphy, Bill Irwin, and the Waymin brothers.

Student Research Projects

- Compare clowning styles, looking for different types of clown masks, costumes, and actions in various cultures. For example, study Japanese *Kyogen* plays, the entr'actes sandwiched between Noh plays; Yoruban *Egungun* from Nigeria; and Hopi katchina clowns of the Southwestern United States' Native American pueblo people.
- Study European clowning during the Middle Ages and Renaissance, as practiced in the courts and theater. Discuss a style in general (such as royal jesters or commedia stock characters), or find biographies of famous practitioners, such as:
  - **Royal Jesters** Triboulet and Caillette (1525–1540, French);

Will Somers (English, d. 1560, King Henry VIII's jester); Richard Tarleton (English, d. 1588, Queen Elizabeth I's fool)
  - **Commedia dell'Arte** Tiberio Fiorelli (1608–1694, Scaramouche); Domenica Biancolelli (1637–1688, Arlecchino/Harlequin); Evaristo Gherardi (1633–1700, Harlequin); John Rich (1692–1761, Harlequin)
- Describe and compare the three main types of clowns found in Western circuses: auguste clowns, whiteface clowns, and traditional clowns. Or find biographies of famous practitioners.
  - **Auguste Clown** A white-faced, big-nosed, dumb comic in a spangled costume, made popular by Joseph Grimaldi and Frank Brown. The white face may be broken up by geometric shapes in various colors.
  - **Whiteface Clown** A kind of fantasy image, a cartoon. The "straight man," or the one who appears serious, graceful, and sophisticated. Often works in partnership with an auguste clown. Look for Jean-Gaspard (French, as Pierrot 1796–1846); and Theodore Hall (1864–1921, known as "Footit"), who worked with auguste clown Raphael Padilla (1868–1917, known as "Chocolat") as his "fall guy."
  - **Character Clown** An exaggeration of an everyday life or stock character, such as the tramp or shopping bag lady, the washerwoman or cleaning lady, the doctor or professor, or the nurse Emmett Kelly, Groucho Marx, and the Waymin Brothers are examples of character clowns.
- Write a biography of a famous nineteenth- or twentieth-century European or American circus clown.
  - Nineteenth-century clowns include Joey Grimaldi, British, (1788–1837); Dan Rice (1823–1900), an American

famous for his role as Uncle Sam and who worked with his learned pig, Lord Byron; and Frank Brown, also known as Flan Blon (1858–1924).
  - Twentieth-century clowns include the Fratellini family of Italy (c. 1900–   ); Charlie Chaplin as the "Little Tramp" (British/American (1889–1977); Emmett Kelly's "Willie the Tramp" (American, 1880–1959); Buster Keaton (American, 1895–1966); and the German clown, Valentin (1882–1948).
- Research the development of clowning in film and television as performed by Charlie Chaplin, Buster Keaton, the Marx Brothers, Jacques Tati, Cheech and Chong, Robin Williams, Monty Python, Jim Carey.
- Follow the development of touring circuses.
  - **The Big Top, Three-Ring Circus** Phineas Taylor Barnum (1810–1891) and James A. Bailey (d. 1906), founders of what eventually became The Ringling Brothers Barnum and Bailey Circus
  - **Circus Nouveau** Clowning styles as found in Canada's Cirque du Soleil, San Francisco's Pickle Family Circus, and New York City's Big Apple Circus
  - **One-Ring** European family-style circus of one ring, such as the Moscow Circus
  - **Medicine Shows** From the nineteenth century to commercials on television

 Exploring the Form

Creating a Clown Character and Routine

1. Direct each Player to find three keys to a clown character: a walk; an image established through the use of one prop, such as a hat or cane; and one gag or routine that suits this image.

2. Give Players time to try out various ideas and to rehearse whatever they choose to do. Have Players work in pairs or teams, watching and directing each other to help figure out how to make their image and routines funny enough to elicit laughter.

3. Have Players share the routines with one another.

4. (Optional) Put these bits and pieces together, to make a clown show, or use them as entr'actes within another performance project.

The following activities will help Players find their clown character and stage business.

Walks

Ask each Player to choreograph a walk. Every clown is recognized by his peculiar walk. Think of Charlie Chaplin's turned out feet and cane display, or Groucho Marx bent over at the waist, with his crossed hands resting on his lower back, pacing

back and forth. This is often the best place to start to find a character.

A clown walk can be based upon the personal characteristics of each Player's everyday walk. Any of the following qualities, exaggerated, can become a bit that turns a walk into something funny or amusing. Have all the Players walk around the space, noticing the following qualities in their walking styles.

Weight Placement Where do they place their weight as they contact the floor (heel first, toe first, with a flat foot, one foot harder than the other)?

Posture How do they hold their spines (leaning forward from the head, tilting backward from the hip, more to the left than to the right)?

Use of Appendages How do they use their arms and hands (do they swing wide, does one swing differently than the other, do they not swing at all)?

Eye Focus Where do they like to focus their eyes (on the floor, at a distance, at eye level, always shifting)?

After Players have analyzed their walks, ask them to choose what they want to exaggerate for their clown characters.

Use of Props

Using Props in Unusual Ways Offer Players a pile of objects and direct each to select one, and use it in a way that is unrelated to its usual function. Objects could include a bucket, umbrella, ball, hoop, rope, broom, ruler, book, or scarf. Once someone has used an object in one way, no one can repeat that idea.

Personifying the Prop Tell Players to give the prop a personality and create a relationship with it. For example, use a broom or chair as a dance partner, an umbrella as a boat.

Formats

Joke Can be visual or verbal; borrowed from joke books or another comic's routines, or jokes with which Players are familiar

Bit/Dialogue Expansion of a joke into a routine for two or three performers

Sketch A longer, more elaborate scene, made by combining several bits; could involve more than two characters, and have some kind of loose plot development

Gag In American circus, a synonym for all clown routines; can mean a comic remark, trick, prop, stunt, scene, and so on, used in performance

Pitch/Monologue/Lecture Can be built up by recycling riddles, puns, rhymes, or other types of oral literature; singing songs and ditties; telling a selection of jokes on a related topic; or following some kind of logical progression, such as a sales pitch or spiel, or a medicine show routine used to sell articles; or a performing ballyhoo, which is an attraction to draw a crowd to see what's going on inside

Comic Actions and Routines

Mimes

- Create illusions with actions, such as an imaginary wall between you and the audience, a four-sided structure that surrounds you, going up and down a ladder, going up and down a rope, or juggling balls.

- A series of falls, slips, and trips that take the clown across the stage or through a series of entrances and exits

- A series of bumps into other characters or things

- Chases: Who chases? Who is being chased? Where are they going and why?

- Sneezes, nose blowing, and crying

- Takes: A response to a surprise or unusual situation that is shown to the audience as a freeze in attitude and/or facial expression, as in a "slow burn" to show irritation or anger. Groucho Marx often used this technique.

Lazzi *Lazzi* is a commedia term for comic routines. A single *lazzo* was defined in 1699 by Andrea Perrucci as "something foolish, witty, or metaphorical in word or action." Lazzi can involve sight gags, word plays, elaborate props, mime, and acrobatics. They are used to interrupt scenes with a bit of foolishness or terror. Sometimes they are used to liven up a dragging scene; sometimes they are a kind of in-house improvised joke made by one actor on another, making it necessary to improvise around the unexpected change. Other lazzi require many actors and stage properties, and are preplanned.

- Feats: human pyramids, leapfrog, relay races, unicycle rides, somersaults, cartwheels

- Mistaken identities, disguises, reversals of gender, age, or class

- Surprises: twenty clowns piling out of a small vehicle, birds pulled out of hats, flowers pulled out of a sleeve, producing a coin from a finger snap

Costume and Makeup Design

Hats Like walks, hats can be the one prop and costume item that gives the key to a character. Ask each participant to bring in a hat, or provide a bunch of hats for Players to choose among. Have a wide variety of styles, including bowlers, hard hats, feather caps, berets, party hats, and straw hats, of various sizes from tiny to huge, so that everyone will be able to find a unique character through the use of the hat. Ask Players to:

- Take it on and off.

- Pass it from hand to hand (develop juggling routines).

- Use it to make cliché gestures.

- Substitute a hat for any object. Hats can be stand-ins for steering wheels, umbrellas, weapons, toys, people, pillows, gifts, and on and on.

Clothing Ask Players to dress their own clown characters. The clothes could be everyday clothes put together in a somewhat strange or unusual way, such as a combination of items that are too large or too small. Or, their costumes could have one exaggerated detail, such as a huge tie that hangs to the floor, silly sunglasses, or oversized shoes. Suggest that Players borrow old clothes from family members or visit a thrift store. Men's long overcoats, vests, and bathrobes make great costumes.

Makeup Have each person design a mask that can be used as his own clown face. (See Researching the Form, pages 175–178.)

Performance Suggestions

Razz-ma-tazz Make a parade of clown walks, waves, bows, and quick interactions with the audience. When you go to the circus, the clowns are usually first seen in the big parade, or *razz-ma-tazz,* that begins the show. Then they reappear throughout the performance, one by one or in groups, vying for the audience's attention amidst all the other distractions.

Enter/Exit Miniplays Use these miniplays to help performers find simple, clear actions to get the audience's attention when they enter and exit.

1. Direct all Players to perform solos that include finding a way to enter, doing one action task, then finding a way to exit.

Examples:

- ENTER HELLO EXIT
- ENTER GOODBYE EXIT
- ENTER GET OUR ATTENTION EXIT
- ENTER INTRODUCE YOURSELF EXIT

2. Direct all Players to combine two or more of the above list of enter/action/exit combos.

3. Have Players perform these actions as solos, duets, or in teams while some other unison activity is being done by the rest of the group.

Examples:

- The group sings a silly song very seriously.
- The group tries standing on their heads while maintaining total concentration on another task, such as a recitation.
- The group makes human pyramids of three, four, or more Players. They collapse in unison, rolling off in all directions. Each Player knows exactly where to go and what to do at every moment.

Entr'Actes A string of running jokes on the same subject (elephant and knock-knock jokes); a string of jokes using the same form (puns, limericks); or running sight gag routines, such as problems with the curtain, chases, a water bucket constantly tipping over, sneezes, water pistols, and so on. (See further suggestions in Entr'Actes, page 211.)

Teaching Notes

Management Tips

Introductory Discussions Start clowning activities with a discussion of what makes Players laugh, smile, or feel amused in daily life. Ask them to share descriptions of professional clowning they have seen in a movie, circus, or on television.

Show Clowning Examples Share illustrations from the history of clowning, through photographs, drawings, or excerpts from videos.

Video Suggestions:

- Films of Buster Keaton, Charlie Chaplin, and Laurel and Hardy
- *The Golden Age of Comedy* (1957) contains an anthology of various clowns
- Marx Brothers films, including *Duck Soup* (1933), *Monkey Business* (1931), *Horse Feathers* (1932), *At the Circus* (1939), *Night at the Opera* (1935), and *Day at the Races* (1937)
- *It's A Mad Mad Mad Mad World* (1963) includes Milton Berle, Jimmy Durante, and Jonathan Winters
- *Popeye* (1980) with Robin Williams
- Jacques Tati in *Monsieur Hulot's Holiday* (1953) and *Mon Oncle* (1958)
- "Monty Python's Flying Circus" (English television series, 1970–1972)

Physical Warm-Ups Before asking Players to experiment with clowning routines that might involve acrobatics and mime, have them do a warm-up involving the whole body. Try stretches, breathing exercises, yoga postures, running in place or in laps, and tag games. See Short Takes, for more ideas.

Connections

History and Social Studies Have Players research clowning as it appeared in the place, culture, and time they are studying.

Language Arts Have Players explore different literary forms that are used to make jokes, including riddles, puns, conundrums, and limericks. Read the work of writers such as Shel Silverstein, Edward Lear, and James Thurber.

Special Needs

Study the differences between the joke-telling styles in American Sign Language and English. Have deaf and hearing students exchange jokes.

Assessment

Teacher Observations

- Were Players able to notice and describe the similarities and differences in clowning styles from different times and places?
- Were Players able to help one another in developing routines, to increase comic effects?

Group Discussion

Ask Players to analyze how humor is communicated in both physical actions and language.

- Is there a difference between what is funny to you and your friends and what is funny to other groups?

Student Activities

Book

pages 111–112 (Overview)

pages 113–117 (Vocabulary)

pages 118–120 (Background Reading)

pages 121–122 (Performance Model)

Journal

Tell Players to keep a log of everything that made them laugh or everything that was amusing to them for one week or one month, and another log of anything they did or said that made their friends and family laugh or smile.

References

Anobile, Richard J., editor. *Why a Duck? Visual and Verbal Gems from the Marx Brothers' Movies.* New York: Darien House, Inc., Avon Books, 1971.

Dennis, Anne. *The Articulate Body, The Physical Training of the Actor.* pp. 193–201. New York: Drama Book Publishers, 1995.

Fo, Dario. *The Tricks of the Trade.* Translated by Joe Farrell. New York: Routledge, 1991.

Murray, Marian. *Circus!* New York: Appleton-Century-Crofts, Inc., 1956.

Senelick, Laurence. *A Cavalcade of Clowns.* San Francisco: Bellerophon Books, 1977.

Speaight, George. *The Book of Clowns.* London: Sidgwick and Jackson, 1980 and 1984.

Stolzenberg, Mark. *Clowns for Circus and Stage.* New York: Sterling Publishing Company, 1981.

Stock Characters

The sum of a person's traits can be called her *character. Stock character* is a theater term for a role presented in bold strokes, as a stereotype or cartoon. Stock character roles are immediately recognizable because of their symbolic costumes and masks, manner of speaking, familiar physical mannerisms, and the predictable nature of their relationships with other characters.

We have been well trained to recognize stock characters, because they are a standard device in both writing and theater. If you hear a character described as a feisty old woman, a tricky used-car salesman, a bragging soldier, a bored housewife, a nosey mother-in-law, or a bratty child, a picture will immediately come to mind, because these are stock characters that have been used over and over again.

There are scriptwriting advantages to using stock characters. The audience can easily identify them and predict their actions and reactions because they know them so well. This means that the writer does not have to waste time introducing each character, and can jump right into moving the plot ahead.

Following is a list of common stock character types used in the theater. You will probably recognize many of their titles from their use in both literature and performance:

Hero Male juvenile lead; the *Innamorato* (male lover)

Heroine Female juvenile lead; the *Innamorata* (female lover)

Soubrette Female flirt or tease

Ingenue Young, innocent girl

Old Man Wise/foolish teacher, doctor, father, etc.

Old Woman Mother, aunt, friend, etc.

Heavy Male or female bully or villain

Wise Servant Male or female; nurse, housekeeper, cook, valet, butler, etc.

Foolish Servant Male or female

Stock Characters suggests a variety of research projects and performance experiences to introduce Players to the concept of stock characters, including their history, how to recognize them, and how they are used in theater.

Researching the Form

This discussion of stock character types includes those from the European commedia dell'arte tradition, Chinese opera, and Japanese Kabuki.

Commedia dell'Arte

Fifteenth-century commedia dell'arte was a professional improvisational theater style with origins in ancient Greek and Roman theater. Commedia companies were often maintained within families, and scenarios were handed down from generation to generation, in oral or written form. The scenarios depended on the strengths of the actors, rather than the leadership of a playwright or director. The actors improvised on the plots, without rehearsal, by following a list of entrance and exit cues. Actors were required to master dance, mime, music, comedy, and acrobatics, integrating all of this material into their improvisations.

The commedia actors' roles, referred to as *masks*, became the dominant image of commedia. Each actor was assigned a stock character to play. The characters relied on traditional gestures and costumes, and used stock business and dialogues to get into or out of any situation. The stock bits of stage business were used to spice up transitions between scenes or at moments when the action on stage needed more excitement. Some famous bits that passed into standard theater business continue to be used in comedy, vaudeville, and cartoons, including catching flies, falling, acrobatics, magic tricks, mock fights with a clacking slapstick to simulate the sound of blows, chases, and word plays.

Many roles can be traced to a particular actor, who developed the prototype. Through time, great actors contributed changes to aspects of a character and its costume. The names of masks changed from language to language. For example, the Italian *Pedrolino* became the French *Pierrot*, and the Italian *Arlecchino* became the French and English *Harlequin*. Women's roles were often played by young men or boys, because women were not permitted to perform in most parts of Italy until well into the sixteenth century. This is how men came to be given the dominant number of roles in commedia, and the most important characters. The effects of this tradition are still being felt in theater today, in the perennial scarcity of strong roles for women, other than those of ingenue and soubrette.

Commedia scenarios utilized many popular plot devices that we recognize today because they were carried over into the Renaissance plays of Shakespeare, Lope de Vega, and Molière, and have continued to be recycled since that time. These devices include mistaken identity; young woman dressing as a man; disguises of one or more characters; young characters who discover they are related and royalty; friends torn between love and loyalty; lovers posing as servants and vice versa, often to save them from marrying rich, old people; the servant who is smarter than the master; and the use of twins or multiple twins.

Commedia characters can be loosely divided into categories; some characters take on a life of their own that defies categorization. Descriptions of stock character types vary from scholar to scholar and period to period. However, three general categories seem to appear with some regularity.

- **Serious Types** The Lovers. These unmasked characters often fueled the plots.

- **Semiserious Types** Eccentric Old Men or masters who frequently thwarted, and sometimes saved, the serious and comic types. They often wore masks.

- **Comic Types or Zannis** Comic servants or valets, often called *zannis*. The go-fers, who confused everybody and generally helped solve the problems of the serious types in the end.

Following are descriptions of the most famous stock characters.

Zannis or Comic Types

Arlecchino (Harlequin) A servant, often to Pantalone, but also to Il Capitano or Il Dottore. Relative of Pulcinella. In love with Columbina. A man-child from Bergano. A trickster, he is sometimes described as intelligent; sometimes described as physically quick, but mentally slow. A skilled dancer, he somersaults to pick up an item he has dropped, stands in a ballet fourth position (toes turned out, one foot spaced in front of the other), and tiptoes in an even three-step pattern. Sometimes, he moves in a bent-over position, caused by carrying heavy bags or sedan chairs. His costume originally had no mask, but later took on a black leather one with a bump on the forehead. He wears a suit of red, yellow, green, and brown patches. His slapstick hangs from a black belt worn low on the hips.

Brighella The boss of the servants. He is a cynical schemer, capable of exploiting any situation or person, who loves to stir up intrigues. He stands in ballet first position (heels together, toes turned out), with bent knees, or one leg bent and the other extended straight. His upper body tilts from side to side as he walks. He wears a white suit—jacket and full trousers—with green braid down the sides and an olive-tinted mask with a hook nose and an elaborate mustache. A purse and dagger hang from his belt. He plays the mandolin.

Semiserious Types

Pantalone or Pantaloon Mean, cheap, and completely gullible, this Old Man plays either father or employer roles and is the guardian or husband of Columbina. He wants to hold on to the old ways. His hands gesture so wildly, almost beyond his control, that he has to anchor them behind his back to keep them still. He is a skinny man who wears a long-nosed mask and has a long, pointed beard that sticks out. He wears the costume of a merchant from Venice, with red stockings and slippers, a short tight jacket, and a long black cloak.

Il Dottore (known by many names, including Graziano, Balanzone, Scarpazon, Forbizone, Boloardo) Pompous Old Man whose speech is filled with gibberish and malapropisms. (This is the same character who appears in the Mummer's plays, who boasts of his travels and his cures, fights over his fee, and who, in the end, brings the hero back to life.) He is a Doctor, and either a bachelor or a widower. He walks in figure-eight patterns with mincing little steps. As he thinks, his body sinks progressively lower, then rises as he solves the problem. He wears a long black academic style robe, black stockings and shoes, and a black skullcap, sometimes accessorized with a white ruff or a wide-brimmed hat. His black mask covers only his forehead and nose, which is bulbous in shape. The actor's cheekbones are usually painted red to infer a drinking problem.

Serious Types

Innamorati Beautiful, young women and men who are always in love with being in love, often with more than with one person. Usually four Innamorati are needed for a scenario (as two sets of lovers). They are very vain, always fixing themselves. They are never alone and are always being spied on. They are essential to the plotting of the zanni's and the Old Men. They stand in ballet positions and walk off-balance, due to the condition of their hearts. Dressed luxuriously in the latest fashions, perhaps changing many times during the course of the play, they wear wigs and use heavy makeup instead of wearing masks. Their props consist of a handkerchief, a fan, or a flower. Female Innamorati are known variously as Flaminia, Silvia, Lavinia, Aurelia, etc. Male Innamorati are known variously as Octavio, Lelio, Silvio, Fabrizio, Leandro, Aurelio, etc.

Isabella More refined and independent than the innamorati but developed from that strain of characters. She can solve her own problems. Usually the daughter of Pantalone.

Other Masks

Pedrolino (Pierrot) A sad, mute, and honest character, he is a loner who suffers from unrequited love for Columbina. He is always tired and falling asleep. He stands with feet in ballet third position (heel of one foot touching the arch of the other foot, toes turned out), and walks in straight lines. He is dressed in a baggy pajamalike outfit with a large collar (suggesting he has to wear hand-me-downs), and is painted white-faced, without a mask. This role was often given to the youngest son in a theater family.

Pulcinella (English Punch, of *Punch and Judy,* is a descendent.) He is a hunchback from Naples who is an egotistical schemer, liar, and scoundrel. Aggressive and inconsistent, he lives by his wits and tells all secrets. He is light and delicate on his feet, and does acrobatic performances on a slack wire or trapeze. He walks with small jerky steps and stands with his weight on one leg. He carries a cudgel and wears a brown or black mask with a long hooked nose and large wart or bump on the wrinkled forehead.

Il Capitano This soldier is the butt of the zanni's jokes. He is a coward and a fake who pretends to be brave, handsome, and good. He usually ends up in a panic, humiliated, and scared to death. He often works with Pantalone on get-rich schemes. He wears a mask with a long, crooked nosed and a flamboyant mustache, and dresses as a soldier with huge boots, a feathered helmet, and a tattered leather vest. He often gestures with his long sword.

Columbine or Colombina A pretty, smart, and independent woman who is a confidante of the heroine. She can think through a problem and schemes for the best solution. She could be the maid of one of the Old Men, a wife or ward of Pantalone, or in love with Arlecchino. In commedia scenarios, she often appears in place of her mistress. She appears unmasked, with eye makeup emphasized.

Scaramouche A Neapolitan who brags and quarrels. He loves women and wine but women are not interested in him. He communicates through mimed gestures, postures, and facial grimaces. He dresses in black and wears no mask. He plays a mandolin.

Due to its bawdy nature, commedia lost momentum by the Restoration Period of the seventeenth century. However, its tradition of *stock characterizations* carried over into the hiring practices of professional theater companies. The word *stock* came into common use in connection with English nineteenth-century theatrical repertory companies. Each actor who performed the repertory specialized in a particular type of role. Actors were hired as generic stock character types and were paid according to their level of responsibility. The Tragedian, who could also appear in comedies, was also the leading man, and he was paid the most. Other stock characters included the Old Man, the Old Woman, the Heavy

Chinese Opera

The roots of Chinese opera are not certain, but storytelling dance dramas were known as early as the Han Dynasty (206 B.C.–A.D. 219), and by the time of the Sung Dynasty (A.D. 960–1279) it was flourishing. Chinese opera was significantly influenced by theater forms of the conquering Mongols, who established the Yuan Dynasty (A.D. 1277–1367). It became and continues to be a popular theater style, combining music, song, dance, speech, martial arts, and acrobatics to tell stories based on history, legends, and folktales. The stories often serve as morality lessons promoting Confucian philosophy, teaching the glory of virtuous behavior and the likely punishment of evil.

Chinese opera is traditionally performed by men. Actors start training as children, taking eight to ten years to master the fundamental skills. These skills are codified into a system called the four *kung* (singing, speech, dancing, and martial arts/acrobatics) and five *fa* (use of the mouth, eyes, hands, legs and body to communicate the character's personality). Students start by studying martial arts and acrobatics, then go on to learn singing, dancing, and speech. Only then are the student actors allowed to train in roles, often specializing in one stock character type.

The roles are classified as one of four main types—identifiable by the style of the masks—called *Sheng, Tan, Ching,* and *Chou.*

- *Sheng* are male characters with unpainted faces (actually they wear some makeup, but so little in comparison to other characters that they are thought of as having none). They can be young or old, from various walks of life, and often need to be proficient in the martial arts.

Father or Heavy Lead (villain), the Heavy Woman, the Juvenile Lead (young hero and lover), the Low Comedian (farcical or clown roles), the Walking Lady and Gentleman (supporting roles), the General Utility who took on minor roles, and the Supernumeraries, who did walk-ons (similar in function to the spear holders in operas and the extras used in films today). There were also specialists, including the Principal Dancer, the Leading or First Singer, and so on. The playbill changed nightly, and everyone in the company played their type, regardless of the script. For example, when a play included a young male hero or lover, such as Romeo, the actor hired as Juvenile Lead was given that role.

Commedia dell'arte is just one of many theater traditions that rely on stock characters. Although the systems for categorizing types widely differ in details, in general they reveal, through masks, costumes, props, gesture, language, tone of voice, and music, who or what each character is and whether they are to be praised or censored as soon as they appear on the stage. Two traditions, Chinese opera and Japanese Kabuki, are examples of other theatrical forms that depend on stock characters.

- *Tan* are the female version of Sheng.

- *Ching* actors have heavily painted faces. The painting reveals their personality, which can be either good or evil.

- *Chou* actors are male clowns, who provide comic relief or give commentary on the action. (Female clowns are called *Tsai Tan*.)

The audience knows, just by looking at the actor's face and dress, if the character is good or evil. In general, red symbolizes integrity, black symbolizes rashness, blue stands for fortitude, green for boldness, yellow for cruelty, purple for strength, white for craftiness, gold for wit, and silver for mysteriousness. Combinations of these colors in a painted facial mask, and the designs of costumes, shoes, and wigs, convey additional meanings to identify each character. When the colors and designs of the mask and costume are combined with gestures and expressions, each character is uniquely defined.

Kabuki

This popular Japanese theater form was flourishing by the end of the sixteenth century. Some of its presentational style comes from the earlier, more formal court theater style called *Noh,* and some from the doll theater that developed around the same time, known in the United States as *Bunraku.* Originating in dance, Kabuki presents dramas with plots taken mainly from domestic life and history, and legends of demons and ghosts. By the nineteenth century, horror plays were added to the repertory.

Kabuki is performed by men only, and includes an onstage orchestra, singer-narrators, actors who are also dancers, elaborate set and costume design, and stage assistants dressed in black who inconspicuously move props, change sets, help the actors change costume, and prompt the actors. The stage is

first seen covered by a formal draw-curtain *(maku)* of alternating vertical colored stripes of reddish brown, green, and black. The three colors contain information about Kabuki history, and refer to the colors of three Edo period companies (1600–1868). As this front curtain demonstrates, Kabuki has evolved a detailed code of symbols that audiences learn to recognize. The curtain opens after oak clappers sound a steadily accelerating beat.

As in Chinese opera style, Kabuki theater style uses color and style of makeup to signal character. However, the meanings of the colors and shapes are somewhat different. In Kabuki, red is used to symbolize strength, manliness, youth, and righteousness. Blue and black are worn by both wicked characters and supernatural beings. Brown indicates a clown. Whiteface is reserved for beautiful young men and female characters. The way the lines are drawn, especially the outline of the eyebrow and eyes, gives further clues, as do the wigs, shoes, hand props, and the colors, fabrics, and cut of costumes.

There are eight principal types of characters in Kabuki plays: the hero *(tachiyaku),* the villain *(katakiyaku),* the old woman *(kashagata),* the young woman *(wakaonnagata),* the young man *(waskashugata),* the old man *(oyajikata),* the comic *(dokegata),* and the child *(koyaku).* Within each category there are subcategories of types. For example, older women's roles include those of high-ranking respectable women, middle class wives, and a rare type of character *(onnabudo)* who acts like a warrior and is given more importance than the hero. Starting in children's roles, actors traditionally played one stock type throughout their adult careers. Today, actors may play more than one stock type, even within one performance.

 ## Exploring the Form

Finding a Stock Character

Ask each Player to think of a character (who could be based on someone they know) and to find one word or phrase and one action that describes this character best. Tell Players to keep repeating their word or phrase and action, trying different rhythms, tones, and dynamics. See Clowns and Clowning (pages 170–174) in this chapter for other suggestions of ways to find a character, especially the suggestions for finding a walk; using a signature costume piece, such as a hat; or using a hand prop to substitute for costume.

Dialogues of Opposites

Have Players work in pairs to improvise a scene by choosing and playing opposite stock character types, such as victim and villain.

- Ask partners to choose stock character roles to play and a situation in which to improvise dialogue and interaction.
  - The scene is a meeting between the two characters.
  - The scene begins with a fall. One character falls, and the way in which he falls helps the other character decide how to react in order to carry the scene forward.

- Whisper directions to each Player, telling them their stock character and situation. Ask both Players to discover the nature of each other's character through their improvisation.

Lazzi Comic Routines

Ask each Player to select one stock character, and to work out at least two or three bits of stage business to use as needed in an improvisation of a monologue, dialogue, or scenario. For example, an old man or woman who keeps forgetting things and looks everywhere to find them; an ingenue who dances and sings; a servant who mimics his master, making fun of him; or a hero who always falls asleep at important moments.

Following are two suggestions for developing a lazzi routine. (Additional lazzi routines are on pages 132–133 of the Student Book.)

Scenario Direct Players to work in teams. Allow them to choose stock characters, or assign them stock character roles. Give teams time to make up a skeleton plot involving their characters. Have teams give improvised performances for one another, during which Players can insert their lazzi routines anywhere and anytime.

Monologue Give Players a topic, or let them choose one, around which they are to improvise at least two monologues, using different stock character types for each monologue. For example, discuss how to cook a chicken as a master cook, using puns, malapropisms, and magic tricks; and as a new, inexperienced cook, using acrobatics and mime. (A rubber chicken could add some dash to this one.)

 Teaching Notes

Management Tips

Stock Characters in Advertising Ask students to bring in advertisements from magazines and newspapers and to identify their use of stock character types.

Physical Warm-Ups When starting a session of improvisations using stock characters, make sure that Players have a physical warm-up, both to protect them from injury and to encourage them to work with total body awareness.

Analyzing Stock Character Portrayal When Players share their improvisations, ask the audience to identify the stock characters that were chosen, and if the actors communicated the roles as intended. For example, is the Doctor coming across as a good guy (the Old Man) or as a villain (Heavy Lead)?

Connections

Language Arts

• Have students identify and describe stock character types in required reading selections, such as short stories, novels, or plays.

• Choose one stock character type and describe what function the character has in a play or novel. Compare two similar types in two different forms. For example, describe how an ingenue looks and acts in a commedia dell'arte play and in a current popular television show.

History Choose a theater style and describe and analyze its use of stock character roles and how they might describe the culture in which the theater style developed. Besides those mentioned in this activity, some other traditions that use stock characters include: South Indian *Kathakali* masked dance dramas; Balinese dance dramas, including the forms called *Legong* (a court dance for young girls), and *Galunggan* (where the witch *Rangda* fights the good lion god, *Barong*).

Special Needs

In discussion, give detailed descriptions of stock characters for blind students.

 Assessment

Teacher Observations

• Were Players able to compare stock character roles?

• Did they understand the relationships and plot function of the various types?

- When playing a stock character role, were they able to use their research information to find action and characterization?
- Did Players use both voice and movement to convey character?

Group Discussion

Discuss a current television dramatic series, situation comedy, or cartoon, and identify the stock character types. How do they compare with the same type of stock characters in the commedia or other styles?

 Student Activities

Book

pages 123–130 (Background Reading)

pages 131–133 (Performance Model)

Journal

Ask Players to write a description and identify the stock character name or type of an anonymous person they observed recently, perhaps on the street, riding public transportation, or in a park or shopping center.

 References

Books

Ducharte, Pierre Louis. *The Italian Comedy.* Translated by Randolph T. Weaver. New York: Dover Publications, Inc., 1966.

Ernst, Earle. *The Kabuki Theatre.* Honolulu: The University Press of Hawaii, An East-West Center Book, 1974.

Fo, Dario. *The Tricks of the Trade.* Translated by Joe Farrell. New York: Routledge, A Theatre Arts Book, 1991.

Gordon, Mel. *Lazzi, The Comic Routines of the Commedia dell'Arte.* New York: Performing Arts Journal Publications, 1983; 1992.

Kawatake, Toshio. *Kabuki, Eighteen Traditional Dramas.* Translated by Helen V. Kay. San Francisco: Chronicle Books, 1985.

Rolfe, Bari. *Commedia dell'Arte, A Scene Study Book.* Oakland, CA: Personabooks, 1977.

Rudlin, John. *Commedia dell'Arte, An Actor's Handbook.* London and New York: Routledge, 1994.

Salerno, Henry F., translator and editor. *Scenarios of the Commedia dell'Arte, Flaminio Scala's Il Teatro Delle Favole Rappresentative.* New York: Limelight Editions, 1992.

T'sao, Kuo-lin. *The Face of Chinese Opera.* Taiwan, R.O.C.: Hilit Publishing Co., Ltd., first English edition, 1995.

Films

Children of Paradise (1944), directed by Marcel Carne, shows Jean-Louis Barrault as a nineteenth century mime.

The Red Shoes (1948), directed by Michael Powell, provides a story-within-a-story showing stock character types in both contemporary and ballet styles.

Dramas

Goldoni, Carlo. *A Servant of Two Masters,* a play in commedia style.

Hwang, David Henry. *The Dance and the Railroad,* a two-character play placed in the United States at the time Chinese men were hired to build the railroads. One of the characters is a former actor in the Chinese opera.

Notes

- There are many theater companies working in commedia style today; videotapes of their performances may be available through your local library, video store, or college drama department. Insight Media, a mail-order service that distributes theater arts videos, includes videos that demonstrate Chinese opera, Kabuki, and Noh.

- The San Francisco Mime Troupe performs original works in a style that is highly influenced by commedia. They tour San Francisco Bay Area parks, for free, as they have been doing since the 1960s.

- The Canadian-based Cirque du Soleil designs many of their costumes and characters on commedia and clown archetypes.

- Italian director, actor, and writer, Dario Fo, and his wife, Franca Rame, perform, lecture and direct plays, touring frequently in the United States.

- Theatre du Soleil, a French company directed by Ariane Mnouchkine since the 1960s, does original work informed by commedia dell'arte style.

- Ballets that use stock characters include *Petrushka, Coppélia, Firebird, The Nutcracker, Giselle, The Sleeping Beauty,* and *Swan Lake.*

- Story operas, including those of Mozart, Verdi, Bizet, and Wagner, use stock characters.

Shadow Plays and Puppets

At some time or another, most of us have played at casting hand shadows on a wall. We are inundated with television, video, advertising, theater and film artists, and music videos using shadows to suggest or abstract information, create a mood and atmosphere, or project images. Alfred Hitchcock, Orson Welles, Akira Kurosawa, and Ingmar Bergman are a few of the film directors who use shadows extensively in their black and white film work. In many parts of the world, young people learn about their culture, ancestral history, and beliefs through shadow and puppet plays. Although we are familiar with shadow and puppet plays, we may not be aware of how they convey information.

Shadow Plays and Puppets contains many choices of activities and projects to introduce Players to the genre of puppet and shadow theater. Players can research and compare different traditions, or they can design and construct a set, puppets, hand props, costumes, and lighting; make a script from an existing or original source; and experiment by operating the lights, animating puppets and props, choreographing shadow dances, and miming or speaking the script.

★ Researching the Form

Shadow Theater

The basic principle in making shadow plays is to throw a shadow image onto a screen. All that is needed is a light source, objects or puppets, and/or performers.

As the performers and/or objects or puppets move between the light source and the screen, the audience sees a shadow form of the images projected on the screen.

One of the most masterful uses of shadow art can be found in the shadow plays of the Indonesian island, Java. Called *wayang,* they are community affairs, sponsored by families to mark life rituals, such as weddings or funerals. These shadow puppet plays tell a story, usually one from the Sanskrit epic poem, *Mahabharata,* the longest poem in the world, written between 500 B.C. and A.D. 500.

The plots are divided into three sections, with a beginning, middle, and end. First, there is a conflict in which the forces of chaos and denial dominate (the "negative forces of the left"); the second section introduces the "positive forces of the right"; and in the third section, the positive forces of the right triumph over the negative forces of the left, and order is restored. These *wayang* plots correspond to man's life and spiritual development: his youthful immaturity and lack of moral judgment, maturity and responsibility in adulthood, and wisdom and tranquillity in old age.

Wayang are performed by one man, a puppeteer *(dhalang)* who sings, manipulates the whole cast of characters (stick puppets made of leather with filigree cutouts), and is the director of a *gamelan* orchestra of ten to fifty players. The orchestra includes mainly percussion instruments, various sizes of gongs, and some flutes and stringed instruments.

The audience sits on either side of the puppet screen: invited guests

of the sponsors usually sit on the shadow side of the performance, and everyone else on the outside, behind the *gamelan.*

Other forms of traditional shadow plays include Moroccan *chleu* boys' dance; Indian *chhau* dances for the ancestors to celebrate the Fight of Rama; the Hebrew *golem* plays; European solstice puppet shows, where straw puppets are thrown into bonfires as symbolic representations of the cyclical rebirth of the seasons; and Chinese shadow theater, which was originally made for women because they were not allowed into the regular theaters.

Puppet Theater

Puppet theater is a highly developed art form, involving elaborate sets, dolls, and prop design. Practitioners train for years to master their craft. Often labeled as children's entertainment in this century, puppetry was traditionally a form of adult folk theater. Many Americans remember the 1950s television puppet shows called "Howdy Doody" and "Kukla, Fran and Ollie," and most are familiar with the more recent puppetry work of Jim Hensen, whose Muppets were made famous on "Sesame Street." The Muppets carry on the puppet tradition of teaching the language and culture of a people to the next generation.

One of the most famous puppet theater styles, begun in the sixteenth century, is the Japanese *Bunraku.* One to three puppeteers manipulate each puppet character while an all-male chorus sings the story, accompanied by an orchestra of drums, flutes, and stringed instruments. The puppeteers are onstage all of the time. Two assistant puppeteers, dressed in black with hoods over their heads, move the legs and left arm. The master puppeteer, whose face is revealed, manipulates the head and right arm of the puppet. The live theater style called *Kabuki* assimilated puppet theater styles and scripts, including the tragic play, *Chushingura,* based on an actual event in 1702.

In Europe and the United States, puppets continue to be a popular form of street theater. One of the most famous hand puppet shows is the British *Punch and Judy.* Marionette theaters, whose heyday was during the European Renaissance, use puppets controlled by strings. They performed on miniature proscenium stages, using set designs of changing painted backdrops and masking flats that create the illusion of perspective. In marionette shows, unseen puppeteers manipulate the strings while telling the story through the voice of each character.

In the 1960s, Peter Schumann revived European carnival-style puppet making in the United States with his *Bread and Puppet Circus* plays and street theater. His day-long pageants involve hundreds of volunteers in the making of papier mâché puppets with cloth costumes, that range in size from finger-length to giants that have to be moved by teams of people. In his shows, Schumann includes banners, masked people on stilts, and six-foot masks that cover a person's body. His ideas have been very influential in the revival of puppetry in this country.

Projections: Film, Video, Slide

Since the 1960s, we have become familiar with the use of projections in industrial promotions, live music concerts, and music videos. Laurie Anderson is a performance artist who experiments with mixing live performance, projections, and shadow play. She believes that electronic equipment is connected to storytelling in much the same way that fires were historically.

For me, electronics have always been connected to storytelling. Maybe because storytelling began when people used to sit around fires and because fire is magic, compelling and dangerous. We are transfixed by its light and by its destructive power. Electronics are modern fires. (*Stories from the Nerve Bible,* New York: HarperPerennial, a division of HarperCollins, 1994.)

★ Exploring the Form

As you begin to explore puppet theater and shadow plays, you will have many choices to consider. You could choose an approach from the following suggestions and include shadow plays, puppetry, or both.

1. Choose the type of stage that fits the scale of your project. (See "Choosing a Stage," page 184.)

2. As a group or in teams, have Players create a shadow or puppet play with characters that convey the time, style, and mood of a period. Make a script or score to perform. Almost any subject or work of literature can be transformed into a shadow and/or puppet play. Take advantage of the form by choosing fantastic themes that might not be as easily performed by live actors, such as fairy tales, myths, fables, or poems.

• Write an original script or score. Refer to activities in Chapter 5, Scriptwriting, and Chapter 6, Scores, to find ways to write a script. See Living Pictures (page 125) for ways to arrange original or "borrowed" images into scores, and Storytelling (page 89) and Scenarios (page 96) for ways to plot story lines.

• Use an existing story or play.

• Adapt an existing story or play.

• Dance and Pantomime: Use movement that may or may not convey a plot.

3. As a group or in teams, create puppet characters and props.

4. You can add a sound environment from live or recorded music.

5. Experiment with and rehearse the score or script. Assemble all the set and prop items so that Players can experiment with everything that will be used in performance.

6. Perform your shadow and or puppet play.

Choosing a Stage

Puppet Theater

- Flat table surface
- Miniature finger-puppet theater
- Medium-size proscenium puppet theater for hand puppets, stick puppets, or marionettes

Shadow Plays Using Puppets

- Puppet theater
- Full stage
- Use one screen
- Use multiple screens
- Shadow plays using human figures and/or puppets on a full stage and one or more screens

Making Puppets

Materials Many materials can be used to make puppets, from simple and inexpensive to elaborate. Use paper, cardboard, large cardboard boxes, parchment, cinemoid (acetate), foam rubber, Styrofoam, leather, fabric and decorative notions, papier mâché, plaster of paris, supporting sticks or wooden dowel rods, bamboo poles, nylon fishing line, tape, glue, paint, magic markers, leather punch, hole punch, paper fasteners, etc.

Hand Puppets and Finger Puppets

You can use the bare hand to create shadow images, or make puppets by painting faces on fingers. Or make covers for the whole hand, the hand and part of the arm, or the fingers only.

Flats as Masks (also called Puppets) Gather large cardboard boxes and, using a matte knife, cut them into flat sections. Or use large pieces of Styrofoam. Consider the characteristics of the object or the style and character of the puppet. For a shadow play, make the images as silhouettes. Draw or paint the shapes of objects large enough to cover the performer's body, partially or completely.

- Flats can be hand-held by Players, attached to sticks, or suspended from poles with nylon fishing line. Flats work very effectively as clouds, trees, houses, trains, cars, sun, moon, stars, mountains, or animals (a flat can be just the animal's head, which is held on a stick above the performer's head, or a mask covering the wearer's head or body).
- When working in shadow, experiment with the placement of Players behind the shadow screen. If they remain to the side or behind the light source as it projects onto the screen, only the flat will be seen.

Stick Puppets These are cutout images manipulated by one or more wooden dowel rods. Attach the dowels to the sections of puppets that move independently, such as the arms, head, legs, or torso. Stick puppets can be made for a small puppet stage, a shadow stage, or be larger-than-life and manipulated by one or more people.

Paperdoll Cutouts These puppets could be hand-held, put on sticks, or hung by nylon fishing string. They work well on miniature stages.

Designing Costumes

- Since all images read as black or grey on a shadow screen, the color of props, costumes, and puppets need be of no concern. Shape is the primary concern. Size will vary according to the size of the shadow theater or shadow screen.

- Small puppets and props can be cut out to resemble and portray a specific period of dress and attitude of character. Experiment with the figures to find what works best for your project.
- When the Players are to be the shadow figures, use hats, street clothing, or draped fabric to suggest historical period costumes. Any old sheet can look like an elaborate period costume, when draped appropriately. Otherwise, have Players wear leotards or street clothing, as appropriate to the piece. Experiment with other costume ideas to find those that work for you.

Designing a Shadow Play

Light Sources for a Shadow Play

The size of the light source is related to the size of screen you are using. Use one or more of the following light sources:

- Ordinary table lamps with a 100-watt bulb (a gooseneck or an architect's desk lamp would work well)
- Strip lights attached to a wooden base and placed on the floor or table of the shadow theater
- Photographer's flood light with a 250/300-watt bulb
- Professional theater lighting instrument, such as a scoop or leko, with a color wheel attached so that you can have the screen change color; or gel frames that cover the light source, if desired
- White or colored light (color can heighten special effects)
- Strobe lights, slide and film projectors, and mirrors are popular tools used to create, distort, or change images
- If you will be performing outdoors, firelight or gaslight can create a storytelling atmosphere

Shadow Play Screens The size of the screen will determine the size of the images: the taller the screen, the greater the potential for large images. Screens can be hung from rope, wire, a pole, stretched on a frame, or even be held by two students. To obtain clear, sharp images, hang the curtain or screen as taut as possible, allowing it to fall to the floor without creasing or wrinkling. Secure the bottom with weights. The most magical screens have no seams. The following materials can be used to make a screen:

- Large bedsheet(s), hung by clothesline or rope
- Professional scrim or drop curtain
- Mylar sheets or plastic drop cloths

Try the following variations for special effects:

- Split the shadow screen into sections and place each section on different parts of the stage.
- Mylar can be cut into large shapes that are hung on different parts of the stage.

Projecting Light on the Screen

Front Projections The figure and light source are in front of the screen.

Rear Projections The figure and light source are behind the screen.

- Performers can choose to not be seen on the screen by standing to the side of or behind the light source while manipulating their puppets.
- The audience may or may not be able to see behind the screen to watch the performers and/or puppets. If the performers wish to remain hidden, use flats or curtains to mask any open space between the screen and the side walls or curtains.

Performance Issues When Working with Shadows

If working with shadows, be aware of the following elements.

Size and Clarity The closer the image is to the light source, the larger and more diffuse the image will appear; and vice versa.

Color The light source can be white or colored light. Change color effects by placing gels of various colors over the light source, or use a color wheel attached to the light source.

Creating Characters for Shadow Images To give life and expression to shadow images, use profiles of the image, similar to the silhouettes that appear on Egyptian reliefs and Greek vase paintings. Experiment to find how the qualities of the character can be portrayed in silhouette to convey the character. In a paper cutout stick puppet, a head bent forward might indicate modesty; a ragged costume, poverty; and a fancy hat might symbolize wealth.

Projecting Clear Images The tips that follow will help Players create clear images for both human and puppet shadows.

- The head needs to be held in silhouetted profile in order for facial features and expressions to register.

- Hands need to be turned so that the palm faces either forward or back.

- Be aware that the audience will see the shadow figures as in a mirror, the opposite of what you see when manipulating the character. If a Player is behind a scrim holding a flat that contains cutouts of letters, the audience will read the letters from left to right, so the Player must hold the flat backwards.

- An object can appear to move on its own if a Player stands or walks behind a light source, suspending the flat by nylon thread from a dowel rod or bamboo pole.

Performance Issues When Working with Puppets

Encourage every puppet operator to find his or her own style. Following are a few basic management tips.

- Ideally, one Player should operate each figure, unless it is a prop that requires more than one operator, such as a wave that has to move back and forth from stage right to stage left.

- If the figures have to cross one another, Players have to rehearse the maneuvers to avoid collision or entangling their puppets.

- If there are more characters than manipulators, let the less important figures remain static.
  – Practice with the size and scale of the puppets' movements.
  – Keep the movements economical. Resist wild action.
  – Use contrasting movement to keep the show alive.
  – Allow for some distance between the characters.

- Assistants may be useful to give or take puppets from the operators; to help keep the puppets organized backstage so they don't become entangled; and to change sound effects, sets, props, light colors, and music.

- Have Players observe the rehearsals to see if the effects are working, or hold or hang a mirror in front of the playing area, angled so that the operators can see what is happening from the audience's point of view.

Variations

Other Projections Project slides and film along with shadow images.

Multiple Light Sources Use more than one light source to get multiple shadow images.

Create _Tableaux_ Make _tableaux_ of puppets, live figures, or cutouts of scenes. This can be very effective for illustrating poems and songs.

Mix Shadow and Live Performers One possibility is to create shadows with rear projection, and show live performers in front of the screen at the same or different times.

★ Teaching Notes

Management Tips

Safety Issues Double-check the safety of all setups before every rehearsal and performance.

- Secure lighting instruments so that they are stable.

- Secure electric cables with gaffer's tape so that no one trips.

- Secure any flats and masking devices with sandbags or other weights so they do not fall.

- Make sure that no lighting instruments are touching fabric, or are placed where someone could get injured while making shadows or operating puppets.

Student Awareness Show Players where to stand in order to work safely in their environment, and how to enter and exit the set.

Set Up a Prop Table Provide a prop table or rack for puppets and props so that objects are not thrown about the backstage playing area. If a table or rack is not available, define an area where students can place their props so that they will not interfere with lighting equipment or foot traffic.

Rehearsal Techniques

- Begin with short, specific tasks, such as moving forward or backward behind a shadow screen; deciphering the right to left ordering (the reverse of what the audience sees).

- Experiment with effects of different timing.

- Have Players alternate being audience and performers.

Connections

Art Research and create various types of puppets that can be used in a puppet or shadow play.

History Connect puppets and shadow plays to a research project useful to your required curriculum. Ask students to identify the costume, speech and language patterns, and events of that particular time. Choose various scenes that you would like to portray. Choose an existing, or create an original, score or play to recreate that time. You could have several scenes, each performed by a team of Players,

in which the audience travels from scene to scene. (See Tableaux Vivants, page 199.)

Social Studies Research cultures that combine puppets and shadow plays with storytelling to pass their traditions on to future generations. Listen to recordings, look at photographs, or watch videos (if available). Compare differences and similarities, discussing the purpose, design, and content of the plays in each form.

 Assessment

Teacher Observations

- Were Players able to understand the basic concepts of how to make a shadow or puppet play, using either themselves or puppets as characters?

- Were Players able to explore the qualities of space and time to create the shadow effect they wanted to convey their text?

- Did Players take advantage of the special effects that can be achieved with Shadow Plays and Puppetry?

Group Discussion

In discussion, ask students to consider how shadow plays can pass on the traditions of a culture to future generations, and how they can convey a culture's history, spiritual beliefs, and political ideas. Discuss how shadows and puppets are used in contemporary media and theater, including popular television shows, movies, and advertising.

 Student Activities

Book

pages 134–137 (Background Reading)

Journal

- Ask Players to watch television or go to the movies to observe how shadows are used in these media. Have them record their observations on how shadow was used. What was the message? Why was shadow used? Who was in the audience? What does the use of shadow say about the film, advertisement, or culture?

- Encourage Players to attend a puppet show. Have them record their observations of the puppets and how they were used. Were they larger-than-life puppets? Was there a miniature puppet theater? Was the show intended for children, or for people of all ages? Did the content involve legends and fairy tales, or historical or current events?

 References

Books

Anderson, Laurie. *Stories from the Nerve Bible,* New York: HarperPerennial, a division of HarperCollins, 1994.

Brecht, Stefan. *The Bread and Puppet Theatre.* Two Volumes. London: Methuen Drama, Michelin House, 1988.

Green, Susan. *Bread and Puppet, Stories of Struggle and Faith from Central America.* Foreword by Grace Paley, Introduction by Peter Schumann, Photographs by Ron Levine and George Lange, edited by Greg Guma. Burlington, VT, 1985.

Reiniger, Lotte. *Shadow Theatres and Shadow Films.* London: B.T. Batsford Ltd.; New York: Watson Guptill Publications, 1970. Reprinted: *Shadow Puppets, Shadow Theatres and Shadow Films.* Boston: Plays, Inc., 1975.

Schlemmer, Oskar, Laszlo Moholy-Nagy, and Farkas Molnar. *The Theater of the Bauhaus.* Middletown, CT: Wesleyan University Press, 1961.

Wilson, Robert. *Robert Wilson's Vision.* Boston and New York: Museum of Fine Arts in association with Harry N. Abrams, Inc., 1991.

———. *The Theater of Images.* Revised Edition. New York: Harper & Row, 1984.

Magazines

Ward, Keeler. "Shadow World of the Javanese." *Natural History,* pp. 68–77, November 1987.

Theater Crafts and Lighting Dimensions can be found in any bookstore that carries theater books.

Films

Look for black-and-white movies, particularly from the Expressionist period of the 1920s and 1930s, although they tend to be of the horror and mystery genre.

- *Mary Shelley's Frankenstein,* a 1931 horror classic starring Boris Karloff.

- Tom Forman's *Shadows,* a 1922 silent classic starring Lon Chaney (includes a shadow play with figures cut by the German silhouettist, Engert).

Anderson, Laurie. *Home of the Brave.* 1986. Depicts front and rear projections and shadows.

Bergman, Ingmar. *The Seventh Seal.* 1957.

———. *Fanny and Alexander.* 1983. Contains a marionette theater scene.

Cocteau, Jean. *Beauty and the Beast.* 1946. Black and white, surrealistic version of the fairy tale.

Curtiz, Michael. *Casablanca.* 1942. Black and white.

Disney, Walt. *Pinocchio,* 1940; *Cinderella* 1950; *Bambi* 1942.

Disney Studio. *The Lion King.* 1994.

Eisenstein, Sergei. *The Battleship Potemkin,* 1925 Silent classic.

———. *Alexander Nevsky.* 1938. Score by Prokofieff.

Hitchcock, Alfred. Any of his black and white films, such as *Saboteur,* 1942; *The Thirty-Nine Steps,* 1935.

Weir, Peter. *The Year of Living Dangerously.* 1983. Takes place in Indonesia; includes a scene from a Javanese shadow play and atmosphere created through shadow.

Welles, Orson. *Citizen Kane.* 1941. Extensive use of shadow to depict mood and suspense.

Wyler, William. *Wuthering Heights.* 1939.

Look for live performances using puppet and shadow including:

- *Mummenschanz,* a Swiss-based mime and puppet theater company that tours extensively and has occasional guest appearances on "Sesame Street."

- Laurie Anderson tours multidisciplinary performances that employ sophisticated technology, involving original music, film and slide projections, lasers, and storytelling.

- George Coates, a San Francisco-based performance artist, uses projections that utilize various technologies in collaborative, multidisciplinary works.

- Other American artists working with puppets include: Julie Taymor, Paul Zaloom, Theodora Skipitares, Peter Schumann's *Bread and Puppet Theater* of Vermont, *Hystopolis Puppet Theater* of Chicago.

Or look at commercial video and film puppet shows, including *The Muppets* and *Tales from the Crypt.*

Masks and Masquerades

Masking is virtually a universal phenomenon. Most of us are familiar with masks, having either worn them or viewed them on others. Masks appear in infinite variety; the bare face can be used as a mask, simply by making funny or strange expressions, or a mask can be a covering that conceals all or part of the face through the use of makeup and costume. Sometimes, masked characters are called *masks*. A *masquerade* is a costume party, masked ball, carnival, or other celebration at which masks are worn.

Mask work is a powerful tool for learning how to find a character. The actor cannot hide behind words or pretend that the mask by itself makes the character. Actors have to find a way to embody the mask so that the character reads as genuine, believable to the audience.

Masks and Masquerades discusses various methods to begin a study of masks to learn about their history and their uses in various cultures. Players can compare their many functions and intended effects, which may not always be evident by simply observing an artifact. Players may design and make their own masks. They could try performing with or as a *mask,* finding out how it influences them to move in new ways. This is partly a result of seeing with a limited field of vision, and partly, because masks are magical. When a wearer puts one on, the mask comes alive, transformed into a living, breathing presence.

★ Researching the Form

The practice of masking is so vast and varied that this lesson can only discuss a few examples from different times and places. Although the origins of mask making are not clear, prehistoric cave drawings offer evidence that masks and other disguises have always been used to transform people into something other than themselves. Masks may function in many ways.

- As disguises, to keep the wearer's identity a secret and to increase the mystery of and belief in the mask persona

- To allow spirits to inhabit the wearer's body

- As part of ceremonies to promote physical and spiritual healing

- To establish kinship ties within a clan or family group; to commemorate the ancestors in memorial parties

- To inspire awe and terror in the enemy during a battle (This was the source of the Chinese opera masks.)

- To pass on sacred or historical traditions

- As individualistic displays, worn for artistic or festive purposes (as in Carnivals), or as proof of power and wealth

- As a theatrical effect, providing the actor with a character

- As protection, from cold, the sun, germs, physical harm

Masks go in and out of favor in both religious and theater traditions. However masks continue to

survive in communities, resurfacing on secular holidays or festive occasions such as Halloween, Mardi Gras, or other carnivals, where revellers disguise themselves as animals, gods and other cosmic entities, constellations, famous people, strange creatures, and so on.

In Western theater legacies, mask traditions were handed down from ancient Greece and Rome, to commedia dell'arte, circus, and mime. Recently, masking has been extended to include animated film characters, who appear in masked human form in spin-off theme parks such as Disneyland or Walt Disney World.

The following discussion gives a few examples of celebratory masquerades from various times and places.

European Court Masques

European court masques were dramatic entertainments, or ballets, usually based on mythological or allegorical themes, that accompanied formal balls and banquets. Masques were popular in the courts of the sixteenth and early seventeenth centuries, traveling from Italy to France and then to England. The performers of the masques were members of the court, often including the reigning king or queen, dressed in elaborate costumes and masks. They carried symbolic emblems and participated in dances and theatrical displays that were often without plot. The spectacles were presented in formal palace gardens and courtyards during good weather, and inside grand halls during winter. They included fireworks, volcanoes, angel-filled clouds, fountains with nymphs and tritons, gargoyles, dragons, monsters, horse ballets, and even grand halls that were flooded to recreate famous naval battles.

In England, masques were referred to as "acted pageants," and were designated for special court occasions such as weddings, birthdays, and victories. Between 1605 and 1618, artist and architect Inigo Jones, inspired by visits to Italy, where masques were in vogue in the courts of the de Medici family, often worked in partnership with poet Ben Jonson. Eventually, Jonson gave up writing masques because, he said, he did not wish to compete with carpenters and scene painters. The collaborations of Jones and Jonson were extremely important to the development of theater design and staging, especially through their influence on William Shakespeare.

Solstice Masques

The origins of solstice masques (a sixteenth-century French term for *mask*) are shrouded in prehistoric times, yet there are still many cultures that have community celebrations or festivals at the time of the winter or summer solstice to celebrate the sun and the turning of the year. Celebratory forms connected to the solstice can be found throughout the world, including parades (Chinese New Year dragon parades and German, Swiss, and Scandinavian First Night processionals); midsummer bonfires and puppet shows (France, Spain, and England); and the mystery plays or *revels* known by various names. (In England they are called *mummers'* plays, the Basques' term is *morisca*, *morisco* in Spain, *moresco* in Italy, and *moreska* in the city of Korcula on the Adriatic coast in the former Yugoslavia.)

These solstice theatrical presentations celebrate the seasonal cycles, frequently depicting the cycles of life and death in nature. Somehow, these stories and traditions mixed together to become mystery plays. They were performed as amulets or prayers to renew the spirits of the community and its leaders at the beginning of a new year; as a prayer for the return of the vegetation gods and the sun; and to help ensure a community's good fortune for the coming year.

The English custom was to perform a little play that traveled through a village from house to house, much as caroling is practiced today. The play, often called a *mummers' play* or *revel,* was enacted in disguise, or in mask, by the villagers. Mummers' plays contain many stock character types. Depending on the place and version, the same character, such as the doctor, can be present in either his good or bad aspect. Most of the plays contain an elected king, and sometimes a queen; a fool; a doctor or magician; and a team of sword dancers. And there is always a hero, who can appear variously under the mask of St. George, the Dragon of Good Fortune, Sir Gawain, Old Barleycorn, the Sun King, or the Grain God. This legendary hero or champion is killed and brought back to life just as the sun is reborn or renewed at the time of the winter solstice, the shortest day of the year.

Carnival

Carnival seasons vary and sometimes overlap with solstice celebrations. They start any time from the New Year to the first full moon of spring, or the day before Lent, sometimes known as "Fat Tuesday."

Carnivals are celebrations with processions of pageant floats, masked and lavishly costumed dancers, stilt dancers, musicians and singers, merry plays, banquets, and balls. Masks are always an intrinsic part of the celebration, allowing people to transform themselves for a short time. Some cities sponsor contests to crown either a king or queen of Carnival, and schools of dancers, musicians, and singers spend months preparing new costumes, songs, dances, and floats to compete for prizes.

Carnival festivities appear throughout the Near and Far East, Africa, and Europe. Some of them were brought to the Americas, including Chinese New Year dragon parades and northern European First Night celebrations. In the Americas, carnivals have often survived in purer form, as exhibited in the major festivals of Brazil, Trinidad, Haiti, Mexico, and New Orleans. The classic 1959 Brazilian film, *Black Orpheus,* set in the world of the samba schools of a Rio de Janeiro carnival, tells its morality tale in a modern version of the ancient myth of Orpheus and Eurydice.

The Dan People of West Africa

The Dan people of West Africa include Ivory Coast Yacuba people and the Gio people of Liberia. The Dan masks, which represent spirits of the forest, can appear beautiful, frightening, or comical. The eyes are the masks' dominant feature. Slitted eyes connote feminine beauty, and protruding, tubular eyes project shock. The Dan mask known as *Gaa Wree-Wre* has a towering presence and is said to have the power to stop a war. It embodies a judge, with legal power to gravely hear and rule on human cases. The mask's movements consist of either sitting or walking with a swaying gait like an aquatic bird. It wears a tall, conical headdress decorated with indigo blue and red embroidery, and cowrie shells; bells hang from a beaded necklace around the jaw; leopard teeth and hairpins are worn above striped indigo shawls, and an enormous raffia skirt completes the costume.

Another Dan mask, called *Gle-Gbee,* is a stilt dancing mask, or "long spirit," who possibly emerged

from the water. The featureless mask has a long fiber tail, and is topped by a conical headdress of fur, cowrie shells, and leather strips. The dancer wears short raffia skirts over striped blue and white pants that cover ten-foot-high stilts. The stilts have supports mounted on their sides, which the dancer stands on to strap them onto his shins, leaving the knees free to perform the rapidly moving dance figures of jumps, giant steps, and tilts. The *Gle-Gbee* are tests of equilibrium, working against the pull of the earth and play of witches, whom they are believed to scare away with their dancing presence.

Tlingit, a People of Alaska's Northwest Coast

In clan memorial parties of singing, dancing, and dining, carved and painted wooden ceremonial masks or hats of a family's crest are brought out as displays of rank, money, and power. A *crest* is a badge owned by the lineage of a family or clan. Crests may be represented as mythical creatures or in animal or human forms.

Chhau Dance

(Orissa Province, West Bengal State, India) One example of a *chhau* dance festivity occurs in the spring, when thirteen masked female dancers, who represent doubles or shadows of the gods, dance a repeating ritual procession for three days, as part of a festival honoring the god, Shiva. They move through the town, wearing full-face, papier mâché, painted masks, traveling back and forth between the temple and a shrine by the river. After three nights, male dancers wearing god-masks perform an epic drama of the Hindu gods—Shiva, Kali, or Durga—involving dances with vigorous leaps, stamps, and acrobatic feats.

Kathakali

In this South Indian style of religious masked dance dramas, actors perform sacred legends outdoors in the streets, with massive costumes and multicolored masks creating their sets. They wear wide, pleated skirts supported by many underlayers, colorful scarves that fly as they twist and turn, tall gilded and painted headdresses, and bare feet that rhythmically stamp the earth. Actors learn special eye exercises to strengthen the eye muscles for rapid and controlled movement of the pupils. They dramatize their painted facial features by enlarging them, accenting them, or deforming them. For demons and supernatural heroes, they put red pepper under the eyelids to redden the eyeballs in performance.

Noh

Noh, a Japanese court masked dance-drama employing dance, mime, singing, and music, emerged around the fifteenth century. The plays are comparable to European mystery or miracle plays, involving gods and spirits, demons and ghosts, human tragedies and comedies. Noh masks are subtle full-face masks of painted wood that appear to come alive when activated by actors who have undergone long and arduous training. Noh style is very abstract, with spare, symbolic movements. For example, a cry is represented by putting the hand in front of the face, as if to dry a tear. Additional actions are considered unnecessary to communicate the emotion. Actors learn how to hold the spine with a particular use of tension, balance, and relationship to space, to use eye focus, and to make subtle shifts that take advantage of the play of light and shadow on the mask. The actors move with a slowly measured, sliding gait, their feet never losing contact with the floor. Perhaps this careful walk developed because they are somewhat blinded by having only tiny eyeholes in their masks, which inhibits their sense of space and balance.

Balinese Topeng

In *topeng,* an actor provides a one-man show in dance, mime, and song. The most excellent practitioners may travel from village to village—and even perform on television. The actor appears as numerous masked characters to teach practical lessons of survival, using historical and philosophical stories that parallel situations in the current life of the village. The actor improvises, using traditional patterns of movement and gesture to depict the roles of a prince or village leader, prime minister, queen or noblewoman, and

various clown servants. The last mask to appear in the *Topeng Pajegan* is Sidha Karya, who chases after the young children, finally gifting one with the yellow rice and Chinese coin offerings that the actor gave at the beginning of the performance. His strangely grinning, ghostly white face embodies a good spirit, who demonstrates his story's moral: Things are not what they appear to be.

 Exploring the Form

Activities to Find Character in a Mask

Walks (Inspired by exercises of master teachers of French mime, Etienne Decroux and Jacques Lecoq.) In classic mime, the part of the body that is most forward in the walk indicates a particular type of stock character. To find a way into the character of a mask, have Players, individually or in teams, walk across a large space several times, leading with different parts of the body. Try the following series of focuses or invent your own.

- First time, ask Players to notice everything about their own walking style.

- Second time, ask Players to lead with their heads.

- Third time, ask Players to lead with their feet.

- Fourth time, ask Players to lead with their chests.

- Fifth time, ask Players to lead with their stomachs.

- Ask Players to lead with an elbow, shoulder, hip, eyes, ears, nose, or other body part.

- Ask Players to move forward, backward, right, or left with either a right or left focus leading the body.

As Players walk, keep moving among them, and, at any time, stop individual Players by asking them to freeze. Ask them to describe how they feel in the posture of the walk, or whether a character has emerged from the walk. If the Player does not see or feel his character, ask him questions in response to what you observed in his improvisation. Help Players understand their characters by asking questions such as: "Do you feel old (stiff, light, sluggish, rushed, happy, angry, etc.)? Then, divide the group in half to observe and discuss one another's various walks and characters. This could be done with or without masks.

Working with an Object Talk the masked Players through the following direction: See an object. Take it. Inspect it. Let it remind you (the character) of something else. Then look at the object and have an idea about it. For example, the character picks up a broom, thinks about the job he has to do with it, examines it, and transforms it in his mind into a time when he was young and dancing with a beautiful partner. So he dances with his broom partner. This activity could be combined with the character found in a walk. Have Players try the same series of actions as different characters.

Reacting to an Imaginary Object Direct Players by talking them through the following process of discovering an object: Enter the playing area and see something. Want it. Look at it. It's funny. It's horrible. It's hot. It's gooey. It's scary. It disappears. Look for it. Find two of it. Be confused. There is a conflict. Which one do you want? Figure out how to solve the conflict.

Choosing a Theme and a Performance Form

Following are some examples.

Pyramus and Thisbe "Pyramus and Thisbe," an excerpt (see Student Book, pages 214–229) from Act V, Scene I, of *A Midsummer Night's Dream,* written by William Shakespeare around 1593 or 1594. This miniature play-within-a-play takes place in Athens. It is performed by a company of six amateur actors, led by the character Peter Quince. The actors are actually servants in the court (or *mechanicals,* as they are known) and characters in a subplot. The servants are ordered to present a pastoral play, in mask, about the lovers, Pyramus and Thisbe, as entertainment on Midsummer Night's Eve. This takes place in the court of Theseus, Duke of Athens, with the courtiers holding a running commentary on the actions of the mechanicals. It can be performed with or without the noble characters.

Shadow Play (See Shadow Plays and Puppets, page 182.) Everything can be personified through a mask. Characters can be human or nonhuman, animate or inanimate. (Doors, clouds, sun, moon, stars, rocks, trees, animals, cars, and trains make wonderful masks.)

Mummers' Play (See Researching the Form, page 189, for references.) Use the traditional folk play forms or make up your own masked play to celebrate the solstice.

Legend, Myth, or Animal Tale Create your own masque by adapting an existing myth, legend, fable, or animal story, or by creating a new one. A story can be told by a single narrator, by a choral group, or by each character speaking his own parts. (See the *Tricky Tales* script, a modern version of trickster tales, told by masked characters from around the world, in the Student Book, pages 230–260.)

Carnival A processional celebration or a masked ball. Make a parade of masks with dancers, singers, musicians, and even floats. (See Researching the Form, page 189, for references.)

Script Based on Masked Characters

Create a script or score based on Players' masked characters and their interactions with one another. Or have masks participate in Carnival-like celebrations.

- **Stock Characters** Participants choose one masked (stock) character to become and make a mask to fit their character (type). (See Stock Characters, page 175.)
- **Original Mask** Offer materials with which to create a mask. Encourage Players to make their masks in any manner they wish. Have Players practice moving with their masks to discover how to embody the mask's character.

Making Masks

There are many materials that are inexpensive, readily available, and easy to cut and decorate that can be used to make masks: white paper plates, grocery bags, cardboard boxes (appliance stores are a source for refrigerator or stove boxes when extra-large shapes are needed), and half-masks made of plastic or cloth and string or yarn. Decorative materials can include crayons, a variety of felt-tip colored pens with different widths, cut paper, stickers, yarn, glitter, or any other materials that can be affixed to the mask base. Players can make masks inspired by a tradition or style, or create a new tradition. Following are some ideas.

Paper Plate Masks Ask every Player to create a mask by painting or drawing a face on a white paper plate. Begin by marking where the eyeholes should be placed.

Cut Paper Masks Direct Players to fold a blank piece of paper in half. Cut out the mouth, nose, and eye holes. The cut-out pieces can be used to decorate or add features to the masks.

Paper Bag Masks Place a grocery bag upside down over the head of the wearer. First draw and cut out half circles at the wearer's shoulders so that the bag will sit easily on the wearer. Mark where the eyeholes should be placed and cut them out. Then have the Players draw faces on the mask.

Papier Mâché or Plaster Masks Make masks from papier mâché or plaster of paris. These masks could be life masks, molded on the Players' own faces. Check your local library or art store for art techniques.

Half-Masks Purchase cloth or plastic half-masks. They are usually available at theatrical supply shops, toy stores, or novelty stores. Direct Players to decorate their masks with paper, yarn, glitter, and any other materials.

Flats as Masks (also called *puppets*) Find large cardboard boxes. Using a matte knife, cut them into flat sections. Draw or paint the shapes of objects large enough to cover the performer's body at least partially, and if wanted, completely. The cut-out shapes can be hand-held or affixed to a stick. Use the flats as clouds, trees, houses, trains, cars, sun, moon, stars, mountains, or animals (the animal head can be cut out and held on a stick above the performer's head or as a mask covering the head). (See Shadow Plays and Puppets, page 182.)

Box Masks Using boxes of various sizes, direct Players to draw and cut out a face on one side of each box. If there is printing on the box and a very clean, simple effect is desired, cut the box so that it can be turned inside out. Tape the box back together inside out, using tape the same color as the box. Players can

also make faces on all four sides or on two opposite sides of their boxes. This is wonderful for characters who have changing natures, or who move around a lot. Use cut paper, bits of jewelry, glasses, paints, tinsel, and other bits and pieces of junk and art supplies to add details to the character's image. It may be necessary to fasten a hat or ties inside the box to anchor it on the wearer's head.

Issues of Comfort and Design

- **Visibility** The first problem to solve is where to put the eyes on the mask so that when it is worn, the wearer can easily see. Once the location is determined, the eyes can be drawn according to whatever style is wanted. Determine eye positions by having one person hold the mask over her face with one hand while touching the eye socket with the other hand. Another person can mark the exact location of the wearer's eyes with a pencil.

- **Comfort** Try to strike a compromise between being able to see, and keeping the mask's mystery. If airholes are desired for the wearer's comfort, other small openings can be cut at the mouth and nose. Have Players punch or poke two holes near both sides of their masks and attach string, elastic, ribbon, or yarn ties so that the masks can be worn comfortably by tying them behind the head. If a mask rubs uncomfortably, have the wearer glue pieces of makeup sponges at the points of contact to help relieve the problem.

- **Fast Changes** If the wearer does not have to talk, and would like to be able to put on and remove the mask quickly, a cork or a piece of rope or plastic tubing can be affixed at the center of the mouth, and the Player can hold the mask in place with his teeth.

- **Effectiveness of Design** Before Players make their masks, explain that all features of a mask must be drawn clearly and boldly enough to be seen, or "read," from a distance. Once Players have all drawn their masks, have each Player put on his mask and walk a distance from the group, and have the other Players check to see if the mask is clearly visible. If not, have Players try using stronger colors, bolder lines, and bigger shapes to solve the problem.

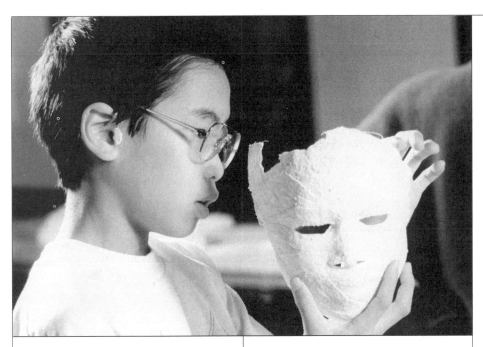

Mirror Image Try having Players wear their masks in front of a large mirror, so that they can study how they appear to others. Ask them to try looking in various directions, changing either the eye focus or tilt of the head. Ask them to notice the way they have to hold the mask in order for the mask to be seen, and how the mask comes alive through changes of eye or head movements. Or walk among the Players as they are working with masks, holding a hand mirror. Catch Players by surprise, showing them a glimpse of themselves as a mask.

Rehearsing with the Masks In general, when learning how to perform with masks in a proscenium theater, and especially when using the flats and paper plate masks, Players need to understand that although some masks can turn and still be seen, many masks cannot. The Masks must remain facing the audience at all times, or they will not "read," and will effectively disappear from view.

The natural tendency, to turn and face whomever you are speaking to, does not work when using a flat as a mask. Tell Players that the flat needs to maintain a frontal focus. The person behind the flat

could incline in the direction of the listener or indicate interest through other physical gestures. Divide the group into two teams and have them watch one another. Then they can see how the masks look when they are held facing flat front or turned at an angle.

The flat front focus is not an issue if an open-theater setting is being used, or if the performance is a parade. Direct Players to share their masks with all sides of the audience. In a parade they can acknowledge each direction with waves, nods, and bows.

Connections

Social Studies and History Choose places and times of celebrations and festivals that connect with your curriculum content. The masks could incorporate design ideas from these sources.

Language Arts When studying myths and legends, try making masks to fit those tales. Read the stories while wearing the masks. (If the masks are full-faced, they can be worn on the top of the head like a hat, or angled on the forehead, in order to not interfere with each speaker's voice.)

Art Collaborate with other teachers on large projects to make masks that fit curriculum or production design problems. Or offer a class in mask making.

 Assessment

Teacher Observations

- In their research, were students able to describe and compare the way masks appear and are used in different cultures and times?

- Did making and wearing a mask help Players develop their understanding of the powers endowed in masks, and the uses for them?

Group Discussion

Discuss masks, showing examples or pictures of examples. The choice of the masks could be related to your social studies curriculum, come from classic theater traditions, or be from contemporary sources (such as an analysis of current styles of street makeup, or "Sesame Street" characters). Ask students to describe their reactions to various pictures of masks or real masks.

Use the following questions to start a discussion about performing in and watching performances in masks.

- Do you like to see masked characters performing?

- Do you feel any difference between performing in a mask or without a mask?

- Describe how you felt when you took off your mask.

Discuss how people mask their faces in everyday life. (See Stock Characters, page 175, for further information about theatrical mask traditions.)

Student Activities

Book

pages 138–144 (Background Reading)

Journal

Ask students to describe any masks they have seen. They can be make-up masks, or be made from another materials, such as plastic, wood, paper, or plaster.

References

Alford, Violet. *Pyrenean Festivals, Calendar Customs, Music & Magic, Drama & Dance*. London: Chatto and Windus, 1937.

Chase, Richard. "Old-Christmas Eve." Chapter 1 in *Grandfather Tales*. Boston: Houghton Mifflin Co., 1948.

Dennis, Anne. *The Articulate Body, the Physical Training of the Actor*. New York: Drama Book Publishers, 1995.

Hill, Errol. *The Trinidad Carnival*. Austin, TX, 1972.

Kirstein, Lincoln. *Movement & Metaphor, Four Centuries of Ballet*. New York and Washington: Praeger Publishers, 1970.

Laliberte, Norman, and Alex Mogelon. *Masks, Face Coverings and Headgear*. New York: An Arts Horizons Book, Van Nostrand Reinhold Co., 1973.

Mack, John, editor. *Masks and the Art of Expression*. New York: Harry N. Abrams, Inc., 1994.

Moore, Lillian. *Images of the Dance, Historical Treasures of the Dance Collection 1581–1861*. New York: The New York Public Library, 1965.

Orloff, Alexander. *Carnival*. Austria: Perlinger Verlag, 1981.

Shakespeare, William. *As You Like It, A Midsummer Night's Dream, The Tempest*.

Slattum, Judy. *Masks of Bali, Spirits of an Ancient Drama*. San Francisco: Chronicle Books, 1992.

Thompson, Robert Farris. *African Art in Motion*. Berkeley and Los Angeles: University of California Press, 1974.

Films:

Romeo and Juliet (1968), directed by Franco Zeffirelli. Contains a masked ball.

Beauty and the Beast (1946), directed by Jean Cocteau; *Beauty and the Beast* (1991), directed by Gary Trousdale and Kirk Wise, Disney Productions.

The Mask (1994), directed by Charles Russell.

Much Ado About Nothing (1993), directed by Kenneth Branagh. Contains a masked ball.

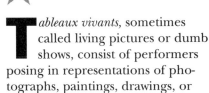

Tableaux Vivants

Tableaux vivants, sometimes called living pictures or dumb shows, consist of performers posing in representations of photographs, paintings, drawings, or sculptures, or as re-creations of street scenes or other events.

Players may learn about the history of this genre, and may experiment by creating *tableaux* as scenes, moments within a scene, or as entr'actes. *Tableaux* provide opportunities for costume and set design and offer intriguing ways to experience art and history.

★ Researching the Form

The first wave of popularity of European *tableaux vivants* occurred when they were used as an integral part of medieval religious mystery plays. In fourteenth-century France and England, *tableaux vivants* were used to honor a monarch's entrance into a city or to provide hints concerning the current political climate. In the elaborate spectacles of seventeenth-century French and English court masques, party disguises helped create displays that included posing and pantomime within promenades and dances. One very famous French image from the period depicts Louis XIV posing as the Sun King, wearing an elaborate corona headdress.

By the eighteenth century, *tableaux vivants* were frequently performed to represent specific works of art, familiar figures from antiquity, or allegorical themes. Performers struck poses, called *attitudes.* The criteria for excellence in the art

of performing *tableaux* was to appear as similar to the original idea as possible.

By the 1850s, *tableaux* had become popular entertainment in European salons and music halls, and soon traveled to similar venues in North and South America. Frequently, *tableaux* were billed in the music halls or vaudeville circuit along with minstrels, dancers, acrobats, and similar attractions. It was common for songs, instrumental music, recitations, and pantomime to accompany and embellish each *tableau.* The performance of the living picture took the form of a pose (*attitude*) followed by a quick change or shift in position to another pose. The most skilled performers were able to trick the observer by making seamless transformations of costume, position, and character in full view of the audience. For example, Venus transformed into Diana, who transformed into the Goddess of Liberty.

By the late 1800s, *tableaux* became increasingly complicated. Machinery and sets that used revolving platforms, movable backgrounds, and lighting tricks, and realistic effects, such as falling snowflakes and waterfalls, were employed to keep audiences returning to see the latest inventions. In spite of these technical attractions, *tableaux vivants* disappeared by the end of the nineteenth century, in the face of competition from melodramas,

concert salons, and plays that showed a lot of skin, called *leg art.*

People continue to be intrigued by this art form, so *tableaux vivants* resurface from time to time. *Tableaux* are still found in community festivals and pageants, musicals, and contemporary performance artworks. (For example, Laguna

Beach, California, presents Pageant of the Masters, an annual display of living pictures that has been a tourist attraction for many years.) The most contemporary, high-visibility evolution of the form is *voguing*, dance contests based on photo images of movie stars and fashion models that surfaced in Harlem clubs during the 1980s and hit the mainstream through Madonna's popularization in her music video, "Vogue." The dance consists of various poses, similar to photo images or film freeze frames, that keep changing from posture to posture.

In Japanese Kabuki theater (flourishing by the end of the sixteenth century), male characters assume poses or friezes, called *mie*, to show their characters' attitudes toward an event. Often used at the moment of climax, it's one of the most popular features of Kabuki style. The chief characteristic of these poses is the intensity with which they are performed. The actors use crossed eyes to emphasize the singular focus, and muscle tension to create a perception of a larger-than-life image. The pillar pose, stone-throwing pose, jerking pose, and play-ending pose are translations of the terms for some of the most famous *mie*. A series of *mie* can be performed as move/freezes in a stationary position, or, within the context of a series of rhythmic steps or stage crossings. They can be performed as solos or by groups. *Mie* can shift time and point of view. For example, as a climactic dramatic action happens, one by one, each main character can assume a pose, revealing his reaction to the action. One resource suggests that many of the *mie* closely resemble Buddhist temple sculpture (beginning in the ninth century and predating Kabuki), and that it is likely that the poses were derived from them.

1. Ask Players to select an image from existing artworks, their own artworks, art books, newspapers, magazines, advertisements, billboards, and posters. Or Players could choose instead to recreate street scenes or other events, or to choose a theme to represent in *tableaux vivants*.

2. Discuss and decide which images to use and how to present them in *tableaux*. You could choose to perform the images in one of the following ways.

• Still lifes

• A series of slow motion scenes, changing details of set or design with each new image

• An alternating pattern of moving and freezing, set on a rhythm

3. Divide your group into teams, or work together as one group, to experiment with forming *tableaux*.

4. Experiment with adding other elements to the *tableaux*.

• Verse (using a narrator to speak or sing)

• Costumes that imitate those in the image being portrayed

• Live or recorded sound to accompany the images

• Props

5. Decide how you want to present the *tableaux* and where to place the audience. Consider whether you want the audience experience to move from image to image, or if the audience should remain stationary, viewing *tableaux* from one perspective. Then assign Players to the place or places in the performing area where their scenes will occur.

6. Rehearse the *tableaux,* using all the design elements (see below) you intend to include in the performance.

7. Have Players perform their *tableaux*.

Audience Placement

Traveling Audience If the audience is to travel from *tableau* to *tableau*, similar to viewing art in a museum or community festival, then place the *tableaux* randomly, in a large pattern (a circle, square, or U-shape) or along a path in the playing area so that the audience is guided by your design setup to view the *tableaux* as a sequence.

Stationary Audience To present *tableaux* to an audience that is to remain stationary, use the following devices to change scenes.

• **Blackouts** The Players perform a static or moving series of images in light. To change an image, the lights go off (blackout). When the lights come on again, a new image is in place. This repeats until all images have been performed.

• **Shadow Screen** The Players perform behind a shadow screen, using a static or moving series of images.

• **Masking Devices** Use masking devices, such as curtains or flats, to mask the changes between tableaux.

• **Move/Freeze** Use a series of images that alternate between a move and a frieze. This could also involve a rearrangement of costumes, props, and set.

Types of Stages

Choose an indoor or outdoor setting in which to present your *tableaux,* such as a cafeteria, proscenium stage, playground, or entrance hallway and staircase. You can also model spatial and set designs on presentations of medieval mystery and morality plays, in which stages, called *stations,* were organized in a large circle or U-shaped formation.

Indoor or Outdoor Setting

• Station individual Players or teams randomly throughout the playing area.

- Station individual Players or teams in a circle or *U*-shaped formation.
- Set up several small platform stages, in a random or specific formation, throughout the playing area.
  - **Stationary Platform Stage** Players perform one or more separate scenes on each stage.
  - **Rotating Platform Stage** Divide a platform, as you would divide a pie, into two or more separate spaces with a masking device, such as curtains or flats. Stage a different scene on each division. As the platform rotates, each scene comes into the audience's view. This appearing and disappearing act continues until all the images have been presented.

Outdoor Setting Use one or more wagons or flatbed trucks as stages that are stationary or that travel along a path. *Tableaux* floats could travel in parades or processionals.

Masking Devices

Several Preset Tableaux Use curtains, flats, or paper to separate two or more preset *tableaux* within one performing area so that the audience sees only one scene at a time.

Changing Tableaux Change from *tableau* to *tableau* within one performing area by masking the changes with curtains, flats, or paper.

Backdrops

Backdrops provide a background for the scene being presented and mask other scenes that the audience should not see at that time. Backdrops can be nonpictorial or pictorial.

Nonpictorial Backdrops Use existing stage curtains, screens, lightweight room dividers, two or more people holding up fabric, or papers attached to one or several poles.

Pictorial Backdrops

- **Roller Backdrops** Affix paper or fabric—on which a series of changing scenes are painted or drawn— onto a roller. This roll of painted scenes is turned to reveal each new scene.
- **Flip Backdrops** Paint or draw separate scenes on separate pieces of paper or cloth. Connect them across the top to a tube, pole, or stick. Flip these separate pieces of paper or cloth over the top to reveal a new scene, in coordination with the Players' sequence of actions.

Performance Suggestions

Tableaux within a Larger Scene Use *tableaux* within a movement activity or scene. Direct Players to use *tableaux* to change the timing in a scene, to emphasize a moment, or to highlight an emotional experience of a character so that the audience can experience the importance of the moment. Create a series of tableaux that occur one after the other, as in a domino effect or motion picture flip book. Or have Players move across the playing area in a series of *tableaux* that segue from one into another.

Tableaux That React to a Tableau As in the Japanese *mie* (see Researching the Form), set up one group *tableau* that represents a moment of high drama or emotion. Have other Players make solo or group *tableaux* that comment on that moment. Each solo or group should show a different reaction to the first *tableau*. For example, the group *tableau* could be the signing of the Declaration of Independence. The solo *tableau* could include the reactions of King George III of England, Betsy Ross, a Yankee farmer, and a Native American.

Altered Images Instead of recreating an image exactly, have Players make tableaux that reflect their point of view on existing photographs, paintings, or sculpture.

★ Teaching Notes

Management Tips

View slides or transparencies of paintings and sculpture. Discuss elements of the images that could be part of a *tableau*.

Sense Memory Warm-Up Have Players study an image for ten to thirty seconds. Remove the image from view and ask Players to draw or describe what they saw. Look at the original again, and compare.

Mural Warm-Up Divide your class in half or into an equal number of teams. Tell one team (Team 1) to begin as audience and the other (Team 2) to begin as performers. Ask one person on Team 2 to take any position, in a frieze, against a wall. Then ask the other Players on Team 2 to determine individually the idea of the frieze and a way to join in the frieze until all members of Team 2 have created a group frieze that looks like a wall mural. Ask members of Team 1 to each memorize the position of a Player from Team 2. One by one, they replace Team 2 Players in the frieze, copying positions as accurately as possible. The replaced Players of Team 2 become part of the audience. This continues until Team 1 has recreated the mural. Team 2 observes the mural and discusses whether the mural looks the way it felt. Finally, both teams have a discussion about what they think was the subject of the mural and decide on a title for the mural.

Adding Design Elements Research costumes, song, verse, and music so that they reflect the time and place of the *tableau*. In addition to the images, try to have on hand items that might help students create their *tableaux*. Provide clothing and small hand props to suggest costume and character, such as scarves, hats, umbrellas, and canes.

Connections

Art and Art History Recreate paintings, sculptures, or photographs. Visit art museums, galleries, wax museums, and diorama displays; find friezes or murals on the walls of public buildings; or research images on ancient buildings, such as the Parthenon, and Aztec, Mayan, or Egyptian temples and tombs; research famous paintings and sculptures. Some of the most popular *tableaux* were recreations of the following artworks: *Washington Crossing the Delaware* by Emanuel Leutze; *The Declaration of*

Independence by John Trumbull; *Penn's Treaty with the Indians* by Benjamin West; *Congress Voting Independence* by Robert Edge Pine and Edward Savage; *Liberty Leading the People* by Eugene Delacroix; the Statue of Liberty; friezes on government buildings; sculptures or paintings of goddesses and legendary women, such as the Three Graces, Aphrodite/Venus, Diana, Cleopatra, and Helen of Troy; or photographs of famous women such as Harriet Tubman, Clara Barton, Eleanor Roosevelt, Marie Curie, and the Suffragettes, including Susan B. Anthony.

History

- Find images of historical figures to use as source material for *tableaux*.

- Use a series of *tableaux* to depict historical events or periods. For example, research the history of your state and select twelve events that can be used to make *tableaux*.

Literature

- Reenact scenes from allegories, myths, legends, fables, and folktales. Research images of mythological figures to use as source material for *tableaux*.

- Research a style of theater that features *tableaux vivants,* such as European medieval morality plays or American community pageants of the late nineteenth and early twentieth centuries.

Social Studies Use images from current media that typify the issues in current events.

Special Needs

This activity is particularly useful for those students who learn visually, need to work on focusing, or have difficulty with reading and memorization.

 Assessment

Teacher Observations

Were students able to locate and analyze images that would work well as *tableaux*? Were students able to recall and recreate images? Were they able to perform a series of images? Was it engaging for students to learn curriculum from visual images of a period?

Group Discussion

Discuss with your students how art can reflect a period of time, place, or culture. Ask them what images they would choose to depict their time and place.

 Student Activities

Book

pages 145–146 (Background Reading)

Journal

Ask Players to each find an image to share with the class. Have them write a paragraph on the history of the image, discussing its time, place, costume, and message. Or suggest that students choose an image that, in their opinion, represents their generation.

 References

Glassberg, David. American *Historical Pageantry, The Uses of Tradition in the Early Twentieth Century.* Chapel Hill and London: The University of North Carolina Press, 1990.

McCullough, Jack W. *Living Pictures on the New York Stage.* Ann Arbor, Michigan: UMI Research Press, an imprint of University Microfilms International, 1981; 1983.

Radio Theater

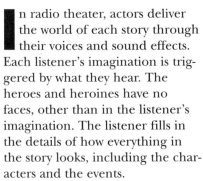

In radio theater, actors deliver the world of each story through their voices and sound effects. Each listener's imagination is triggered by what they hear. The heroes and heroines have no faces, other than in the listener's imagination. The listener fills in the details of how everything in the story looks, including the characters and the events.

Radio theater provides a perfect medium to consider the use and effects of sound design. Interestingly, although the theater world commonly thinks of using sound and music for isolated effects, it has only recently begun to think of the sound environment as a cohesive design element.

Since the scripts of radio plays are generally read by actors in the recording studio, radio plays can be considered a form of readers' theater. This activity introduces the history of radio plays, ways to think about the nature of sound and sound production, and provides ways to experiment with performing in the genre of radio theater.

★ Researching the Form

From the 1920s through the 1950s, radio plays were an important part of life in the United States, causing as much discussion and loyalty as do the most popular shows on television today. They used a variety of formats, including soap operas, thrillers, westerns, science fiction, situation comedies, documentary style dramas (docudramas), and vaudeville. Titles of some of the most popular shows were "Inner Sanctum," "Amos 'n' Andy," "Tom Mix," "The Lone Ranger," "Ma Perkins," "Stella Dallas," "Sherlock Holmes," "Captain Midnight," "Jack Benny," "My Little Margie," "Superman," "Little Orphan Annie," "Sam Spade," Gene Autry's "Melody Ranch," "Terry and the Pirates," "Fibber McGee and Molly," "Our Miss Brooks," and "Helen Trent."

An example of the potential power of radio theater can be found in the public's response to Orson Welles's 1938 broadcast, "Invasion from Mars." Welles posed as a reporter delivering news bulletins, reporting a Martian attack on Earth and the United States Army's response. People panicked, jammed phones lines to Washington, and some actually ran to the hills in fear. The broadcast resulted in Welles having to go on the air to make a public disclaimer, assuring people that this was only a fictitious story.

★ Exploring the Form

Performing a Radio Play

1. Choose an existing radio play script or write an original monologue, dialogue, or scene with a plot to be performed "on radio."

2. As a group, read the script together. Ask Players to look for any sound cues that are inferred by the text, such as a door slamming, a scream, a telephone ringing, a doorbell, crickets, or traffic. Decide whether to create the sounds onstage live or use recorded sounds.

3. Decide how to lead into the show and how to exit. This can be accompanied in many ways, including using an announcer; creating and inserting advertisements; inserting news bulletins; giving a station call signal; or designing a signature theme for your show by using music, a jingle, or a sound effect loop.

4. Make acting and technical crew assignments. While the actors rehearse the script together, have the sound crew gather materials to make sound effects and edit them to fit the cues.

5. Have actors and sound technicians rehearse together to set cues, refine timing and timbre, and adjust sound levels.

6. Have the Players perform and/or record their radio drama.

Collecting Sound Effects and Music

Decide whether to create the sounds onstage live, make live recordings in the field, or use existing compact disc (CD), record, or tape formats.

Live Sound Effects Onstage or offstage sounds made without the use of recording equipment. Following are some suggestions for making certain kinds of sounds live.

- **Footsteps** Fill a tray with a substance that sounds like gravel, snow, or mud, then have someone walk or run in place in the tray.

- **Rain** Drop sand or rice in a tray or tambourine that has a reverberating surface.

- **Thunder** Shake a piece of sheet metal.

- **Sea Sounds** Shake dry peas around a tambourine or small drum.

- **Fire** Crumple cellophane (you may have to amplify this with a microphone).

- **Breaking Glass** Rattle broken glass inside a closed box.

- **Prerecorded Sound Effects** Thousands of recorded sounds are available. Libraries often have sound effects on long-playing records, cassette tapes, and compact discs that you can borrow. Re-record them in the format you will be using for your radio play. If you need a sound effect to last longer than is recorded, it will be necessary for you to do several recordings back to back, in a loop, to extend the duration of the sound effect.

- **Field Recordings** Make your own tapes of sound effects by going out and recording live sounds, such as traffic noises, bird songs, and dogs barking. Experiment with various solutions. Many times one sound can represent another. For example, running tap water can provide a waterfall sound effect.

- **Electronic Sounds** Synthesizers or other keyboards often have sound effects built into their programs, such as water dripping, wave sounds, bird sounds, bees buzzing, hands clapping, car horns, gunshots, scraping, shock alarm, emergency sounds, or telephone rings. Experiment by adjusting to different pitches, timbres, and durations to create atmospheric effects that indicate time passing, impending doom or suspense, or provide an exclamation. For example, bend or sustain a sound, or add vibrato or reverberation. These can be recorded or played live.

Cueing Sound Effects

You will need to assign at least one person to be the sound engineer, whose job is to run the recorded or live sound effects. You might need a stage manager to give the cues indicating when to begin and end each sound, and one operator who actually runs the cues. These technicians will need to organize the sound effects and cueing system. Following are some organizational ideas.

- **Reel-to-Reel Tape Recorder** Most professional theaters use this format to record and store magnetic tape. Each sound cue is recorded on tape, then all cues are edited together on one reel by splicing leader tape between each cue.

- **Cassette Tapes** Use one cassette tape for each sound cue. You can buy ten- or fifteen-minute cassette tapes for this purpose.

- **Technical Concerns** In the performing space, technicians will need to set sound levels, balance speakers so that the sound levels are equal, and reduce feedback and distortions.

- **Cue Sheets** Set up an order to run the sound cues. Make a chart that indicates when each cue happens and the level, location, and duration of each sound effect.

★ Teaching Notes

Management Tips

Listen to a Radio Play Have Players listen to a radio play. Your local radio station may produce radio theater programs, which can be assigned as homework and discussed in class. (Garrison Keillor's radio program, "Prairie Home Companion," currently broadcast on most Public Radio stations, generally contains short skits

that can be taped to use as examples for the class.) Otherwise, try to borrow recordings from the library.

Test Recordings As soon as possible, run a test of all recorded sound effects, listening to them in the performing space and at the volume level that will be used in performance to make sure that there are no unintended noises or distortions. Re-record, if necessary.

Using Microphones If you will be using microphones in performance, have students listen to one another on and off mike to help them become sensitive to how microphones affect articulation and tone. Before each rehearsal and performance, adjust the volume levels so that they are appropriate for each speaker on each unit, so all performers are in balance. Have one operator monitor the volume control throughout the performance, adjusting levels as needed.

Coordinating Cues for Recording If recording the radio play, put one person in charge of coordinating cues, such as the director or stage manager. Have all Players agree upon visual cues or some other system, such as American Sign Language, to communicate without sound. This will keep the company in focus, and help you avoid having to edit unnecessary sounds from the tape.

Connections

History Chronicle the history of radio: its invention; the plots and characters of popular radio theater shows; the changes of standard formats that are popular at one time or another (such as the current rise of talk shows).

Science

- Have students study and explain how humans hear sound, what radio waves are, and how radio signals are transmitted.
- Ask students to make diagrams or explain how sound transmission works, including amplification, feedback, and modulation.
- Ask students to describe how sound equipment works, such as recorders, amplifiers, microphones, or speakers. Have them investigate new technology by learning about the latest tools that help produce and record sound, such as the digital audio sampler called MIDI (Musical Instrument Digital Interface), or multitrack mixers.

Computers Investigate computer software programs designed to help produce sound environments, such as Sound Designer, Pro Tools, Sound Edit, Alchemy, Deck, Metro, and Performer.

Foreign Languages and ESL Read and perform bilingual stories or perform in the language being studied.

Special Needs

Since this activity is structured as primarily a sit-down activity, it provides performing and technical opportunities for students in wheelchairs or with limited physical mobility. Braille text needs to be provided for any blind students. Provide sign language interpreters for deaf students.

Teacher Observations

- Were students able to determine which source material would be effective as radio theater?
- Did students understand how to make the stories come alive through the techniques of sound effects and voice modulation?
- Were students able to communicate character through voice and create setting through sound effects?

Group Discussion

Use the following questions to generate a discussion about radio theater.

- Do you think that television plays are as captivating as radio plays? Why or why not?
- As a radio performer, did you use your voice and body differently than in live theater performances?
- As a listener, did you use your imagination more with radio theater? Why or why not?
- Did you enjoy not seeing the audience? Why or why not?
- Did working in radio theater increase your awareness of sounds in the environment?

 Student Activities

Book

page 147 (Background Reading)

pages 148–149 (Performance Model)

Journal

Have Players list ways to write descriptions of at least five different qualities of sounds. For example, wind: *whoosh, swisssshhhh, ooooooohhh, hurricane, a calm wind*

References

Harmon, Jim. *The Great Radio Heroes.* Garden City, NY: Doubleday and Company, Inc., 1967.

Kaye, Deena and James LeBrecht. *Sound & Music for the Theater, The Art and Technique of Design.* New York: Backstage Books, Watson-Guptill, 1992.

Theatre Crafts Directory and Theatre Crafts, a monthly magazine that gives listings of suppliers and current information in the field of design and technical production.

The BBC and CBS provide anthologies of sound effects in various formats. They can be found in public libraries or ordered directly from the companies.

Look for famous radio play scripts in your local library. Recordings of old radio programs are also available.

Readers' Theater

Readers' theater is a performed reading of an entire text from a literary source not originally intended to be a script. The Players decide how to take a short literary form, such as a short story or poem, and make it into a live performance. The basic rule is to speak every word as written, omitting or changing nothing in the text. Since the performance is the reading of the text, there is no pressure to memorize lines.

There are many ways to perform readers' theater. In some performances, Players remain seated the whole time, using voice and gesture to emphasize dramatic qualities of the story or poem. In others, Players combine a seated reading with staged blocking of short scenes involving dialogue and action. Sometimes production values, such as musical backgrounds or sound effects, hand props, and changes of costume are added to heighten interest.

★ Researching the Form

The following information offers ideas on how to direct Readers' Theater. There are no specific rules to follow, other than those stated above.

1. **Select the Text** Choose an existing short story, poem, speech, or essay. Or have participants write their own.

2. **Sit-down Readings** Ask the group to sit together in a circle, closely enough so that Players can see and hear one another easily.

Read the selected text aloud together, at least two times.

- **First Reading** Go through the text, reading section by section. Stop to correct pronunciation, provide definitions of words, note and correct typographical errors, or to answer Players' questions. (If there are many words that need to be defined, you might want to provide a glossary.)

- **Second Reading** Read the text together, without stopping, so that Players can hear the flow of the words.

3. **Discuss the Text** Identify the given circumstances: the *Who, Where, When, What,* and *Why* of the work.

4. **Identify the Theme** After the group is familiar with the text, ask them to summarize the story in a word, phrase, or sentence. Choose the one idea that can serve as the theme on which to focus the performance.

5. **Assign Parts** Decide how to divide up the reading of the story so that every word comes alive in a performance. If there are more Players than characters in the text, there are many ways you could divide up performing tasks, so that everyone can be part of presenting the actions and characters.

- **One Role Performed by Several Players**
  - Two or more Players speak the dialogues and others speak the monologues.
  - Some Players are the movers who never speak, personifying the characters through action. And some Players are the speakers, who never move.

- Players speak any text related to the characters given through the author's or narrator's voice.

- **Speakers/Movers** Half of the Players are speakers, or readers of the text; the other half of the Players are movers, using pantomime to communicate the text.

- **Text/Subtext** One group speaks directly from the text. Another group performs what is implied or hidden, but not directly stated, in the text. See Doubles (page 60) for ideas of how to work this way.

- **Chorus of Narrators and Individual Characters** Some Players read any narrative material, such as descriptions of place, people, and time. Other Players take on the character roles.

- **Experimental Approaches** Try alternative ways to assign lines among the Players, instead of dividing the text up by character or narrator parts. Try orchestrating readers like a chorus, listening for interesting combinations of pitch or tone, or by contrasting group and soloist; or use a series of soloists, assigned to lines randomly, in a "round robin" approach.

- **Sound Effects**
  - Assign one or more Players to make sounds that communicate all punctuation marks in the story.
  - Ask Players to create any sounds that are inferred in the text, such as bird calls, whistles, traffic noises, whispered voices, telephones ringing, and so on. (See Radio Theater, page 201.)

Variations

Story Extender Change the basic rule and allow Players to break off the story at the climax, then have them write and perform their own ending.

Memorization As Players begin to familiarize themselves with the lines, they will begin to commit some of the lines to memory. Encourage them to do this as it will strengthen and add interest to the performance. If the Players can handle more memorization, choose certain scenes to be played without script in hand. This can really highlight important scenes of dialogue.

Performance Suggestions

Perform for Another Class Perform for another class that is reading the same material. Or agree with another teacher to exchange performances, with each classroom performing the same or different required texts.

Add Production Elements If taken into performance, you might want to add sound effects, live or recorded music, small hand props, and suggestions of costume.

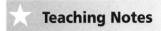 **Teaching Notes**

Management Tips

Text Length Choose a short text so that an entire work can be presented, rather than an excerpt of a larger work.

Materials Each participant should have a chair. Supply individual copies of the text to each person in the group.

Cross-References See further discussion on selecting the text, sit-down readings, discussing the text, identifying themes, and assigning parts in the Introduction to Chapter 5, Scriptwriting.

Reading the Text If possible, have Players read the text individually before they read it aloud together.

Rehearsal Techniques To help Players relax into reading the lines naturally, release them from the page by substituting improvisational activities that will help them understand the sense of the text and develop their characterizations and relationships.

- **Gibberish** Have Players read the whole text, substituting their own gibberish for the written words while still communicating the sense of the text.
- **Mock Opera** Have Players sing the text.
- **Ad-Lib** Challenge Players to perform the meaning of the text, without using the text itself. Have the Players use their own language to have dialogues with each other and tell the story. This will help the Players understand relationships between their characters and increase their understanding of the story.
- **Pantomime** Ask Players to communicate the entire story through movement and gesture language that physicalizes the emotions, feelings, and events.

Connections

Language Arts Choose existing texts that are required readings. Or have Players write original stories. They can be published in a magazine that can then be used in your classroom the following year.

Foreign Languages Perform texts written in the language being studied, or translate and perform a text into the language being studied.

ESL Perform the text in more than one language.

Social Studies Use Readers' Theater to help students study documents, speeches, and diaries from a particular time and place.

Special Needs

Provide materials in a format accessible to deaf and blind students, through use of Braille readers or interpreters.

 Assessment

Teacher Observations

- Were students actively engaged in the choice and analysis of reading materials? For example, were students analyzing, evaluating, and constructing meanings from text in their classroom dramatizations?
- Did students use basic acting skills to develop and portray characters? Did their characters interact in the scenes?

Group Discussion

Use the following questions to generate a discussion about their experience with readers' theater.

- Did the text stand up to dramatization?
- Would the text have been more effective if read silently on the page, or was it helpful to make it into a live performance?
- Through the process of actively performing the story, did the emotions feel more dramatic, and was the meaning clearer?

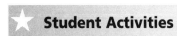 **Student Activities**

Book

page 147 (Background Reading)

Journal

Challenge Players to write a story or poem, or make a list of stories and poems, that could be performed as a readers' theater piece.

Melodrama

Melodrama, one of the most popular forms of theater ever conceived, was originally drama underlined and emotionalized by the addition of music. The elaborate plots of melodramas hinge on the suffering of the virtuous at the hands of the villainous, and take many twists and turns on their way to the usual triumphant ending of good winning over evil. Melodramatic stories may have some familiar historical theme or cultural experience as their foundation. The roles are drawn as stock characters, and played with exaggerated actions that make everything larger than life, to ensure that no one misses the chance to cry or cheer for the hero or heroine, or hiss and boo at the villain.

This activity gives performers a chance to really "ham it up." Players will have a lot of fun while learning how to make up story plots and play stock characters. Depending on how the actors play the characters, the plots can be interpreted as either comedies or tragedies. Melodramas provide a playful forum for discussions of the effects of style on content.

★ Researching the Form

Melodrama, originally an opera term, referred to an eighteenth-century European style of play that became the source of many opera libretti. It consisted of music, singing, and some spectacular effects. In Germany, melodrama referred to a spoken passage with musical accompaniment in an opera, and, in France, to a musical passage in which the character says nothing while the music expresses emotion. Sometimes, even live animals became part of the performance, a connection to circus spectacles, another source for the form.

By the nineteenth century, the emphasis on music and singing gradually shifted to the more spectacular aspects of events. Because of technical advances that came with the Industrial Revolution, theaters could reproduce earthquakes, horse races, forest fires, train crashes, and snowstorms. Codified systems of gestures and body positions were developed to indicate emotions and feelings. Actors studied particular body postures, and audiences recognized their various cues for denial, wonder or surprise, promise, anger, gentle or earnest entreaty, menace, duty and respect, resignation, supplication, fright, and grief.

A popular revival and transformation of the melodramatic form occurred in the silent films of the early twentieth century. Their live musical accompaniment underscored the emotion and drama enacted on the screen. Today, melodramas are still extremely popular, often appearing in the guise of soap operas, thrillers, and cartoons. They continue the sensationalism of struggles between the virtuous and the villainous, as revealed in their characterization, dialogue, and situations.

★ Exploring the Form

1. Discuss with your group the meaning of the term *melodrama*. Then show scenes from films made in melodramatic style.

Examples:
- Lillian Gish's silent movies, such as *Home Sweet Home* or *The Villain Still Pursued Her*
- Early Charlie Chaplin movies, such as *The Immigrant*
- Films based on the novels of Charles Dickens, including *Oliver Twist, Nicholas Nickleby,* and *Great Expectations*
- *Gone With the Wind* (1939), directed by Victor Fleming; from the novel by Margaret Mitchell
- *Who Framed Roger Rabbit?* (1988), directed by Robert Zemeckis

2. Choose a topic to perform in melodramatic style.

Examples:
- Exaggerations of daily life actions
- Newspaper articles
- Familiar events from the present or past
- Novels or short stories (Those by writers such as Edgar Allen Poe, Nathaniel Hawthorne, Charles Dickens, Margaret Mitchell, and Harriet Beecher Stowe, and modern romance novels, are consistent with the style.)
- Spin-offs on the characters and plots of present day television soap operas, movies, and plays

3. Have Players write scenarios in melodramatic style. Ask Players to supply a plot outline of five to ten events arranged in a sequence. It can be based upon a chosen source, or not. (See Scenarios, page 96.)

4. Ask Players to improvise on the melodrama scenarios. Ask for volunteers, divide the group in half, or have teams perform for one another.

Variations

Standard Gesture Language Have Players develop their own gesture language that everyone will use when performing the melodrama. Direct them to think of gestures for specific emotions (such as anger, fear, and hope) and words (such as *yes, no, don't, never, why,* and *please,* all pronouns, and sound effects and sayings, like "tsk,tsk, tsk," "pssst," or "Curses! Foiled again!") that occur often in their melodrama.

Add Singing Have Players sing the speeches.

 Teaching Notes

Management Tips

Learning to Exaggerate Gestures Ask a Player to perform one gesture. Ask for a volunteer to enlarge the gesture, then ask another volunteer to enlarge the enlargement. Or, have all Players stand in a circle. Ask each Player to perform a small gesture, one by one, which everyone repeats three times, enlarging it with each repetition. This game also provides a good physical warm-up. See the game, Clichés (page 58), for more about gesture language.

Performing a Short Melodrama The following bit is a quick illustration of melodramatic plot development. Ask Players to improvise on the text. This could be rehearsed in teams, with teams performing their solutions for one another. Discuss and compare the solutions.

Villain: I come for the rent, the rent, the rent.

Ingenue: I don't have the rent, the rent, the rent.

(This exchange is repeated three times, each time growing more hysterical.)

Villain: You must pay the rent, the rent, the rent.

Hero: *(suddenly appearing)* I'll pay the rent.

Ingenue: *(to the Hero)* My hero!

Small hand props, costumes, set pieces, and music or sound effects can be added.

Connections

Literature Read and discuss novels with melodramatic plots, such as the Charles Dickens's novels *Oliver Twist* or *Nicholas Nickleby,* or view videotapes of movies, such as those mentioned in Exploring the Form.

History Research political events that occurred during the period being studied in class and write a scenario for a melodrama consistent with that period.

 Assessment

Teacher Observations

- Were students able to make scenarios for a melodrama based on a historical event or daily life event from the period?

- Were students able to invent character behaviors that used an exaggerated gesture language to punctuate the text?

- Were students able to apply research from a historical period to create a dramatic text.

Group Discussion

Following are some discussion-starters for a variety of topics related to melodrama.

- Ask students to identify a melodrama from television or films and to discuss what makes it a melodrama.

- Start a discussion about the concepts of being a hero or heroine, and heroism; or being a villain and villainy.

- Ask Players to consider how caricatures of good and evil and the stereotyping of male and female roles in melodrama can persuade audiences to respond in a predictable manner.

- Discuss the fine line between comedy and tragedy and how style can turn the tone of a text from tragic to comic, or vice versa.

- Ask Players to discuss how melodrama reflects particular times and cultures. How is melodrama related to daily life, family, society, and culture?

- Analyze the emotional and social implications of the popularity of this form in both the present and past.

 Student Activities

Book

page 150 (Background Reading)

Journal

Have students write a melodrama scenario.

 References

Winter, Marian Hannah. *The Theatre of Marvels.* New York: Benjamin Bloom, Inc., 1962.

The Thespian Preceptor, or A Full Display of the Scenic Art including Ample and Easy Instructions for Treading the Stage, using Proper Action, Modulating the Voice and Expressing the Several Dramatic Passions, etc. Boston: Joshua Belcher, 1810.

Romance novels

Early silent movies

Television soap operas, situation comedies, and courtroom dramas (such as "Perry Mason")

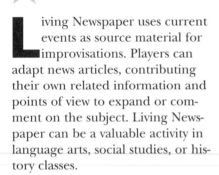

Living Newspaper

Living Newspaper uses current events as source material for improvisations. Players can adapt news articles, contributing their own related information and points of view to expand or comment on the subject. Living Newspaper can be a valuable activity in language arts, social studies, or history classes.

Researching the Form

Living Newspaper plays were popular in the United States from 1935 to 1939, during Franklin Roosevelt's presidency. They were a unit of the Federal Theatre Project, a program of the Works Progress Administration (WPA), set up to create a national theater.

Under the Federal Theatre Project (FTP), hundreds of actors, writers, and directors were employed. They produced sixty thousand performances of some 924 plays for thirty million people in parks, school gymnasiums, and theaters. Most performances were free, although some cost a dollar admission. Many major American actors and directors learned their craft in the FTP, collaborating on performance projects that ranged from Shakespeare, Chekhov, T. S. Eliot, and Sinclair Lewis to group improvisations.

One of their most famous experiments, a dramatization of current events, was called *Living Newspapers*. Starting with news bulletins presented as a series of *blackouts* (short episodic scenes) on subjects like local murders and robberies, actors took subjects hot off the newsstands and presented them on stages in Chicago and New York City. Eventually the form became more elaborate, employing open staging, visual projections, puppetry, crowd scenes, pantomime, dance, vaudeville, *agitprop* (a shortened term for agitation propaganda, or political propaganda dispersed through literature, drama, art, or music), satire, and fragments of authentic speeches and documents. The live theatrical effects of Living Newspapers are comparable to effects used in film, radio, and newsreels, such as narrators and commentators and supertitles of text over image.

The Living Newspaper became a unit of the FTP, allied with the Newspaper Guild. It became truly investigative social theater. One-act plays to full-length scripts were written on various concerns, such as economics, the environment, politics, racial equality, health issues (including food and drugs), and social reform.

A popular character, called the *Voice of the Living Newspaper,* sat to the side of the stage and commented in the style of a newscaster. The amplified Voice gave the time, date, and location of the dramatic actions and interrupted and commented on stage events, sometimes taking a different perspective than the one shown in the staged action.

The frequently controversial content of these productions helped lead to the end of the FTP. Richard Watts, Jr., of the *New York Herald-Tribune* reviewed *Medicine Show* on April 21, 1940, when it opened as a commercial theater production after the demise of the FTP.

You probably know about the technique of the Living Newspaper. More illustrated soap-box than conventional. . . its viewpoint has always been progressive to radical, and its manner is to dramatize its subject by means of illustrated lecture, caricature, case history, a lantern slide or two, perhaps an occasional graph, a touch of symbolism, a bit of tub thumping, and a little savage irony.

The Living Newspaper genre has been kept alive by improvisational theater companies such as Second City and The Improv (both located in Chicago) and television's "Saturday Night Live," which has become a popular home for improvisational theater company graduates.

Exploring the Form

1. Ask Players to collect and bring in newspaper or magazine articles that they think could be presented onstage. Each person should be responsible for bringing at least one article to class. The articles could be selected randomly, or relate to a specific topic or problem. Tell Players to look for articles that:

- are full of action
- are one scene or consist of only a few scenes
- can be performed by three to five people
- include a surprising turn of events
- avoid extreme violence

2. Ask Players to read their news stories aloud to the group. Have Players improvise short scenes using one or more of the following methods.

- A speaker reads the story while the other Players act out everything in the story as they hear it.

- After listening to a reading of the story, Players act it out from memory.

- Leader as Director: After listening to the reading, assign a character for each Player to play, or have each Player choose a character to play. As a group, decide where the story happens and what relationship each character has to the news story. Then create an improvisation of the story combining what the Players remember of the article, quoting exactly or paraphrasing.

- Player as Director: The Player who brings in the article reads it aloud and acts as director. The director assigns the characters and describes how the performers can establish the setting and plot. Characters improvise dialogue. Director can participate as "Voice of the Living Newspaper," keeping the story on track and filling in facts for the audience.

3. Have the group choose which stories to develop further by deciding which ones offer the most interest to the group.

4. Divide Players into small groups to develop and present short scenes. Share the following suggestions with them.

- Improvise, referring to the text to build up characterizations and actions.

- Develop plot and dialogue by setting the order of events and each character's reaction to them.

- If necessary, add appropriate characters so that everyone can participate, such as turning one lawyer into two or more, or adding children to a family.

- Add quotations from other related reference materials, such as authentic speeches and documents.

- Use the device of a commentator (the "Voice of the Living Newspaper").

- Between episodic scenes, splice in a typical, but nonfactual, representation of the effect of these news events on the audience.

Performance Suggestions

Add Production Elements Add dances, visual effects, graphs, agitprop devices, and other embellishments to develop the Living Newspaper improvisations into a full-scale theatrical production. For example, use signs, slogans, or supertitles to further convey the message.

Combine Scenes into One Piece Have all the groups present their skits as one large piece. Use the "Voice of the Living Newspaper," move signs of headlines across the stage, or other devices to make transitions between scenes.

Teaching Notes

Management Tips

Refer to the Source Materials To help students find dialogue, use direct quotations, building out from the source, if needed. Use accompanying photographs to inspire a set design or create the stage picture.

Write a Script If you decide to make a performance project, write a standard script from improvisations, using character names and setting dialogue.

Connections

Social Studies Ask students to bring in articles that relate to current events. Ask your class to write news articles or editorials about current events in their lives.

History Ask students to research and bring in articles that were published at the period of time that you are studying in class. When making an historical period piece, you might have to help students learn how to find newspaper and magazine articles in the library, or books containing old newspaper articles.

Foreign Languages Ask students to find articles that are written in the language they are studying in school.

Special Needs

Students who have difficulty reading could research images or cartoons that contain political propaganda or a specific point of view.

Assessment

Group Discussion

Discuss with your students how images and text can convey political and social messages, and how specific audiences are targeted to promote a message. Discuss with them how a writer conveys his or her point of view to the reader. Ask them to analyze their articles to determine if the writer is also conveying the culture's point of view, or in some way describing the culture. Include in the discussion how the targeted audience, choice of language, and placement of image in relation to text or to other images can influence points of view. Include a discussion about how the authors' points of view influenced what they wrote.

Teacher Observations

• Were students able to understand how point of view can be conveyed through text and image?

• Were they able to understand the concept of how an audience is targeted to promote a specific point of view?

• What kinds of articles were chosen by the students, when given the option of random selection?

 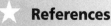

Student Activities

Book

page 151 (Background Reading)

pages 152–153 (Performance Model)

Journal

Ask Players to describe the effect of acting out the news articles.

• Did it make the events seem more real, or more emotional?

• Did the performers' points of view alter the content?

References

Brown, Lorraine, editor. *Liberty Deferred and Other Living Newspapers of the 1930s, Federal Theatre Project.* Fairfax, Virginia: George Mason University Press, 1989.

Entr'Actes

When a group has developed several unrelated short performance events, commonly referred to as "bits and pieces," the pieces can be linked together in a single performance. One of the most tried and true ways to connect a performance of several events is to add entr'actes as transitions. Historically, *entr'actes* referred to intervals between two acts of a performance, often taking the form of musical entertainments, comedies, or other diversions in an attempt to please as many tastes as possible. Frequently performed in front of the downstage house curtain, entr'actes had the practical function of amusing the audience while scene changes were being made behind the curtain.

Entr'actes function as glue, giving consistency to the look of a show. They provide opportunities to feature special talents and interests of group members. Performances by singers, rappers, dancers, gymnasts, jugglers, magicians, and comics can be worked into these scenes-between-the-scenes. The entr'actes can be completely different, or can connect in some way to the theme of the performance.

★ Researching the Form

Entr'Actes from Different Forms and Times

Entremes Spanish term for events that took place between courses of a banquet. They were dramatic or nondramatic, frequently comic in nature, and ended with music and dance. By the 1600s, *entremes* developed into a comic or farcical one-act play form, as used by Cervantes in *El viejo celoso* and *El retablo do las maravillas*.

Intermezzi (or Interludes) Italian Renaissance term for a series of spectacular pantomimes interspersed with *madrigals* (unaccompanied part songs for two to three voices, following a strict poetic form), placed between performances of comedies. The seed from which opera took its origin.

Kyogen Japanese farces or comic plays that are used as humorous skits between two Noh plays and are performed on the traditional Noh stage. The titles of two *kyogen* are *Gan Tsubute* (A Goose and a Pebble) and *Fumi Yamadachi* (The Cowardly Bandits).

Pitches Short farcical or comic dialogue performed for free in front of a theater to attract an audience to the show inside. For example, a talk given by a pitchman in a medicine show or a circus.

Olios Entertainments between the acts of a burlesque or vaudeville show, which were performed in front of a curtain or drop while a scene was being changed behind it.

Knee Play A term coined by Robert Wilson and used for divertissements or "joints" that were set between the fifteen scenes of *The Civil Wars,* his epic multinational opera, developed in the 1980s. Conceived as dance plays and choreographed by Suzushi Hanayagi, the knee plays provided three- to six-minute visions or poetic commentaries on the fully staged main actions, and were toured separately as a full evening's work.

 ## Exploring the Form

Using Entr'Actes in Performance

Use entr'actes to contrast, complement, or comment on the main event, which could be a play, a choral reading, or an instrumental offering.

Show of Unrelated Entr'Actes
Combine unrelated entr'actes to make a show consisting of only entr'actes. This is basically the organizational structure for many popular entertainments, such as variety shows and music hall extravaganzas, which offer programs of many independent acts. Performances of one-act plays, songs, dances, animal acts, and joke routines were assembled into an order intended to build in excitement from the opening to the last act of the show, which often used all the performers.

Show of Related Entr'Actes
Organize a program of related entr'actes, held together by style, theme, or image.

- Use a theatrical genre, such as a minstrel show, a medicine show, or an operetta.
- Use a unifying theme or image to hold the program together. The show can be conceived without the main event, so to speak, referring to an unseen work of literature or historical event. The

source provides inspiration for a variety of responses involving many different arts disciplines.

Forms of Entr'Actes

Following is a list of some possible entr'acte choices. (See Clowns and Clowning, page 170, Tableaux Vivants, page 197, and Choral Dances, page 38, for additional ideas.)

Sight Gags Adopt clowning or classic commedia style physical jests such as falling down, sneezing, swatting imaginary flies, performing hat tricks, and so on. Or have Players invent new sight gags.

Running Gags Routines using related jokes or sight gags that are interspersed throughout the show. They could be a string of knock-knock jokes or elephant jokes; a frustrating problem, such as a water bucket that constantly tips over, or a performer who gets swallowed by or caught up in the curtains; sneezes; or water pistol fights.

Chases Fast entrances and exits of running, running plus jumping, runs plus a slide or two to change direction, and so on. Chases should contain lots of surprises. They can be performed by duets, trios, or a large group.

Run-Around An organized frenzy of various locomotors that travel in a spiral, zigzag, circle, or other floor pattern. This run-around could be connected to the changing of set pieces, props, or scene. If so, assign everyone a task and a path to follow as objects are taken on and off the playing area. If lighting is available, here's a time to have fun.

Chorus A chorus of Players serve as commentators on events that have happened or will happen in the performance. The chorus could function as the master of ceremonies or as news commentator. (Derived from the Greek

Chorus, in which a group of actors/dancers commented on the action of the play.)

Solos Individual Players could perform monologues as a news commentator/anchor or as a storyteller.

Master of Ceremonies Called the *Interlocutor* in minstrel shows. Have one Player serve as Master of Ceremonies to introduce acts and provide transitions between bits.

Dialogue/Bit Joke exchanges or short skits that could involve straight man and fall guy routines (See Clowns and Clowning, page 170). Could be done as a call and response with Players or the audience.

Sketch Make a longer, more elaborate scene by combining several bits. It could involve more than two characters, and have some kind of loose plot development.

Social Dances, Folk Dances, Movement Games Recreate pairs, group, line, or circle formations from various eras, or use dances currently in vogue.
Examples:
- Play parties: Singing and dancing games developed in nineteenth-century Appalachian American communities where couple dancing was not an accepted social activity
- Singing and clapping games, including jump rope and double Dutch routines.
- Unison group routines: Drill team formations; mass entrances and exits
- Clogging and other country dances
- Line dances: stroll, bunny hop, conga line, electric slide, etc.
- Partner dances: waltz, polka, tango, boogie, two-step, etc.
- Dances from various cultures, times, and places

Dance Performances Ballet, modern, jazz, and tap dances: solos, duets, or group numbers

Drill Team Routines High-stepping, leg-kicking movements and formations in the style of the Radio City Music Hall Rockettes

Advertisements Players write and perform product advertisements in the style of past or current presentations on radio or television.

Magic Tricks Invite any magic experts to share their talents.

Feats Have Players perform acrobatics, such as somersaults, cartwheels, back flips, and pyramids; baton twirling; juggling; rope jumping (single rope and double Dutch); stick dances; and other physical feats that will please and amaze the audience.

Performance Suggestions

Parades Use parades as a way to enter or exit the performing area, or to pass through the audience. Have Players travel in single lines, parallel lines, circles, spirals, zigzags, or other patterns, performing a series of move/freeze actions or locomotors. Parades could also be performed in character. The following suggestions can be adapted to many performance styles and functions.

- **Prologue** Performers travel through the audience to the performing area or across the stage in full costume to introduce the coming event to the audience. Embellish the parade with singing, dancing, clapping, or playing instruments.

- **Razz-Ma-Tazz or Ballyhoo** Use a parade as a grand-opening number to attract a crowd to a performance and build excitement for the show. Such a parade can also occur just before an intermission. Add tambourines, dance steps, drums, and gongs.

- **Bridge** Stage a parade between sections or scenes in a larger performance.

- **Epilogue or Ending Bow** Use a parade as a recap at the end of a show, featuring all the performers and events. Or use a parade to serve as the performers' bow and exit.

 Teaching Notes

Management Tips

Safety Issues

- To maintain order and safety in chases, runarounds, and sight gags, carefully choreograph and stage all entrances and exits, onstage paths, and any surprises

or jokes (such as "accidently" bumping into one another). Actions can be performed in small groups of two or three Players. A larger group will require more organization.

- Clear all entrance and exit areas. Make sure that lighting equipment is securely anchored and cables are stabilized to the floor with duct tape. Advise your performers to use these areas only for entrances and exits (not to watch the show); advise the crew to keep these areas clear and free of props or any extraneous debris.

- If there is a high-speed chase or a flying leap that goes straight into the wings, station "catchers" in the wings to slow down the speed of the exiting Player or guide the leaper to safety.

Program Order Post a performance order in one or more places backstage, listing all scenes in order and the names of the Players involved in each scene. Players can consult the list during performance, to remind themselves of their cues.

Connections

Literature

- Choose some short pieces to develop into entr'actes, such as poems, fables, or legends. Or, choose and read a play for which to create entr'actes.

- Direct existing plays, using entr'actes to connect scenes and cover set changes.

History

- Research the type of entr'actes that might have been performed during a production in a particular period of history.
  - Study Renaissance court masques, where *tableaux vivants* were used as entr'actes between large allegorical or historical action scenes.
  - Study commedia *lazzi* routines, which are still used today in circuses and television variety and comedy shows. (See Clowns and Clowning, page 170.)
  - Research the kinds of entr'actes used in American vaudeville, popular in late nineteenth and early twentieth century. Look for related routines in circus and television programs.

Social Studies and Arts

- Study the folk dances from specific regions and cultures and include them in your production as entr'actes.

- Ask your students to attend a community festival in which entr'actes appear as part of the celebration, such as a Revels production that celebrates a solstice.

- Attend a live performance in your community that uses entr'actes as part of the performance.

Collaborations If your school is putting on a talent show, or some other variety show format, ask that each class be responsible for producing one short skit and an entr'acte. Or string together several entr'actes from different classes to create one production. Or, have one class be responsible for the entr'actes, and let the other classes create the acts.

Assessment

Teacher Observations

- Were Players able to understand the concept of entr'actes and how they are used in theater?

- Were Players able to identify the various forms of entr'actes?

Group Discussion

Discuss how entr'actes reflect the life of a particular time, place, and culture, basing your discussion on research or after viewing a performance using entr'actes. Compare how entr'actes are used in television, live theater, community celebrations, and circuses. Ask your group what kinds of entr'actes are most appealing to them, and why.

Student Activities

Book

pages 154–156 (Background Reading)

Journal

Have Players keep a log of their favorite jokes, or anything else they think is funny, that could be used in an assembly or as part of a class performance. They could also keep a log of other quick ideas that could be used as entr'actes.

References

Wilson, Robert. *The Theater of Images.* New York: Harper & Row, Second Edition, 1980; 1984.

See Clowns and Clowning (page 170) and Masks and Masquerades, (page 189) for more references.

Short Takes

This chapter contains various quick warm-up exercises to use in classes, rehearsals, and preparation for performance. These games and activities will help Players develop individual and group trust; focus, and teamwork skills; individual awareness through centering; physical endurance, strength, and flexibility; and clear vocalization. Before creating a project together, a group needs to build these skills. They cannot navigate the uncertainty of new work without this common base.

At the start of a new session, caution participants to take responsibility for themselves and make sure that their actions do not injure others so that everyone can have fun without getting hurt. Ask Players to inform you about any injury or condition that might prevent them from participating in certain exercises. Let Players know that if they start an exercise and discover that it causes pain, cramping, or exacerbates an existing condition, they should slowly cease the exercise. If possible, offer alternative ways to work on any exercise. Of course, you must be eternally vigilant of possible injurious situations and try to circumvent them.

Players often arrive at rehearsals with their daily lives in tow, not thinking about theater; maybe they had a good day, maybe they had a hard day. In order to meet together in a positive atmosphere, ask Players to leave their private lives at the door and focus on making theater.

Just as orchestra members have to tune their instruments and warm up before they can play together, theater performers must prepare themselves to work together through physical and vocal warm-ups and centering and focusing activities.

It is useful to begin a session with a ten- to twenty-minute warm-up. Have Players stand in a circle formation to try some of the movement warm-ups in this chapter, or use relaxation techniques, yoga, body conditioning, dance exercises, or pantomime. Music—your choice or Players' choice—can add a relaxing or energizing feel to the exercises. Once Players are warmed up, work on focus, concentration, and ensemble skills by playing theater games and practicing trust exercises. Then move to games that explore ideas through improvisations that are appropriate to the upcoming project. After several weeks, this random group of individuals will become an ensemble, ready to work on a larger theater project.

The following games and exercises are assembled into eight categories: movement warm-ups, vocal warm-ups, traditional games, trust exercises, observation and recall exercises, focusing exercises, rehearsal energizers, and rehearsal preparation.

Stretches

In a circle, one by one, have Players share their favorite stretches and/or relaxation exercises. Everyone copies each Player's idea for a while, then the next Player demonstrates a new idea. Try to have each Player offer a new way of warming up.

Dance Steps

In a circle, one by one, have Players share their favorite dance steps. Everyone copies each Player's step for a while, then the next Player demonstrates a new idea.

Run-Around

Have everyone run around the room in a circle seven times (or some other designated number of times). Besides a circle, the floor pattern could be a triangle, a square, the letter shapes of each person's name, number shapes, or any other shape. Encourage everyone to use all of the space available.

When they have completed their laps, Players should freeze in a pose, maintaining the frieze until everyone has finished and is in a frieze. Then have Players repeat the run-around and freeze, reversing directions.

Obstacle Course

Set up a path, inside or outside, that includes a variety of terrains, such as stairways, wide-open spaces, and obstacles such as cones, ropes, or hoops laid on the floor. Set a time limit and have everyone keep moving along the obstacle course until time is up.

Keep Moving

Set a time limit and tell Players to keep moving, in any way they like, until time is up. Add and change music to change the dynamics.

Locomotor Series

Ask for suggestions or provide a series of three to four actions that mix locomotor movements with another quality of movement. The basic locomotor movements are skipping, jumping, walking, running, leaping, hopping, and galloping. Other qualities of movement might include turning, falling, rising, and so on. Divide the group into small teams and have each team create and demonstrate a series to share with the rest of the group.

Daily Life Actions

Ask Players to perform one or all of the following actions: lie, sit, stand, walk, run. The actions may be performed in any order and changed at any time. Remind Players to maintain awareness of their performance. Have Players perform the daily life actions as simultaneous solos, in one or more groups, depending on the space available and the size of the group.

Continue the exercise until you feel the performers understand their connection to what they are doing. One of the main purposes of this exercise is to help participants remain in the present. This is achieved by having them become more aware of their energy levels moment to moment, and how it influences their choices of action and performance dynamics. By choosing such pedestrian movements, the issue of skill is removed.

Shadow Boxing

Ask Players to scatter throughout the space. Warn them to make sure that they will not come into contact with another person when they extend their arms and legs. Tell Players to fight with the space around them, using arms, legs, head, and back.

Imaginary Fight

Divide the group into pairs. Tell partners to have an imaginary fight, without ever physically contacting each other. Each should react to imaginary blows as though contact had been made.

Speed Changes

Have Players fight space or each other in slow motion or accelerated time, or to a series of timing changes.

Slow Motion

Ask Players to move around the space in slow motion. Suggest that they try a variety of movements, such as lowering to the floor, rolls, walks, and runs. You may wish to set up this activity as a race, in which the winner is the one who comes in last.

Gentle Shake-Out

Ask Players to stand in place, then gently shake the right hand, and then the left hand. Repeat, shaking the foot, the whole arm from the shoulder joint, and the whole leg from the hip joint. Make combinations, mixing right and left. This exercise can also be done while lying on the back, with legs or arms extended at right angles to the torso.

Rotations

Ask Players to stand in place while they gently rotate their joints, including ankles, knees, hips, shoulders, and wrists. Then ask Players to place their hands behind their knees, with wrists crossed, and to rotate their knees in both directions. Next, release the leg and rotate the hips in both directions. You can add moving the hips in a forward and backward diagonal direction. Progress upward through

the ribs and shoulders. These exercises are called isolations. Instruct Players to move smoothly and slowly. Be aware that some people cannot circle various parts of their spines, and that the neck area is particularly vulnerable to injury. Ask these Players to take responsibility for finding another warm-up while the rest of the group does their rotations.

Tense-Up

Coach Players to stand in place and move their shoulders up to their ears and then release them. Repeat two or three times. Then tell them to contract, or clench, all the muscles of the body from the soles of the feet to the top of the head, including the muscles of the face. Have them hold in contraction for a few seconds, then release everything at once. Repeat.

Feats

Feats are presented in the form of challenges, dares, demands, or invitations. A feat may involve physical skill or a particular performance quality. It can be performed independently or in teams. Each feat should be chosen to offer challenges appropriate to the age, physical abilities, and focusing skills of the group so that it is possible for Players to accomplish or better the challenge. In working out each challenge, performers may demonstrate physical skill, awareness of timing, and a sense of humor that

often shows up in a witty interpretation of the challenge.

Feats provide easy, fast transitions that can be used to energize a group between study tasks or other activities. They can also be used for positive disciplining—to motivate a group to work together, to arrive on time, to prepare themselves for work, or to try harder.

1. Set up boundaries, time limits, or any other parameters for feats.

2. Call out a command, question, or challenge.

3. Have Players perform the command or challenge one by one, simultaneously, or in teams, depending on the time available, the nature of the challenge, and the size of the working space.

4. Give as many challenges or commands as time allows or as you think will be necessary to achieve your purpose.

Physical Feats

• Call out a single physical feat for Players to perform, such as a locomotor (jump, leap, walk, run, skip, gallop, hop) or another physical action, such as a fall, turn, flip, or freeze. Have Players repeat the challenge at least two times.

• State a challenge as a question.
  – After you run, jump, fall, and spin around, can you stop on a dime?
  – How many _____ can you do in one place? For how long?

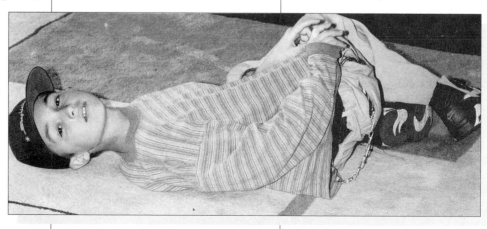

Timing Feats

These challenges involve a time limit. Players must start at one point and get to another point in a specified amount of time.

- Climb the stairs in ten seconds.
- Go from the house to the stage in thirty seconds.
- Specify a place and a time limit to arrive onstage: five seconds to go downstage; four seconds to go centerstage; ten seconds to go upstage left.
- Take one minute to get up from a chair.
- Take one minute to go from a crouch to a standing position.
- Monologue: Keep talking without stopping for one minute.

Activity Feats Challenge Players to continue an activity for a specified amount of time.

- Sing for thirty seconds.
- Sing and dance for thirty seconds.
- "Die" for one minute.
- Freeze for thirty seconds.

Quality Feats Ask Players to work on a specific quality.

- How smoothly can you slide?
- How loudly can you scream?
- How softly can you sing?
- How funny can you look?

Imaginary Feats

- Ask Players to perform some extravagant, impossible task.
- Ask Players to show off their most fabulous skills.

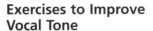
★ Vocal Warm-Ups

Exercises for Jaw, Lips, and Tongue

- Make funny faces.
- Gently waggle the jaw up and down, side to side, forward and backward.
- Stick out your tongue: wiggle the tongue; try to touch your nose with your tongue; try to touch your chin with your tongue.
- Hold the tip of the tongue between your thumb and first two fingers while talking.
- Blow air through loose lips, making a sound like a motorboat.
- Puff out the cheeks with air for a few seconds.
- Using tones or words, direct the voice around the space: in front, behind, to the right, to the left, to a particular person.

Exercises to Improve Vocal Tone

The Chord Everyone stands in a circle or clump, arms around each other's shoulders or waists. Each person listens to the others' breathing and at some time begins to hum or sing on any tone or pitch. The chord can start quietly, like a drone, then build up in volume and duration before returning to silence. There is no leader. The group decides when the chord is over. (Developed by the Open Theater, directed by Joe Chaiken.)

"Me-May-My-Mo-Moo" Starting on a low tone, sing all five long vowel sounds. Then go up one interval, and sing all five sounds on that interval. Continue up the scale, singing the five long vowel sounds for at least one octave's worth of pitch intervals.

"Ah, Oh, Aa, Eee" For each sound there will be five tones to sing. Choose a tone to begin singing "Ah." For the second tone go one interval above that tone; return to the tone; sing one interval below that tone; return to the tone. Proceed through "Oh," "Aa," and "Eee" in the same manner. That completes one series. Repeat the entire series one interval higher. Proceed up the scale. The sounds can be changed by adding any consonant to the vowel sounds.

Exercises to Improve Enunciation

The following tongue twisters are amusing ways to practice clear enunciation. It's also fun to make up your own tongue twisters—just think of a sentence in which all the words start with the same letter or sound.

- Peter Piper picked a peck of pickled peppers.
- She sells seashells down by the seashore.

- Frenzied fleas fly frantically forward.
- Quick quotes quell querulous questions.
- Peggy Babcock, Peggy Babcock Peggy Babcock . . .
- Moses supposes his toeses are roses
But Moses supposes erroneously;
For nobody's toeses are posies of roses
As Moses supposes his toeses to be.

 ## Traditional Games

Traditional Games are games that have been played for many generations, in many different cultures and places. Although the details of a game may vary from place to place and from time to time, the very title of the game should bring instant recognition to everyone.

Tag Games

Traditional Tag One person is "It." Everyone else tries to keep away from "It," who is trying to tag someone. When a person is tagged, she becomes the new "It."

Freeze Tag The person tagged freezes for a few seconds, and then becomes the new "It."

Explosion Tag The person tagged "explodes."

Connection Tag When a person is tagged, he remains stuck to the tagger, until all Players are "stuck" to one another.

Slow Motion Tag The game is played in slow motion.

Lemonade Tag

1. It is usually helpful to begin this game with a discussion about what kinds of jobs there are in theater work, and what each job entails. Theater jobs include actor, director, singer, musician, dancer, set designer, choreographer, stagehand, costume designer, dresser, stage manager, lighting designer, box office manager, usher, and audience.

2. Set home boundary lines for two teams, placing a team at either end of the space. Each team secretly decides on a theater job to pantomime for the other team, which will try to guess the job.

3. Teams walk toward each other, chanting the following jingle in a call and response pattern, until they arrive in the middle of the space, facing each other.

Team 1: Here we come.

Team 2: Where from?

Team 1: _____ (city name)

Team 2: What's your trade?

Team 1: Lemonade

Team 2: Give us some.

4. Team 1 pantomimes a theater job until someone from Team 2 correctly guesses what the job is.

5. Team 2 chases Team 1 to their home base. Anyone who is tagged from Team 1 joins Team 2. Caution Players to only touch tag each other. No tackles or pushing allowed.

6. Reverse the activity so that Team 2 begins the game. Continue playing rounds indefinitely. The winning team is the one with the most people when the game ends.

Follow the Leader

Follow the Leader gives each person in a group the opportunity to be the Leader and to have his or her ideas run the show. The Leader performs a movement and/or sound, and all the Players must follow the Leader as closely as possible. Follow the Leader is an excellent device to build group cooperation and teamwork. When this game is repeated over a period of time, it helps groups develop ways to work together, honor each individual's ideas, become more accepting of themselves and others, adapt to variations in energy level, and explore new ideas.

1. Choose one person to be the first Leader. Have Players stand front to back in a line behind the Leader.

2. Ask the Leader to perform a movement and/or sound, either moving through space or remaining in place. Explain that the other Players must copy, or follow the Leader, as closely as possible. The Leader can change the movement and/or sound at will.

3. Indicate when it's time to change Leaders. The Leader moves to the end of the line and the next person in line becomes the new Leader. The game continues until everyone has had a turn at being Leader.

Call and Response

Call: The Leader demonstrates the action and/ or sound.

Response: The rest of the Players repeat the action and/ or sound.

Team Follow the Leader

Break up into teams of three to four Players. Each team plays the traditional game. Teams can interact by using floor patterns that intercept or weave through and go around each other. Or teams may make physical contact or react to each other's actions. For example, one team may be standing with their hands extended, palms up. Seeing this, another team Leader reacts by leading her team down the line with a high five.

Characterizations Have Players perform the same action while assuming the roles of different characters.

Examples:
- Players walk a tight rope as different characters in a story.
- Players become spies, trailing a case.
- Players become monsters.
- Players leave a burning building.

Musical Chairs

Talking Chairs and Singing Chairs are two variations on the traditional game, Musical Chairs. They are all great fun to play, work well as orientation games, and draw in participants who normally might be reticent about joining a performance game.

1. Set up chairs in a line or circle formation. In a line formation, alternate chair facings. In a circle formation, chairs should face out from the center. The total number of chairs should be one less than the total number of participants. Ask Players to stand in a circle around the chairs.

2. Explain the game rules (Steps 3 through 5).

3. Start the music. When Players hear the music, they should walk around the line or circle of chairs.

4. Stop the music. All Players should try to sit on a chair. The Player without a chair is out of the game.

5. Remove one chair from the line or circle. Repeat this process until only one chair remains. The Player who sits in the last chair is the winner.

Talking Chairs In this variation, music is substituted by one person speaking a monologue. The Players' cue to stop and claim a chair

occurs when the monologue stops. The subject of the monologues can be chosen by you or the group. During Talking Chairs, the Player who loses out on claiming a chair becomes the next speaker. The preceding speaker can either rejoin the game (allowing everyone to play at all times) or stay out of the game until one Player remains who is declared winner, as in Musical Chairs.

Singing Chairs Replace the music with one or more persons singing a song in recitative style (halfway between singing and talking).

 ## Trust Exercises

Group Trust Exercises

Blindfolded Tour Have everyone close their eyes or put on blindfolds. Instruct everyone to walk anywhere around the workspace, taking care of themselves and one another. Be prepared to intervene if you notice a potentially dangerous situation. You may wish to ask several Players to help you "spot" the blindfolded tour.

Circle Trust One Player stands in the center of a circle made by everyone else. Players stand close enough to support and guide the center Player as he falls around the circle. The center Player's task is to start by falling backward or forward, visualizing his body as a straight line from head to feet and holding his arms against his sides. Players pass him around the circle. Several Players should work together to catch and pass. Caution Players to handle the falling Player gently and carefully, and not to push him too hard. Stop the game if Players become unruly.

Visual Trust One Player walks around the inside of a circle

of standing Players, keeping eye contact with each person she passes for as long as possible. She chooses one Player with whom to exchange places, indicating her choice through eye contact only. The chosen Player remains in eye contact until he is inside the circle ready to begin his turn.

Blind Crossings Ask Players to form a line at one end of the room. One at a time, Players cross the length of the room with their eyes closed. Other Players "spot" the traveling Player, protecting her from walking into any obstacles, and telling her when to stop. When Players are confident walking across the space, challenge them to try walking backward, running, leaping, jumping, or any combination of locomotor movements.

Partner Trust Exercises

Guides Divide the group into pairs. One partner guides the other, whose eyes are closed. They walk around the room, beginning very slowly, with the guide cueing the "blind" person when any changes in turf—steps, walls, meeting other people—are about to occur. They speed up only when the "blind" partner has physically relaxed into trusting his guide. Then have partners reverse roles.

Support System Have partners work with each other to discover as many ways as possible each can support the weight of her partner. Caution partners to take great care of themselves and each other by moving slowly and carefully and by discussing what they are going to do before trying it. You may wish to establish a rule that no one can completely pick up her partner.

Catching and Falling Have partners take turns falling and catching each other.

Observation and Recall Exercises

Sense Memory

Sense memory is Stanislavsky's term for the memory bank of information learned through the senses, and our reactions to sense perceptions. These exercises will increase Players' awareness of their senses. They can also function as concentration and relaxation techniques.

Sight Memory Tell Players to each choose and look at one area of the space for one minute. Then have them turn away from their observed spaces, perhaps by sitting in a circle with other group members. Have them take turns sharing with the group everything remembered from what was seen.

Sound Memory Have Players sit on the floor or ground and tell them to listen to all the sounds that occur during one minute. Ask them to be as silent as possible during the exercise. Then have them take turns sharing with the group everything they heard. (Players could close their eyes during this exercise.)

Observation Recall Assign Players to take a walk. During the walk, they should observe carefully and try to notice everything. When the group meets again, make a list of what was seen, heard, and smelled on Players' walks.

Character Recall Go to a public space where it is easy to observe people. Tell Players to observe all of the people in the space, or to choose an individual to focus on. They should note physical characteristics, including the way people walk and their gestures, facial mannerisms, and any idiosyncratic habits. When Players return, have

them each become one or more of the characters they observed. If you wish, have Players develop their recall improvisations into a script, scenario, or scene to perform for the group.

Color Memory Assign Players to choose a different color to notice every day. Instruct them to spend at least ten minutes a day observing, trying to notice everything in the environment or any objects that are the chosen daily color.

Visualizations

Room Recall Ask Players to visualize a room in their own home, a relative's home, or a best friend's home. Tell them to recreate the sense of that space by "living" in the performing space as though they are in that room. Players should move through the space as though all walls, furniture, and other objects are there. Players should concentrate on seeing the room, touching the furniture, manipulating objects, hearing the sounds that occur, and smelling the scents.

Journey Have the group lie on the floor with closed eyes, then read them the following instructions: "Visualize a journey you have taken, or would like to take. In your mind, travel through space to that place. Notice textures of objects, sounds, smells, and tastes that are part of the experience."

Short-term Memory Instruct Players to take a minute or two to visualize a recent experience, such as lunchtime, getting ready for school, or a dream. Tell them to try to remember as many details as possible of their actions during this experience. Have Players take turns performing the experience, recreating it in "fast forward" mode.

Focusing Exercises

Observing an Event

Divide the group into at least two teams to observe an imaginary event. Allow each team to decide what imaginary event to observe. It could be a sports event, a movie, a parade, or any other event that includes an audience. Then locate where the event will occur in the space. Choose an exact spot such as a bulletin board, the particular lines of a basketball court painted on the floor, or an exit sign. On an agreed-upon signal, the event begins and one team of observers gives focus to the event. While maintaining their focus on the event, Players also use peripheral vision and careful listening so that it appears as if all are observing the same event as the rest of their group. The remaining team or teams of Players act as audience. When the performance is done, the audience can guess what event is being observed. (This exercise is based on Viola Spolin's game, "Seeing a Sport.")

Newscaster

Divide Players into pairs. Tell them that one partner will perform as a newscaster or reporter, who tells a story as quickly as possible. The other partner mimes the story she hears, moving as slowly as possible. Partners choose who will be the newscaster and who will be the mover. Then have partners reverse roles. (Newscaster is based on a game in Keith Johnstone's book *Impro, Improvisation and the Theatre.*)

Two People Equal One Storyteller

Have the group divide into pairs, which take turns performing for the group. During each performance, partners stand facing the audience, one in front of the other. The front partner stands with his hands behind his back, masking the back partner from the audience's view. The audience sees the back partner's hands, which wrap around the front partner to appear as though they belong to the front partner's body. The partner seen by the audience tells a story while the hidden partner gestures the story with his hands. The roles can be reversed during the story.

The illusion can be created by various devises. The person telling the story could stand on a chair, with the other person hidden behind them, so only their hands can be seen. Or, if available, a cloth or coat can be draped around the two performers so that the speaker's head and the mover's hands are all that the audience can see.

Four Tasks

Ask Players to choose four physical tasks. (*Examples:* sit cross-legged; turn a cartwheel; lean against a wall; pick up a telephone and listen.) The actions should be completely unrelated to each other. Each action should be performed for its own sake. Tell Players to decide the *beginning* (the impulse to move), *middle,* and *end* (completion of the task) for each action. When Players can easily repeat their four actions as a series, tell them to add an unrelated vocalization of a poem, a song, or a speech from a play or elsewhere to deliver simultaneously with their performances of the four tasks.

 ## Rehearsal Energizers

When the workshop begins preparing for public presentation, the work methods need to shift into production mode. Instead of explorations of materials for script and score structures, the focus changes to how to present the structure that has been developed.

Although when mounting original productions that are made by ensemble process nothing is ever set in stone, at least a feeling of repetition now becomes necessary. It is the Director's job to find ways to help keep the performers interested and energized.

Throughout rehearsals and in performance, encourage everyone to keep searching for new ways to deal with their performance structure, thereby ensuring that the performance will always sparkle by being true to the present moment.

If Players are taught to believe it is impossible to make mistakes, they learn to work with what is actually happening on stage at every moment.

Opera

Sing the script, in operatic style, with arias and recitative.

Gibberish

Perform the script in gibberish.

Animal Play

Play the script as animals.

Deaf Play

Play the script as though the audience is deaf. The Players perform the script in silence, thinking their lines. They include everything in the script, maintaining the rhythm and all stage business. This should not become a pantomime of the script.

Rewrite

After the Players have read the script enough to be familiar with the structure, and before they have memorized their lines and stage business, have them perform the script using their own words and actions. You will easily be able to see if the ensemble is in agreement about their understanding of the structure and the characters.

Style Transformations

Play the script in the style of another theater form, such as vaudeville, circus, thriller, newscast, sitcom, or documentary.

Improvisations to Find New Information

Use improvisations to find fresh motivations for character, new stage business, and new relationships to other characters.

Examples:

- Have the Players improvise in a new setting or situation that would be consistent with the story and their characters but does not exist within the script or score.
- Have the Players change the outcome of the script. For example, what would happen if the hero lives, instead of dying; what would

happen if the heroine left home, instead of remaining with her family?

Switching Parts

Have all Players perform the script as a character other than the one they have been assigned to play. This encourages Players to understand and see another character's point of view, and may give them new insights into their own characters.

Entrances and Exits

Have Players determine the *Where* and *Why* for each one of of their entrances and exits. This could be done as an improvisation, or as a mental warm-up by each Player. Or it could be done as a question and answer session between Director and Players. For example, while standing backstage, the Player is thinking, "I am in a meadow now *(Where)* to gather berries for supper *(Why)*, and I'm about to enter the forest *(Where)* in order to get home *(Why)."* The Player can add motivation. For example, hunger is the reason she is in the meadow, and she is afraid of going through the forest to get home.

This exercise will help prepare Players for their roles, and will help them enter the performance already in character.

★ Rehearsal Preparations

Character Biographies

When performers are playing as characters, it is helpful to construct imaginary life histories of their characters. The histories should be built from information given in the text or script, adding more information that is consistent with, but may not be part of, the text. Each Player should discuss his ideas with other performers whose characters may intersect with his character's life.

This activity can be written, done as an interview, or a "This is Your Life" presentation. Everything should be discussed in first person; the performer is the character. In interviews, other characters ask questions of the one who is being interviewed, as though they were on a talk show, or as though they were in court. Everyone takes a turn being interviewed.

The biographical information is for use in performance, to help the performer play the total character. Even though the audience may only see a few moments in the life of this character, the performer can construct a full life from which to live as the character.

The more facts a player decides about his character, the more he has to play. For example, an actor waits backstage to enter the stage. He will look and feel differently if the character knows where he just came from and why he is entering the performing space, rather than entering as an actor entering from the backstage onto a stage.

It enriches the performance if all performers know one another's biographies and use the information in performance.

Performer's Log

Direct each performer to make a chart of what she does in each scene, including entrances and exits, and what props and costumes she will be using.

Example:

Scene	What I Do	Props/Costumes
Preset	Standing DSR wing	Chair, DSR
Scene I	I am a tiger.	Mask, mitts, tail
	I enter from DSR.	
	I join a totem.	
	Intro speech after snake.	
	I exit to my DSL home position.	

Communication Ball

Players stand in a circle. Holding a real or imaginary ball, one person makes eye contact with another person to whom he intends to send a message. He throws a ball to that person at the same time that he speaks the message. The message could be a line from the play or an improvised message based on a character in the play. The thrower continues talking until the other person catches the ball. The message is completed when the ball is caught; the catch signals that the message has been received.

The catcher then chooses another person by eye contact, throws the ball to her, while sending another spoken message in character. The game continues until everyone has had at least one turn.

Running Cues

Working independently, each Player goes through his performance from beginning to end, remembering all details. This can be done by literally "running" their cues on stage, or it can be done in the mind.

Beginnings and Endings

All Players perform only the transitions of the performance, section by section or scene by scene. Include any cues that involve changes of set, lighting, and other productions elements.

 Student Activities

Book

page 157 (Overview)

pages 158–159 (Vocabulary)

pages 160–163 (Performance Models)

pages 164–166 (Writing Models)

CHAPTER 11

Showtime!

Showtime! guides you on how to think about going into production if you and your group have decided to expand a project into a public performance, or if putting on a show is part of your job description. The chapter is divided into five main sections.

Preparing the Players for Performance

contains information on how to shift from creative, process-oriented work sessions to performance mode. It suggests ways to reach agreement concerning work habits and expectations, including how to use rehearsal time effectively to refine details and increase performers' confidence; the importance of using standard theater vocabulary as a common language; establishing rules of behavior;

maintaining focus both on and off the stage; and procedures for conducting final rehearsals.

Setting the Stage Picture: Blocking Devices offers directing techniques to organize Players so that they know what to do while onstage. There are suggestions of how to block large groups, including dividing Players into teams; keeping everyone involved by making them part of the stage picture, either as *tableaux* or set; and spiking the stage to help Players orient themselves onstage and to know where to place set pieces.

Designing a Production presents suggestions for producing effects that will help set mood, depict setting, provide background, give energy to images, or add cohesion to a production. It introduces choices involving both sound and visual design elements, including lighting, projections, masks and curtains, hand props, makeup, costumes, platforms, and special effects. Considering Technical Needs advises you on how to think about and plan for the technical requirements of the show. It considers what questions to ask, such as: Is the theater safe for Players to navigate? Will it accommodate your electronic equipment? Should there be a program? Have you provided for the special needs of performers and audience?

Assigning a Technical Crew gives you job descriptions for the stage manager, lighting designer and light board operator, sound operator, property manager, wardrobe manager, and production stage crew.

Experiencing Showtime includes information on how to direct final rehearsals and performances. It discusses the necessity for performer and crew preparations prior to curtain time, dressing the lobby, handing over the responsibilities of the production to cast and crew, and striking the show after the final curtain. The chapter concludes with a section on how to have closure with your group, once the performance has completed its run.

Going into Rehearsal Mode

Once the decision has been made to go public and invite an audience to watch a performance, a shift in dynamics begins to occur. Collaboration and experimentation change to consolidation and repetition through rehearsals that establish exactly what will be performed.

Establishing One Director The director has to begin to make unilateral decisions about what works for the performance and the audience. It simply becomes too chaotic to have everyone continuing to offer directorial opinions. Close to performance deadline, the speed of the process accelerates so that there is little time or tolerance for continuing experimentation.

It is your job as director to prepare Players for the transition from free experimentation to setting a performance piece. Used to the free play and open invitation to contribute to the decision-making process, performers may not understand the need to give up their decision-making powers, and may get hurt, angry, or even try to take over as director. Try to anticipate these feelings by explaining to the participants the reasons for the change. Most Players will understand the necessity for a single director. Explain that the director is the only one who can see the work from the audience's point of view, and ultimately, choices have to be made from that viewpoint. (Players have an opportunity to direct a short poem-play, see Student Book, pages 196–199.)

Rehearsing Effectively Players must also understand the importance of rehearsals. To get performers to the peak of their energy takes a steady diet of disciplined work. Mastery of the material only comes with repetition. Rehearsals can be compared to the training regimens used in the sports world to bring athletes to their peak level of performance at the time of competition.

The old theater truism, "What you rehearse is what you perform," holds true, to a large extent, even when performing improvisations. To rehearse effectively, performers must do everything intentionally. They must think about and make conscious decisions about a myriad of details, such as where and when entrances and exits occur, their relationships to other characters, what props are needed and where the props are to be placed or set, what stage picture is being presented to the audience, and even how to keep from scratching an itch while on stage. The reward of going through all this hard work is that, in performance, whatever was rehearsed gets even better.

It helps to have the students take the audience point of view during rehearsals. Have them take turns coming out of the performance space to watch one another so they can see and understand why certain directorial choices are made, what effect the images are having, and what works most effectively.

A video record serves the same purpose, and has the additional benefit of allowing each performer to see and critique herself performing each detail. If the equipment is available, try recording rehearsal sessions, so that Players can see themselves on tape.

Using a Standard Performing Arts Vocabulary

To facilitate the rehearsal process, stress the use of standard theater vocabulary when identifying parts of the stage, stage movements, portions of the script, theater styles, rehearsal techniques, and production elements. (See Glossary, page 241.) Not only will this ensure that all participants understand what is said, but they also will be able to transfer the terms to other performing arts experiences.

It is probable that your group will also develop new vocabulary terms that are particular to their piece. For example, if the piece revolves around songs, then the identifying vocabulary, such as titles for scenes and the actions within scenes, might come from the titles of the songs or elements introduced in those songs. Try to use appropriate musical terms when possible, such as *beats, coda, vocal chorus, instrumental bridge.* If the piece revolves around movement, sections and actions within the sections can be identified with standard dance terms or with a label that describes the way an action feels or looks to the performers, using kinesthetic, emotional, or other references. For example, a walk could be called *commuter walk, slow motion walk, elephant walk, frantic walk, two-step walk, march,* or *promenade.*

Establishing Rules of Behavior

During the often chaotic process of setting a production, there's no room for playing around, experimenting with equipment, gossiping backstage, fussing with each other's hair, playing "I'm the boss," or having attitude problems. In order for rehearsals to progress as smoothly and positively as possible, make sure the Players understand and agree to specific rules of behavior for participating in rehearsals and performances. These rules should encompass safety tips, proper theater etiquette, and common courtesy. All performers need to learn how to live safely in any theater home in both backstage and onstage areas. (See Rules of Theater Safety, pages 172–174, in the Student Book.)

There are only a few basic backstage canons, which Players should learn and begin incorporating in rehearsals.

- If you can see the audience, they can see you.

- Do not peek through stage curtains or move them—unless it's part of the show.

- Be quiet while standing backstage or waiting for your turn to perform. Assume that the audience hears everything.

- Know and avoid the location of lighting equipment backstage. Stage lights are hot. Cables can trip you.

- Props can only be moved by the person who is responsible for them.

The following idea should be emphasized during rehearsals: If everyone takes care of himself, we will all be fine. If Players start bossing each other around onstage it is not helpful to anyone or to the performance. Instead, encourage them to help one another through their own performances. Performers should be prepared to bail each other out of dropped cues, technical failures, and other problems by finding solutions that are consistent with a character or situation and maintain the style of the performance.

Maintaining Focus

The most exciting performances are those in which the performers are present in the moment and aware of everything that is happening onstage. Strong performances come from concentration, a skill that needs constant attention. It is easy to go out of focus: a change of place, a sudden noise, a new audience, an intrusion of daily life, or anything unexpected can take a performer's concentration away from being present in the performance. Performers must remain aware of and open to change, since performers' histories, characters' histories, audience reactions, and other performers' energy and delivery will keep changing during the course of a production.

Defining the Performance Objective
Help the performers maintain a common focus by defining the performance objective up front. As a group, discuss the overall intention of the piece. Come to an agreement that can be stated in as few phrases or sentences as possible. This discussion could be preceded by an individual writing assignment. The performance objective could become the basis of some very effective publicity for the production. The Players can learn to write a press release that reflects their language and point of view. They can begin to learn about publicity and public relations by sending out releases, calendar listings, and public service announcements to local newspapers and other media.

Focusing on Character
There are many ways Players can prepare for a performance that will help them maintain focus. One way is to explore and create character histories. Have each performer think of and answer questions about her character and her character's relationship to other characters and events and places in the performance. (See Finding a Biography for Your Character, page 165, in the Student Book.) Once a performer has worked through all of her character's history and circumstances, then she is free to let the character live. In performance, she can focus on other characters' behaviors, and react in the present to whatever is seen, felt, and heard.

Warming Up for Performance
Just before entering the stage, it is essential for performers to become focused and prepare themselves, mentally and physically, for the upcoming performance. (See Movement and Vocal Warm-Ups, pages 160–163 in the Student Book.) Doing vocal warm-ups and mentally running cues can bring a performer into full performance energy and focus. To prepare for an entrance while waiting backstage, performers can ask themselves questions that help them focus on their characters' motivations, so that when they enter the stage they are already in character. In nonlinear text deliveries (those that don't have a story line), such questions may not apply.

In preparing for pure dance performances or other nonlinear performance forms, it is just as necessary to be in the present and to begin the performance in the offstage area. This may be accomplished just by warming up the body, mentally running cues, and standing in the wings ready to go. Often, the entering movement begins in the backstage area, so that when the performer appears onstage, he is already moving with high energy.

Focusing Onstage
When performers feel that they have lost their concentration, some of the following suggestions might help to bring them back into focus.

- Listen to the other people onstage.

- Watch what is happening onstage, noticing any new and/ or unexpected changes.

- Ask yourself a question appropriate to the situation.

  Examples:
  - Who is this other person onstage with me?
  - What is this scene about?
  - The other character just forgot his lines. What am I going to do about it?
  - The taped sound cue is late. How do I enter?

(See Keeping Your Focus and Concentration, page 175 in the Student Book.)

Posting the Order of Scenes

Make a list of the scenes, written in bold letters, and post it where everyone can view it easily. If there is space, also list, scene by scene, the names of individuals responsible for being onstage. This list will lessen the anxiety some people feel when memorizing.

If the performing space has a backstage, place the order of scenes in both the right and left backstage wings. If necessary, provide a backstage reading light. If there is no backstage, find a place where the performers can see the list while onstage, such as on the wall behind the audience.

Conducting Final Rehearsals

The most effective way to a successful performance is to intensify rehearsals close to performance, and, if possible, go full out every day of the week leading up to a performance. At least one final rehearsal should run exactly as the performance will run—with no interruptions by the directors or technical crew for any reason. This is the time to let the performers deal with any difficulties as they happen onstage.

Make sure that notes go home listing rehearsal times, requests for materials, and detailing other responsibilities of the performers, such as deadline dates for memorization and bringing in costumes.

Also post bulletins reminding all performers when to bring in costumes, props, and any other necessary equipment. These bulletins should repeat the announcements that are sent home. Let Players know they are responsible for all deadlines and rehearsal times.

Follow through on your requests. In rehearsal, have performers try out everything that will be used during the performance, such as props and music. If something is not present at rehearsal, it probably should not appear in the performance, either. Remember, *what is rehearsed is what is performed.* Costumes that do not present any performance problems could be an exception to this rule.

Continue to encourage the performers to keep working on their own, outside of rehearsals. Suggest that they try looking in a mirror to see how they look doing bits, moving in their costumes, and working with their props. They need to find a way to feel comfortable with new props and costumes and to visualize the blocking. Explain that they can work anywhere—in their backyard, on their way to school, in the shower, or during breaks with their friends—in any way that they can to keep connecting to the material.

If Players feel embarrassed about rehearsing in public, remind them to try visualizing techniques (see Short Takes, page 221)—no one can see what a person is thinking. If possible, set up a place and times where performers and crew members can meet informally to help one another work on lines, choreography, technical cue sheets, and technical problems.

Repetition during rehearsals is essential, especially if the performance involves memorization of movement, text, or program order. However, if the performance is to be an improvisation, somewhat the reverse is true. During rehearsals for improvisations, keep changing some of the elements—vary the sound environment, the spatial relationships, the timing, or the costumes and props—to ensure that performers' responses to the structure don't become habitual and the work continues to be fresh.

To honor the nonstop rule of final rehearsals, address problems by taking notes and reading them back to the whole cast and crew at the end of the rehearsal. Discuss what you saw, what worked, and what needs help or a change. Agree when to work out changes, if they need onstage time. If time will not allow for a group discussion, try writing up the notes and handing them out to the cast and crew.

It's very helpful to have an audience present during the final rehearsals, to give the Players the feeling of going public with what has probably so far been essentially a private process, experienced only by the performers, designers, and crew. Even one or two watchers make the performers aware of the coming reality of an audience. You can ask the audience to take notes, too. Often, young performers listen more carefully to comments and criticism from their fellow students.

Setting the Stage Picture: Blocking Devices

One of a director's biggest jobs is setting the stage picture for every moment of a production. Placing performers onstage, keeping them in the stage picture, and blocking their movements are tasks that require a lot of planning, cooperation, and rehearsal. Following are some directing suggestions for accomplishing these goals.

Dividing Players into Teams

Grouping and moving Players in team units is a blocking device that can have many beneficial effects. Not only does this device enable you to move large groups efficiently; team structures also give Players the security of being part of a crowd and provide the opportunity for peer tutoring. It is often useful to organize teams so that older team members can take care of the younger members, or so that the able can assist the disabled.

Once teams are established, the staging can be organized into a system for moving the groups, thus greatly facilitating the director's job. For example, *the green group enters SR and the blue group enters SL; group A does one scene while group B does another.*

Keeping the Performers Onstage

There may be various reasons to keep all or most of the performers onstage throughout the performance.

- There might not be a backstage or offstage area where performers cannot be seen by the audience.

- It might be easier to maintain discipline if everyone remains onstage throughout the performance.

- The performers could be used as part of the set or visual design to enhance the stage picture.

Having everyone onstage throughout a performance helps project an ensemble image, in which everyone is active and feels important to the show. If Players believe that everything onstage is equally necessary to set the stage picture, then they will not feel that certain performers are featured over others.

Making All Players Part of the Stage Picture

All performers need to know that as long as they are onstage, they are still part of the stage picture. There might be some confusion as to what performance attitude should be when performers are not the main focus. Players may understand how to find this performance attitude if you draw analogies to lighting or camera effects: the main action is what is in the spotlight, while the rest of the action is not; in terms of video or film camera techniques, a close-up is used for the main action, leaving the rest of the image slightly out of focus as background.

When performers are not the focus of the action, they should maintain a neutral, relaxed, and quiet stance, giving their focus to the main action. Or, they could continue an activity quietly, as part of the stage picture.

Set Focus Points The director's task is to keep the audience's eye on the main action, while giving other onstage performers something to do. Following are some focusing devices for accomplishing this.

- In unison work, it may be appropriate for everyone to agree on an architectural detail to look at. You could also suggest that Players look at a point above and behind the audience.

- Advise Players to look in the direction of the main action, unless, of course, there is a reason their characters would not do so.

- Suggest or provide some prop Players can hold onto or a set piece that they can look at or to which they can maintain a spatial relationship. For example, a Player can hold a hat or lean on a table.

Create Tableaux Using teams or small groupings, block the performers into close proximity to each other (a cluster). The effect of these clusters can be simply to create a pleasant stage picture, or to present an image that relates to the text. The actions or monologues/dialogues can occur from these clusters. Sometimes, in order to heighten a moment or bring focus to a speaker, it helps to have individuals step out of their cluster positions to perform, and then return to their group or take up a new position.

Examples:

- In a scene about childhood memories that was performed by students, three teams played three different childhood games. Following an assigned order, speakers stepped out from these clusters to share a childhood memory with the audience, and then rejoined their teams' games.
- In another scene about parents, teams created three "family photographs" with friezes that changed in the transitions between each monologue. By the last monologue, everyone formed one large family photo.

Organize Line Formations Have performers scatter themselves equidistantly throughout the stage. Set these locations so that each time the performers enter onstage they know exactly where to go. Rehearse entrances and stage positions a few times until Players are clear about their spatial orientation. If you change performance sites, reset these line formations according to the particulars of the space.

Example:

A blocking device traditionally used in staging some folk plays, such as the mummers' play of St. George, has performers stand against the back wall of the playing area. Each comes forward when it is his turn to perform and returns to his back wall position when his turn is finished.

Use Players as Part of the Set Have performers play everything in the scene, including the environment. Players can use their bodies to create the shape of a place (a forest, a river, a castle, a table, a classroom, a bus) so that the audience can see what is indicated by the text.

Spiking the Stage

Sometimes, it helps to *spike,* or mark performers' positions on the floor with tape, so the performers know exactly where they need to arrive to play a scene. For general positioning, it is also helpful to spike three points on the downstage curtain line: center and the right and left quarter divisions, as measured from the center stage marker to the stage edges. Performers can use these spike marks to judge their positions and movements.

When working with large groups of inexperienced performers, it is useful to spike the audience sight lines to indicate the boundaries of the stage or playing area, and to illustrate for performers where they can no longer be seen by the audience. You can determine the audience sightlines by having Players sit in various locations in the audience area to tell Players moving to various locations onstage when they can and cannot see them. Spike the outermost area that is still within the audience's sight.

 Designing a Production

Imagine a movie without the sound score. Without a musical cue, how would you know whether the person running down a street is afraid or exuberant? Imagine a stage filled with a realistic set, or filled only with light. These examples illustrate how much the design elements affect and become intrinsic to any performance. The following suggestions are ways to begin thinking from a total theater perspective. (Also see Production Design Elements, pages 182–186 in the Student Book.)

Creating a Sound Environment

Sound environments can be used to set mood, depict setting, provide background, give energy to images, or add cohesion to the production. (An example of using sound to add cohesion is using music during transitions or between sections or scene changes.) To create a sound environment, use existing recordings or tapes; live music provided by a single accompanist, several percussion instruments, or an entire orchestra or band; or create sound effects by making field recordings, borrowing tapes from a public library or radio station, or assigning stage crew members to produce them live in the wings. (See Creating a Radio Play, pages 148–149 in the Student Book.) Ask a music group in your school to write songs or music to accompany spoken text in the piece. Sometimes a musical parent, teacher, or outside professional may be willing to help you create a sound environment for your production.

Creating a Visual Environment

Lighting Lighting is one of the most powerful, if not the most powerful, design elements available in theater today. It is also the most flexible, because it shapes and transforms open space. Lighting effects are created through manipulation of angle, level of intensity, choice of color, shape, and timing of cue changes.

Lighting can be used as a set, filling an empty performing space with a suggestion of place, time, season, and mood. It can draw attention to specific areas. It can also be used as a transition device, to indicate the beginnings and endings of scenes, and to segue from one scene to another with fades, cross-fades, and blackouts.

Lighting design and execution requires technical training so that performers, technicians, and the theater itself are safe. This book is not able to provide enough space to guide you with practical informa-tion on electric circuitry, types and uses of lighting equipment and stagelighting systems, how to make lighting plots, use color, and so forth. There are many excellent texts that can be consulted, and most college drama departments offer production training courses. It may be possible to volunteer at a local community theater to apprentice with someone with professional training. Or there may be a knowledgeable parent or volunteer willing to assist with hanging instruments and patching them into the circuitry.

For many activities in this book, stagelighting is not an issue. If you want to design lighting, there is no standard method to copy. You may choose to follow a general rule of thumb for lighting dance and pan-tomime, which is: give the dancers' bodies full definition by using side lighting; and for theater: keep faces lit to reveal expressions. No matter what lighting design you use, you will need to set and rehearse all cues during technical rehearsals, in order to ensure a smooth running performance.

The following suggestions offer various solutions to lighting a performance.

- Natural light in either an indoor or outdoor situation
  - Daylight only
  - Daylight plus supplemental fill lighting, such as ceiling lights, flashlights, or a follow spot (a light instrument that can be manipulated to follow the actor's movements)

- Stagelights: Some type of system may already exist in your school theater, gymnasium, or cafeteria. You can also rent complete systems. If you are thinking of purchasing equipment, ask for expert advice from your local electricity board and fire inspectors familiar with stagelighting.

– Low-tech production: Provide a basic setup used for the entire event, using an even wash of light throughout the playing area. Set only lights on/lights off cues. This basic setup could be supplemented with extra lighting, such as a follow spot, or a specifically focused instrument, to produce some special effect.

– High-tech production: Lighting design with multiple instruments, dimmers, color gels, and so on. It is possible to produce a very adequate lighting design with a few instruments, cables, and a dimmer board.

If there is no lighting equipment available in the performing space, this does not necessarily mean that a show cannot be lit. Instead, challenge students to create their own lighting system. This will especially appeal to those who love to experiment and make science projects. The problem to solve will involve designing a lighting system that can be safely operated using the existing electrical circuitry in the building. Interesting effects can be created using such equipment as baby spots, blacklight or other standard light bulbs, strobe lights, strings of Christmas tree lights, two-pound coffee cans to focus a beam of light, dimmer connections to create fades, metal trees and clamps or other ways to hang the lights, and lots of cable. All these items can be purchased in hardware and variety stores or gathered from homes. Some experimenting needs to involve testing the system in the space to see if it is safe to operate and whether or not it provides adequate illumination and sufficient equipment for the effects desired.

Projections Make slides of drawings, photographs, or other visual information that relate, juxtapose, or comment on the action. Or ask participants to bring in images they want to use. You can create your own film, video, or slides, including painting or scratching images on film stock; or use already existing materials such as family home movies and archival materials that can be borrowed from television stations, libraries, or other sources. Some of these materials are out of copyright; if they are still covered by copyright, you will have to get a permission release.

Slides, films, or videos can be projected against the back wall of the performing space. The projections can span floor to ceiling, or as large as is possible, in order to create the environment within which the performers live. Or, the projections can be as small as a rectangle, a "window" that is part of other set or lighting design elements. The projections can also be focused on strips of mylar, plastic curtain, or cloth that are hung where desired in the performing space. The projections can be made as rear or front projections.

Masks and Curtains One large curtain, or sections of curtains, can be painted, collaged, or quilted, as inspired by ideas/images. Hang as a backdrop, scrim, front curtain, or as dividers within the performance space. Use curtains or flats to hide whatever you do not want the audience to see (backstage, mechanical devices, costume changes, and so on) or to indicate a change of scene.

Hand Props Make or gather small hand props, puppets, and masks. Ordinary, familiar objects can become powerful poetic statements. Even small hand props, such as a handheld mask or a cane, can make a large visual statement. Use props to help focus and organize action for the performers. Props also give people onstage something to do when they are not the center of attention.

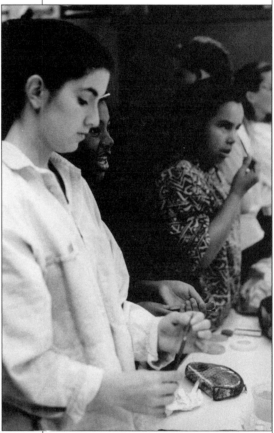

Makeup When performing in daylight or in an intimate space where the audience is close to the performers, there is no need for makeup. But if stagelights are being used, which can remove all the shadows and planes from the face, or the performance is in a large space with the audience at some distance, it is often necessary for performers to wear makeup, especially if it is important for the audience to read facial features.

For many young people, putting on makeup represents a lot of the magic of theater. It is a wonderful device to calm performers down and center them as they prepare themselves for the moment of performance. (See Stage Makeup, pages 187–193 in the Student Book.)

Water-based brands (such as Kryolan or Mehron) are the least irritating to skin and easiest to remove (all you need is water and soap). They are available in theatrical supply stores or mail order catalogs. If you have to use grease paint or standard commercial products, they should be removed with a nonirritating oil before using soap and water.

Water-based makeup has an endless shelf life. So if students will be doing a lot of theater, find out if it is possible to ask them to purchase their own basic supplies. It is best that students use a base that, when applied, looks exactly the same as their own skin color. So a field trip to a theatrical supply store or an experimentation session where a variety of color choices are available would be the optimum way to learn what to purchase.

There are many excellent books that illustrate how to apply stage makeup. Be aware that grease- and water-based makeups each require somewhat different techniques of application, blending, and removal.

Costumes

- **Uniform Costumes** Choose a uniform outfit that everyone is most likely to have in their wardrobes, such as blue jeans and white tee shirts. Or wear only a certain color scheme, such as all white, all earth colors, all red and black, all black and white with details of red. Have everyone bring in oversized tee shirts, white or colored. Use fabric paints, tie-dye, or silk screening to decorate them. Add pants, leggings, sweats, or tights of any color or one color.

- **Random Costumes** Have everyone choose to wear anything they want out of their closets. Since young people today generally dress with a strong awareness of image and sense of costume, when it is appropriate to the content of the performance, just ask them to choose anything they have to present themselves most strongly.

- **Community Resources** Check out the possibility of borrowing or renting costumes from college or community theater departments. It is sometimes possible to get donations from local businesses, especially those that market to families or young people. Promise them a mention in your program, or give them an advertisement. It is best to be specific about your needs: a hundred pairs of high-top sneakers, twenty hooded sweatsuits of varying colors. Or they may tell you what is available.

Platforms Use platforms to indicate change of level, space, or scene areas. Several platforms can define several scenes at one time.

Mechanical Devices Following are some ideas for moving two- or three-dimensional cutouts of images or puppets.

- Have performers hold images, masking all of their body or parts of their body. The images could be placed on sticks.

- Attach the images to a pulley system to move them up and down or side to side.

- Hang the images from a pole by fishing line; the person manipulating the pole may or may not be seen by the audience.

- Encase the performers in oversized cardboard boxes, constructions of wire and papier mâché or fabric; plastic sheeting; or other material.

- Enlarge images by using stilts, constructions that extend body extremities (make wings, tails, giant heads), or other structural means. A Player's body could be enclosed, or not. Some of these constructions will require teams of performers to manipulate.

Special Effects Theater productions, film, and video use mirror reflections, stage machinery, projections, screens and curtains/scrims, holograms, and virtual reality tricks to change reality for special effects. Masks and costumes, puppets, and flats can help create strange illusions. If you are lucky enough to have a stage with trap doors, revolving platforms, a fly space large enough to bring large pipes in and out of stage view, and other stage machinery that is sometimes present in theaters, you can have a field day creating illusions. Special effects could start as a science, carpentry, computer, or art class design project that utilizes individual skills to invent images and machinery to create the images. Participants can get very excited about experimenting with lighting, sound, and photography equipment; building set, prop, and costume constructions; and using computer graphics and programming. It's a good idea to ask Players to make mock-ups or models before getting into the larger expense of realizing creative ideas.

Considering Technical Needs

Long before you take a show into production, you must think about and plan for all of the technical details of the show, remembering to think out the backstage logistics, as well as the onstage ones. Following are some questions to get you started. Determine ahead of time how these needs will be accomplished.

- Do you need a stage crew? If so, what jobs are absolutely necessary to ensure a smooth production? Do you want a stage manager, sound operator, lighting board operator, curtain pullers, backstage crew? In other words, who will be running the show?

- Are there set pieces, musical instruments, hand props, or any other equipment that needs to be in place onstage or offstage for any scene? Who will be responsible for this job—the performers or the stage crew?

- Where will the cables for electronic equipment be positioned?

- Where are the outlets for the cables, and will the circuits carry the extra electricity load?

- If there will be live music, where should onstage musicians be placed? If they need outlets for electronic equipment, will there be outlets nearby, and do they need extension cords and power surge protectors?

- If using taped music, who will be responsible for running the tapes? On what format must the tapes be recorded?

- Should there be a program for the event? If so, who will be responsible for making it? By what date?

- What safety measures will help protect the crew and performers?
  - Secure cables to the floor with duct or gaffer's tape.
  - Mark stairs clearly with glow tape.
  - Keep all entrance/exit channels clear of objects.

- Do you need interpreters for performers, both backstage and onstage? Do you need interpreters for the audience? Where can the signer be positioned so that he can be easily seen by performers and the audience without interfering with the onstage action? (Downstage right or left usually works well.)

- Can the performance be done on one level plane to accommodate the needs of students who use wheelchairs, walkers, crutches, or have other physical needs?

- Do blind or visually impaired performers need to have guides to lead them into and around the performing space?

- Would it be advisable to provide guides for students with spatial perception problems, to help them find their stage positions for entrances and exits?

⭐ Assigning a Technical Crew

The size of the technical crew can vary according to the needs of the production and the number of people available to work. In a very small production, the actors may take over many technical jobs, and the stage manager may cover everything else. It is good training for actors to consider design and technical problems as part of the total picture of their performance. Actors should at least take responsibility for their own props, costumes, and perhaps the construction and placement of set pieces.

But if there are people other than the performers who are available and interested in handling these aspects of the performance, everyone will feel better knowing there is a backup person to take responsibility for each aspect of the production: the set, the props, the costumes, the sound, the lighting, the actors' cues, and so forth.

Middle school students will seek out tech crew positions. Working backstage offers all of theater's creativity and excitement without the anxiety some people experience when appearing in front of an audience. Many students will consider it great fun to be able to hang and focus lights, talk over headsets, build sets, and be given permission to give directions to their fellow classmates (as a stage manager). The more you can hand over responsibility for all aspects of the production, the more excited and free the performers and crew will feel in creating and running their own show. As a director, aim to sit in the audience, watching the show.

The following outline gives a quick, simple description of the production jobs that help a production run smoothly. (Also see Design and Production Job Descriptions, pages 176–181, in the Student Book.) It is intended as an introductory guide; if possible, consult reference books on stagecraft and technical theater. Several are listed in the Bibliography, and there are many others in libraries and bookstores. If your budget allows, consider hiring a consultant to come in, or find parent volunteers or students from a local college drama department who would be willing to help.

Stage Manager

The stage manager is in charge of everything backstage. In a small production, the stage manager might have to do most or all of the crew jobs, such as designing lights; painting sets; supplying props, set pieces, and sound effects; and running the control desk during the show. Even in a show with very few technical demands—such as one performed in daylight with no set pieces—it is extremely helpful to have someone, other than the director, take over organizational responsibilities.

It is essential for the stage manager to have the respect of the cast and the maturity to take on the job, because it does require the ability to follow-through from beginning to end with infinite patience and attention to details, plus a willingness to act as cheerleader, policeperson, parent, and authority figurehead without hurting feelings or intruding into Players' performance focus.

Following is a list of the specific duties of a stage manager.

- Keeps copies of the script, the theater ground plan, the set design, and the production schedule.

- Acts as liaison between all members of the production: writer, director, performers, designers, and technical crew. Calls production meetings, at first to coordinate design concepts, special effects, and to discuss everyone's particular responsibilities; later to find out where help is needed and to be a troubleshooter.

- Assembles and maintains a *prompt book* that includes:
  - **Cast and Crew List** Names and telephone numbers
  - **Suppliers' List** Includes type of goods or services, names, telephone numbers, hours, and includes such information as personnel involved in the management of the performance space, designers, costumers, and equipment rentals.
  - **Cue Sheets** For sound, lighting, special effects, props, set changes, and costume changes. There can be two kinds of cue sheets: a *master cue sheet,* which notates all changes involved in each cue; and *individual cue sheets* for each operator, notating only his particular responsibilities. There is no universal system of notation in making cue sheets; they can be tailored to fit each particular system and the personal preference of the stage manager. They do need to have consistent symbols and abbreviations so that anyone may read them and understand the system easily. The cues need to be organized in a system so that they can be located quickly, with the moves to execute each individual cue laid out in sequence.

- Becomes a Prompter: During rehearsals and performance gives warning cues to tell actors time for entrances.

- Checks preset of set and props.

- During performance, calls sound, curtain, and light cues to the light board operator and sound operator—through headset or signal arrangement.

If the stage manager is running the show alone, with too many details and responsibilities for one person, then have the actors take care of their own props, help each other with costume changes, and carry on and off any set pieces during the course of the performance. Everyone helps with the load-in and load-out of a performance.

Lighting Designer/ Light Board Operator

(Can be one person, or if available, more than one.)

- Attends production meetings for discussion of total design concept, direction, scheduling needs, special effects, and so on.

- Designs and executes lighting plot, working with crew to ensure proper hanging, patching into circuitry, focus setting, and to choose and place color gels for all instruments.

- Prepares cue sheet, with stage manager, that covers lighting aspects of production from preset to final curtain.

- Returns lighting instruments to theater storage area, unless given permission to leave the design hanging.

Sound Operator

- Attends production meetings for discussion of total design concept, direction, scheduling needs, special effects, and so on.

- Collects sound equipment and effects. This can involve preparing tapes of existing sound/music, making sound effects tapes from archival recordings or going out into the field to make original recordings, or creating live sound effects for use in the production.

- Prepares sound cue sheet, with stage manager, so it is possible to follow the show independently. Although the sound operator will probably be connected to and receive calls from the stage manager, she should also be able to follow visual cues from actors' actions or lighting changes, in case there is a technical problem with this method of communication.

- Checks preset of all sound equipment before the performance. ("firing up the system") Start by properly placing and plugging in equipment, noticing if anything has been moved since last used. Turn on the amplifiers last, to avoid an electronic "pop," which is loud and hard on speakers. Check any controls that are normally left in one position during the show, to make sure they are accurate. Set spike marks by using a grease pencil or small piece of tape cut in the form of an arrow to mark the correct setting)

- Operates sound during technical rehearsals and performance. Operating sound well requires timing and style. It is frequently connected to lighting cues, with the operator sensing the timing of the fade-in, fade-out, or other cue.

(When a cue doesn't play when called, the stage manager will be aware of it as soon as the sound operator is. The stage manager will determine whether to pass over the cue, or layer it on top of what is going on. If the problem is an incorrect volume, it's best to get it to the proper audio level. The point is to try to cover mistakes as smoothly as possible, so that the audience isn't aware of a noticeable jump in the audio level.)

- When the show is over, leaves the booth and equipment in as good or better condition than it was found. Returns all tapes to the director, along with the cue sheets.

Property Manager

- Collects and maintains all properties.

- Presets props. This can be done by arranging a prop table in an offstage area, or onstage, if appropriate, where props can be taken from and returned to as needed. Or, props can be preset onstage or in the wings (out of traffic corridors).

- Takes care of removing props during set strike and returns them to owners or storage.

Wardrobe Manager

- Takes measurements and records sizes of all performers, if needed.
- Collects and maintains costumes.
- Checks for any needed repairs, cleaning, proper hanging, and ironing of costumes during the run of production.
- After production, cleans and returns all borrowed items. Stores items that belong to the production.

Production Stage Crew

- By agreement with or assignment by the stage manager, each crew member should know exactly what his job will be for each cue, set, or scene change. Organization of the jobs can be determined by figuring out the way to accomplish the tasks with the minimum number of stage crosses necessary to get the job done. No one should stand around doing nothing.

- Help prepare, set up, and maintain scenery and props.

- Hang and focus lights, following the directions of stage manager or lighting designer.

- Before the performance, arrange a system for storing objects offstage, and decide who places each piece onstage.

- Make individual cue sheets if working a show where there is no intercom, or where there is no backstage area. Each member of the stage crew needs to have a script, with all the tech cues indicated, so that each can be independently responsible.

- Move set pieces into position during preset or as part of the show; remove pieces not needed.

- Keep all entrance and exit areas clear of any costumes, props, actors, or themselves.

- Spike or mark the stage floor for the exact placement of set pieces or to indicate where people should stand for *Specials* (lighting instruments focused so they can be used for a particular purpose during the performance).

- Arrange flats or curtains to cover the backstage areas from audience view.

- Clean and prepare the stage and house of the theater before the performance. If possible, and especially if the floor is dark and shows dust marks, wet mop the stage area, leaving enough time for it to dry before curtain time. If not, at least sweep the floor and dry mop it. Also, check the house to be sure that all personal items of cast and crew are removed, sweep the house, set or straighten the chairs, mark reserved seats.

- Assist the actors backstage, as needed.
  - **Dresser** Helps actors in quick costume changes, working out a dressing system with actors in advance.
  - **Prop Assistant** Hands actors props, or takes them from them, keeping all entrance and exit wings clear of objects.

- During the show, may be responsible for lighting duties, such as running the dimmer board or operating the follow spot.
- Produce special visual effects by operating equipment such as slide, video, or film projectors, smoke or fog machines, remote controls for onstage props, offstage pipe system to let curtains and objects fly in and out.
- Produce hand-operated sound effects, according to cues from sound operator or stage manager. This could include constructing and using special effects such as a wind machine, gunshots, thunder sheet, doorbell, and door slams.
- Help strike the set.

Experiencing Showtime

In a sense, projects are never finished—they just get presented in the best form you are able to realize by a certain date. Stop making changes in the production when you sense the performers need to stay with the choices made up to that point. However, even during a performance, encourage Players to try new ideas within the details of their own performances. Even after opening night, many companies keep adjusting the script, stage business, and technical cues until they get it "right."

When the day of the performance arrives the anticipation is infectious. Everyone is excited and nervous, including those who may

pretend otherwise. Tell them that it's good to be nervous—it shows they care. One way to alleviate performance anxiety or stage fright is to let Players know that, in theater, a mistake only happens if they decide to tell the audience, through their own actions or reactions, that one has occurred. Martha Graham, the renowned choreographer, was fond of saying, "If you have to make a mistake, make it BIG." This philosophy really works. Players can relax onstage and begin to enjoy performing if they understand that it is not really possible to make a mistake. A performer can always use a problem as a gift to find something new, or play it so broad that the "mistake" appears to be intended. Audiences love to be included in problems. Because everything is new to them anyway, they probably won't even notice if something unplanned occurs.

Getting Ready to Perform

Plan to get to the theater as far ahead of time as possible, especially if you are going to a site other than your usual workspace. *Calls* (time to arrive at the theater) usually are set at least two hours ahead of curtain time to allow performers and crew to prepare before the audience enters the house.

Technical Crew's Preparations The technical crew needs to check out all equipment to be used in the performance, making sure that everything is in working order and preset so that it is ready to go. The stage and house need to be cleaned up. The stage floor should be wet mopped or swept, and if there is a lobby, that should also be tidied up.

Performers' Preparations The actors need to carefully set their props, apply their stage makeup, run through their cues, warm-up their voices and bodies, and put on their costumes.

Dress the Lobby If possible, it is festive to dress the lobby with information that the audience can enjoy looking at, either while they are waiting to enter the house or during intermission. If you want to arrange a display, it can be set up during this time. Photos of everyone in the cast and crew are standard. Rehearsal photos and photos or programs from past productions provide background information and validate the group's work. Be sure to arrive with your supplies, including scissors, push pins, and masking tape; or bring prearranged boards that can be set on tables or leaned against walls. The art classes may want to participate in this effort, and take the opportunity to display their work.

Performing the Show

A director's time to shine is during the process of making a work. For the performers, the big rush comes at performance time. Although some people find rehearsals boring, others find them reassuring and necessary, and even fun. But most agree that the more spectacular rewards come with performance. This is when everyone finally understands what they are doing. It is at this point that the directors separate to become audience members. Whatever happens from this point on is the responsibility of the technical crew and performers—now they can truly own their performance. They've invested in themselves and shared their vision. Everybody becomes a star.

Completing the Experience: Post Performance

After the performance, it's a nice gesture to present everyone with some small token, such as flowers, as thanks for all of their hard work. Then the audience comes backstage to offer their congratulations. However, there is one more job to do before everyone can leave.

Striking the Set Make sure to previously warn everyone, including parents, that performers and crew are expected to stay after the show to strike the set.

A *strike* means to clear the performance out of the theater. This is in compliance with traditional theater etiquette, which requires each group to leave the theater in a state of readiness for the next event and its performers. To complete the strike, all production gear should be removed from the stage, backstage, and dressing room areas.

- Actors can take responsibility to see that garbage is put into trash bins; dressing tables are washed off; and costumes, set pieces, and hand props are packed and moved out of the theater.

- Crew members take responsibility for their specific job areas. The section Assigning a Technical Crew outlines the strike responsibilities of the lighting and sound operators and the stage crew. Many theaters ask that all lighting equipment be returned to its storage area; some theater managers may do that for you, or ask you to leave it as is.

Achieving Closure After a performance, it's a good practice to have some closure, otherwise your hard work feels unfinished. Arrange to meet with all participants on another day to discuss the performance. If you were able to videotape the performance, this is the perfect time to watch it as a group. However, be sure to remind Players that they are looking at a live performance through a two-dimensional video format, and since the performance was not made for video purposes, it will not have the same effect and may not capture the magic that was felt in live performance.

Ask how everyone felt about the performance: their personal feelings about the show and their own performing experience—and discuss what they heard from people in the audience. You may wish to also have Players fill out written evaluations of the show and/or the whole theater experience. If applicable, discuss future projects and performance opportunities.

Conclusion

Collaborative ensemble events made in school or community arts centers offer rare experiences that many professional artists and performing companies would love to emulate. Some of our greatest performing arts experiences have occurred in these venues. There are many elements that create this magic. One is the opportunity to work on a big scale, with a large cast of performers that generally includes many races and kinds of people. Another is that in original collaborative productions, where everyone can be playwright, performer, director, and designer, there is no middleman interpreting other people's ideas. You cannot make performing more authentic than that.

Creating something from nothing is magical. When an audience shares a universe created by this kind of energy, the stage becomes electric with vitality and a sense of immediacy. It's wonderful to watch.

★ Student Activities

Book

pages 167–168 (Overview)

pages 169–171 (Vocabulary)

pages 172–174 (Rules of Theater Safety)

pages 175–195 (Background Reading)

pages 196–199 (Performance Model)

Journal

Have Players read over their journals and write a final entry summarizing what they learned about themselves through their experiences in *Live On Stage!*

Glossary

A

act *(n)* The divisions or sections of a play, each of which may contain one or more scenes. *(v)* To make something happen. To do or perform something.

acting positions Terms that describe the actor's onstage positions on a proscenium stage relative to the audience and/or the other performers:

blend in Performer adjusts body position slightly, in relation to other actors.

full front Performer directly faces the audience.

full back Performer's back to the audience.

open up (turn out) Angle front of body more toward the audience.

profile (left/right) Performer is positioned so that audience sees only half of the face.

shared scene (cheat) Performers angle toward each other, halfway between full front and profile (one quarter right/left) in order to share their conversation with the audience.

actor/actress Male/female performer. One who participates in the action. Currently, *actor* is used to identify both male and female performers.

agitprop A shortened term for *agitation propaganda,* or political propaganda as dispersed throughout literature, drama, art, and music.

assemblage A visual arts technique that takes objects from the environment and combines them in paintings, sculptures, and new environments.

aside An acting convention in which the actor speaks a line that the other actors onstage are not supposed to be hearing.

B

beats (1) A way to break up long speeches or scenes. (2) A series of scenes within a scene. (3) A measure of time (one second or ten minutes), designating when to begin and end an idea.

blocking (floor plan) A way to organize the action onstage. A rehearsal device to clarify script, character, and stage picture by arranging floor patterns and performers' spatial relationships to each other and the set. Usually designated by the director. Performers follow blocking in performance.

body music Sounds made by using the body as an instrument, as in clapping, stamping, or doing the hambone.

business (see *stage business*)

C

call and response A repeating pattern, used in music and literature, in which one voice (call) is answered by another voice or group of voices (response).

canon A musical form in which the same melody is repeated by one or more voices, overlapping in time in the same or a related key.

Carnival A celebration, which happens in many parts of the world, with processions that may include pageant floats, masked and lavishly costumed dancers, stilt dancers, musicians and singers, merry plays, banquets, and balls. Carnival seasons vary and sometimes overlap with solstice celebrations. The season may begin any day from the New Year to either the first full moon of Spring, or the day before Lent.

chance system A way to interpret information in a performance structure that has been determined, at least in part, by random selection.

character (role) An actor becoming a person, animal, or object through physical expression, including sound and movement.

Chinese opera A highly costumed, masked form of storytelling; dance-drama, performed mainly by men. Known as early as the Han Dynasty (about 200 B.C.–A.D. 219), it combines music, song, dance, speech, martial arts, and acrobatics to tell stories based on history, legends, and folktales.

choral dances Any group dances done mainly in unison, making formations of line and circle patterns.

clichés Popular sayings or catchy phrases or ideas, which, by virtue of long use and repetition, become truisms or familiar ideas. May also refer to gestures and facial expressions that have taken on specific meanings.

clown A funny fellow. A jester, fool, buffoon, or trickster who entertains with jokes, tricks, pranks, and other wild antics in a circus, play, or other presentation. Beginning in the nineteenth century, clowns in Western circus traditions were categorized as:

auguste clown A white-faced, big-nosed comic in a spangled costume. Face may be broken up by geometric shapes of various colors. The "fall-guy."

character clown An exaggeration of an everyday life or stock character. The tramp or bag lady, the doctor or professor, the nurse or the cleaning lady.

whiteface clown A fantasy or cartoon image. The straight man, or the one who appears serious, graceful, and sophisticated.

collaboration A creative process in which all participants work together.

commedia dell'arte An improvisational comedy style with origins in ancient Greek and Roman theater. Became popular in fifteenth century Italy, during tours of professional, family-maintained companies. The plays' plots, scenarios, and stock characters were handed down from generation to generation in either oral or written form. Continued to be influential all over Europe into the eighteenth century. The traditional plots and characters have carried over into present-day theater, video, and film.

contact improvisation A form of "dance sport," developed around 1972, in which partners give and take each other's weight by carrying, wrestling, lifting, falling, finding and losing balance. Incorporates elements of martial arts, social dancing, sports, and child's play.

corps de ballet The dancers in a ballet company who perform as a chorus, in contrast to the soloists.

cue A prearranged signal to enter or exit the stage, or to begin or end an action, stage business, dialogue, light, sound, or set changes.

cue to cue A rehearsal technique generally used in setting stagelighting plots, in which the actors perform only the beginning and ending of each cue,

rehearsing each scene in sections. Cues begin with a cue for "stand-by" and conclude when the technical effect is finished.

running cues A rehearsal technique to physically or mentally review performance tasks. Performed solo or in ensemble.

cue sheet A list of effects (particularly sound, lighting, properties, scene changes) used to organize the technical aspects of the production.

cut and paste Scoring technique: collecting visual and/or verbal information from various sources and recombining them to create a score.

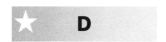

D

dialogue Two or more speaking/vocalizing actors.

director Person responsible for coordination, guidance, and development of all aspects of a production so that performance represents a unified vision. Conducts planning sessions, auditions, and rehearsals; attends production meetings; supervises technical production, schedule, and all budget expenditures.

doubles A term used to describe a way of portraying a theatrical concept called "internal action," in which the actors decide what motivates a character, or what is the meaning behind his/her actions and words in the text. To do this in a performance, at least two actors portray different aspects of the same character; one embodies the text (or *substance*) and another the subtext (or *shadow*).

duet Any interaction between two people.

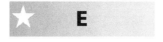

E

ensemble (teamwork) A group of people who regularly perform together. A no-star system in which all players are equally important.

entr'acte Any short piece that comes between scenes or acts of a performance. Music or sounds played during the intermission of a play. In musical terms, referred to as a *bridge*. Known by other names, such as *divertisement, intermezzi,* and *knee-play.*

F

focus (concentration) Attention paid to a specific action, person, place, or event.

fourth wall A theater convention that refers to an imaginary glass wall or window that separates the audience from the performance on a proscenium stage, allowing them to see what is happening on stage. "Breaking the fourth wall" means that the performer goes through the imaginary wall.

fractured texts Retelling any fairy tale, myth, famous writing, or commercial from a different point of view; revising the story in a more contemporary or outrageous fashion.

frieze *(n)* A motionless hold or pause in the action (as in a photograph or sculpture).

G

game An activity based on a set of rules by which the actors agree to play.

gesture A movement that expresses or emphasizes a feeling or idea. A communication signal.

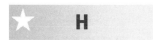

H

horse ballet A choreographed spectacle for horse and rider, using intricate and precise patterns and processionals. An equestrian pageant, popular in the great courts of seventeenth-century Europe, which survives in the displays of the Royal Lippizaners of Austria and the Royal Canadian Mounted Police. The groupings used for the *corps de ballet* are a direct descendant of this form.

huddle An improvisation device, which allows Players a short time to solve problems in the improvisational structure, or cue each other. Players gather together in a circle, with heads to the center, in the same way a football team huddles to decide the next play.

I

improvisation (improv) A spontaneous creative process in which the performer simultaneously originates and performs his material. Immediate response—with no preparation—to rules, space, sound, other performers, or other elements for solving the performance problem. An exercise in "thinking on your feet." Used as a training, rehearsal, or performance technique.

open improvisation Completely unrehearsed improvisation in which all decisions are made spontaneously.

predetermined improvisation Rehearsed performance structure in which performers agree on the order of rules or actions for the improvisation.

installation A human-made construction that is placed in an existing environment. It can modify or make a significant change in a particular space and can function as a set design or sculpture.

J

jester A European clowning style from the Medieval courts.

jingle A simple, repetitious, catchy rhyme or doggerel, similar to advertising slogans, cheerleading calls, and jump rope chants.

K

Kabuki A popular Japanese masked theater form flourishing since the end of the sixteenth century, which originated in dance, using stylized movements, and songs. Male actors present lavishly costumed dramas with plots taken mainly from domestic life and history, legends of ghosts and demons, and history and horror plays.

Kathakali A South Indian style of religious masked drama in which actors perform sacred legends outdoors in the streets, with massive costumes and multicolored masks creating their sets.

L

lazzi Term from *commedia dell'arte* for stock comedy routines or stage business (see *stage business*). Can involve sight gags, word plays, elaborate props, mime, and acrobatics.

Living Newspaper A theater form that dramatizes current events, both past and present. Became popular in the United States, starting in 1935, with a wing of the Federal Theatre Project known as the Living Newspaper Unit. Can be performed simply as an illustrated lecture or soapbox, or elaborately, with improvisation, dance, satire, puppetry, pantomime, crowd scenes, and visual projections.

locomotors Physical actions that take actors and dancers from one place to another by means of walking, running, skipping, hopping, galloping, leaping, or sliding.

M

mask Usually refers to a disguise for the face, but can also include disguises for the rest of the body. Masks are made in various ways. Most frequently, they conceal all or part of the face through the use of makeup and costume. The bare face may be considered a mask if it is used to make funny or strange faces. (Sometimes, masked characters are called *masks.*)

masque A spectacular production performed by professionals and amateurs in mask. A festival of disguised guests, bearing presents, who join their hosts in a ceremonial dance. Practiced in sixteenth-century France, Renaissance Italy, and Tudor and Elizabethan England (where the more popular style was called *mummers' plays*).

masquerade A costume party, masked ball, carnival, or other celebration at which masks are worn.

measures In music, the metrical unit between two bars on the staff; a bar of time, measured in 3/4, 2/4, or 4/4 rhythm, for example.

melodrama A dramatic form, using exaggerated suspense, romance, and sensational plot twists, which generally ends happily. Originally a music

theater form, still popular today in television soap operas and films.

monologue A single speaking/vocalizing actor.

N

Noh A fifteenth-century, Japanese court, masked dance-drama, using dance, mime, singing, and music to present mysterious plays of gods and spirits, demons and ghosts, human tragedies and comedies.

P

pantomime (mime) A performance that communicates an idea or action without words or sound.

part form A musical term for a way to analyze, break down, or deconstruct ideas from a composition into sections or component parts.

performance art A term used since the 1970s to describe the public work of artists performing outside the confines of a particular form. It involves multidisciplinary combinations of visual arts, dance, theater, film, video, and music. Often improvisational and collaborative, its origins include storytelling, cabaret, and conceptual art.

performance game *Live On Stage!* term for experiential, process-based improvisational structures using various performing and visual arts disciplines.

performance map A diagram of a site that indicates boundaries and distinguishing characteristics. On the map, performers are shown how to use the performance space.

plot (1) Describes the action of a play and sequence of events. (2) A list of cues for effects used in the play.

point of view (1) A metaphor to describe many kinds of physical, social, and psychological relationships to events. (2) The particular physical vantage point from which we look at something. (3) Opinions, judgments, and attitudes that influence our perceptions when we look at something from a particular physical vantage point.

R

razz-ma-tazz A circus term for the big parade, or runaround, that starts the show.

rehearsal Practice in preparation for a public performance. Repetition to perfect the show.

dress rehearsal Total run-through of the performance. This should be considered a real performance, in which all production elements are used: costumes, hand props, makeup, lighting, set, sound, bows, etc. **(Note:** This can be divided into more than one level of expectation: e.g., first, second, and full dress rehearsal.) Frequently used as a "preview" to which audiences are invited.

run-through Rehearsal technique in which the actors go through the complete performance from beginning to end without stopping.

walk-through Rehearsal technique in which the performer indicates the complete performance, especially noting cues and blocking. Completed with less than full performance energy.

technical rehearsal Run-through of the technical aspects of the performance in which lighting, sound, set, and property needs are resolved in order to set the technical cues.

rescue squad An improvisation device and variation of transformations (see *transformation*).

ritual A form of action that implies a repeating pattern or series of actions. Used in the context of a repeated warm-up, rehearsal, class, or performance structure.

round A short musical composition for two or more voices in which the same melody is repeated by one or more voices at equal time intervals. Once each soloist or group has joined in, they complete the melody at least one time.

S

scenario (treatment, skeleton plot) An outline of a dramatic work, from which actors can improvise a whole play. A scene-by-scene synopsis of the action, or series of beats, that actors fill with

dialogue and stage business (see *stage business*). Term originated with the skeleton plots of the commedia dell'arte.

scene The subdivision of an act in a play, identified by place and time.

score A performance structure, to guide the performer. An arrangement or recording system for a series of actions to be interpreted by a performer. It can take many forms: a scenario; a collection of photos, drawings, or words; a series of verbal cues or rules; a map; a series of dance or pantomimed actions that are recorded in a shorthand system of symbols or descriptive words, and so on.

script The text of a stage play, film, or radio broadcast. Can include technical and directing suggestions, cast of characters, suggested set design, and list of props.

segue To make a direct transition from one scene to another.

sense memory Stanislavsky's term for the memory bank of information learned through the senses, and one's reactions to sense perceptions. Sense memory exercises can increase awareness of sight, hearing, touch, smell, taste, or can function as concentration and relaxation techniques.

shadow play An entertainment or pantomime, featuring actors, puppets, or flat, cut-out figures, which move between a light and a translucent screen. The audience sees them on the other side of the screen as shadows. Created by rear projection or front projection.

side An abbreviated script form. Each actor gets a script that shows the full speeches of his/her character, and a few words of the preceding speech, which are the actor's cue.

site specific Refers to artworks conceived for, installed in, and/or performed in a particular space.

skit A short act or sketch; often refers to a comic scene.

slapstick Literally, a comic weapon, originally called a *batte*, comprised of a pair of lathe paddles, or long pieces of wood, fastened together at one end. Used by comics (especially in commedia dell'arte, English pantomime, and vaudeville) to create a great deal of noise with a minimum of danger when a person is struck. In vaudeville, the slapstick was often placed in the orchestra pit with the drummer who cracked it to make slapping sounds in synchronization with actions on stage. Used to refer to a broad style of comedy.

stage business Physical actions used by actors to develop and intensify the action, or to define characterization.

stage picture What the audience sees on stage. A series of living photographs or *tableaux* which are blocked in rehearsal.

station Specific place on stage where an actor must be at a particular time in a production. In medieval theater, referred to miracle and mystery plays performed on pageant wagons, which were placed at different points, or stations, to which the audience traveled during the course of the performance.

stock character A theatrical and literary term for a character presented in bold strokes. A stereotype or cartoon, immediately recognizable because of familiar mannerisms, ways of speaking, and predictable relationships with other characters.

storyboard In theater, a series of images drawn to show what a sequence of actions will look like on stage. In film, it is used to design the setup of a series of shots.

structure The overall organization or framework of a production. In a production that uses a script, it can refer to the order of acts and scenes. In an improvisation, it can refer to the rules or score which the performers follow to make their piece.

subtext What the actor is thinking while performing the text.

take Originally, a comic reaction to heighten a comic effect. Four basic takes are:

body take Similar to the double take, but the entire body is used in the motion.

double take A somewhat slower realization that things are not as they should be. The initial glance is followed by a more definite turn of the head and focus on an object or situation.

skull The most sudden reaction, usually involves a snap of the head in the direction of the other performer.

slow take A delayed reaction.

tableau (tableaux, pl.) A technique in nineteenth-century theater whereby a dramatic pose was struck by members of the cast at the start or end of a play or scene to convey mood or to underscore a dramatic moment. Commonly used to convey entire scenes as if they were living pictures.

task A term used in improvisation to describe the job a performer is asked to accomplish.

tempo The rhythm or speed at which a musical composition is played. Can also be used in terms of the rhythm of a script.

text The script, score, or rules of the game that the actor performs.

traditional games Games which have been played cross-culturally for many generations. Details of the game may vary from place to place and time to time. The title of the game should bring instant recognition. Examples include Tag, Follow the Leader, Musical Chairs, and Tug of War.

transition Moments of change necessary to go from scene to scene, act to act, place to place, activity to activity, or movement to movement.

transformation An improvisation device used to make a fundamental change in any element of the performance—the *Who, Where, When, What, How,* or the style.

treatment (scenario) May infer an extended plot synopsis. Frequently used in television and film industries.

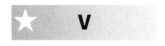

visualization Using familiar images that will evoke a feeling or sensation. A training and rehearsal technique to aid the actor in finding ways to play a beat or character.

warm-up A series of vocal and/or movement exercises to prepare for rehearsal or performance.

A way to protect the body from injury and to bring focus to the work to be done. Performed solo or in ensemble.

Wild Card Title given to a Player who is asked to join the action in a scene as a new character. An improvisation device to bring new information to the scene.

Types of Performing Spaces

open theater (arena stage) A nonconventional performing space of any shape in which the audience sits on at least two sides and possibly four sides. There is no proscenium (see *theater in the round*).

proscenium arch theater A conventional theater with a proscenium arch, usually without a forestage (see *apron*).

theater in the round Acting area with audience on all sides.

thrust stage Type of stage that projects into the auditorium and enables audience to sit on at least three sides of the stage.

Parts of the Performing Space

Proscenium Stage Areas The stage is commonly divided into six (or nine) acting areas, which are formed by two equidistant imaginary lines that run from downstage to upstage and perpendicular to the curtain line or footlights.

For convenience, directors and performers use the following terminology to identify the imaginary stage areas. All terms are given from the performers' point of view as they face the audience, not from the director's or audience's point of view. Therefore, Stage Right is to the actors' right—to the left for the director and the audience.

Stage Left (SL) All areas left of center stage.

Stage Right (SR) All areas right of center stage.

Center Stage (CS) Area in the middle of the stage, equidistant between Stage Left and Stage Right.

Downstage (DS) The area on the proscenium stage that starts from the edge of the stage closest to the audience and goes to center stage.

Upstage (US) The area on the proscenium stage that starts from center stage and goes to the back wall.

These stage area terms come from theaters with sloped stage floors, where the back of the stage is actually higher than the front of the stage. This was a common architectural style for theaters dating from the nineteenth century and earlier. Its purpose was to help the audience see better and to enhance the illusion created by scenes painted in perspective. Today, most auditorium floors are put on the rake and the stage floors are flat.

Standard Names for the Proscenium Stage (6–9 Playing Areas)

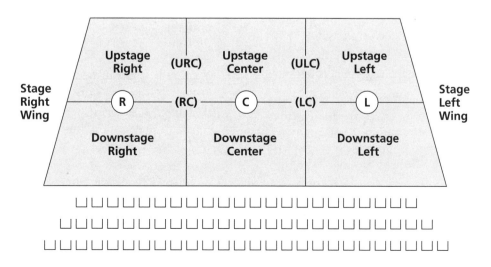

apron (frontstage) The part of a stage that extends in front of the curtain and proscenium arch. Also called a *forestage*, or *thrust*, when it extends forward enough to provide a substantial acting area.

backstage The area, generally not seen by the audience, to the sides or back of the stage. Accommodates dressing rooms and storage space for props and set pieces when they are not needed on stage.

crossover Backstage passageway where performers can cross to the right or left wings without being seen by the audience. Usually behind the cyclorama (see *cyclorama*).

curtain line An imaginary line directly under the front curtain or proscenium arch.

cyclorama (cyc) A large curtain or wall, usually concave, placed or hung at the rear of the stage.

flies Space above the stage, hidden from the audience, where sets, curtains, and lighting equipment are hung from pipes, which can be lifted from the stage, or *flown*, by manipulation of ropes on pulleys.

Green Room Area where cast and crew wait to be called.

house (auditorium) (1) The area in a theater where the audience sits. May include the box office, foyer, and any adjacent space in front of the curtain that separates the backstage areas. (2) Personnel in charge of the house, including house manager, box office personnel, ticket takers, ushers, and maintenance staff.

leg Cloth suspended vertically from the flies (see *flies*), used to mask the sides of the stage.

offstage Refers to a position close to the stage but not seen by the audience. To "be in the wings."

onstage In view of the audience.

proscenium A permanent or semipermanent wall dividing the auditorium from the stage in a modern theater. An open frame for the stage picture. The front curtain is hung from this area.

rake The slope of a stage floor away from the horizontal. It is higher upstage than downstage. The house can also be placed on a rake so the back of the house is higher than the front.

sightlines Lines of vision between the actors onstage and the audience. The director should set blocking so that it is seen from as many seats in the auditorium as possible. If everyone in the audience can see everything onstage, a theater is said to have "good sightlines."

teaser (tormentor) Short flown border used to mask scenery or equipment.

wings The sides of the stage, concealed from the audience's view, where actors await their cues to enter the stage; one or more masks or curtains placed on each side of the stage to hide the backstage area from the audience's view.

Production Equipment and Other Technical Theater Terminology

blackout A total darkening of the stagelights. Signals the beginning or end of a scene, act, or play. Can be a strong change within a scene. Can be used instead of opening and closing a curtain.

blackouts series of quick scenes that begin and end in a blackout. Often used in vaudeville and film.

cue sheet A record of all the stage manager's responsibilities: sound, actors' entrances, changes in light, etc. Sound and lighting operators frequently have their own cue sheets specific to their jobs. Somewhere backstage, visible to anyone, it is useful to have a running cue sheet listing order of scenes, or sections, and performers involved in those scenes or sections.

drop A suspended, unframed piece of scenery, usually made of canvas. First used about 1690.

front projection screen A light source and lens placed in front of a curtain. Usually located in the house or on the downstage center edge. Projects the shadow of a performer, puppet, slide or filmed image onto the screen.

gel (gelatin) Colored Roscolene or other plastic, see-through material used to color stage lighting.

house lights Lights in the audience area that are turned off when a production begins. "House lights up" means the house lights are on. "House lights down" means lights are turned off.

loading door A backstage door leading outside the theater. Used to load heavy props and equipment.

mask (1) Curtains, flats, or scenery used to conceal either areas or machinery from the audience. (2) An expression that describes one actor unintentionally obscuring another.

property (props) Items used by the actor onstage.

hand props Items small enough to be carried by the performer.

set props (pieces) Pieces of furniture and scenery used during a play.

stage props Items used onstage.

rear projection screen A light source and lens placed behind a curtain on the side opposite the audience. Projects the shadow of a performer, puppet, slide, or filmed image onto the screen.

set *(n)* Scenery and furniture, or *pieces,* arranged onstage during a performance. A *set piece* is any individual item onstage, such as a chair or door. *(v)* To prepare the stage before a performance or before a scene; to place any prop, set piece, or actor onstage.

special A lighting instrument used to create a particular effect.

spike Mark the position of scenery, property, or a performer's position on the stage floor. Temporary spikes are made with masking tape or chalk. For blackouts, use fluorescent tape, which glows in the dark, to help the actors or stagehands find their places.

strike To clear the stage or performing area, either after a scene, or at the end of a performance.

Bibliography

Directing

Barker, Clive. *Theatre Games, A New Approach to Drama Training.* London: Methuen Drama, 1977. Reprint. 1989.

Brook, Peter, *The Shifting Point, Theatre, Film, Opera 1946–1987.* New York: Harper and Row, 1987.

———. *The Empty Space.* New York: Atheneum, 1987.

Chaikin, Joseph. *The Presence of the Actor, Notes on the Open Theater, Disguises, Acting, and Repression.* New York: Atheneum, 1987.

Cole, Susan Letzler. *Directors in Rehearsal, A Hidden World.* New York and London: Routledge, A Theatre Arts Book, 1992.

Dean, Alexander, and Lawrence Carra. *Fundamentals of Play Directing.* 4th ed. New York: Holt, Rinehart and Winston, 1980.

Grotowski, Jerzy. *Towards a Poor Theatre.* New York: Simon and Schuster, 1968.

Johnston, Keith. *Impro, Improvisation and the Theatre.* London: Methuen, 1979. Reprint. 1981.

McCaffery, Michael. *Directing a Play.* Macmillan Publishing Company, Schirmer Books, 1989; Oxford: Phaidon Press Ltd., 1988.

Mekler, Eva. *The New Generation of Acting Teachers.* New York: Penguin Books, 1987.

Rabiger, Michael. *Directing, Film Techniques and Aesthetics.* Stoneham, MA: Butterworth-Heinemann, 1989.

Spolin, Viola. *Improvisation for the Theater, A Handbook of Teaching and Directing Techniques.* Evanston, IL: Northwestern University Press, 1963. Updated with a new preface, 1983.

———. *Theater Games for the Classroom, A Teacher's Handbook.* Evanston, IL: Northwestern University Press, 1986.

Suzuki, Tadashi. *The Way of Acting, The Theatre Writings of Tadashi Suzuki.* Translated by J. Thomas Rimer. New York: Theatre Communications Group, Inc., 1986.

Movement Activities: Dance and Pantomime

Banes, Sally. *Terpsichore in Sneakers, Post-Modern Dance.* Boston: Houghton Mifflin Company, 1980.

Blom, Lynne Anne, and L. Tarin Chaplin. *The Moment of Movement, Dance Improvisation.* Pittsburgh: University of Pittsburgh Press, 1988.

Dennis, Anne. *The Articulate Body, The Physical Training of the Actor.* New York: Drama Book Publishers, 1995.

Hamblin, Kay. *Mime, A Playbook of Silent Fantasy.* Garden City, New York: Doubleday/Dolphin, A Headlands Press Book, 1978.

Rolfe, Bari, ed. *Mimes on Miming.* Los Angeles: Panjandrum Books; London: Millington Books, 1981.

Steinman, Louise. *The Knowing Body, Elements of Contemporary Performance and Dance.* Boston: Shambhala Publications, Inc., 1986.

Acting

Barr, Tony. *Acting for the Camera.* New York: Harper and Row, 1982.

Boleslavsky, Richard. *Acting, The First Six Lessons.* New York: A Theatre Arts Book, 1949. Reprint. 1993.

Mekler, Eva. *The New Generation of Acting Teachers.* New York: Penguin Books, 1987.

Pasoli, Robert. *A Book on the Open Theatre.* New York: Avon Books, 1970.

Stanislavsky, Constantin. *An Actor Prepares.* New York: Theatre Arts Books, 1946. Reprint. 1948.

Improvisation

Banes, Sally. *Terpsichore in Sneakers, Post-Modern Dance.* Boston: Houghton Mifflin, New York, 1980.

Coleman, Janet. *Compass, The Improvisational Theatre that Revolutionized American Comedy.* Chicago: The University of Chicago Press, 1990. Reprint. 1991.

Dennis, Anne. *The Articulate Body, The Physical Training of the Actor.* 193–201. New York: Drama Book Publishers, 1995.

Jenkins, Janet, ed. *In The Spirit Of Fluxus.* Minneapolis: Walker Arts Center, 1993.

Johnston, Keith. *Impro, Improvisation and the Theatre.* London: Methuen, 1979. Reprint. 1981.

Pasoli, Robert. *A Book on the Open Theatre.* New York: Avon Books, 1970.

Sandford, Mariellen R., ed. *Happenings and Other Acts.* London and New York: Routledge, 1995.

Spolin, Viola. *Improvisation for the Theater, A Handbook of Teaching and Directing Techniques.* Evanston, IL: Northwestern University Press, 1963. Updated with a new preface, 1983.

Steinman, Louise. *The Knowing Body, Elements of Contemporary Performance and Dance.* Boston: Shambhala Publications, Inc., 1986.

Sweet, Jeffrey, ed. *Something Wonderful Right Away.* New York: Avon Books, 1978.

⭐ Scriptwriting

Take advantage of your public and local college libraries and borrow their generous collections of jokes, poetry (including limericks, conundrums, jingles), plays, songs, music, folk tales, fairy tales, games new and old, and picture books of art and photography.

Blacker, Irwin R. *The Elements of Screenwriting, A Guide for Film and Television Writing.* New York: Macmillan Publishing Company, Collier Books, 1986.

Charlip, Remy. *Arm in Arm.* New York: Macmillan Publishing Company, Four Winds Press, 1969.

Charlip, Remy, Mary Beth Ancona, and George Ancona. *Handtalk Birthday, A Number and Story Book in Sign Language.* New York: Macmillan Publishing Company, 1987.

Charlip, Remy and Jerry Joyner. *Thirteen.* New York: Macmillan Publishing Company, Four Winds Press, 1975.

Conrad, Edna, and Mary Van Dyke. *History on the Stage, Children Make Plays from Historical Novels.* New York: Van Nostrand Reinhold Company, 1971.

Kennedy, Adrienne. *People Who Led to My Plays.* New York: Alfred A. Knopf, 1987

Lawson, John Howard. *Theory and Technique of Playwriting.* 1st ed. New York: Hill and Wang, 1936. Reprint. 1960.

Singleton, Ralph S. *Film Scheduling, Film Budgeting.* Beverly Hills, CA: Lone Eagle Publishing Co., 1984. Reprint. 1989.

⭐ World Theater

Alford, Violet. *Pyrenean Festivals, Calendar Customs, Music and Magic, Drama and Dance.* London: Chatto and Windus, 1937.

Anderson, Laurie. *Stories from the Nerve Bible.* New York: HarperCollins, HarperPerennial, 1994.

Anobile, Richard J., ed. *Why a Duck? Visual and Verbal Gems from the Marx Brothers Movies.* New York: Avon Books, Darien House, Inc., 1971.

Brecht, Stefan. *The Bread and Puppet Theatre.* 2 vols. London: Michelin House, Methuen Drama, 1988; New York: Routledge, 1988.

Brown, Lorraine, ed. *Liberty Deferred and Other Living Newspapers of the 1930s, Federal Theatre Project.* Fairfax, Virginia: George Mason University Press, 1989.

Richard, Chase, ed. *The Jack Tales and Grandfather Tales.* Boston: Houghton Mifflin Company, 1943. Reprint. 1971.

Dennis, Anne. *The Articulate Body, The Physical Training of the Actor.* New York: Drama Book Publishers, 1995.

Ducharte, Pierre Louis, translated by Randolph T. Weaver. *The Italian Comedy.* New York: Dover Publications, Inc., 1966.

Ernst, Earle. *The Kabuki Theatre.* Honolulu: The University Press of Hawaii, East-West Center Books, 1974.

Fo, Dario, translated by Joe Farrell. *The Tricks of the Trade.* New York: Routledge, A Theatre Arts Book, 1991.

Glassberg, David. *American Historical Pageantry, The Uses of Tradition in the Early Twentieth Century.* Chapel Hill and London: The University of North Carolina Press, 1990.

Gordon, Mel. *Lazzi, The Comic Routines of the Commedia dell'Arte.* New York: Performing Arts Journal Publications, 1983. Reprint. 1992.

Green, Susan, with Foreword by Grace Paley and Introduction by Peter Schumann. Photographs by Ron Levine and George Lange. *Bread and Puppet, Stories of Struggle and Faith from Central America.* Vermont: Green Valley Film and Art, Inc., 1985.

Harmon, Jim. *The Great Radio Heroes.* Garden City, New York: Doubleday and Company, Inc., 1967. Reprint. 1993.

Hill, Errol. *The Trinidad Carnival,* Austin, TX: [Publisher?], 1972.

Hopkins, Albert A., ed. *Magic, Stage Illusions and Scientific Diversions Including Trick Photography.* New York: 1897. Benjamin Bliom, Inc., 1967.

Kawatake, Toshio, translated by Helen V. Kay. *Kabuki, Eighteen Traditional Dramas.* San Francisco: Chronicle Books, 1985.

Kirstein, Lincoln. *Movement and Metaphor, Four Centuries of Ballet.* New York and Washington: Praeger Publishers, 1970.

Laliberte, Norman, and Alex Mogelon. *Masks, Face Coverings and Headgear.* New York: Van Nostrand Reinhold Co., An Arts Horizons Book, 1973.

Mack, John, ed. *Masks and the Art of Expression.* New York: Harry N. Abrams, Inc., 1994.

McCullough, Jack W. *Living Pictures on the New York Stage.* Ann Arbor, Michigan: University Microfilms International, UMI Research Press, 1981. Reprint. 1983.

Moore, Lillian. *Images of the Dance, Historical Treasures of the Dance Collection 1581–1861.* New York: The New York Public Library, 1965.

Murray, Marian. *Circus!* New York: Appleton-Century-Crofts, Inc., 1956.

Orloff, Alexander. *Carnival.* Austria: Perlinger Verlag, 1981.

Reiniger, Lotte. *Shadow Theatres and Shadow Films.* London: B.T. Batsford Ltd.; New York: Watson Guptill Publications, 1970. Reprinted under the title *Shadow Puppets, Shadow Theatres and Shadow Films.* Boston: Plays, Inc., 1975.

Rolfe, Bari. *Commedia dell'Arte, A Scene Study Book.* Oakland, CA: Personabooks, 1977.

Rudlin, John. *Commedia dell'Arte, An Actor's Handbook.* London and New York: Routledge, 1994.

Sachs, Curt. *World History of the Dance.* New York: W.W. Norton and Company, Inc., 1937. Reprint. New York: Norton Library, 1963.

Salerno, Henry F., ed. and trans. *Scenarios of the Commedia dell'Arte, Flaminio Scala's Il Teatro delle Favole Rappresentative.* New York: Limelight Editions, 1992.

Senelick, Laurence. *A Cavalcade of Clowns.* San Francisco, CA: Bellerophon Books, 1977.

Shakespeare, William. *As You Like It, A Midsummer Night's Dream, The Tempest.*

Slattum, Judy. *Masks of Bali, Spirits of an Ancient Drama.* San Francisco: Chronicle Books, 1992.

Speaight, George. *The Book of Clowns.* London: Sidgwick and Jackson, 1980. Reprint. 1984.

Stolzenberg, Mark. *Clowns for Circus and Stage.* New York: Sterling Publishing Company, 1981.

Thompson, Robert Farris. *African Art in Motion.* Berkeley and Los Angeles: University of California Press, 1974.

T'sao Kuo-lin. *The Face of Chinese Opera,* 1st English ed. Taiwan, R.O.C.: Hilit Publishing Co., Ltd., 1995.

Wilson, Robert. *The Theater of Images.* Cincinnatti, OH: The Contemporary Arts Center, 1980. Revised. New York: Harper and Row, 1984.

———. *Robert Wilson's Vision.* Boston and New York: Museum of Fine Arts in association with Harry N. Abrams, Inc., 1991.

Winter, Marian Hannah. *The Theatre of Marvels.* New York: Benjamin Blom, 1962.

★ Technical Theater

Buchman, Herman. Photographs by Susan E. Meyer. *Stage Makeup.* New York: Watson-Guptill Publications, 1971.

Corson, Richard. *Stage Makeup.* 5th ed. New York: Appleton-Century-Crofts, 1975.

Fraser, Neil. *Lighting and Sound.* Oxford: Phaidon Press Ltd., 1988. New York: Macmillan Publishing Company, Schirmer Books, 1989.

Gruver, Bert. Revised by Frank Hamilton. *The Stage Manager's Handbook.* New York: Drama Book Publishers, 1952, 1953, 1972.

Hoggett, Chris. *Stage Crafts.* New York: St. Martin's Press, 1975.

Holt, Michael. *Stage Design and Properties.* Oxford: Phaidon Press Ltd., 1988. New York: Macmillan Publishing Company, Schirmer Books, 1989.

———. *Costume and Makeup.* Oxford: Phaidon Press Ltd., 1988. New York: Macmillan Publishing Company, Schirmer Books, 1989.

Kaye, Deena and James Lebrecht, with Foreword by Peter Sellars. *Sound and Music for the Theatre, the Art and Technique of Design.* New York: Watson-Guptill Publications, Backstage Books, 1992.

Menear, Pauline, and Terry Hawkins. *Stage Management and Theatre Administration.* Oxford: Phaidon Press Ltd., 1988. New York: Schirmer Books, a division of Macmillan, 1989.

Theatre Crafts Directory and Theatre Crafts, a monthly magazine that lists suppliers and current information in the field of design and technical production.

The BBC and CBS provide anthologies of sound effects in various formats, which can be found in public libraries or ordered directly.

★ Education

Cratty, Bryant J. *Active Learning, Games to Enhance Academic Abilities.* 2d. ed. NJ: Prentice-Hall, Inc., 1971. Reprint. 1985.

Gardner, Howard. *Creating Minds, An Anatomy of Creativity Seen Through the Lives of Freud, Einstein, Picasso, Stravinsky, Eliot, Graham, and Gandhi.* New York: HarperCollins, BasicBooks, 1993.

———. *Frames of Mind, The Theory of Multiple Intelligences.* New York: HarperCollins, BasicBooks, 1985.

Goldberg, Meryl Ruth, and Ann Phillips, eds. *Arts as Education.* Cambridge, MA: Harvard Educational Review, Reprint Series No. 24, 1992.

Haggerty, Brian A. *Nurturing Intelligences, A Guide to Multiple Intelligences Theory and Teaching.* Menlo Park, CA: Addison-Wesley Publishing Company, Innovative Learning Publications, 1995.

Jennings, Sue. *Remedial Drama.* New York: Theatre Arts Books, 1973; Reprinted with revised appendices, 1984.

Lopate, Phillip. *Being with Children.* New York: Doubleday and Company, Inc., 1975.

McCaslin, Nellie. *Creative Drama in the Classroom.* 4th ed. New York: Longman Inc., 1968, 1974, 1980, 1984.

General Reference

Costello, Elaine. *Signing, How to Speak with Your Hands.* New York: Bantam Books, 1983.

Fluegelman, Andrew, ed. *The New Games Book, Play Hard, Play Fair, Nobody Hurt.* San Francisco, CA: The Headlands Press, Inc., 1976.

Goldsworthy, Andy. *A Collaboration with Nature.* New York: Harry N. Abrams, 1990.

Hartnoll, Phyllis. *The Theatre, A Concise History.* New York: Harry N. Abrams, 1968. Reprinted as *The Concise History of Theatre.* England: Thames and Hudson, 1985.

———. *The Oxford Companion to the Theatre.* 3d. ed. London: Oxford University Press, 1967.

Raffe, W. G. *Dictionary of the Dance.* New York: A. S. Barnes and Company, 1964.

Reed, Ishmael, general ed. The HarperCollins Literary Mosaic Series. Nicolas Kanellos, ed. *Hispanic American Literature,* 1995; Gerald Vizenor, ed. *Native American Literature,* 1995; Shawn Wong, ed. *Asian American Literature,* 1996; Al Young, ed. *African American Literature,* 1996. New York: HarperCollins College Publishers.

Schlemmer, Oskar, Laszlo Moholy-Nagy, and Farkas Molnar. *The Theater of the Bauhaus.* Middletown, CT: Wesleyan University Press, 1961.

Sternberg, Martin L. A. *American Sign Language Dictionary.* New York: Harper and Row, 1981. Reprint. 1987.

Tiberghien, Gilles A. *Land Art.* Princeton, NJ: Princeton Architectural Press, 1995.

You might also review the broad selection of theater magazines, such as *Drama Review, Dance Magazine, Contact Quarterly, Dance Ink, American Theatre, Theatre Crafts, High Performance, Lighting Dimensions,* and *The Act.* The *Smithsonian, National Geographic,* and the Sunday edition *of The New York Times* also frequently contain articles describing performance practices throughout the world.